SOUTHERN BIOGRAPHY SERIES

WILLIAM BLOUNT

WILLIAM BLOUNT

William Blount

By

WILLIAM H. MASTERSON

LOUISIANA STATE UNIVERSITY PRESS

BATON ROUGE

MANUFACTURED IN THE UNITED STATES OF AMERICA
BY THE VAIL-BALLOU PRESS, BINGHAMTON, N.Y.

TO VETTA

PREFACE

THE BIOGRAPHER in American history may be attracted to a subject by any of a variety of interests. A Washington may intrigue by his accomplishments, a Hamilton by his brilliance, a Jefferson or Franklin by his versatility, an Arnold or Burr by the complexities of personality. The subject of this study is interesting for yet other reasons. William Blount's accomplishments, though not inconsiderable, were equaled by many of his contemporaries; his mind, alert and of some breadth, was not extraordinary, and his personality was entirely consistent. He is arresting primarily because he typified so exactly a vital segment of past and present American society—the businessman.

Blount represents a class which was just emerging in eighteenth-century America and which has steadily maintained its importance in society until today it has become to many other nations the personification of our national character. True it is that earlier societies had produced these men and they had participated powerfully in the direction of affairs. But the close of the colonial period saw the resources and opportunities of this continent perhaps first fully recognized. The era of predominantly subsistence economy was closing, and the first age of "big business" about to dawn. Further, the removal of the British governing groups together with the imperial restrictions on business activity meant that a new governing class must step forward to fashion their own rules for a game in which the stakes were high and the prizes enormous. The political freedom of 1783 was accompanied by an economic freedom no less heady, less ardently sought, nor narrower in its implications for society. Within these new freedoms moved Blount and his contemporaries. Their influence was enormous, their roles significant and too often ignored for the more arresting picturization of political principle or party slogan.

No out-of-focus Marxian determinism is implied in such a study; neither is praise or blame meant to be invoked on business or businessmen past or present. What is attempted in this work is an illustration of a significant and all too often ignored American type, and of the important part played by one of this type in the history of his locality and in some respects of the nation. Secondarily, an attempt is made to describe the career of an individual of major significance in North Carolina and Tennessee history in the last quarter of the eighteenth century.

Every research student will recognize the many acknowledgements due in a study such as this. The thanks due to many individuals for courtesies and assistance in various libraries and archives, while suitable, would perhaps be tedious. Outstanding co-operation and courtesy from Robert T. Quarles, Jr., of the Tennessee State Archives, Christopher Crittenden, State Archivist of North Carolina, Miss Pollyanna Creekmore of Lawson McGhee Library, Professor Stanley Folmsbee of the University of Tennessee, and Frank Burton and his staff in the North Carolina State Department of Archives and History must, however, be recognized with appreciation. The work of Dr. Alice B. Keith on the Blount manuscripts and on her doctoral thesis on Blount business affairs was most helpful. The interest and co-operation of these helpful friends has been of great assistance and inspiration to the writer.

TABLE OF CONTENTS

LIST OF ILLUSTRATIONS

THE FAMILY

It was a good house, a comfortable house. In summer, its long porch and wide halls offered relief from the clammy North Carolina low country heat; on a late winter evening candlelight in its little dormer windows and curling smoke from its two chimneys promised cheer and warmth to the cold, wet homecomer.

In the rear, barns, slave quarters, harness rooms and stables, lacking, perhaps, the modest distinction of Blount Hall, sturdily housed the myriad activities of a ceaseless battle to maintain the Hall against the wilderness. For, though adjacent stump-studded fields represented local victory, the home clearing still stood surrounded by untouched legions of pines, gums, and sycamores, ever ready to reclaim the terrain which had so recently been theirs; and back of these rose more and more in endless array, covering the province with but local interruptions for countless miles from seacoast swamp to mountain crest.

Still, Jacob Blount was a worthy opponent of the wilderness, possessing as he did a full background of enterprise and endeavor. Two Norman ancestors had sailed with William the Conqueror, one commanding the invading fleet. From their services the family had prospered; and their offices and honors and manors were soon scattered over the broad fields of Suffolk and Lincolnshire. As years passed, the Blounts, though not of the first rank of nobility, were always active and partisan, and the family served causes as their interest and loyalties directed. So William le Blount, sixth Baron Ixworth, fell battling for Simon at Lewes, and a later Sir Walter of Soddington served Charles I too well during the campaigns of the civil war. For this service brought no rewards but suffering and imprisonment at Oxford and the Tower. Moreover, the restored Stuart's gratitude proved greater than his largess, and Walter Blount had four ambitious sons and four daughters to equip and dower. Ever enterprising, several Blounts had been among the gentry interested in the establishment of the colony of Virginia, and two of Walter's sons, James and Thomas,[1] now turned toward this new field for those of high design and low prospects. They arrived in Virginia with family crest and some financial supply in 1664 and settled in Isle of Wight County.

Here the Blounts fell to the congenial task of acquiring and prospering. Quick minds, hard work, and fortunate marriages transformed these younger descendants of lesser English nobles into something approaching local magnates in the nascent society of the wilderness. Moving with that current of Virginians who sought better or cheaper lands, the first American Blounts soon turned south into Chowan Precinct in present North Carolina. James Blount entered a tract on Albemarle Sound as early as 1669 and in 1684 patented another on which rose Mulberry Hill, a showplace home with fresh-water springs and carefully planted orchards. The owner, though a leader in Culpeper's Rebellion, was a burgess, a member of the governor's council, and a leading citizen.

[1] Worth S. Ray (ed.), *Index and Digest to Hathaway's Historical and Genealogical Register* (Austin, 1945), 19; Charles McClung Papers (Lawson McGhee Library, Knoxville), XIV (Part 1), 227.

Following this rising magnate, a son, Thomas, carried on the family traditions most characteristically. After some Indian-harried years on his wife's plantation in Perquimans, he moved to Kendrick's Creek in present Tyrrell County on Albemarle Sound in the winter of 1698–99. Here he built Cabin Ridge plantation and stimulated an activity which would have done credit to a New England village. Thomas Blount was a planter, blacksmith, carpenter, shipbuilder, and worker in metals. In the latter capacity, he made the casts to stamp the first set of weights and measures brought to the colony. His mill, at one time the only such in the province, produced boards for the first church at Edenton, and the first courthouse. Together with the other vestrymen of St. Paul's he planned the first church building at Edenton; he fought in Indian wars and represented the colony in Indian treaties; and in 1703 he sat in the legislature for his district. Meanwhile his landholdings grew. By marriages, by transporting people to the colonies, by purchasing, and by trade came Cabin Neck, two "middle plantations," and a score of undeveloped tracts.

To this accumulation of wealth and dignities a son, also named Thomas, added further. Marriage to Anne Elizabeth, daughter of the successful Lionel Reading, brought this restless Blount new estates and valuable connections, and, carrying on the quest for affluence, he moved to Beaufort Precinct in Bath County, and located on the Tar River. An aggressive fighter like his forebears, he was once indicted for "an Assault & greivous battery" on one Robert Campain, whom he "did beat Batter bruise and Sorely wound with Sticks Clubbs and fist insomuch that his life was despaired of." [2] But no disgrace followed;

[2] William L. Saunders (ed.), *The Colonial Records of North Carolina* (Raleigh, 1886–90), II, 695. (Hereinafter referred to as *Colonial Records.*)

the family, now known as the Tar River Blounts, continued to lead and prosper, and on Thomas Blount's death,
four sons, Reading, James, John, and Jacob, received the
usual ample heritage.

Thus, from the first purposeful James to the hot-
headed Thomas, the motif was "Advance." With modest
capital the emigrant younger sons had set the pattern for
a family of affluence and leadership. No title-flaunting,
inept émigrés, the Blounts served with both hand and
brain the community and themselves. Blount land and
slaves were not only bought and sold, they were also leased
and worked on shares. Blount mills ground the essential
corn or sliced the boards of the community for cash or
barter. Blount carpenters and coopers made wagons, hogs-
heads, staves, and shingles for a neighborhood increasingly
engrossed in planting; and Blount forges served, for a
price, the farmer in peace and the soldier in war. Land
was the theme, but variety was the counterpoint.

Young Jacob Blount was restless. In 1753, life in the
home of his father-in-law had the graces one expected in
the residence of John Gray, a Scottish gentleman of Governor Gabriel Johnston's suite, and of his wife Mary Bryan
Gray, a daughter of Virginia gentry.[3] "Rosefield's" schedule was hospitable and gracious. With his own family,
Jacob was increasingly happy. On Easter Sunday, March
26, 1749, at "Rosefield," in Bertie County,[4] his wife,
Barbara Gray Blount, had presented him with their first-
born, a son named William. Next came a daughter, Ann,

[3] Helen M. Blount Prescott, *Genealogical Memoir of the Roulhac Family
in America* (Atlanta, 1894), 62; Rodman Papers (in the possession of Mr.
William Rodman, Washington, North Carolina), *passim*; Stuart Hill, "The
Hill Family" (manuscript in the North Carolina State Library, Raleigh), IV,
passim.

[4] Rodman family Bible in Rodman Papers; Hill, "Hill Family," IV.

followed in 1752 by a second son, John Gray. Too, his business career in Tyrrell County was thus far gratifying. As a rising businessman and well-connected justice of the peace, Jacob Blount was always welcome at the Pollacks' on Chowan River or the Worleys' or the Holts' or the Blounts' in Albemarle. The few score homes of Edenton offered the young couple dinners and teas and a polite society which mixed talk of the classics and of the *Spectator* with that of stock raising and tobacco prices. Other social pleasures included boating, dancing, horse racing, backgammon, or a "preaching." More interesting to Jacob Blount were the town's sail-cluttered wharves and warehouses, pungent with tobacco or tar, or perhaps a chat over plans for the next Assembly with young Joe Hewes or Sam Johnston. Always there was the absorbing game of land. It had begun with a 500-acre grant on Contentnea Creek acquired for him at the age of nine years. Succeeding years saw additions such as the 640 acres bought from the Bryans in Craven County, or the 350 acres in Anson.[5] Thus a life of modest affluence, respect, and friendships moved busily along. More honors were to be expected— the Assembly was talked of for next year.

But the human tide was sweeping ever more strongly southward, where lay promises of richer, higher lands, busier commercial towns, better opportunities for the young man of business. Those good lands of Craven County, sandy for tobacco or river-bed black for almost any crop, had drawn like an international magnet Huguenots, Swiss, Palatines, and English since the very beginning of the century. The Tuscaroras, once a savage peril that had burst upon and swept back early venturers, were shattered now

[5] Saunders (ed.), *Colonial Records,* IV, 75, 353; VI, 82, 1082; John Gray Blount Collection (North Carolina State Department of Archives and History, Raleigh), P.C. 898, *passim.* (Hereinafter referred to as Blount Collection.)

and the survivors had drawn off. With mounting momentum the white current had for thirty years been flowing back to rebuild and reclaim. Now Bryans, Coors, Herritages, Reeds, and their like were fast carving out in the Neuse area a civilization to compare with that of the old Albemarle section. To ease his wife's doubts, Jacob Blount could point out improved roads, ferries, a widening settlement on the Neuse, schoolteachers, a church with the Reverend James Reed, and even a newspaper in James Davis' North Carolina *Gazette*. Besides, the new governor, Arthur Dobbs, was rumored to favor the Cape Fear region yet further south, which meant still more incidental development for the Neuse-Pamlico neighborhood. To Blount, who already owned lands and a comfortable house in Craven County and had two young sons and a daughter, the attraction of the south was as irresistible as the similar call had been to his forebears.

So, as in the past, the call was answered. In the spring of 1753 the household goods were collected, the heavy lumbering wagons and the carts loaded, the stock gathered, the slaves instructed, and the long winding trip begun over jolting roads, across numberless creeks, and always through the endless trees, until at last through friendly fields the "road" became a lane that led to the Hall.

CHAPTER I

THE EASTERN CONSERVATIVE

THE HALL BECAME IN TIME a place of myriad activity. For the growing family it provided not only the shelter of a home, but also an invaluable economic and social training. Jacob Blount's activities were many. With slave labor he farmed cotton and tobacco; he bought and sold cattle and hogs; he either produced or bought for re-sale tar, pitch, and turpentine; and he loaned money and credit to his neighbors, for whom his mill ground corn. Thus, from their earliest boyhood, the Blount boys were accustomed to versatility of enterprise.[1]

Of equal significance for their futures was their social training. Like most rural families, the Blounts were family-conscious. The Hall was the focal point of their lives, and their activities there bred a closeness of spirit that continued throughout the lives of William, John Gray, and Thomas Blount. Whether in business projects or in social intercourse, Blounts acted in concert and with a constant family interest.

The absence of a "settled" schoolmaster in the neighborhood worried Jacob Blount, for it was not until 1764, in William Blount's fifteenth year, that teacher Thomas Tomlinson was welcomed by the parents of Craven County, and hence the boys' early training was necessarily carried

[1] Blount Collection, *passim*; Rodman Papers, *passim*.

on by their parents.[2] Religious instruction was more sporadic. As befitted a descendant of Anglo-Virginia gentry,
Jacob Blount was an Episcopalian, and, moreover, an active one. A vestryman of Christ Church Parish, he sought
financial and moral support for the clergy,[3] though New
Bern was forty miles away—too far for regular attendance
—and the family usually attended the small chapel at the
nearer hamlet of Ayden to hear the Reverend James Reed
on his visits there.

But it was the increasing activity of Blount Hall that
most absorbed the boys. The widening pattern of their
father's enterprise was reflected early in their lives. The
routine and the skills of farm, mill, and shop, all practiced at the Hall, became in them inherent knowledge. They
learned both to labor and to direct labor, both to act and
to listen; above all, to observe. On social occasions such as
horse-racing days on the Hall's track, the boys undoubtedly watched and listened while their father, amidst a
knot of friends of similar gentry status, talked weights and
handicaps and made and collected bets. In the evening a
chosen group of these friends and neighbors might sit
around the dining table sipping Jacob Blount's Madeira
and talking of crops, colts, merchandising, the doings of
the assembly, or speculating on prospects when young
Lieutenant Governor William Tryon replaced the aging
Arthur Dobbs.[4]

The passing years widened the world of William and
John Gray, as they observed their father absorbed in the

[2] Saunders (ed.), *Colonial Records,* VII, 35–36; Samuel A'Court Ashe,
History of North Carolina (Greensboro, 1908), I, 390; Francis H. Cooper,
"Some Colonial History of Craven County," in *The James Sprunt Historical
Publications,* XVII (1922), 53; Lachlan Cummings Vass, *History of the
Presbyterian Church in New Bern, North Carolina* (Richmond, 1886), 74;
Alice B. Keith, "Three North Carolina Blount Brothers in Business and
Politics" (Ph.D. dissertation, University of North Carolina, 1940), 37.

[3] Saunders (ed.), *Colonial Records,* VI, 230; IX, 61–62.

[4] Blount Collection, *passim*; Rodman Papers, *passim.*

Blount Hall in Craven County, North Carolina

many activities incident to his rising status. As militia officer, Jacob Blount rode on muster days to New Bern for gatherings more convivial than military, but within the revelry of the ranks and the quiet chats of the gentlemen officers throbbed that vital pulse of public sentiment to which all Blount ears harkened. On the second Tuesdays in March and September, Justice Blount presided with his fellows at the New Bern district court. Here there was little formality but much common sense as quarrels were adjusted, fines imposed, delinquents warned, and future rates assessed. On still other occasions the never-ending battle with the highways went on as Blount checked off his own and his neighbors' labor in "*a just account* of work that is *missing* on the *roads*." The active squire's little journal expanded with the minutiae of his busy life:

get calico for Henry Cannon . . . things left with Tisdell the Silver smith in New Bern to sell for me . . . rent of my plantation at Cosby £6 . . . memo to rent 8 negroes at best price possible for Sam'l Cornell . . . skins to go to Philadelphia . . . lists of brands for barrel heads . . . memo to buy vinegar, onions, needles, buttons, nutmeg, coffee, indigo and Apples at New Bern . . . Deborah Anderson come before me and made oath that John Merron begot a base born child by her . . . a loan to Blackledge to buy pork . . . cargo lists of hides tallow and fat, for Philadelphia . . . memo: hire atty for man accused of stealing.[5]

With all these came the duties of executor to estates, cases to be prosecuted at court, monies to be collected for transporting felons to the jail at New Bern.

The earliest recollections of the boys also included memories of their father's absences on assembly duty.[6] There, like an able politician, Jacob served both his own neighborhood and the province at large. For individual constituents, he secured exemptions from taxes and services, he interested himself in acts to facilitate navigation

[5] Blount Collection, P.C. 904.
[6] Saunders (ed.), *Colonial Records,* V–IX, *passim.*

in the ports, to establish a school and build a better jail at New Bern, to destroy pests of farmers, to build yards and fences, to collect strays, or to secure better government for New Bern. He also served the committees on claims—indispensable builders of political support. For the province at large he worked steadily in the collection of quitrents, the establishment and regulation of the superior and county courts, the delineation of parishes and vestries, the obtainment of a public printer, the printing of laws, the establishment of towns and warehouses, the building of roads, the proper preparation of export commodities, and the regulation of fees.[7] Though an increasing use of New Bern as the seat of the assembly made possible quick trips to the Hall to keep in touch with activity there, absences from home were inconvenient and sometimes impossible.[8] On the other hand, the increasing development of the Craven-Pitt area meant both more rival groups and more aspirants for offices, and it dictated attention to the game of politics. Allied with the increasingly wealthy and powerful Bryan family and the rising Richard Caswell, Jacob Blount steadily maintained and augmented an already strong position. Thus before the attentive gaze of young William and John Gray, the people and politics of the countryside became familiar by personal acquaintance or by conversation at New Bern or the Hall.

And with the faces of the people they learned the face of the land, for Jacob Blount's growing wealth was reflected in his increasing acres. As it did for thousands of other specie-starved subjects of King George, land for him became security, wealth, power, and avocation. It reflected

[7] *Ibid.,* V, 243, 244; VII, 363, 386, 387, 392, 418, 571, 573, 580, 589, 593, 625, 641, 942, 953–54; VIII, 318–19, 324, 454.
[8] Saunders (ed.), *Colonial Records,* VI, 164, 662–63, 801.

his judgment, it colored his politics, it permeated his existence. The steady growth of Blount lands was his chief measure of success: May, 1754—240 acres on North Contentnea; March, 1756—400 acres in Anson County; June, 1758—325 acres on the north side of the Neuse; September, 1759—350 acres in Craven; May and November, 1761—385 acres in Craven.[9]

In August, 1761, Jacob Blount and Richard Blackledge made the significant purchase of a store at the forks of the Tar River, a site of which the commercial possibilities were not lost on his sons.[10] The last years of the 'sixties saw the list of purchases lengthen: two lots in New Bern from Richard Cogdell; 500 acres east of Contentnea Creek; 200 acres from Abraham Giddens; 214 acres in "Black Swamp"; 600 in Craven; another 640 in Craven; 200 from Marlowe in Pitt County; 200 on the Neuse; 217 at the mouth of Great Contentnea; 144 on Grindel's Creek.[11] So acreage increased in this decade of personal prosperity and advance.

Nor did Jacob Blount buy merely to hold. He acquired, rather, to sell and realize profit. Equally long was even a partial list of sales: to Robert Fellow, 160 acres on the south side of Little River; to William Millender, Jr., 200 acres on Cabin Branch for £50; to Samuel Powell, 200 acres in Pitt County for £20; to Dennis Cannon, 150 acres on the west side of Cash Swamp for £20; to Ethelred Peters Taylor, a 100-acre plantation on the south side of Great Contentnea Creek for £50; to Samuel Granger, 200

---

[9] Craven County Deeds, Book 15, p. 232, State Land Office (Raleigh); Blount Collection, P.C. 898, *passim*.

[10] Jacob Blount Day Book, Blount Collection, P.C. 899.

[11] Blount Collection, P.C. 898; Rodman Papers, *passim*; Pitt County Deeds, Book B, 490; Craven County Deeds, Books 12–13, p. 353; Book 14, p. 336; Book 15, pp. 11–12, 34–36, 37–40, 91–93; Book 17, pp. 94–96; Book 18, pp. 189–92; Book 21, pp. 54–55.

acres.[12] So there unfolded before the growing boys a constant pattern of land transactions, and such activity in time naturally absorbed them likewise.

Meanwhile the Blounts experienced the ordinary joys and sorrows of a family. In 1755, soon after arriving at Blount Hall, the family was increased by a second daughter, Louisa, followed in 1757 by a son, Reading, and two years later by Thomas. In 1763, another daughter, Barbara, was born, but the endemic fevers and the cares of the growing family were too much for the mother, and she survived the arrival of her namesake daughter but fifteen days, dying on April 8, 1763. This, the children's first great sorrow, occurred in William Blount's fourteenth year. The motherless brood waited for two years before Jacob Blount, on November 26, 1765, married Hannah, widow of William Baker of South Quay, Virginia, and daughter of Colonel Edward Salter, an influential early settler. This marriage brought Mrs. Blount's son, Ned Baker, to the Hall to join his step-brothers and sisters, and from the marriage were born two sons, Willie Blount and Jacob Blount, Jr.

In the year 1765 other events occurred which affected the family. On March 28, Governor Arthur Dobbs died while preparing to return to England, and on April 3, he was succeeded by the energetic and popular William Tryon. The latter had arrived in New Bern in the previous December, amid the rejoicing of the New Bern burghers, and the Blounts had gone down to watch the town outdo itself in welcoming the new Lieutenant Governor's arrival with "handsome" illuminations, nineteen-gun salutes, and congratulatory addresses by the mayor and his council. In the evening a great ball had been staged in the courthouse,

[12] Craven County Deeds, Books 12–13, p. 136; Book 16, p. 232; Book 18, pp. 182–84, 345; Book 22, p. 1; Blount Collection, P.C. 897, *passim*.

with "near one hundred" gentlemen and ladies present, and at about ten in the evening "a very elegant collation" was laid for the elite in the Long Room while "plenty of liquor was given to the Populace." [13]

The confidence of the burghers was not misplaced, for upon assuming the governorship Tryon lost no time in securing an appropriation from the assembly to begin the erection of the "Palace" at New Bern, thereby assuring an influential future for the Neuse-Pamlico citizens. While the magnificent new palace arose in New Bern, Jacob Blount made his usual purchases of slaves and land, marketed his crops, and engaged in business with Sam Cornell, or David Barron & Company, or Richard Ellis. He worked increasingly hard in the assembly with Alexander Lillington, the Ashes, Cornelius Harnett, and others from the Cape Fear region, with Joseph Hewes and Stephen Cabarrus from Edenton, with the Joneses of Halifax, and, above all, with the pushing Richard Caswell of Kinston. The new governor was tactful and able, and despite a few quarrels the assembly served with him in harmony.

Nevertheless, the prosperity and general harmony of the easterners did not disperse lengthening shadows from the west. There a long history of extortionate fees, packed juries, venal officers and lawyers, and general eastern disregard for the problems or difficulties of the westerners had recently erupted in explosions in Mecklenburg, Halifax, and Granville counties. For a time Governor Dobbs' proclamation forbidding illegal fees had quieted affairs, but in the Spring of 1768, the west flared up anew over tax seizures in Orange County. Tryon and Colonel Edmund Fanning assembled the militia at Hillsboro to protect

---

[13] *North Carolina Magazine or Universal Intelligencer,* December 21-28, 1764, in *North Carolina Historical Review,* VI (1929), 413-14.

the courts, and before this force the "Regulators" wilted. The east applauded, and in December, 1768, Blount carried from assembly to council a bill to pay for suppressing "the late Insurrection on the Western Frontiers." [14] But the west would not down. Although this assembly erected Tryon County from Mecklenburg as the Regulators desired, other measures on debt, triennial assemblies, and taxation were lost. In addition, the eastern-minded group, stirred by anger, printed a strongly anti-Regulator sermon.

The Spring of 1769 was a troubled one. Petitions arrived in New Bern from Anson, Mecklenburg, Tryon, and Chowan counties, and scattered attacks on officials continued. On September 7, a hurricane roared in from the Atlantic to blast New Bern for two days. The tide rose twelve feet in a few hours; ships, wharves, houses, tanneries, stores, and the distillery were destroyed, and six citizens lost their lives. Nearly two thirds of the city was swept away, and costly damages soared.

On October 23, 1769, therefore, Blount journeyed to the battered town to take his place in a nervous and unstable assembly. The house contained many new faces as the Regulators, disappointed in the assembly and defeated in the courts, had turned to the polls. Of seventy-eight members, forty-three were new men.[15] Nevertheless, it was a moderate group of legislators, and reasonable reform measures were introduced, only to be lost as news arrived of grievances in the north. On November 2, the house received resolutions of the Virginia house of burgesses directed against the Townshend Acts, resolutions which had occasioned the summary dissolution of the Virginia house by the royal governor. The Carolinians, after con-

---

[14] Saunders (ed.), *Colonial Records,* VII, 982–83.

[15] John Spencer Bassett, "The Regulators of North Carolina," in American Historical Association *Annual Report,* 1894 (Washington, 1895), 184.

sideration, passed in their turn five loyal but spirited resolutions, claiming for the assembly the sole right of
taxation, affirming the right of petition to the Crown,
denouncing transportation overseas for trial, and presenting a petition for royal redress.[16] Tryon, ill and anxious
for favorable Whitehall opinion, rebuked the assembly
and dissolved it, and Blount and his unrepentant fellows
rode home.

A lull followed. Then in September, 1770, the western
storm broke. Visitors at the Hall told of outrages at Hillsboro; of friends and relatives—John Williams, Edmund
Fanning, Thomas Hart, Alexander Martin—beaten by
mobs; of Judge Richard Henderson fleeing while property
was ruined and mock trials were held in the captured courtroom. In November came reports that Judge Henderson's
home, barns, and stables had been burned, that the mobs
were marching on New Bern to secure redress and to bar
Fanning from his assembly seat. The little capital was in
an uproar. The attorney-general hastened to the governor
to confer on the law of treason, Blount and other justices
of the peace were ordered to take depositions on the outrages, the militia was to be called out between Hillsboro
and New Bern, and the Craven County militia was ordered
to protect the capital.

Amidst these alarms and excursions, the Blounts' excitement rose with the rest. Friends and relatives had felt
the mob's lash and had lost property to its fury, and the
Hall lay directly in the path of an invasion of New Bern.
Defenses had to be prepared and movables made ready for
evacuation while Blount and the older boys were involved
in militia strategy. The assembly met for the first time
in the new palace in December, 1770, and Jacob Blount
prepared to take active part in support of law and gov-

[16] Saunders (ed.), *Colonial Records*, VIII, 121–24.

ernment. With Fanning, he repaired to the palace to inform the governor of the assembly's readiness to proceed to business, and his friend, Richard Caswell, was elected speaker.

Tryon asked both for redress of grievance and for punishment, including the raising of troops against the "seditious mob." The two houses, trying to be moderate but panicky from rumors, expelled and imprisoned Hermon Husband and enacted a severe riot act.[17] Meanwhile, the governor pressed for action, and when a grand jury on February 2, 1771, failed to indict Husband and others, he called another for March and virtually chose its membership. The "gentlemen of the first rank, property and probity" thus personally selected included Jacob Blount and his closest associates, Joseph Leech, John Hawks, Richard Cogdell, Richard Caswell, James Glasgow, and Edward Salter. They and Judge Henderson met at New Bern with the foreordained result of sixty-two true bills and not one exculpation.[18]

The governor immediately prepared for a military expedition into Orange County, and Blount and the other merchants left the courts of justice for the marts of trade. The little capital hummed with martial bustle. Stores and blacksmiths' teemed with soldiers-to-be purchasing clothing and equipage. A sloop from New York brought two fieldpieces, drums, colors, leggings, and cockades. Richard Blackledge became commissary, John Hawks, paymaster general. Jacob Blount, now paymaster for the Craven County troops, also furnished one of the scarce wagons for transport.

Such activity was needed, for on March 19, 1771, Tryon called on the colonels of the counties for 2,550 men.

[17] For the journal of this session, see *ibid.*, 302–46, 385–479.
[18] *Ibid.*, 511, 528–32, 546–47.

A column under Hugh Wadell was to march from Cape Fear to Hillsboro via Salisbury; the second, under the governor, from New Bern directly to Hillsboro. On April 21, the Carteret troops arrived at the capital, and next day Craven mustered three companies under Colonel Joseph Leech and one company of Rangers under Captain Christopher Newle. On April 24 the column proudly paraded from an admiring town with two fieldpieces, six swivel guns, sixteen wagons, and four carts. Among the troops rode Jacob, John Gray, and William Blount.[19]

Hillsboro was reached without incident on May 9. Two days later, the column was in motion again, and on May 14, reached the banks of the Alamance. A day of rest followed, and on May 16 the brief battle ended victoriously for the government. Then followed the reprisals and the triumphant homeward march. Neither Blount nor his young sons figured prominently in the confused events of the day, but the father's accounts illustrate his active program:

Sent to Capt. Holt's 6 shirts, 2 jackets, 3 prs. Breeches, 3 prs thread stockings to be washed. . . . Pade Mr. Holt for washing 6 shilling . . . Paid Cogdell his part for finding . . . horse. . . . lent Richard Cogdell at the Moraveens town six pounds to pay for a mare. . . . pade at Hillsborough for one horn 6s 6d. . . . pade Smyth at Hillsborough for mending my cart. . . . received field gun from the Governor and let it to the following. . . . received guns from Mr. Clare and lent them to the following persons . . . . List of Rich Blackledge's company against the Regulators, April 1771, List of Capt Johnstons company. . . . Capt Samuel Smyth's company. . . . a memorandum of monies pade to the troops that the Governor ordered for their part of the plonder taken from the Regulators the day the battle was fought at Grate Alamance May 26, 1771 . . . which was 2/6 each man.[20]

[19] Walter Clark (ed.), *The State Records of North Carolina* (Raleigh, 1886–1907), XIX, 837–38. Hereinafter referred to as *State Records*. Persistent traditional and family accounts place William Blount in Tryon's army, though no direct evidence has been discovered to prove this.

[20] Jacob Blount Day Book, Blount Collection, P.C. 899.

And so the merchant-soldier kept accounts, purchased, and made loans while he marched to uphold the authority of his King. It was a busy experience, a typical experience, and a legacy of policy to his attentive sons: law and order must prevail; gentlemen will see it done; business need not suffer.

In a larger sense, too, the Alamance was significant for the Blounts. As the little army wound back through the wooded hills to New Bern in the hot July, an era was ended, though they did not know it. Tryon had already returned to the capital; in little over a month, this able, politic champion of the east had gone to his new post in New York. In the critical years to come, his place was to be filled with a far less astute man. The King had lost a shrewd conciliator among his increasingly less pacific, if still loyal, subjects in his province of North Carolina.

CHAPTER II

THE MERCHANT SOLDIER

THE LAST YEARS of North Carolina's loyalty to the Crown saw the beginning of mature activity for young William Blount. He watched closely and participated increasingly in the varied activities of his father, for Jacob Blount was never busier nor more prosperous. Accompanying him to New Bern's races or sales, supervising the farm labor, buying and selling for father or self, William Blount, no longer a gangling youngster, now met his father's associates as client or purchaser. Names known from childhood—Bryan, Cogdell, Person, Hooper, and Leech—became persons with views and interests to be estimated, assessed, and used. His father's wealth, and especially his credit, made the transition easy. The name of William Blount became familiar not only to merchants and farmers in the Carolinas but to business firms as far away as Philadelphia.[1]

John Gray Blount at times seemed closer to his father. It was John Gray whose name appears most often in the Memorandum Book, who clerked at the Assembly in 1770, 1771, 1773, and 1774. The second son's tastes were more nearly those of the father. The give and take of commercial dealings, the haggling, the keen appraisal of value

---

[1] Craven County Deeds, Book 18, pp. 184, 345; Lida Rodman manuscript, in Rodman Papers.

were more congenial to him. William's was the polish, the ingenuity, the geniality, the study of the personalities and foibles of men. More open views, opinions, and sympathies in John Gray kindled deeper and wider friendships, for towards him men felt admiration edged with envy. The more secretive and reserved William inspired respect tinged with caution. Between the two, mutual esteem never diminished, for William's energy, originality, and ambition commanded his brother's approbation, while John Gray's keen sense of values and mastery of detail evoked from William a respect he denied virtually all other men.

Both brothers felt the steady hunger of ambition. Both had learned well the value of shilling and pence as well as of pound and guinea, though William would spend more readily than his brother. Both had supremely developed the sense of speculation—of risk balanced against reward; in John Gray it was tempered with more judgment, in William it was burnished with more ingenuity. Both, too, were closely attuned to the public mind, both felt the current of opinion keenly, and ignored it only for the superior pressures of wealth or power.[2]

This sensitivity to public feeling, as the opening years of the 'seventies slipped by, gave mounting warning of crises to come. Tension was building up in the commonwealth, increased by mounting pressure from without. On August 11, 1771, Josiah Martin assumed the governorship. His virtues were his vices. Plain, blunt, honest, and loyal, he lacked completely the diplomacy, ingratiation, and astuteness which Tryon used so successfully. Too impolitic to create a government party, Martin proceeded at once in line of duty to antagonize the eastern group of which Tryon's party had been created. So completely were the personal interests of this class ignored that no other basis

[2] Blount Collection, *passim.*

for adhesion to the government's policies remained save blind loyalty to the Crown. This was enough for Scottish merchants, British officials, and Highlanders of the Cape Fear region. It was not enough for ambitious, assertive yeomen, in many of whom tradition, race, and blood abhorred the name of Briton, and whose principal interest in life, untrammeled individualism, was now denied and threatened in the name of loyalty.

The clash was not long in coming. The Blounts, Caswells, and their fellow moderates in the assembly of 1771 were agreed that the west should be mollified, and so suggested pardons for the Regulators, established new counties, provided for a western road, and fixed rates for fees. But Martin in 1771 went too far when he traveled to the west, issuing pardons to the Regulators and visiting with them and with the unassimilated, competitive, and Tory Scots of the Cape Fear region. To eastern businessmen this appeared an excess of brotherhood, especially from a man who openly disparaged Tryon the Conqueror.[3] Although the legislature (to the delight of speculators) paid for the Alamance campaign by a £60,000 debenture issue, the prosaic clerk of the committee on accounts on December 6, 1771, cast the apple of discord. He reported that a poll tax and certain import duties on liquors enacted to meet appropriations of 1748 and 1754 had raised a surplus over the appropriations. Here was a situation which no responsive merchant-politician could ignore. If the tax were discontinued, constituents would be pleased, currency contraction prevented, friendly sheriffs unfortunately in arrears could be relieved of embarrassment, and a restraint on trade removed. The assembly stopped the

---

[3] Ashe, *History of North Carolina*, I, 396–98; Enoch Walter Sikes, *The Transition of North Carolina from Colony to Commonwealth*, in Johns Hopkins University *Studies in History and Political Science*, Series XVI, Nos. 10–11 (Baltimore, 1898), 10.

tax, and the wily Richard Caswell, sensing gubernatorial opposition, proposed a resolution to indemnify the sheriff for not collecting it. Martin, as expected, reacted violently, vetoed the law as fraudulent, and dissolved the legislature. When Speaker Caswell sent the resolution to the sheriffs anyway, the governor threatened them with suits, and the issue was open.[4] The dissolution did not come, however, before a second explosion occurred, this time over the running of the boundary with South Carolina on terms which meant loss of territory. Tryon had diplomatically delayed this unpopular measure, but the imperceptive Martin, despite angry protests from the assembly, by proclamation ordered it to be run.

In 1772, the unpopular line was surveyed during a summer of severe drought and crop failures. The assembly met January 18, 1773, in a fretful mood. When the legislators turned to fashion a new judiciary bill to replace an expiring one, the long-standing quarrel over an attachment clause, which allowed seizure of the property of debtors living in England, caused such a wrangle that no judiciary bill was passed, and the assembly was dissolved on March 9, with both sides angry. The province was in a condition to accentuate ill temper; with few courts in existence and the jails filling, even the more sober citizenry grew disturbed. Martin chose then to issue commissions of oyer and terminer to clear the jails, and with infrequent sagacity, asked the Whig leaders Maurice Moore and Richard Caswell to serve as judges. Accustomed to office and stirred by ambition, both men accepted the posts only to meet such a wave of public criticism as to amaze even these veteran politicians. It was a lesson in public sentiment which Caswell never forgot.

[4] Saunders (ed.), *Colonial Records,* IX, xvi–xviii; Sikes, *Transition of North Carolina,* 12; Ashe, *History of North Carolina,* I, 399–400.

In fact, in three short years, unbending, loyal Martin had deeply antagonized the strongest elements in his colony: he had insisted upon pursuing deflation in a chronic debtor-speculator society; on giving away land and population to a supercilious rival province; on withholding their just dues from Carolina merchants, though it meant the release of that lawless element which Tryon had marched to suppress. A leadership of self-conscious loyalty found its private interests and its social order menaced while its sovereignty was flouted for the interests of English "gentlemen" who would not pay their debts, and of South Carolinians who recognized North Carolinians only to despise them. From the history of this polyglot colony of so many racial origins and religious hues, a number of episodes might have warned the wary. The names of Culpeper and of Cary bore a tradition of civic restlessness and clashing discord in leadership, but the monitions of domestic history were unheeded.

Also, not only the leadership, but the generality of Carolinians bore old grievances. The westerner, so long denied a nearby county court; the debtor, refused the paper-money key to freedom; the Granville District farmer or the small landholder, hounded for quitrents for an absent English landlord or enclosed by the idle land of English speculators—these saw much virtue in a change of things. Similarly, the inland merchant, pressed by canny Tory competition; the smuggler, threatened with more vigilant customs officers; the speculator, eyeing forbidden Indian lands—these envisioned greater wealth from a new order. In agreement were others: the disappointed politician; the would-be governor; the Baptist preacher, struggling for a legal congregation; the dispossessed, the envious, and the unaccepted. All of these had seethed for decades past. Now to their unformed ranks came those

who were accustomed to lead: Bryans, Coors, Blounts,
Harnetts, Joneses, and Harveys. The combination was
fatal to the status quo.

In their response to external pressures, people and leaders had already reacted clearly. In 1765, the Stamp Act
officials had been met with demonstrations, seizures of
stamps, burning effigies, and coercion, and the repeal of the
act brought public rejoicing. In 1768, the assembly had
taken no official notice of circular letters from Virginia
and Massachusetts, but this lack of action had been denounced by the influential and conservative Samuel Johnston as "great pusillanimity," and John Harvey privately
assured Massachusetts of North Carolina's co-operation.
Meanwhile, the assembly composed an address to the King
and instructed their agent in England to present it.[5] In
short, increasing anti-British activity to the northward had
deeply stirred the Carolinians, and they reacted like their
northern counterparts with extralegal committees, Sons of
Liberty, and unending oratory.

So, with long-standing discontents, with new fears
within and alarms from without, the province of North
Carolina in March, 1773, was loyal but disturbed. The
observant Josiah Quincy, passing through Wilmington
early in the year, dined with a group of leaders at William
Hooper's and stayed with Cornelius Harnett, whom he
characterized as the "Samuel Adams of North Carolina."
Quincy came to talk committees with the gentlemen, and
he left well pleased.[6] The next assembly, after a quarrel-

[5] R. D. W. Connor, *Colonial and Revolutionary Periods,* Volume I of
(no ed.), *History of North Carolina* (New York, 1919), 321–30, 331–33;
Ashe, *History of North Carolina,* I, 346–48; H. I. Crumpler, "Craven County
in the Revolution," in *North Carolina Review,* July 7, 1912, p. 11; Alonzo
Thomas Dill, Jr., "Eighteenth Century New Bern: A History of the Town
and Craven County, 1700–1800," Part 7, in *North Carolina Historical Review,*
XXIII (1946), 326.

[6] Dill, "Eighteenth Century New Bern," *loc. cit.,* 326; Ashe, *History of
North Carolina,* I, 410.

some and short life, again met dissolution, and the leaders opened systematic correspondence with the North.

During the 1773–74 winter of tension and strategy planning, young William Blount, along with his family and other conservative leaders, was slowly forced into a choice of loyalties. Men of business rather than of the courts, and more and more engaged in the multifarious activities of money-making, William and his family had hitherto stood as moderates. But the threat of lawlessness, the pressure of debt, the influence of relatives and associates, the promise of wider activities and prospects, and, above all, the increasing volume of Whig sentiment, worked decisively on them. Of the younger brothers, Reading Blount, most martial of the family, was already deep in militia affairs, while the excitement of the volatile Thomas rose daily. William and John Gray, like their father, moved less exuberantly though just as surely in the direction of rebellion.

On March 1, 1774, the assembly convened, only to be quickly prorogued amidst another burst of irritation. Speaker Harvey roared, "Then the people will convene themselves," and he, with Edward Buncombe, Sam Johnston, and Willie Jones talked methods of calling a popular meeting, while Hooper was delegated to broach the matter in Cape Fear to Harnett, Ashe, and others.[7]

Into this scene of disgruntled indecision burst galvanic news. Breathless horsemen sent express from correspondents in the North brought fact, alarm, and rumor: the port of Boston had been closed, the powers of the Massachusetts assembly had been curtailed, overseas trials were provided, and more British troops had been sent to Massachusetts to be quartered by force on the civilians. Here was material

[7] Ashe, *History of North Carolina*, I, 414; Allan Nevins, *The American States During and After the Revolution* (New York, 1924), 41.

in plenty for the Carolina leaders to work with, and the response was electric. Letters went forth to the Northern colonies approving the cutting off of commercial relations with Britain and the convening of a congress of all colonies. Under Hooper's guiding hand the first provincial congress, despite the thunders of Martin, met at New Bern on August 25, 1774. In session three days, this body passed resolutions asserting rights of taxation, representation, and judicial procedure, condemned England's acts relating to Boston, and adopted nonimportation and nonexportation agreements. Approving of the Continental Congress, the congress selected Hooper, Hewes, and Caswell as delegates, provided for county committees to be set up for the enforcement of their resolves, and outlined a procedure for being recalled into session.

Thus the colony of North Carolina swung into the stream of "rebellion" as the governor termed it, of "protest" in the minds of most leaders. For, though Hooper wrote to James Iredell of the colonies "striding fast to independence" and building an "empire upon the ruins of Great Britain," yet Caswell, a representative politician, still retained the confidence of the suspicious governor.[8]

During the following winter of crisis, committee work kept Jacob Blount increasingly engaged, while his two oldest sons mixed usual business pursuits with heady politics. As the months passed, the county committees assumed absolute authority. Oaths of loyalty were demanded, known Tories roughly handled; at Wilmington, imported tea was locked up in the customhouse, and powder was distributed to the troops now being drilled and outfitted.

[8] William Hooper to James Iredell, April 26, 1774, in Griffith J. McRee, *Life and Correspondence of James Iredell* (New York, 1847), I, 197; C. B. Alexander, "Richard Caswell, Versatile Leader of the Revolution," in *North Carolina Historical Review*, XXIII (1946), 119–20; Ashe, *History of North Carolina*, I, 422–23.

In Craven, the committee disarmed all who would not support the Continental Association and even requested the vestry to discharge the much-respected Reverend James Reed for refusing to conduct services on the fast day appointed by the Continental Congress.[9] In November, Jacob Blount was appointed by a Pitt County committee "to assist the gentlemen of Saint Michael's parish to raise aid and relief for Boston." Morale at home, too, had to be kept up, and on March 4, 1775, he, with his fellow members of the New Bern committee, exhorted the citizens to stand firm in support of the Association and damned Britain with ringing fervor. Meanwhile, Jacob, William, and John Gray Blount acquired a desirable land grant from the governor, and watched with great interest the preparations of their friend, speculator Richard Henderson, to purchase a vast tract in western North Carolina and Virginia, in which scheme they planned to invest with their cousin Thomas Hart.[10]

Governor Martin returned from a visit to Tryon in New York on January 15, 1775, to find the committees directing affairs. Embittered and sorrowful over the third loss of a child, he sought and obtained appointment as land agent for the Granville District, only to be faced with the competition of Henderson's lands acquired by illegal western purchase. The governor then called an assembly to meet at New Bern on March 29, 1775, and on February 11, the ill but watchful Harvey again sent forth handbills for a convention at the same place, to meet on April 3.

Both sides girded for the final test. Samuel Ashe,

[9] Ashe, *History of North Carolina*, I, 425–27; Connor, *Colonial Period*, 354–58; McRee, *Life of Iredell*, I, 256.

[10] Craven County Deeds, Book 19, pp. 391–94; Book 21, pp. 282–84; Book 22, pp. 12, 269, 307; Book 24, pp. 103, 104; Blount Collection, P.C. 898, *passim*; William Blount to John Gray Blount, June 4, 1777, in Alice Barnwell Keith (ed.), *The John Gray Blount Papers* (Raleigh, 1952), I, 3–6. Hereinafter cited as *Blount Papers*.

Cornelius Harnett, James Moore, and Alexander Lillington worked in Cape Fear overawing recalcitrant antiasso-
ciationists, while in the Neuse area, Abner Nash, the
Blounts, and others stirred up public feeling, as did Willie
Jones in Halifax, and Samuel Johnston in Edenton. On
April 4, both congress and assembly organized and made
a quorum, with identical leadership and virtually identical
membership, while the elder Blount and the other members
of the two bodies worked together closely.[11] The assembly,
dissolved in four days, accomplished as little as was expected. The congress thanked its delegates to the Continental Congress and re-elected them, ratifying the acts
of that body. It then made provision for its reassembly
and adjourned.

The climax came on May 6 when New Bern heard
the news from Lexington. Speeding on a messenger to
Onslow County, the Craven leaders acted. Men drilled
in the squares of New Bern, messengers rode forth night
and day, rumor and fact flew through the little town and
swept the country like its indigenous malarial fever. The
cornered governor fought back, but his emissaries to the
Scots were watched, and his letters to General Gage, with
their damaging requests for arms, were opened. When
he dismounted and collected the cannon on the palace
grounds, Abner Nash led an angry group of protest. Rumors rose that the governor planned to arm the slaves,
and the crowds grew larger and louder, culminating in
a mob that seized the cannon and bore them off, while
young John Gray Blount hurled a lightwood knot at the
governor.

Still, if his son was impetuous, Jacob Blount was not.
As at Alamance, his grievances were less in politics than
in economics, his interest less in personal violence than

11 Nevins, *American States,* 77–78.

in the preservation of order, less in political theory than in economic practicality. He might harangue the militia with flaming Whiggism, he might sign the Association, serve on the Pitt County Committee of Safety, and bind himself to obedience to the Continental and North Carolina congresses, but he maintained relations with the governor, and his home was open to the frightened, departing Loyalists, many of them his lifelong friends. The businessman would not be stampeded, and his public efforts were in the less martial committees of ways and means or in settling accounts.[12]

Because the crowding events of the summer of 1775 absorbed the attention of their father, more direction of business fell to William and John Gray Blount. Keen judgment was required to buy and sell in a quaking economy. The political portents and potentials of the congresses had to be weighed, shrewd purchases made from timorous émigrés, supplies sold to the nascent Whig forces. Outside contacts had to be kept up and commercial lanes used before they perhaps shared the fate of Boston. Never were there fewer established canons to guide young merchants. The most respected leaders of the mercantile world, Thomas MacKnight, Archibald Hamilton, Samuel Cornell, John Cruden, were smeared with Toryism and driven out. Old markets collapsed with old regulations. The commerce of the colony, not seriously affected by the earlier Association, was almost stricken down by 1775.[13] Under the scarcity of goods and the increasing flood of paper, the whole economic system was twisted, and popular feeling, lashed by scarcity, rose against all merchants. At home, too,

[12] Speech of Jacob Blount, Blount Collection, P.C. 906; Saunders (ed.), *Colonial Records*, IX, 1143–44, 1181; X, 38, 171–72, 504, 507.

[13] Charles Christopher Crittenden, *The Commerce of North Carolina* (New Haven, 1936), 116, 117, 142; Arthur M. Schlesinger, *The Colonial Merchants and the American Revolution, 1763–1776* (New York, 1918), 535.

duties pressed, for Blount Hall must be directed, and Jacob
Blount insisted on their attention there.

It was this atmosphere of political and economic upheaval that set the mold of the mind and methods of William Blount. To the versatile opportunism and powerful
economic motivation of his youthful training were now
added the experiences of life in a re-forming economic and
political system. The many opportunities to be seized, the
plunge to gain or lose all, the gamble—whether in paper
money, corn, or political allegiance—all became immanent
characteristics of the young Whig's thinking. In business
and politics the times called for a leadership of expediency,
gamble, and maneuver, and Blount's nature responded
in a manner which became a lifelong pattern.

In the last days of May, 1775, Governor Martin fled
to Fort Johnston on the Cape Fear and thence in July to
a British warship. Clouds of Loyalists followed, while
rumors spread of Scots descending on Wilmington from
Cross Creek. All this made new Whig moves necessary,
but the first divisions in that group were now appearing.
To Samuel Johnston, James Iredell, Allan Jones, William
Hooper, and other lawyers and conservatives, the music
of freedom now began to carry the discord of anarchy.
Loyalist friends were being pillaged, mobs were too frequent, doctrines of leveling filled the air. Among the gentlemen assembled to guide the colony appeared Timothy
Bloodworth, the ex-blacksmith; Thomas Person, the ex-
Regulator; and Griffith Rutherford, the Tory-hater. Yet
events had to be met. Caswell hurried from Philadelphia;
and in July, Johnston, to enlist western support, called a
congress for August 20, 1775, at Hillsboro. This body
raised two regiments, issued money, formed the usual temporary government of hierarchical committees, promised

bounties for manufacture, and sent emissaries to ex-Regulators and the Cape Fear Scots.[14]

The winter of 1775–76 was one of mounting excitement. In February came the Whig victory at Moore's Creek, crushing the Loyalists and raising Caswell on the waves of military popularity. It also redoubled Whig efforts and confirmed the beliefs of many, including the Blounts, in independence.[15] Still, the congress which met at Halifax in April, 1776, faced grave problems: large numbers of disaffected citizens, expiring terms of the Minute Men, and the need for more troops, arms, and money. In addition, Governor Dunmore's forays caused anxiety, especially as rumors persisted that Governor Martin and General Clinton, standing off Wilmington with a fleet of forty sail, daily expected Cornwallis and seven regiments. The economic necessity of a more permanent government was urged by Jacob Blount and the merchant group, but neither Johnston with his Conservatives nor Jones and Person with the Radicals were ready for a contest.[16] Hence the matter was postponed, though the Radicals succeeded in replacing Johnston with Willie Jones on the state

[14] Sikes, *Transition of North Carolina*, 45–53; McRee, *Life of Iredell*, I, 263; Connor, *Colonial Period*, 370–79; Thomas M. Pittman, "The Revolutionary Congresses of North Carolina," in *North Carolina Booklet*, II (1902), Pt. 6, p. 14.

[15] Samuel Johnston to James Iredell, April 5, 1776, in McRee, *Life of Iredell*, I, 275; Ashe, *History of North Carolina*, I, 507–508; Connor, *Colonial Period*, 381–84, 395–98.

[16] Saunders (ed.), *Colonial Records*, X, 515; Henry M. Wagstaff, *States Rights and Political Parties in North Carolina: 1776–1861*, in Johns Hopkins University *Studies in History and Political Science*, Series XXIV, Nos. 7–8 (Baltimore, 1906), 9–10; Nevins, *American States*, 130–31. For parties in the period, see *ibid.*, 358–62; Delbert H. Gilpatrick, *Jeffersonian Democracy in North Carolina, 1789–1816* (New York, 1931), 12, 22–24; Stephen B. Weeks, "Thomas Person," in *North Carolina Booklet*, IX (1909), 27–28; Ashe, *History of North Carolina*, I, 527–29, 530, 556–57; Fletcher M. Green, *Constitutional Development in the South Atlantic States, 1776–1860* (Chapel Hill, 1930), 66, 75–76.

Council of Safety. The congress also provided for four new battalions to add to the troops raised the year before, and instructed their delegates at Philadelphia to act with the other states in a declaration of independence. To the apprehension of the Conservatives, the emission of another $1,000,000 in paper money was ordered.

Yet it was a moderate congress, and the moderates received recognition. On April 17, Jacob Blount was appointed paymaster for the Second North Carolina regiment and subsequently paymaster of all North Carolina troops.[17] Next day William Blount was appointed to a committee to purchase and otherwise procure firearms for Craven County troops, and on May 3, probably at his father's request, he succeeded Caswell as paymaster of the New Bern District militia. The congress also made Reading Blount a captain and Thomas Blount an ensign in the Continental battalions.[18]

Meanwhile John Gray Blount was engaged in another enterprise of profound consequence for the future of the family. This was a trip to the Kentucky country with his cousin, Thomas Hart, and a purchase with him of lands in Richard Henderson's huge Transylvania Company acquisition. The economic interests thus acquired—and increased by those of Jacob Blount's second wife, who inherited Transylvania interests—were the first elements in William Blount's preoccupation with the West.[19]

The year 1776, however, kept most of the Blount family close to their home. Crowded, bustling little New Bern was thronged. Prisoners of war, felons, and Tories

[17] Saunders (ed.), *Colonial Records*, X, 524.

[18] *Ibid.*, 518, 524–25, 584.

[19] Reverend John D. Shane (ed.), "The Henderson Company Ledger," in *Filson Club History Quarterly*, XXI (1947), 22, 40; Archibald Henderson, "The Transylvania Company, a Study in Personnel," *ibid.*, 238; William Blount to Thomas Hart, May 18, 1798, in Thomas J. Clay Collection (Division of Manuscripts, Library of Congress).

filled the jails, while vestries examined yet more suspects. Civilian-soldiers and officers swarmed the streets. With Wilmington blocked and Beaufort once attacked, the commerce of the colony funneled through Ocracoke Inlet, crowding old and new wharves. On the river, Fort Caswell rose. John Wright Stanley, Richard Ellis, David Barron, and their brother shippers hurried off their brigs and sloops to foreign ports for supplies, or transformed merchant ships into privateers. Commissioners scoured the country for sulphur, iron, gunpowder, and especially salt. To secure this precious item, Richard Blackledge, senior, established a salt works, and John Gray Blount, returning from the Kentucky region, took ship in early 1777 for the French West Indies.[20]

While some North Carolina troops moved south, first to Wilmington, thence to Charleston, and others under Griffith Rutherford started westward against the expected Indian attacks, William and Jacob Blount worked with Richard Caswell and the state Committee of Safety in the unending task of securing and paying out money. The scarcity of this item, save in depreciated paper, the widely scattered positions of the troops, and the uncertainties arising from the new militia law all made the paymaster's work tedious and demanding. In June came heartening accounts of the defeat of Sir Peter Parker's fleet at Charleston, and in late July the expected news of a declaration of independence at Philadelphia.

Meanwhile, political winds in the new state grew bitter. The widening breach with England, the growing savagery of Whig and Tory raids, the pressure of debts, the old East-West animosities, the clash of race and creed in the

<hr />

[20] Saunders (ed.), *Colonial Records*, X, 984–85; John Gray Blount to Governor Caswell, March 4; 1777, in Clark (ed.), *State Records*, XI, 406; R. L. Hildrup, "The Salt Supply of North Carolina during the American Revolution," in *North Carolina Historical Review*, XXII (1945), 411.

heterogeneous population, all these evoked and pointed up divisions in Whig ranks. On August 9, 1776, Willie Jones reminded all Radicals of the coming congress, which was to make the constitution. The Conservatives waged a vigorous campaign, and riotous elections ensued. The rising after-battle smoke disclosed carnage in Conservative ranks: Samuel Spencer defeated in Anson County, John Campbell in Bertie, and leader Samuel Johnston rejected and burned in effigy. On November 12, at Halifax, the Radical victors assembled to form a constitution which was to last for over fifty years, and to excite the disgust of conservatives for over twice as many.[21] Yet, though dominated by Radicals, and following Radical ideas in general, the congress accepted unofficial advice from Johnston, and the constitution was in several respects a compromise. Also, the moderate Caswell was chosen interim governor.

To the busy but observant William Blount, the convention and its handiwork taught two things: the strength of the Radicals in the state, and the omnipotence of the assembly—lessons well learned. More immediately for his future, the congress on December 11, 1776, named him paymaster of the Third North Carolina battalion of Continental troops.[22] The origin of this appointment lay in both public military and private economic policy. With the removal of danger in the south, movement to the north was indicated for the North Carolina troops, and northward lay markets for Blount merchandise. Also, increasing issues of Continental money lent prestige and advan-

[21] Samuel Johnston to James Iredell, December 9, 1776, in McRee, *Life of Iredell,* I, 338–39; Nevins, *American States,* 141. For an analysis of the constitution, see Earle H. Ketcham, "The Sources of the North Carolina Constitution of 1776," in *North Carolina Historical Review,* VI (1929), 215–36.

[22] Saunders (ed.), *Colonial Records,* X, 966; North Carolina Revolutionary Army Accounts, IV, V (North Carolina State Department of Archives and History, Raleigh).

tage to the merchant-paymaster. Wild inflation demanded cash, and chaotic markets offered splendid advantages to the man with the ready money or official credit of a paymaster. In the dual role of businessman and paymaster, therefore, William Blount acted and prospered through the following years.

In early 1777, the Philadelphia Congress voted $500,-000 to pay the North Carolina Continentals, but as the troops were ordered to join Washington, Jacob Blount declined to go north, and William was chosen to receive the new funds on going to Philadelphia with his battalion. Deep in plans for acquiring one fourth of a "Pilate Boat" for privateering, he left by ship after the battalion, arriving at Williamsburg on June 4. In this busy capital he visited friends, markets, and shipping offices as usual, and also wandered into a session of the Virginia legislature in time to be irritated by a proud member's reference to that body as "the Highest Court of Judicature on the Continent," but the nettled Carolinian soothed his feelings at a passably good concert. More important, embattled speculator Richard Henderson dropped in to visit, and informed Blount that, as he wrote his brother, "our titles to the Transilvania lands shall stand or fall with his own," and that although the future of the speculation was in doubt, still, "all the entries will be made good to the Adventurers, whether he looses the proprietorship or not." [23]

In Philadelphia, while the American army watched Howe and listened for reports from Burgoyne, Blount exchanged the Carolina troops' nearly worthless paper for Continental money, and dispatched $300,000 in new funds to Caswell by a messenger, who promised to advise John Gray Blount of its arrival before delivering the money to

[23] William Blount to John Gray Blount, June 4, 1777, in Keith (ed.), *Blount Papers*, I, 3–6.

the governor. Further to be sure of prior advantage, Blount wrote his brother to apply to Caswell at once to get debts due the Blounts paid in Continental money while it lasted. He then remained in the vicinity of Philadelphia transacting financial affairs for his family and his battalion and witnessing the vain attempts of the army to keep Howe from Philadelphia. In October he returned to North Carolina.[24]

In his absence the state had been fairly calm save for depredations of deserters and threats of Tory uprisings, but factional politics continued. The first session of the first state assembly in April had elected Caswell governor, but expressed its partisan feeling by replacing congressman Joseph Hewes with Radical John Penn, to the intense disgust of the lawyer-Conservatives, and Hooper refused to serve in consequence.[25]

The second session, meeting at New Bern on November 15, 1777, was equally ill-tempered. A judiciary law written by James Iredell was passed, but the selection of two of the three judges—John Ashe and Samuel Spencer—was scarcely calculated to soothe Conservatives. Angers of the assembly spilled out into street and tavern, and on November 27, the sergeant at arms of the assembly haled before the bar of the house William Blount, charged with "high insult and indignity" to the house "and a breech of the privilege thereof, by committing a violent, deliberate and

[24] John Penn to Richard Caswell, July 12, 1777, in Clark (ed.), *State Records*, XI, 736, and XII, 591-92; William Blount to John Gray Blount, July 12, 1777, in Keith (ed.), *Blount Papers*, I, 6; Account of Jacob Blount, in Book of Settlement of North Carolina Accounts, in Records of the Office of the Adjutant General (National Archives, Washington, D.C.); Richard Caswell to Captain William Caswell, November 11, 1777, in Caswell Papers (University of North Carolina).

[25] James Iredell to Hannah Iredell, April 28, 29, 1777, in McRee, *Life of Iredell*, I, 358-59; "Creed of a Rioter," *ibid.*, 335-36; Samuel Johnston to Thomas Burke, (n.d.), in Connor, *Colonial Period*, 424; William Hooper to Robert Morris, May 27, 1777, in *North Carolina Historical Review*, IV (1927), 97-99; Nevins, *American States*, 363.

premeditated outrage on the person of the Honourable the Speaker in the streets of Newberne." Blount acknowledged the "outrage," but declared that he "had no intention to insult or offend the House," whereupon, asking pardon of the speaker and the house, he was discharged, "paying costs." Still, the insult rankled, and the house refused to clear the Paymaster's Philadelphia transaction "for want of sufficient proof." [26]

For the remainder of the year Blount was busy in army duties and private land purchases with his father. Frequently, too, he took the road to Wilmington, where lived Mary Grainger, the engaging, lively daughter of the late Caleb Grainger, a landowner-merchant of the Cape Fear region. The family was an old one, as prominent as Blount's own, though it was now harassed by problems of settling the father's estate. Mrs. Grainger, a somewhat inept if headstrong lady, welcomed the business advice and help of the astute young New Bern merchant, even as the heiress, Mary, looked favorably on her suitor's handsome face and social graces. Under these circumstances, Blount's war-pressed courtship moved swiftly into marriage on February 12, 1778. With dark, vivacious "Molsey" he began life at "Piney Grove," his comfortable farm at Martinsborough, acquired from the estate of his grandfather Thomas Blount.[27]

To maintain this home, to participate in a wartime business economy, and to fulfill official duties demanded Blount's free time and energy for the following two years. In January, 1778, the family was pleased by the release of young Thomas Blount from military line duty to serve as assistant paymaster, and in September a second wedding caused rejoicing when John Gray Blount married Mary

[26] Clark (ed.), *State Records,* XII, 308, 697.
[27] Rodman Papers, *passim.*

Harvey, thereby aligning two powerful families. John Gray took his bride to his home in Washington, North Carolina, where he operated the store earlier acquired by his father, and the disturbed times did not prevent visiting and correspondence between the members of this close and devoted family.

Military matters took much of William Blount's time. In April of 1778, a more responsive legislature (Nathan Bryan of Craven being on the committee of claims, and old friends Benjamin Hawkins and Richard Cogdell on that of accounts) paid Blount's Philadelphia account, and he continued his army duties, disbursing funds to both Continental and militia troops. He was made increasingly busy by the reorganization of the North Carolina battalions and their journey to South Carolina for the defense of Charleston, but, though active in facilitating this campaign, he was not present at Charleston on its fall and so, like his brother Reading, escaped the capture which befell Thomas Blount.[28]

Meanwhile, the career of the private merchant became increasingly exacting. With John Gray at Washington, William at Martinsborough, and Jacob at Blount Hall, the Blount establishment presented a widespread and well coordinated system to engage a large part of mid-Carolina commerce and merchandising. The elimination of British merchants, the high cost and danger of inland transport, the destruction of other and more usual buyers (in Virginia by British raids, in South Carolina by invasion) all threw the North Carolina producer on the mercy of the seacoast merchant of his own state. Meanwhile inflation soared, as

---

[28] Revolutionary Series Manuscripts, in War Department Records (National Archives); Account of William Blount, October, 1778, in Book of Settlement of North Carolina Accounts, Records of the Office of the Adjutant General; Cornelius Harnett to Richard Caswell, October 24, 1778, in Clark (ed.), *State Records*, XIII, 249–51; Rodman Papers.

finished goods disappeared from the markets and floods of paper money rose constantly higher. Choice purchases and the opportunity for virtual debt repudiation presented themselves to the New Bern merchants as anti-Loyalist legislation took effect in 1779. Hence, with established credit and capital, with facilities for warehousing or resale, and with close official and military connections through such men as Harvey, Nash, and Caswell, the Blounts rode the crest. To them came countrymen with tar, pitch, lumber, staves, shingles, and tobacco for whatever price the Blounts would give. To them also came agents, commissariats, and generals to get the salt, the cloth, the shoes, the weapons, the multitudinous supplies necessary to keep an army in the field. Buying shrewdly and generally only for immediate resale, guarding the better money and disbursing the more worthless, purchasing at low cost and selling at high prices, William Blount prospered.

Complaints there were, some open and bitter, some wry and facetious, as that from Cousin Thomas Hart:

I have (Once more) Sent a waggon and two Hhd^s. tob^o. to your place, and what will you send me in Return, I Suppose a half Bush^1. Salt, or Gall^n. of Rum for a 100^{wt} Tob^o, Something like this, I make no doubt,—What a Sett of Atheistical fellows must there be in New-bern that thinks there is Neither God nor Devil to punish them in a Nother World, for their usury to us in this, I must send down Debow Once more to preach up the Doctrine of Regeneration or the New Birth to you, for If ever there was a Sett of men on the face of this Globe, who stood more in Need of being Regenerated and Born anew, I wonder trully how many poor Sons of Bitches with tears in their Eyes have I Seen within these Six weeks past, Coming from your place, Some with 5 or 6 Bush^{ls}. Salt in their waggons, Some [with?] 8 or 10 Gall^s. of Rum, and others with Cargoes [of less?] Vallue, all declaring themselves Broken [miserably] but None of them without a Good Store of [curses which] they bestow (with a very Liberal hand) on the Good folks of Newbern . . . can you expect to thrive Under the Heavy Curses of the Rightious folks of this Country, had Not you better try to do Something that may

entitle you to Our Blessing Instead of Our Curses, come do (for
Godsake) begin with me, and let us See what you can do. . . .[29]

This semiserious adjuration was probably ignored
along with others more bitter, for Blount considered a
complainer as "an envious man, who was disturb'd Only
with his Own [mis]fortune, which forbid him Reaping
equal [amounts with] those he envy'd. . . ."[30] So, despite criticism and ill feeling, the Blounts bought prize
cargoes, speculated in paper money issues, sold supplies
to the Southern states, purchased land, traded with individuals, and throve.

Increasing economic influence inevitably brought
thoughts of political activity. Lawyer-conservatives were
political enemies because the rising merchant-speculator
espoused paper money issues, but the strength of these foes
was at Edenton and Wilmington. Governor Abner Nash
was a Craven man, and the friendship of Caswell was
steady and valuable. Members of the more radical wing,
such as John B. Ashe, were to be won over by the hospitality and well-filled cellars of Blount Hall.[31] Hence, in
1779, when the house of commons member from New Bern
resigned, William Blount announced for the office. His
opponent was young Richard Dobbs Spaight, rising hope
of the conservative faction, and the election was violent
even in a period of fierce contests. Both candidates coun-
tenanced illegal voting, the sheriff's rulings on eligibility
were capricious, and the "Tin Cannister without a Top"
which served as a ballot box was unsealed and unguarded.

[29] Thomas Hart to William Blount, January 25, 1780, in Keith (ed.),
Blount Papers, I, 8–10. For Blount prices, see also Archibald Maclaine to
George Hooper, February 5, 1784, in Clark (ed.), *State Records*, XVII, 128.

[30] Thomas Hart to William Blount, January 25, 1780, in Keith (ed.),
Blount Papers, I, 8–10.

[31] John B. Ashe to John Gray Blount, March 11, 1780, in Blount Collection; James Iredell to Hannah Iredell, May 18, 1780, in McRee, *Life of
Iredell*, I, 445.

Spaight won, but Blount protested; the committee on privileges and elections declared the election illegal, whereupon the house set it aside and neither aspirant was re-elected in time to take his seat in that session.[32]

In fact, as the year 1780 opened, Blount's energies were turned from politics by the increasing pressure of darkening military events. The reorganized Carolina Continentals left the north in late 1779, and, though augmented by further levies, were engulfed in American disasters at Savannah and Charleston, involving Blount finances, both public and private.[33] Along with a patriot reverse at Waxhaws on the twenty-ninth, these defeats laid North Carolina open to the British, and panic swept the state. Leaders were faced with gigantic problems. The state was already burdened with a paper money emission of $6,500,000 on which depreciation ranged from 32 to 1, to 150 to 1. Although taxes had risen steadily to six-pence per pound, inefficient collection and inflation reduced the revenue. Along with the valueless money, the almost complete absence of finished manufactures brought astronomical inflation: $20 for a string of fish, £100 for a barrel for corn, beef at £48 per pound, and bonds for some officials rose to £1,000,000.[34] The manpower problem was equally grave. Legislators of this commonwealth of strident individualists had never devised a tight system of draft or of adequate enlistment. Now, faced with invasion and bled by losses at Charleston, the legislature turned to bounty, and offered for enlistment in the Continental troops $500

[32] Clark (ed.), *State Records*, XIII, 919, 928–29; Speaker Benbury to the Sheriff of Craven County, May 15, 1779, in Papers of the House of Commons, October 18–25, 1779 (North Carolina State Department of Archives and History).

[33] Bond of John Gray Blount and William Blount, May 20, 1780, in Simon Gratz Collection (Pennsylvania Historical Society, Philadelphia).

[34] Nevins, *American States*, 486–87, 496, 513–14; Crittenden, *Commerce of North Carolina*, 134–36; Dill, "Eighteenth Century New Bern," *loc. cit.*, 356.

at the end of each year of service, and for a service of three years or the war's duration 200 acres with a prime slave at the end of the war. The measure, destined to fail in its objective, was nevertheless big with significance, for it laid off a military tract west of the mountains for the payment of this bounty.[35] Meanwhile, to complete the misery of the poverty-stricken and fear-ridden people, swarms of Loyalists, emboldened by British successes, roved the countryside committing outrages, while state commissary masters, made frantic by need, almost equaled Tory enemies in insolence and violence.[36]

In these chaotic circumstances, Governor Nash and Generals Sumner and Caswell acted with energy. Makeshift factories were established, and new militia levies called up. Purchase, impressment, and specific taxes slowly increased the trickle of military supplies, while on June 2 the Tories were held in check by a guerilla clash at Ramsaur's mill. As the administration wrestled with its tasks, William Blount continued his public and private roles. He still acted as paymaster of the slowly reforming Continentals, and upon the arrival of General Horatio Gates with Virginia and Maryland troops fresh from the victories at Saratoga, Blount became the General's official commissary. As did all such agents, he found his chief source of supplies in the prizes brought into New Bern, and his mercantile interests there enabled him to buy in quantity for the new army. Into New Bern and into South Quay, Virginia, privateers and prizes still came laden with precious stores of stockings, canvas, shoes, linens, osnaburgs, arms, and powder, and Blount was vigilant and

[35] Clark (ed.), *State Records,* XXIV, 337–39.

[36] For conditions in North Carolina, see Hardy Murfree to J. Sumner, July 24, 1780, in Emmett Collection (New York Public Library); Clark (ed.), *State Records,* XIV, 198, 504–505, 508, 513–14; W. P. Palmer (ed.), *Calendar of Virginia State Papers* (Richmond, 1875), I, 376ff., 398 (hereinafter cited as *Virginia State Papers*).

active. Colonel Parker, the Marquis of Bretigny (purchasing agent of North Carolina in Martinique), and Peter Mallet, an old mercantile friend now clothier general, sold at sharp but current prices, and Parker, at least, gave preference to Gates' young commissary over private buyers. Thomas Blount served as messenger between his brother William and General Gates, and strove to arouse martial ardor in the frightened population while he endeavored to keep John Gray Blount from the dangers of combat. In the desperate scarcity and dire need of goods, the procuring of supplies was a cutthroat enterprise. Blount's connections with both merchants and his old friend Benjamin Hawkins, now a commissioner of trade, enabled the commissary to acquire goods at the expense of angry civilian authorities, while his imperious nature did not shrink from actual seizures.[37] In this business, he profited three ways: as an officer he drew a salary, as a merchant he made profits through sales of his own and John Gray Blount's products, and, meanwhile, he and his father paid off their debts to Loyalists in depreciated currency, as the law permitted. On the other hand, he was in camp near Camden on the disastrous August 16, 1780, and in the confusion of that military debacle, lost $300,000 of the soldiers' payroll, for which he was accountable.[38]

[37] William Blount to General Gates, September 5, 18, 24, November 9, 1780, in Clark (ed.), *State Records*, XIV, 591–92, 625, 644–46, 731–32; Joseph Clay to General Gates, October 23, 1780, *ibid.*, 706–707; Board of War to Benjamin Hawkins, December 21–24, 1780, *ibid.*, 479; General Gates to William Blount, September 10, October 7, 1780, in Thomas Jefferson Papers (Division of Manuscripts, Library of Congress); Thomas Blount to John Gray Blount, October 26, 1780, in Blount Collection.

[38] Receipts of John Sitgreaves, Commissioner of Confiscated Property for Craven County, August 20, 1780 (North Carolina State Department of Archives and History); Isaac S. Harrell, "The North Carolina Loyalists," in *North Carolina Historical Review*, III (1926), 587; Clark (ed.), *State Records*, XVI, 36–37; William Blount to Governor Alexander Martin, July 8, 1781, in Governors' Papers (North Carolina State Department of Archives and History).

Through the fall and winter the military picture became a mottled pattern of light and darkness as Cornwallis advanced in September only to fall back after King's Mountain, to return again in January reinforced by troops from Virginia. Meanwhile rumors and alarms shook Whig resolution, with guerilla warfare raging in the west and threatening in the east. Immediately after Camden the frightened legislature superseded the governor's military powers with a three-man board of war, thus merely tripling the inadequacies and confusion of the executive department. At the same time, the assembly, reacting to defeat, replaced Richard Caswell with General William Smallwood of Virginia as commanding officer of the militia, whereupon the ambitious and affronted ex-governor retired from the army and resigned from the board of trade to retire to his "Red House" plantation at Kinston.

Amid these confusions and angers, Blount reached a decision. Immediate family responsibilities were growing. His first child, a son named Cornelius for Whig leader Harnett, was soon to be joined by another, and his wife keenly felt his absence.[39] The virtual disintegration of the Continental battalions, the state's changes in policy, and especially the retirement of Caswell made further military participation distasteful, especially as Reading and Thomas Blount still represented the family in that component. On the other hand, membership in the legislature offered a chance to direct public affairs to the aid of private enterprise. If the assembly could make and unmake men, then the assembly was a desirable goal for an ambitious young man. As speculators in commodities, debts, money issues, and land values, the Blounts consistently needed further paper money issues and new property transfers in

[39] McClung transcript of Colonel William Stephens genealogy, in Charles McClung Papers (Lawson McGhee Library).

which to gamble. Furthermore, new political leadership was in prospect; Abner Nash was due to retire from the governorship, Harnett remained inactive in Wilmington, Johnston was attending Congress, Penn was innocuous on the board of war. Hence, when the New Bern representative vacated his commons seat to accept a place on the council, Blount successfully campaigned, and at Halifax on January 27, 1781, took his seat in the third session of the 1780 house. No tyro, at thirty-one he was cognizant of affairs in the key states of Pennsylvania, Maryland, and Virginia through business connections, personal trips, and attention to newspapers. In his own state he was thoroughly familiar with politicians and political procedure, both in the grass-roots county courts and in the legislature. His personal business was established, and he could rely on the powerful assets of his father and his brother John Gray. Thus equipped, the businessman left the military battlefield [40] to enter that of politics, the campaigns of which would absorb his close attention to the end of his life.

[40] Clark (ed.), *State Records,* XVII, 715. The precise date of William Blount's resignation from the army has not been ascertained.

CHAPTER III

LESSONS IN FINANCE
AND POLITICS

O N THE EVENING of January 17, 1781, the little
hamlet of Halifax was crowded to its utmost capacity. The
sixty or so houses, already burdened with refugees, were
now bursting under an additional load of fifty-odd delegates to the assembly. The crowded inhabitants, pinched
for the necessities of living, charged the visitors the highest prices they dared, and speculated privately whether this
assembly might be the last. Fear hung over the town like
a night mist, and rumors of disaster mingled with con-
jectures on the course of the session.

Still, the atmosphere of power was transforming. It
converted the plain, weatherboard courthouse into a mecca
of hopes and an arena of combat. It gave importance to
the otherwise casual members who trooped into the un-
adorned, chill "big room" to sit on hard benches and listen
to unrewarding oratory. It charged debate with acrimony
and occasional excitement. The white-hot fury of Maclaine, the ponderous logic of Hooper, the smooth, facetious
quips of Willie Jones, the furious energy of Person, the
hate-filled phillipics of Rutherford—these lit the dullest
sessions with interest. For here lay the authority of the
sprawling, diverse state. Here laws were made for good

or ill; here governors and generals, commissioners and
clerks, all officers high and low received their offices and
whatever power they might hold. Officials could be made
or broken in one day's session; plain citizens made rich,
famous, or bankrupt by the wording of an enacted phrase.
In sum, here sat the rulers of the state, answerable only to
their often apathetic constituents. Their individual influence in their respective localities was overwhelming;
their collective power supreme.

On the eve of this 1781 session the legislators sensed
the tension and the emergency. A distracted state awaited
guidance. The British were known to be advancing—
Cornwallis on Greene, and the redoubtable Tarleton on
Morgan. The state's militia was almost totally disorgan-
ized, the Continentals shattered. Worse, the direction of
affairs was chaotic as the unpopular board of war enraged
the governor and quarreled with his subordinates. Crucial
problems of supplies remained unanswered, and the quartermaster department confessed total inadequacy, while
the drastic impressment of supplies enraged farmers and
produced little. Inflation soared, and counterfeiting added
to the flood of worthless currency. The state officers, paid
little and often nothing, ceased acting, and in whole counties civil administration collapsed, while bands of Whigs
and Tories seared the state with fire and blood. In the midst
of chaos, speculators created alarms to influence private
operations, and the quantity of confiscated property seized
by the drastic law of 1779 was a standing inducement to
fraud of every kind.

Their popularity shaken by these conditions, Radical
leaders prepared to act swiftly. Willie Jones, just returned
from a brief sojourn at the Continental Congress, was
not present, so leadership devolved on Edward Starkey,
Thomas Person, Timothy Bloodworth, Matthew Locke,

and John Macon. The usual Conservative leaders, except for the Hawkins brothers, were absent, though Hooper arrived a week before adjournment. Yet as a whole, the leadership, chastened somewhat by events and tempered by the presence of such middle-ground men as Bryan and the Blounts, reflected a revival of the moderating influence of Richard Caswell, who sat in the senate.

The house convened on January 27 and on the next day heard the governor's angry message. Nash prophesied invasion, condemned impressment of supplies, criticized General Smallwood, and flatly threatened to resign unless the board of war was abolished. As the legislature turned to its work, Blount was immediately appointed to a joint committee under Caswell which sought to control the soaring commodity prices. He was not on the steering committee, but his mercantile knowledge was recognized by membership on a committee to examine the accounts of the commissioner of trade.[1]

Cheered by the news of the American success at the battle of Cowpens, the assembly passed a bill to fill the Continental battalions by volunteers and by draft from the militia, ordered $26,250,000 in debentures printed to pay for bounties, and completely reorganized the militia.[2] The powers of the quartermaster were enlarged at the same time that impressment of supplies was made less drastic; also a tariff was by unanimous vote laid on imports, in order to raise revenue and to encourage importation of arms and ammunition by excepting these cargoes from the tax. The militia were distributed after considerable argument, largely according to the wishes of Richard Caswell.[3]

This leader's influence now began its upward course,

---

[1] Clark (ed.), *State Records*, XVII, 721, 722.

[2] *Ibid.*, 726; *ibid.*, XXIV, 367–73.

[3] *Ibid.*, XXIV, 380–81, 381–82, 383; Charles Johnston to James Iredell, February 8, 1781, in McRee, *Life of Iredell*, I, 485.

guided by Blount and his other followers. In response to
another blast from Nash on the "disgraced condition of
the Executive department" a joint committee was appointed including Caswell and his son William. As a result
of their work and of Richard Caswell's suggestion, the
board of war was abolished, and replaced by a temporary
three-member council extraordinary. Before proceeding to
Caswell's triumph, however, preliminary moves had to
be made to satisfy that able but sensitive statesman. On
February 2, the ex-governor's friends, led by Blount, put
through a commons resolution appointing Blount, Hawkins, and others of their number to act with senate conferees "to prepare and draw up a Resolve declaring the
intention of the General Assembly in precipitately appointing General Smallwood to the Command of the Militia of
this State in the room of Major General Caswell." [4] The
senate, in spite of Caswell's presence, objected to the reference to precipitate action, but agreed to acquiesce in "a
less condemnatory statement of the resolution." The commons replied that the resolution of the past September
replacing Caswell had by its "Ambiguity" been construed
"much to his prejudice," and they now proposed to "explain" it, to which compromise the senate agreed, and appointed its committee members. The inevitable result was
the reinstatement of Caswell as brigadier general, with
apologies for any supposed affront, and a sop of thanks
to Smallwood for his services.[5]

To complete his triumph, four days later Caswell was
elected to the council extraordinary, and the New Bern
delegates were rewarded for their votes by the choice of
their city as the site of the next assembly. The new council
represented left center, with but one Conservative mem-

[4] Clark (ed.), *State Records*, XVII, 743–44; XXIV, 378–79.
[5] *Ibid.*, XVII, 670–71, 746, 747, 755, 772, 773–74.

ber, and Cornelius Harnett and Archibald Maclaine among the defeated candidates.[6]

This rehabilitation and triumph of Richard Caswell was of the greatest importance for Blount. Caswell's leadership of the state was henceforth virtually unchallenged until his death in 1789, and his protection and guidance were vital elements in Blount's political career. But his friend's reinstatement was only a part of Blount's activity in 1781. With Person and others he passed on public accounts; with Hawkins he reported to the house on the governor's conduct of affairs since the last session; and on other committees he served his apprenticeship in examining claims against the state.[7]

For his own interest, Blount championed two causes. In the first he introduced a bill to establish district auditors to settle claims against the state. This interesting bill created, in each of the six districts of the state, one or more boards of auditors, which were to sit until May 1, 1781, and which were empowered to settle claims against the state by issuing tax free certificates which would bear 10 per cent interest and be receivable for taxes. It also named the auditors and set the price of goods sold to the state. All purchases were hereafter to be made in specie or the equivalent at the time, and the boards' certificates were to be redeemed in like manner, while tax collectors were forbidden to foreclose on any public creditor before May 1. Finally, the existing single board of auditors was likewise empowered to issue certificates. No more perfect bill could have been drawn to benefit merchant creditors of the state, cash-needy speculators, or office seekers. It passed its third reading in the commons on February 10, and subsequently became law.[8]

[6] *Ibid.,* 785–86.   [7] *Ibid.,* 726, 755, 767.
[8] *Ibid.,* 744, 770; XXIV, 373–75.

Blount's other personal interest involved the officers and soldiers of the Continental line. One reason for this interest was his family's war service. Another was an act of the April session of the 1780 legislature which had granted, among other bonuses, two hundred acres of land to a three-year volunteer, and had specified that the acreage should be in a reserve north of the Tennessee River and west of Cumberland Gap.[9] Political attention to the soldiery was also dictated by policies of simple justice, further enlistments, and personal popularity with a view to future benefit. In response to an officers' memorial, Blount's committee recommended further paper money emissions and more prompt issue of supplies, but a bill for this purpose was lost at the session's close for lack of a quorum.[10]

Meanwhile, though successfully blocking Blount's paper money issue, Conservatives suffered defeat in the rejection of their bill to redeem past issues of currency, and another disappointment by the commons' refusal to pay the salaries of the judges or of the attorney general for the coming year.[11] On the question of Loyalists, a compromise omnibus bill emerged. Property forfeited by the 1779 act could be seized by commissioners or county officers, but land and slaves were to be rented out yearly, and the operation of the drastic 1779 act was again suspended. On the other hand, sales or contracts made to evade confiscation were ex post facto declared illegal, and entries and trespasses on forfeited property were made actionable. Sheriffs were empowered to pursue transferred personal property outside of the state, and Loyalist suspects were denied the franchise. Finally, in order to enlist speculator

[9] Ibid., XXIV, 337–39.
[10] Ibid., XVII, 701–702, 738, 742–43, 777–79.
[11] Ibid., 780, 792–93; XXIV, 382.

support, a rider extended the deadline for filing land surveys for twelve months.[12]

Then, after congratulating Isaac Shelby, John Sevier, and other leaders on their military successes in the west, providing for emergency government in case of invasion, and voting unanimously to defend the state to the last man, the members dispersed. The session, though it aroused the wrath of Conservatives, had not been, as one of them charged, "a corrupt, or what is worse, an idiot Assembly." [13] The west was noticed with an act to quiet titles on the new Virginia boundary, the state's ablest leader was restored to public service, and neither the conservative nor the radical element triumphed too far at the expense of the other.

For Blount, the short session had meant much. Besides marking him as an outstanding lieutenant of Caswell, his legislative debut had given him opportunity to work with and be known to such majority leaders as Willie Jones, Thomas Person, the Caswells, Matthew Locke, and Timothy Bloodworth. His auditor law meant that he might expect the votes of merchants, public creditors, and cash-short speculators. His efforts for the army were on record, and he had supported laws favoring land speculators and debtors. On the strength of such a record, the persuasive, courteous, and affable young legislator could expect much from the future.

Nevertheless, the legislature saw no more of him during the busy months of 1781. Greene returned from Virginia in February, and Cornwallis moved forward from Hillsboro; the two armies clashed at Guilford Courthouse on March 15, after which the British general moved to

[12] *Ibid.,* XXIV, 376–78.
[13] William Hooper to James Iredell, February 13, 1781, in McRee, *Life of Iredell,* I, 487.

Wilmington to refit. Greene turned to South Carolina, and Cornwallis, on April 25, marched into Virginia. These maneuvers shook the state, but upon the departure of the armies, worse befell as civil war racked the countryside until November. British forces, operating from Wilmington, burned, captured, and foraged in wide sweeps, plundering even New Bern. Whig leaders John Ashe and Cornelius Harnett were made prisoners, and fear paralyzed the South. At the same time the notorious guerilla leader David Fanning carried on other and more savage forays, culminating in the capture of the newly elected governor, Thomas Burke.[14] British control of Wilmington and the plundering of New Bern, as well as Cornwallis' northward march, including the capture of Halifax and South Quay, Virginia, all heavily afflicted the mercantile community, and Whig and Tory bushwhacking made life and property unsafe.[15]

Under these conditions, though Reading Blount continued to serve in the army with Greene, his brother William was immersed in private affairs. With John Gray and Richard Blackledge, he shipped boxes of "Spanish white sugars" to the Continental prisoners off Charleston. He journeyed to the treasurer's to pay taxes. When glad tidings came that Cornwallis was "Burgoynaded" and British shipping was concentrated on the York, William and Thomas Blount attempted to secure a commission for their "Tyger Gally" for privateering. As the year neared its end, the ex-legislator began redeeming specie certificates for

[14] Connor, *Colonial Period,* 481–86, 487–92; McRee, *Life of Iredell,* I, 499, 503–504; Mrs. Blair to James Iredell, May 29, 1781, *ibid.,* 516–17; Clark (ed.), *State Records,* XVI, vi–ix; Hugh Williamson to James Iredell, May 1, 1782, *ibid.,* 613; Crittenden, *Commerce of North Carolina,* 152–54.

[15] Pierce Butler to James Iredell, April 27, 1781, in McRee, *Life of Iredell,* I, 505; John Johnston to James Iredell, May 3, 1781, *ibid.,* 507; Thomas Burke to Governor Nelson, August 30, 1781, in W. P. Palmer and S. McRae (eds.), *Virginia State Papers,* II, 371–72; William Savage to John Gray Blount, July 23, 1781, in Keith (ed.), *Blount Papers,* I, 15–16.

cash and buying farm tools to redeem the neglected fields of Piney Grove, where the slaves did not "work to advantage for the want of axes."

Indeed, these months of private life, harassed as yet with warfare, were of vast significance for Blount and his brothers. The close of the war saw the systematization of wartime expediency into a life-long pattern of activity for the whole family. John Gray Blount, whose home and successful store and wharves were at Washington, North Carolina, now formally associated William and Thomas with him in his active business. Lots were purchased in Tarboro, a mercantile hamlet farther up the Tar River, and here the volatile and warm-hearted Thomas Blount with his more business-minded youngest brother, Jacob, set up a thriving branch of the Washington store. Thomas scoured the county for tobacco, corn, naval stores, and forest products with which to load Blount ships for the West Indies, Europe, or the northern ports. To neighboring farmers went sugar, salt, rum, cloth, hats, and hardware. The flat swampy coastland brought frequent illness, and a voyage to the Indies "almost ruined" Thomas Blount, who sometimes yearned for the more carefree soldier's life again; but he worked hard and with his characteristic conscientiousness. Such work under the skillful direction of John Gray brought prosperity, in which partner William shared. Occasional horse races, billiard games, and small parties broke the tedium of labor, and the family visited frequently, despite wretched roads and inclement weather. In early 1782, Thomas' mercurial emotions rose to new heights with the culmination of his courtship of Martha Baker, cousin of John Gray's wife, Mary. Plans and arrangements multiplied, with John Gray furnishing horses and William, after considerable persuasion, parting for a time with his coveted carriage.

Necessary, too, was the repairing and refinishing of a home for the bride, which called forth more consultation with and advice from the older brothers. Finally, the awful ordeal of the ceremony: "I much dread the parade & would willingly expose myself to a heavy cannonade [o]ne hour to be exempt from it & have the [bus]iness as effectually done." [16]

In the Spring, however, public affairs again thrust themselves into private events. On April 13, 1782, the assembly met, and William Blount, though not a member, journeyed to the session. Spurred by Tory attacks, flushed with the success of Yorktown, and angered by Tory guerilla raids, the Radicals teamed with the speculators for drastic action. All confiscated property seized by the acts of 1777 and 1779 was now thrown open for sale by credit or depreciated currency at 150 to 1 on issues before 1781, or 800 to 1 since. The sale was to continue until all property was sold, and sales had to be completed by the ensuing January 1. These huge amounts of property for quick sale in depreciated currency offered tremendous opportunity for the Sheppards, Glasgows, Armstrongs, Caswells, and Blounts, all expert dealers in paper and in land, and they responded with great activity.[17]

The same friendly assembly directed the auditors to make allowance for Blount's losses at Camden in settling his accounts. At the prompting of speculators, a memorial of the North Carolina line was drawn up requesting pay in lands. The assembly appointed a joint committee headed

[16] Blount Collection, 1777–82 R, *passim*; Thomas Blount to John Gray Blount, April 21, 1782, in Keith (ed.), *Blount Papers,* I, 24–26.

[17] Clark (ed.), *State Records,* XXIV, 424–29; T. P. Abernethy, *From Frontier to Plantation in Tennessee* (Chapel Hill, 1932), 42; Harrell, "North Carolina Loyalists," *loc. cit.,* 585–87; Bessie M. Steinle, "The Confiscation of Royalist Property During and After the Revolution in North Carolina" (M.A. thesis, University of Texas, 1935), 63; Papers of the Commissioners of Confiscated Property, 1780–86, *passim*; Robert O. DeMond, *The Loyalists in North Carolina During the Revolution* (Durham, 1940), 243, 244, 250.

by speculator Hugh Williamson to study the problem of
depreciation of soldiers' pay, and the upshot was a law
which raised the land bounties of 1780 to greater amounts
(640 acres for a private to 12,000 for a brigadier) and
appointed surveyors Absalom Tatum, Isaac Shelby, and
Anthony Bledsoe to lay off the western tract. While granting pre-emption to the settlers already there, the act by
implication destroyed the last remnant of Judge Henderson's pretensions, though the commons recognized a claim
for compensation. Four and one-half million acres were
by this legislation opened to holders of military warrants,
three fifths of which the speculators could buy for a song.[18]
Blount's 1781 interest in soldiers' welfare now paid off in
his being named to serve on a committee to settle the soldiers' claims for pay and clothing deficiency, an unparalleled position for contact with the military warrant
holders.

Before the possibilities of the post could be realized,
however, other opportunities beckoned the speculator. At
Philadelphia, in the Continental Congress, Conservative
Benjamin Hawkins had long been North Carolina's sole
delegate, and since his departure in March, the state had
been totally unrepresented. A new delegation was therefore
to be selected, and Blount was interested. Besides the
prestige of such a post, its advantages were manifold. The
Blount firm, despite constant search, found local commerce increasingly stifled by wartime difficulties. Largely
credit operators, the brothers eyed the strong financial
houses of the East with admiration and longing. A firm
member in Philadelphia could make valuable contacts on

[18] Clark (ed.), *State Records,* XXIV, 419–22; Abernethy, *Frontier to
Plantation,* 42–43; Martin Armstrong to General Sumner, February 26, 1782,
in Clark (ed.), *State Records,* XVI, 524–26; Hardy Murfree to General
Sumner April 9, 13, 1782, *ibid.,* 588–89, 592; William Russell to General
Sumner, April 9, 1782, *ibid.,* 587–88; Governor Martin to General Greene,
May 24, 1782, *ibid.,* 688.

the busy wharves and in the countinghouses of the capital. To William Blount, the social life and political air surrounding Congress was likewise attractive, especially amid rumors of a peace treaty. Hence he announced himself available, and on May 3, 1782, was elected with Abner Nash, Hugh Williamson, and Benjamin Hawkins to the Congress. Two of the newly elected delegates were urged to go up at once, and Blount and Williamson agreed to do so. Armed with £800 from the sale of a Loyalist lot and slaves, Blount left home July 2, and took his seat July 22, 1782. He delivered a map of the boundaries of the state, sent by Governor Alexander Martin to Robert Livingston in order to furnish the secretary with information on North Carolina's claims,[19] then began his legislative duties.

As the impotent and faction-ridden Congress grappled with postwar problems, the North Carolina delegates, like their colleagues, adopted as their polestar the interests of their state in matters great and small. Their first problem was one of public relations. North Carolina had paid nothing on her quota of the Continental debt from 1777 to 1779. From December of the latter year through June 15, 1780, she had paid $2,380,000 in paper, which though overvalued by Congress still left her in arrears by $18,230,000. She had then done nothing on the requisitions of late 1780 and 1781, totaling $555,260, and her total Continental debt had risen to nearly $19,000,000.[20] As a result, Blount and Williamson found that North Carolina had "long been viewed in a very unfavorable point of light," the more so

[19] William Sharpe to James Madison, May 25, 1782, in Elizabeth G. McPherson (ed.), "Unpublished Letters from North Carolinians to James Madison and James Monroe," in *North Carolina Historical Review*, XIV (1937), 156–57; Worthington C. Ford *et al.* (eds.), *Journals of the Continental Congress, 1774–1789* (Washington, 1904–1937), XXII, 404 (hereinafter referred to as *Journals of Congress*); Alexander Martin to Robert Livingston, June 24, 1782, in Clark (ed.), *State Records*, XVI, 342–43.

[20] Clark (ed.), *State Records*, XVI, 405.

as the distraught and poverty-ridden Congress was attempting to enlist public sentiment against delinquent states by a monthly publication of money received on state accounts. Resolved that if their state "suffers for the future in the voice of Fame, it shall not be from the want of a friend to advocate her cause," the businessmen-delegates fought propaganda with propaganda. They drew up and had printed in the *Pennsylvania Packet and General Advertiser* a persuasive account of the May assembly's legislation on taxes, enlistment, and supply for the army, and on August 6, this was supplemented by an account of the 20,000 acres voted to General Greene by the assembly.[21]

The Carolina propagandists were next faced by a strongly backed Congressional resolution demanding the reduction of the size of the army. Blount and Williamson knew this meant that "almost every Officer in the North Carolina Line would be deranged" by the reduction, which was, however, approved by an overwhelming majority of states and indorsed by Washington. In no position to do otherwise, they acquiesced, but by skillful delay, political maneuvering, and the use of rumor, they secured for the North Carolina troops an exemption from the demobilization order at the judgment of General Greene. "Thus," the delegates gleefully reported, "our Troops continue on the same footing they would have stood if no Resolves . . . had passed. If the General needs them he will keep them in the Service, and if . . . not wanted they will be requested to march home and try to replace the numerous Soldiers and Citizens we have lost during the War by [be]getting more." [22]

21 William Blount and Hugh Williamson to Governor Martin, August 3, 1782, *ibid.*, 388; *Pennsylvania Packet and General Advertiser*, August 3, 6, 1782.

22 Ford *et al.* (eds.), *Journals of Congress*, XXII, 451–55; XXIII, 642; William Blount and Hugh Williamson to Governor Martin, November 9, 1782, in Clark (ed.), *State Records*, XVI, 455–57.

With all their interests in military arrangements, however, the two businessmen-delegates were most absorbed, like the Congress as a whole, with the question of finance. By July 1, 1782, when $4,000,000 was due on the latest requisition, only $50,000 had been paid by the states, and it was apparent that the chronic financial anemia of Congress would soon prove mortal. A grand committee was appointed on July 22, but, by October 10, it recommended nothing more than an appeal to Rhode Island and Georgia for an affirmative answer to the question of a Continental impost power. Meanwhile, Congress had long perceived the potential value of the Western lands as a means of revenue, if these lands could be secured by cession from the states. The protracted struggle which had ensued over this question of cession had been complicated by jealousies, conditional cessions, conflicting claims, and the ambitious inhabitants of the Vermont area. A Northern-sponsored bill to urge Western land cessions without guaranteeing prior state grants, and another to tax land, polls, and liquors were narrowly defeated soon after the North Carolinians' arrival. Deeply concerned both as businessman and Carolinian, Blount fought the Northern program. He favored seeking to borrow abroad rather than resort to taxation, for his constituents, starved for specie, could pay no cash excise, either on liquor or poll. If borrowing abroad should fail, he advocated tariffs, since North Carolinians, producing bulky products, could not easily find ships, and so the state's relatively small commerce would bear less share of taxation. Toward the land tax, his feelings were mixed. Since by the eighth article of the Confederation, land was to be taxed by value, North Carolina, with few cities, would profit over the more urban North; yet the state's "located," i.e. surveyed, trans-Allegheny lands would raise her quota. At this point Blount's private interest and his state's benefit merged. The cession of her western lands to Congress would remove an extra burden of taxation from North Carolina and raise the incomes of speculators Blount and Williamson. For, while present income from sales was small both to state and speculators, a transfer to Congress would raise the value of the lands through the promise of a national defense and Indian policy and at the same time reduce state taxation even further.

Moved by these considerations, the delegates proposed to Governor Martin that many problems could be solved by a conditional cession. The stipulations were, among others, that Congress assume the cost of past Indian expeditions, that a valuation be made of the lands and also an accounting of state credits and debts, and that any new state created from the lands should assume part of North Carolina's debt. The two speculators did not publicly add that private claims should all be made good, but they worked for that end.[23] These weighted arguments, however, found their recipient totally unsympathetic. Governor Alexander Martin, as avid as any man for popularity and profit, was at this time a rabid champion of state sovereignty. In reply to the delegates' implications, he violently opposed a cession to Congress as "a vile *Agrarian Law* the Romans antiently made in vain . . . which tho' often attempted in Democracies as a principle object to obtain equality among Citizens could never be of any duration. . . ." A cession, he said, would not be to "our interest or policy . . . on any terms yet proposed," and

[23] William Blount and Hugh Williamson to Governor Martin, October 22, 1782, in Clark (ed.), *State Records,* XVI, 434–41; Hugh Williamson to Governor Martin, September 2, 1782, *ibid.,* 406–407; Ford *et al.* (eds.), *Journals of Congress,* XXIII, 604–606. For North Carolina's position, see St. George L. Sioussat, "The North Carolina Cession of 1784 in its Federal Aspects," in Mississippi Valley Historical Association *Proceedings,* II (1908), 35–62.

the conditions which the delegates suggested were "no great favour . . . but a matter of right & Justice." [24]

Finding the matter so powerfully opposed at home and not immediately pressing in Congress, the delegates dropped the subject for a time, but they continued to guard the state's interests closely. They warned the governor that North Carolina's disordered finance would lead to speculation in Continental money; they urged that the state hasten to draw up its claims against the Continental treasury; they gave full reports on the progress of the peace negotiations; and they urged the calling of an assembly as soon as possible. Blount attended the dreary sessions with considerable regularity. He voted to relieve his former superior, Gates, of an inquiry into the Camden fiasco, and also to urge separate collection of Continental taxes, but he kept well in the background, observing but not leading. [25]

All was not official duty, however. Philadelphia was hectically gay in the winter of 1782–83. The social-minded delegates had a wide choice of theaters, suppers, balls, dances, and the homes of cultured friends, such as the successful and charming Dr. Nicholas Romayne, whose future was to be so dramatically linked with Blount's. [26] Dr. Romayne's interests, like the delegate's, were various and speculative, and their frank exchange of ideas created fateful impressions of mutual abilities. Beyond society, however delightful, business beckoned, and Blount responded with hours of conferences with merchants Stuart, Barr, or Pollock, of Philadelphia; Toomer, late of Wil-

[24] Governor Martin to the Delegates, January 28, 1783, in Clark (ed.), *State Records*, XVI, 732–34.

[25] Ford *et al.* (eds.), *Journals of Congress*, XXIII, 466, 669.

[26] Hugh Williamson to James Iredell, December 2, 1782, in McRee, *Life of Iredell*, II, 29–31; Power of Attorney of Nicholas and Susan Romayne, Craven County Deeds, Book 25, pp. 289–90.

mington; and many others. John Gray Blount might occasionally groan at the opulent style of his brother's living, but he had to admit that his business contacts were useful.

Blount also sought private advantage through official information, and merchant, privateer, and politician occasionally merged. On December 30, Congress, at the request of Generals Greene and Wayne, confirmed an agreement of Wayne's at the surrender of Savannah by which British merchants were given six months' protection from seizure of their goods. The sharp-eyed Carolinian noted that the Congressional approval was technically invalid through a wrong date and that in any case the guarantee of protection would soon expire and British merchant vessels on the Savannah River would be exposed. Therefore, to John Gray Blount he sent an utterly characteristic letter:

. . . . I suppose you have left our Blank Privateers Commissions. I hope you have . . . An Ocracok Pilate Boat or any other will cost but little Money and may I suppose be easily procured. A clever Fellow to affect the Seizure is a hard thing to be got. . . . It will be quite immaterial whether he is a thorough Seaman or not. He ought to be a Man of Address and Boldness who would not be frighted by Party and one who would understand how to deal with lawyers and Judges and one who might have address enough if party work was the fashion as it always was in Georgia to raise a party also in his own Defence. . . . imploy who you wish let the Commission be in his Name and all the Business in his Name but take Care that you have a sufficient Instrument of writing whereby you will come in for a good share of the profit . . . it may be necessary for you to go on to Savannah under pretense of some other Business & you may stand behind the Curtain & give the Necessary Directions. . . . if its possible to have . . . [the captured ship] condemned in Georgia either by party, Bribery or any other Way it will be best & then the British Merchants will be the Appealants. . . . John Cruden who fitted out the Vessels that plundered Beaufort last Spring, has a good deal of Property at Savannah. . . .[27]

[27] William Blount to John Gray Blount, January 7, 1782 [1783], in Blount Collection.

Despite such advantages of Congressional service, several circumstances now turned Blount homeward. The four delegates were to serve six-month terms in pairs in order that the poverty-ridden state could pay their salaries in installments, yet have sufficient representatives always present to vote effectively; hence, with the arrival of Nash on November 4, and of Hawkins on December 21, Blount and Williamson were free to leave.

Another important determinant in Blount's return was the increasing scope and volume of his brother's business operations. John Gray Blount had prospered exceedingly in the past two years. He had bought lands in North Carolina, kept up his land interest in Kentucky dating from the early trip with Boone, and planned to open a company to sell Cumberland River lands.[28] The basis of this prosperity was his ever-widening orbit of trade. The partnership of John Gray & Thomas Blount, Merchants, had continued to thrive in William's absence. They now owned outright shares in larger ships—the brigs *Young, Richard,* and *Nancy,* first of a rapidly growing list of marine investments. The young firm's connections were solid and far-flung, and its correspondence wide. Letters flowed in from Titus Ogden or Christopher Neale, leading merchants of New Bern, over a cargo of salt or over tar, tobacco, prize captures. Others from William Campbell in Wilmington urged sending a speedy ship to Europe on the first word of a peace treaty. Prospectuses and lists of prices current arrived from merchant firms in Philadelphia, Charleston, Leghorn, London, and Amsterdam, offering their services as consignees. Occasionally, bad news came in letters from Blount captains in Jamaica telling of their capture by

[28] Pitt County Deeds, Book G, 69–74; Thomas Hart to John Gray Blount, January 29, 1780, in Keith (ed.), *Blount Papers,* I, 11–12; William B. Smith to John Gray Blount, May 6, 1782, *ibid.,* 26–27; Samuel Henderson to John Gray Blount, August 12, 1782, *ibid.,* 28–29.

British privateers, or from New York or Baltimore describing a glut in the market for the cargo's items or an account of the spoilage of a cargo of tar or corn. Increasingly, requests for financing, credit, advice, or the apprenticing of children in Blount homes testified to the rising fortunes and reputation of the firm.[29] All of this meant the need of William's presence, since the approach of peace was bringing new problems of policy to be decided and, above all, new opportunities to be seized.

Of these opportunities by far the greatest presented itself in connection with the coming meeting of the North Carolina assembly. Having failed to meet in the Fall, the legislature was to be faced with many issues in its April session, and among these none loomed larger for the businessmen than the disposal of the Western lands. Blount's plan of combining personal profit with a federalistic cession had been rebuffed by Governor Martin. The Congressman now proposed to drop federalism and combine profit with the prevailing state-first policy of the governor's followers. Hence, he planned ahead for his departure and on January 24 left Philadelphia for North Carolina, arriving, after delays and visits, on March 2, 1783.[30]

Plunging into the preliminaries of the assembly meeting, Blount found North Carolina politics at its whitest heat. The cumulative effects of eight years of warfare had left deep fissures in the society of a ravaged land. Despite the virtual cessation of a successful war, the state

---

[29] Letters of Thomas Blount to John Gray Blount, 1780–84, in Blount Collection, *passim*. For details of Blount trading interests, see Keith, "Three North Carolina Blount Brothers," *passim*.

[30] William Blount to John Gray Blount, January 7, 1783, in Keith (ed.), *Blount Papers*, I, 32–33; Thomas Blount to John Gray Blount, March 2, 1783, *ibid.*, 41–43; Abner Nash to James Iredell, January 18, 1783, in Edmund C. Burnett (ed.), *Letters of Members of the Continental Congress* (Washington, 1921–36), VII, 19; *ibid.*, lxxii.

WILLIE JONES.
Member of the Continental Congress

WILLIE JONES

seemed on the brink of ruin, with a worthless currency, mountainous debts, and an empty treasury. From 1775 to 1783, North Carolina had issued $7,855,000 in paper, and with the exception of $250,000 of it, no taxes had been levied to redeem it. In 1781 alone, the state had issued $26,250,000 in certificates which, by 1783, were of no value. Purchasing agents and quartermasters had disbursed certificates lavishly and had often failed to keep records, receipts, or accounts. In the welter of paper, counterfeiters throve, adding further financial uncertainty. No one knew the amount of the public debt, but all knew the state's credit was gone.[31] With its trade disrupted, its prosperity destroyed, and its passions aroused, the populace of the state reflected its antagonistic interests through its political leaders.

The old political divisions had formed largely on the bases of personal political philosophies. In addition, there had always existed in North Carolina, as in other states, the inevitable antipathy between two economic classes with widely varied interests. A plantation-owning, largely Episcopal, oligarchy of planters, merchants, and lawyers of homogeneous stock was set against a Western society of diverse creeds and small farms, whose economic ties were in this instance with Virginia or South Carolina, and who, as in all states, resented their political inferiority. To these quarrels the war years had added new bitterness. Eastern Conservative lawyers wrangled bitterly with assembly-appointed Radical judges more learned in Whiggism than in jurisprudence. The eastern merchants, never popular, now bore the general resentment against soaring prices and broken trade patterns. Bound by many

---

[31] Albert L. Bramlett, "North Carolina's Western Lands" (Ph.D. dissertation, University of North Carolina, 1928), 85–86; Sioussat, "The North Carolina Land Cession," *loc. cit.,* 37–38.

ties with Loyalist and pro-English families, a number of the easterners fought incessantly to relieve their clients, relatives, and friends from proscription and confiscation. In 1783, they looked hopefully to this first postwar assembly for relief, but at this very time the boldest returning Loyalists were arousing intense antagonism among the Tory-haters and holders of confiscated property. Finally, creditors and professional men saw inevitable ruin from the headlong inflation, and they strove mightily to create popular sentiment for redeeming past currency issues and for paying state debts and Continental quotas.[32]

In such an arena the Spring elections of 1783 were hotly fought. The fact that the courts and assembly sat at the same time continued to hurt the Conservatives' cause, since many lawyers like Iredell forsook the latter for the former, and the defeat of Hooper through a political indiscretion of his aristocratic-minded supporters also dimmed Conservatives' hopes.[33] Nevertheless, both sides were well represented, the Conservatives with Archibald Maclaine, Joseph Hawkins, and Richard Spaight; the Radicals with Timothy Bloodworth, Waightstill Avery, and Thomas Person. The business element was also present in the persons of William and John Gray Blount and Richard Caswell.[34]

The house assembled April 18, 1783. On the first day Blount's resignation from the Continental Congress was laid before the house by the governor; on the next day, he was named to the steering committee, together with

[32] Ashe, *History of North Carolina*, II, 23–24, 26–27; Abernethy, *Frontier to Plantation*, 44–45, 60–63; Archibald Maclaine to George Hooper, March 12, 1783, in Clark (ed.), *State Records*, XVI, 943–46; *id.* to James Iredell, August 25, 1783, in McRee, *Life of Iredell*, II, 69–70.

[33] James Iredell to Hannah Iredell, April 1, 1783, in McRee, *Life of Iredell*, II, 41; Archibald Maclaine to James Iredell, February 21, 1783, *ibid.*, 39–40.

[34] Clark (ed.), *State Records*, XIX, 233–34; Abernethy, *Frontier to Plantation*, 47–48.

Archibald Maclaine, Richard D. Spaight, Matthew Locke, and others—an appointment indicative of powerful influence.

As the days slipped by in committee meetings, votes, and speeches, two things became apparent; the first was that the Radicals still controlled the legislature. Maclaine and his Conservatives failed in all their major objectives. The act of pardon for Loyalists was so exception-ridden as to be useless. The date of the sessions was not changed, nor was the government seated at Cross Creek, as the Cape Fear lawyers wanted. An assessment bill included taxes on stock in trade, and not even a powerful combination of merchants and lawyers could defeat or amend it. Likewise, this assembly was in no federal mood. Maclaine's bill to repeal all laws conflicting with the British peace treaty was rejected, the 4 per cent impost duty granted Congress was repealed, and clauses in a depreciation act excepted Tory debts from the statute of limitations. While more paper currency was issued, a tax bill for the purpose of redeeming past issues was defeated. Even in personal politics, the Conservative leaders were beaten, for, though he unseated Thomas Bloodworth on a technicality, Maclaine's similar attempt against the stronger brother, Timothy, failed, and a counterattack kept the Wilmington lawyer busy defending himself. Personalities, indeed, brought sharp clashes, especially when Caswell sought to regain the governorship. Martin, grown fond of the office, fought back, and, with the aid of the revenge-seeking Conservatives, defeated his rival, though his victory meant little to the Conservatives.[35]

[35] Clark (ed.), *State Records*, XXIV, 475–78, 489–90; XIX, 282, 292, 304, 305, 308, 317, 340, 348, 349–50, 362; Archibald Maclaine to George Hooper, March 24, April 29, June 12, 1783, *ibid.*, XVI, 947–50, 956–58, 965–67; Richard Caswell to William Caswell, May 4, 1783, *ibid.*, 958–60; James Iredell to Hannah Iredell, April 10, 1783, in McRee, *Life of Iredell*, II, 42.

The second major characteristic of this assembly was that its members were deeply engrossed in personal interests, and for many, such as the Blounts, this had come to mean land. With the dislocation of commerce and physical losses of the war as yet neither adjusted nor regained, there arose among postwar Carolina businessmen a tremendous interest in the exploitation of land for profit, further stimulated by the vast quantities of confiscated property suddenly put on the market. Failure of the British-Indian attacks, Western migration, glowing reports of Western fertility and climate, and the removal of old royal restrictions also contributed after 1783 to the incitement of a mania of land speculation which engaged the best efforts of the business leaders of North Carolina and her sister states for decades.[36] Hence, to the old legislative efforts of the Blounts for paper currency, the soldiers, and the West, there was now added the family tradition of the pursuit of land, and in all four phases their exertions were notably rewarded.

To furnish the resources for the new Western enterprise, William Blount on May 6, 1783, introduced a bill for emitting £100,000 in paper currency. Like all his measures, it was written to attract the widest possible support. For official patronage, it provided that the money was to be used for the payment of the present assembly and executive departments, and for no earlier ones. For the army, it enacted that any unpaid soldier might on application secure one fourth of his dues in the new currency. For Conservatives' appeasement, the bill detailed restrictions to avoid fraudulent emission and laid a tax

[36] Aaron Morton Sakolski, *The Great American Land Bubble* (New York, 1932), 29–30; Abernethy, *Frontier to Plantation*, 19; Bramlett, "North Carolina's Western Lands," 54, 113–15; A. P. Whitaker, *The Spanish-American Frontier, 1783–1795* (Boston, 1927), 4–7.

of threepence per pound on property to redeem the paper.[37]

Having thus provided the means for speculation, Blount on the next day opened the game with his bill to "amend" the former soldiers' reserve. During the past winter, the surveyors appointed to lay off the Western military reserve had journeyed with a considerable party to the Tennessee country and had run off the reservation as directed, fifty-five miles north of the southern boundary of the state. In laying off this tract, and others for themselves and associates, they discovered the land to be Indian-infested and inaccessible and so reported to the 1783 assembly military committee, of which Blount was a member.[38] Neither soldiers nor speculators were satisfied with such a bounty, and hence Blount's present bill changed the reservation area to fifty miles south of the Virginia boundary, the reserve to be bounded by lines drawn south from Cumberland Gap and from the intersection of the Tennessee River and the Virginia line. The act also established the procedure for obtaining grants, opened a land office at Nashville under speculator Martin Armstrong, and named a highly respected new board to settle army accounts. Besides making provision for the surveyors and their party and enlisting Governor Martin's aid by a grant of 2,000 acres, the bill made all soldiers with two years' service eligible for claims. The way was thus cleared for vast speculation, since few if any of the soldiers would go through the lengthy procedure for obtaining a grant, nor did most of them possess capital to move and set up homes in the wilderness. Thus the debt-ridden soldier would be

[37] Clark (ed.), *State Records,* XIX, 307; XXIV, 475–78.

[38] Governor Martin to the Commissioners, October 2, 1782, *ibid.,* XVI, 713; James McCallum, "The Early History of Giles County," in *American Historical Magazine and Tennessee Historical Society Quarterly,* II (1897), 312–14 (hereinafter referred to as *American Historical Magazine*).

glad to sell his claims to the Blounts, Caswells, Ruther-fords, or Donelsons.[39]

While William Blount thus furnished capital and im-plemented the soldiers' reserve plan, his brother flung open a far wider field. On April 28, the younger Blount pre-sented a bill which opened the Western land offices, closed since 1781.[40] Although William Blount had previously realized that selling the unprotected lands would bring little revenue to the state, this act was announced to be for that purpose, as well as for discharging debts of cur-rency and arrears to the army. In reality, it was a specu-lator's measure. It declared for sale at ten pounds per one hundred acres all lands west of the mountains all the way to Mississippi, except the military reserve and a small Indian reservation. The money made receivable for lands was all rated above its actual value, whether by scale of depreciation or a nominal value, and amounted in all to less than five dollars per hundred acres. All previous entries were nullified, and the land office (presided over by John Armstrong as entry-taker) was established, for the convenience of businessmen, at Hillsboro. The whole act was a flat violation of all Indian treaties, justified on the grounds of Indian alliance with the British in the late war. The Indians' trade and their land reservation, re-duced now to a small southwestern area between the Tennessee and Big Pigeon rivers, were piously safe-guarded.[41] Thus the western lands were disposed of in accordance with Governor Martin's state-first policy and a vast market opened for speculation.

Besides a depreciation act which aroused Maclaine's

[39] Clark (ed.), *State Records*, XIX, 320; *ibid.*, XXIV, 482–85; Payson Jackson Treat, *The National Land System, 1785–1820* (New York, 1910), 245; Abernethy, *Frontier to Plantation*, 43.

[40] Clark (ed.), *State Records*, XIX, 277, 311.

[41] *Ibid.*, XXIV, 478–82; Abernethy, *Frontier to Plantation*, 50.

ire, a final piece of interested legislation was, in part at least, Blount handiwork. When the house received from the senate Richard Henderson's petition asking compensation for his lost Transylvania land in Tennessee (in which the Blounts were financially interested), four large landowners, including John Gray Blount, were appointed house conferees on a committee to study the claim. Griffith Rutherford on May 7 reported for the committee that the memorialists "ought to have as a compensation for their expenses Trouble and Risque" four hundred thousand acres in Powell's Valley. The senate agreed, but the house rejected the compensation and substituted two hundred thousand acres, which, despite an attempt at further reduction, became law. Thus were friends, relatives, and Blounts rewarded.[42]

But while William Blount the statesman was thus engaged with his brother in legislation for himself and his associates, William Blount the businessman entered into a private enterprise of considerable moment. When the surveyors of the military reserve had reported to Blount's committee of the legislature—or possibly before the report —they had informed the interested land-dealer-legislators that the rich land within the great southern bend of the Tennessee River lay in Georgia and possibly South Carolina and not, as formerly supposed, in the Tennessee country. This several-million-acre tract, long coveted by Carolina Chickasaw traders, was valuable for farming and trade with both the Indians and the whites of the Mississippi Valley. A trading post established there at the Muscle Shoals would enjoy profits from navigation up and down the Tennessee River and hence connection with settlements on the Holston, Cumberland, Kentucky, and Illinois rivers; at the same time a short portage would

[42] Clark (ed.), *State Records,* XIX, 192, 283, 325, 326, 351, 354.

link it with the placid Alabama River and furnish an access to the Gulf superior to the harassed Mississippi route. A trading post had in fact been located there earlier in the century, and the site had attracted the covetous eyes of speculator John Donelson since 1778.[43]

To secure this prize, Blount acted swiftly. With Richard Caswell, John Gray Blount, and James Glasgow, he agreed to secure legal titles from the states and buy goods for the Indian treaties while John Donelson and Joseph Martin secured the land by private treaties.[44] This latter was the more easily accomplished since Virginia had already commissioned Martin, Isaac Shelby, and Donelson to hold a public treaty meeting with the Chickasaw and Cherokee at Nashville. The plan thus swiftly set on foot was to have unexpected consequences.

As the legislative session drew to a close, many of the members were far more engaged in private than in public matters. The significance of the Blount legislation throwing open the West was lost on none. Some, more farsighted, had already made agreements with Western surveyors and had tracts surveyed. Thus, Caswell and secretary of state James Glasgow had engaged Stockley Donelson, surveyor of Sullivan County and son of Colonel John Donelson, to survey the French Broad country, and they were ready to present surveys as soon as the land office should open in October. Governor Patrick Henry of Virginia was also a foresighted land-seeker through his

[43] A. P. Whitaker, "Muscle Shoals Speculation," in *Mississippi Valley Historical Review*, XIII (1926), 365–66; A. W. Putnam, *History of Middle Tennessee* (Nashville, 1859), 62.

[44] Joseph Martin to Patrick Henry, May 21, 1783, in William Wirt Henry, *Patrick Henry: Life, Correspondence and Speeches* (New York, 1891), III, 243–44; John Donelson to William Blount, September 24, 1783, in Keith (ed.), *Blount Papers*, I, 111–12; William Blount to Joseph Martin, October 26, 1783, in Draper Collection (Wisconsin Historical Society, Madison), 4XX17.

personal land agent, Joseph Martin.[45] Blount, likewise,
worked swiftly in order to be ready to profit from his
legislation.

Before leaving the assembly in order to purchase
the Tennessee bend from the Cherokee, the veteran John
Donelson sought Blount influence to secure for his sons
the lucrative surveyorships under the new land act. As a
Western surveyor was an ideal partner, a typical East-
West agreement was made: Donelson and his sons would
locate lands on the French Broad in Tennessee; Blount,
Caswell, and Glasgow would register the lands in Hillsboro on October 15 while attending the next session and
were to use their influence for Donelson's boys. The services of Thomas Polk and his son William, veteran Western
surveyors, also were engaged, to secure Western lands for
a company of Easterners under Blount's direction.[46]

On May 17, the assembly rose, and members with
mixed feelings began their wearisome journeys homeward.
Conservative members, frustrated at almost every point,
found little to commend. Important figures were still pro-
scribed as Loyalists, aid to Congress had been repealed,
the capital was unsettled, the laws were unrevised, and
suits for recovery and debt had been suspended for a year.
State-first men such as Governor Martin were in high
humor.[47] Above all, the speculators in land and paper had

[45] Richard Caswell to William Caswell, May 4, 1783, in Clark (ed.), *State
Records,* XVI, 959–60; Joseph Martin to Patrick Henry, May 21, 1783, in
Henry, *Patrick Henry,* III, 243–44.

[46] William Blount to John Donelson, May 17, 1783, (copy) in Keith
(ed.), *Blount Papers,* I, 57–58; Samuel C. Williams, *History of the Lost
State of Franklin* (Johnson City, 1924), 306 (hereinafter referred to as
Franklin); Thomas Polk to William Blount, July 5, 1783, in Keith (ed.),
Blount Papers, I, 67–68.

[47] James Hogg to James Iredell, May 17, 1783, in McRee, *Life of Iredell,*
II, 45–46; Governor Martin to Benjamin Hawkins and Hugh Williamson,
April 30, 1783, in Clark (ed.), *State Records,* XVI, 783.

triumphed. Vast realms had been opened for exploitation and money furnished with which to act, while the coming of peace would surely mean new land markets at home and abroad.

For William Blount, especially, a new era had opened. Though his interests in merchandising, trade, and politics continued, now land, the never-ceasing pursuit of acreage, and the search for profit in every acre from town lots to imperial domains became his paramount life-long objectives.

CHAPTER IV

THE BUSINESSMAN MEETS
THE WEST

THE FALL MONTHS of the year 1783 were crowded with activity for the Blount brothers. Thomas Blount went to Philadelphia on mercantile business, his aims to find a Philadelphia firm of liberal credit policies to buy North Carolina products and to replenish depleted stocks for the Washington, North Carolina, store and buy goods to pay the Indians for the Bend of the Tennessee lands.

Armed with letters of introduction to Philadelphia firms, young Blount in September tramped the streets and wharves of the metropolis. He found the Eastern merchants most polite, but the credit offered was too short, the tar and pitch on the Blount's *Richard* came too late, and the Carolina tobacco was poorly packed. Wharfage, insurance, pilotage, and cooperage ate up the slim profits, leaving little with which to trade, but Blount ordered goods on credit and faithfully relayed information to his merchant brothers:

The Americans are not at liberty to trade to Havanna—Agreeable to Wᵐ. Blounts instructions I shall make particular enquiry respecting the Trade to Tenereffe & other places. . . . Mr. James Barr . . . says that Staves are never worth less than £18 Sterling P M at Maderia, Tenereffe or Lisbon . . . and that from the Latter we may import China or any other kind of Goods, particularly India,

cheaper than from any other part of the World. . . . I am in treaty
with a young Irishman, who is well recommended as a Book-keeper
for you—his terms will be about £100 P Year—but his Country
makes so much against him that I am yet doubtful whether I will
employ him or not . . .[1]

After a visit to his young half-brother Willie Blount and
neighbor William Blackledge at Princeton, the mercantile
scout returned well-informed to Carolina in the late
Fall.

For John Gray Blount in Washington, too, the Fall
of 1783 was crowded with an appeal to Congress on his
British-captured *Speedwell,* a struggle for the contract
for goods for a proposed Indian treaty, pressure on the
North Carolina treasurer to pay the salaries of friends
Hawkins and Williamson in Congress, lawsuits over Negroes, instructions to the Tarboro branch store, hiring
slaves, and advice for friends on the value of new currency issues.

Like a skillful sailor, William Blount used the winds
of opportunity that swept across the state this busy Fall.
He mobilized family resources by reorganizing into a more
formal partnership the firm of John Gray & Thomas
Blount, Merchants, in which he was now a silent partner.[2]
At Piney Grove his sawmill sliced boards, his kiln poured
forth barrels of tar under its clouds of black smoke, his
slaves moved back and forth down the long rows of corn.
He read attentively the letters of Thomas Blount from
Philadelphia and those of young Jacob Blount from a
trial cruise to the West Indies, and he watched the markets
of New Bern, Hillsboro, and Wilmington. For the firm,

[1] Correspondence of Thomas Blount, August 20, 30, September 2, 9, 11,
23, 1783, in Keith (ed.), *Blount Papers,* I, 86, 95–96, 99–100, 102–105, 109–
111; Blount Collection, P.C. 829, 830, *passim*; Keith, "Three North Carolina
Blount Brothers," 142–43.

[2] William Blount to John Gray Blount, August 21, 1783, in Keith (ed.),
Blount Papers, I, 86–89.

he conceived a plan for selling sweet potatoes on the Philadelphia market and hired a sloop and chose with great care the consignees—the "Whigs of property," Ramsey & Cox. He urged John Gray Blount to import iron plate from Philadelphia for the manufacture of weeding hoes, "a very good article in this county," to sell below the English price. He secured a local monopoly in the rising tar market, buying on futures through the neighborhood, and engaged cargoes for Blount ships by offering Governor Martin 50 per cent interest in the enterprise. He obtained for John Gray & Thomas Blount the contract for Indian goods for the state's treaty with the Cherokee. With the radical Whigs Henry Montfort and Captain Read, he bought a Loyalist's confiscated ship, they buying for revenge, he for profit.[3]

Especially did Blount watch the vital and fluctuating money market. He had a thorough mastery of the value, or lack of it, of each of the multitudinous North Carolina currencies and certificates. In addition, through long experience, he had mastered the process by which cheap state currency or official warrants were used to buy goods to be shipped north and sold for hard money or manufactures which, sold in North Carolina, brought profits in paper or commodities. He understood minutely the uses of credit in a variety of forms and dealt constantly and easily in the futures market.

Because of this mastery, new sources were opened to the firm. Hugh Williamson, Richard Dobbs Spaight, Benjamin Hawkins, and other Carolinians, often away at Philadelphia, willingly gave the partners the use of their salaries in warrants in order to secure profits or hard cash. Williamson, especially, served in Philadelphia as factor, agent, and banker for William Blount.

[3] Blount Collection, P.C. 829, 830, *passim*.

Land, however, remained that speculator's supreme interest, and this in the Fall of 1783 was a passion shared by many. William Blount's military reserve act and John Gray Blount's land sales act had opened a kingdom, and those who sought to inherit it were neither the poor nor the meek. Every traveler across the mountains and every express rider east or west bore instructions or surveys between Eastern financiers and Western surveyors. Companies such as Blount's and Caswell's burgeoned throughout the Carolinas, containing the most prominent names in the state—William Polk, Memucan Hunt, Griffith Rutherford, Thomas Person, Pleasant Henderson, James White, and others.[4] Across the mountains Indians watched with rising anger as surveyors' axes slashed new high marks of the whites' rapacity. No spot was safe, for lands of the peaceful Chickasaw on the Mississippi were entered as fast as those of the unappeased Cherokee in the eastern areas. On the seaboard, speculators scoured the countryside for depreciated paper with which to buy colossal totals of acreage. The law of 1783 limited each entry to five thousand acres, but nothing prohibited the amalgamation of several entries for a far larger total, and entrytakers and surveyors, as well as one secretary of state, could be bribed, while warrants were easily forged. Furthermore, by allowing entries to be "removed" to other locations if located on a prior entry, the law provided a loophole for limitless acquisition, and the illegal sales on credit by entry-taker John Armstrong led to enormous frauds. The amount of land entered under John Gray

---

[4] Williams, *Franklin,* 20–22; agreement of William Polk, Anthony Bledsoe, and others, October 28, 1783, in Thomas Ruffin Papers (University of North Carolina); protest of William Tatham, December 22, 1787, in Clark (ed.), *State Records,* XX, 294–95; Abernethy, *Frontier to Plantation,* 53–54, 58–59; Whitaker, *Spanish-American Frontier,* 4–7; Bramlett, "North Carolina's Western Lands," 90–92, 96–97, 102.

Blount's act was estimated to be three million acres.[5]

Into this frenzied and fabulous contest William Blount plunged with zest. He had perceived in the influential James Robertson of middle Tennessee a perfect Western partner. Robertson's knowledge of and influence in the West was equaled only by Blount's opportunities in the East. Thus by agreement Blount bought military warrants from soldiers, and Robertson surveyed and located them in the military district to the amount of at least fifty thousand acres.[6] Meanwhile, already established associations functioned. Thomas Polk from Charlotte presented to the Blounts his bill for services in purchasing sixty thousand acres of land for £2,250. John Donelson, engaged in Virginia's Chickasaw treaty, nevertheless sent his son, Stockley, to William Blount with "a memo of some lands to be located for our joint interest." The Bend of the Tennessee Company was expanded to include "useful" members, such as John Sevier of Tennessee, Wade Hampton of South Carolina, and Griffith Rutherford of North Carolina, while Joseph Martin from the Indian country sent lists of goods to be secured for the purchase price of the Bend. In August, Richard Caswell reported that Donelson and Martin had, as commissioners of Virginia, met the Cherokee, and while negotiating an Indian boundary had purchased Cherokee claims to the Bend for £1,000, to be paid in goods in December. Donelson urged a trip to the

---

[5] James Clarence Posey, "William Blount: The Land Speculator" (M.A. thesis, Vanderbilt University, 1929), 26–28; Carl S. Driver, *John Sevier, Pioneer of the Old Southwest* (Chapel Hill, 1932), 65–66; Williams, *Franklin*, 21; A. V. Goodpasture, "Education and the Public Lands in Tennessee," in *American Historical Magazine*, IV (1899), 213, 216; Clark (ed.), *State Records*, XXIV, 682–83.

[6] Theodore Roosevelt, *The Winning of the West* (New York, 1894), III, Pt. 1, 248–49; William Blount to Nathaniel Lawrence, January 11, 1787, in Dreer Collection (Pennsylvania Historical Society); William Blount to James Robertson, April 29, 1792, in "Correspondence of General James Robertson," *American Historical Magazine*, I (1896), 392–93 (hereinafter referred to as "Robertson Correspondence").

Georgia legislature to secure legal title from that state.[7]

All these operations demanded paper—military warrants, depreciated bills, indents, and certificates. The military warrants were easily obtainable; their number was legion and was increasing as ex-officers indulged their wartime comrades with careless or false certificates of service. More difficult was the problem of obtaining specie and of exchanging it for satisfactory amounts of certificates in order to pay for surveyors' services or for Western purchases. Whatever the problems, they were Blount's, and the shortening Fall days found him often in the saddle. On one of his horses, General or Titus, or in the much-coveted carriage, he crossed and recrossed the state, bouncing over the rutted clay roads, through bridgeless streams, up and down the long red hills, across the swampy flats. Through pelting autumn rains and endless miles of forests, from home to home and town to town, he rode in search of paper, of credit, of profit. Sales for the firm, land entries for himself, paper currency for the company, all were constant objectives. Halifax, Kingston, Hillsboro, Wilmington, and New Bern, all saw him in these busy months, even though he managed time for considerable periods at Piney Grove, directing the growing business of his mill and kiln.[8]

The year's end brought a longer journey. John Gray Blount needed manufactures for the postwar market, and Donelson and Caswell were now insisting that a company member should get title to the Bend from the Georgia

[7] John Donelson to William Blount, September 24, 1783, in Keith (ed.), *Blount Papers*, I, 111–12; William Blount to John Gray Blount, June 20, August 21, 1783, *ibid.*, 63, 86–89; William Blount to Joseph Martin, October 26, 1783, in Draper Collection, 4XX17; copy of petition of William Blount, February 7, 1784, in Blount Collection; Abernethy, *Frontier to Plantation*, 65–66.

[8] Blount Collection, P.C. 829, 830, *passim*; John Sitgreaves to Captain John Davis, June 18, 1783, in Southern History Association *Publications*, VI (1902), 509–11.

legislature. Meanwhile, Blount heard of rival South Carolina's claims to Western lands, a development he regarded with keen pleasure, as the dispute would be "very favorable to our Designs of obtaining the Georgia Title or the South Carolina Title and either will answer our Purpose equally well for we shall surely settle the Country before the Dispute can be determined and in Order to procure a Title from one or both of those States I will certainly attend both their next Assemblies and I have not the least doubt but I shall succeed. . . ." [9] Thus, optimistically, the manipulator of men turned south to buy goods for his brother and a legislature for the company. The goods to purchase the Bend from the Indians had been secured in Philadelphia and shipped to the firm at Washington. Blount sent these to the Moravian settlement to be transported to the treaty ground, and then turned south. He stopped briefly to transact business at Wilmington, then sailed for Charleston, arriving January 4, 1784. In the capital he found that South Carolina was indeed pressing claims for the Bend lands, and that the legislature was slowly convening. Judging it inexpedient to act, however, he moved on to Georgia, where on February 7 he drew up and two days later presented to the legislature a petition on behalf of himself and his associates,[10] requesting title to approximately three hundred thousand acres in the Bend, on condition of settling three hundred families in three years. The petition was referred to a committee of speculators, who on February 20 made a favorable report. Influenced by the South Carolina claim and by rumors that the Spanish were occupying the region, the house, after

[9] William Blount to Joseph Martin, October 26, 1783, in Draper Collection, 4XX17.
[10] Allen D. Candler (ed. and comp.), *The Revolutionary Records of the State of Georgia* (Atlanta, 1908), III, 492; copy of petition in Blount Collection, P.C. 881.

making some amendments, adopted the committee's recommendations. These called for the election by the legislature of seven commissioners to examine the lands and report to the legislature. The commissioners were also given authority to grant warrants of up to one thousand acres per person at one eighth of a dollar per acre. Most important to the company, the commissioners were empowered to make very generous grants to it.[11]

Blount worked hard to name all seven commissioners, and such was his influence, judiciously secured, that he named three, Donelson, Martin, and Sevier, and influenced the selection of the others, Lachlan McIntosh, Jr., William Downes, Stephen Heard, and John Morrell, all exceedingly land-minded gentlemen. On his return to Charleston he sent copies of the petition and resolution to his associates, accompanied by a revealing letter:

. . . . a Majority of The Commissioners from Georgia are as well disposed (I believe) to the Interest of the Company as I could wish them, they *themselves* have a thirst for a Piece of the Tenesee land also—The Commissioners in the State of N°. Carolina were nominated by myself in the fullest Confidence that each of them will act for all depends on a Majority of the Commissioners being in the Co's Intrest—You will observe by the Resolutions that they have power *to make the Company such Compensation as may be adequate and Satisfactory*—A strong Reason why neither must fail in any Pretext whatever—What will most readily influence the Georgia Commissioners to grant a large quantity of Acres will be an appearance of many People being about to go immediately to that Country to settle therefore you will necessarily keep up a Report of as many being about to go as you possibly can whether true or not. . . . You will observe the Commissioners have power to appoint Militia Officers If the Commissioners of N°. Carolina have no Objection I should like to be appointed Colonel those of Georgia have already given their Voice in my favor and will bring up the Commission for me . . . You will see I have made Use of Bledsoes Name altho he never signed the Articles my Reason for so doing was because he

---

[11] Candler (ed. and comp.), *Revolutionary Records,* III, 525–26; Whitaker, "Muscle Shoals Speculation," *loc. cit.,* 367–68.

was Known to be an over mountain Man of much Interest consequently in the Eyes of the Assembly of Georgia gave Weight to the
Petitioners—You must mention this circumstance to him—Downs
and Herd . . . will on all occasions be with you in Sentiment the
other two are Young men who I really think are well disposed also
but if they are not [are] very easily managed. McIntosh is a sensible
young Man. . . .[12]

One assembly conquered, the lobbyist hurried homeward to assume the formal role of legislator in another,
and, after a short stay at Piney Grove where he purchased
oxen and tools and collected cash, he left for Hillsboro and
the house of commons.

For the assembly which convened April 19, the eastern
Conservatives had made concerted preparation. They took
an unusually sustained interest in electing their candidates,
and strove to rally support for their program by mass
meetings and by pamphlet warfare. Rewards came in the
election of a strong delegation, headed by the veterans
Samuel Johnston, William Hooper, and Archibald Maclaine, and strengthened by the growing conservatism of
some moderates such as Benjamin Hawkins. The Radical
group lost some strength but was still ably led by Thomas
Person and Timothy Bloodworth. The Blounts, Abner
Nash, and William Bryan represented the speculators.

As the delegates gathered in the sleepy little town it
was clear to all that the major problem of the session would
be North Carolina's relationship with the Philadelphia
Congress. This issue had been featured in the Conservative
election campaign. In the assembly it was emphasized by
the presence of such men as Johnston, Blount, Nash, the
Joneses, Hawkins, and Spaight, all of whom as members
had observed the problems of Congress at first hand. The
question was advanced by Governor Alexander Martin's
address to the legislators, and it was the subject of a

[12] William Blount to ?, March 9, 1784 (copy), in Blount Collection.

considerable proportion of the legislation recommended by the steering committee.[13]

This whole matter of closer ties with Congress contained, however, component parts on which factions in the assembly split. The merchant-lawyer eastern group, generally creditors and loosely called Conservatives, supported all measures to strengthen the Congress; the western farming group, generally debtors and termed Radical, although not so cohesive a voting bloc as the Conservatives, on the whole supported few if any such measures. So nearly the same were the two factions' numbers in this legislature that the balance lay with the "third force," the Independents, as represented by the Blounts.[14] The legislature of April, 1784, and its predecessor in 1783, in fact, marked the high tide of William Blount's personal influence in the assembly.

This power of decision Blount used with a shrewd eye to his friends, his state, and himself. He personally conceived the proper policy for the state in its federal relationships largely in Conservative terms. Through experiences at Philadelphia and the natural width of view of an interstate merchant, he and his associates joined the Conservatives in support of several successful measures. Three of the most notable—those granting Congress an impost duty, the right to control foreign commerce, and the proceeds of a six-pence-per-acre tax on land—succeeded but failed to assist the feeble Congress because denied by other states.

In another measure, which he personally sponsored

[13] Ashe, *History of North Carolina*, II, 28–30; Nevins, *American States*, 386–87; William Hooper to James Iredell, March 15, 18, 1784, in McRee, *Life of Iredell*, II, 94–96; James Iredell to Hannah Iredell, March 28, 1784, *ibid.*, 96; Clark (ed.), *State Records*, XIX, 494–99, 542–47.

[14] For parties, see Chapter II, note 16; also, Abernethy, *Frontier to Plantation*, 44, 45ff.

and which was the most important of the session, Blount
also received Conservative support. This was the cession
of Western lands to Congress. Already heavily invested
in tramontane land, he was convinced that Congressional
ownership of the land would not only reduce state burdens,
but—more important—it would raise land prices.[15] Since
his Congressional term in 1782 he had supported such a
cession on favorable conditions, and he therefore on May 7
moved the cession of all North Carolina lands west of the
mountains on certain terms, including, of course, the
guarantee of all entries already made.[16]

A bitter battle resulted. Not only many Radicals and
Tennessee country delegates, but also even certain independent speculators feared loss of economic opportunity
in the West through "foreign" control. Conservatives Maclaine, Hooper, and Johnston, with typical aversion for the
quarrelsome West, stood for Blount's cession. Another
source of support was the Virginia cession, since North
Carolina statesmen were always influenced by the decision
of their northern neighbor, and the latter's cession, con-
ditionally made in October of 1783, finally had been accepted after long quibbling on March 1, 1784.[17] On May
18, a surprise Radical coalition forced an amendment re-
ducing the ceded lands to those beyond the Cumberland
River, but Blount rallied his forces and the original limits
were restored. After final fiery debate led by Person and
William R. Davie, Blount's supporters defeated a motion

[15] William Blount to John Donelson, Joseph Martin, and John Sevier,
May 31, 1784 (copy) in Keith (ed.), *Blount Papers*, I, 167–69.

[16] Hugh Williamson and William Blount to Governor Martin, October 22,
1782, in Clark (ed.), *State Records*, XVI, 434–41; XIX, 567–68; XXIV,
561–63.

[17] *Ibid.*, XIX, 643–44; F. J. Turner, "Western State-Making in the Revolutionary Era," in *American Historical Review*, I (1896), 254, 257; Henry,
Patrick Henry, II, 94–96; Driver, *John Sevier*, 82.

to postpone the question by a narrow 47–46 vote, after
which the bill safely passed 52–43. Defeated Radicals
and the state-first party consoled themselves with a biting
dissent and promises of retribution to come.[18] The passage
of Blount's act was clearly the work of large speculators,
with eastern support, and was commonly recognized as
interest legislation. Its natural corollary was an act closing the land offices at Hillsboro but allowing incomplete warrants to pass into grants, legislation which
aroused even greater opposition against the speculators.[19]

The successful coalition of speculators and Conservatives was, however, doomed to split upon the rock of Loyal-
ism. The supreme goals of Maclaine, Hooper, and Johnston were a relaxation of the confiscation laws and an
adherence to the treaty articles in the matter of debts owed
to Loyalists. Land, taxation, even Federal relations were
secondary in Conservative minds to these aims. On the
other hand, Blount and the speculators, as holders of
confiscated property, had nothing to gain but much to
hazard if the Loyalists gained prewar status. In addition, their own Whiggism and that of constituents argued
against leniency. Therefore, although he agreed with the
rest of the steering committee in recommending repeal of
all laws contrary to the treaty and to a revisal of the confiscation laws, Blount prepared to fight his erstwhile allies
on the house floor. Events also aided his plans to defeat
the Loyalist cause, since Hugh Williamson and Richard
Spaight wrote from Congress construing the Loyalist
clauses of the treaty as not binding on the state, and as

[18] Clark (ed.), *State Records*, XIX, 612–13, 621–22, 642–44, 711–14.

[19] "Extract of a letter from a Gentleman in North Carolina to his friend
in the Western Country," August 5, 1784, in *Gazette of the State of South
Carolina*, November 8, 1784, printed in *North Carolina Historical Review*,
III (1926), 372; Clark (ed.), *State Records*, XX, 294–95; Abernethy, *Frontier to Plantation*, 58–59.

more Loyalists returned they increasingly excited popular anger.[20]

Conservatives' hopes were chilled by the refusal of the house of commons to accept the steering committee's recommendation for conformity with the treaty. Nevertheless, they introduced bills to return unsold confiscated property and to repeal laws inconsistent with the treaty. A battle royal followed. William Hooper from Orange, William Cumming of Edenton, and Benjamin Hawkins from Warren fought in the van. Samuel Johnston in the senate spoke long with unusual vigor and "much sound solid reasoning." The irascible Maclaine was lost to his cohorts when an untimely attack of gout confined his invective to his infirmity, but unexpected aid came from Radicals Willie Jones, Ed Starkey, and Thomas Person, who by personal conviction or for political purposes joined their former foes.

The Independents, now with Radical allies, fought back. Governor Martin gave administration support, Griffith Rutherford boomed against the Loyalist "Imps of Hell," Abner Nash argued, and Blount maneuvered. As the debate raged, Conservatives denounced "ambitious discontented spirits whose existence depends on fanning the passions of the common people," while the Radicals countered with cries of hard times, heavy taxes, aristocratic cliques, and speculation. From the Radicals in the senate came a bill to dispose of all confiscated property remaining unsold; in the commons, Blount and Nash led the fight for a comprehensive bill of banishment, and on this, speculator and Radical gleefully united. The governor added his creditors' names, Rutherford, his enemies; and

---

[20] Clark (ed.), *State Records,* XIX, 545–46; Archibald Maclaine to George Hooper, June 14, 1784, *ibid.,* XVII, 144–47; Richard D. Spaight to Governor Martin, March 12, 1784, *ibid.,* 20–21; Hugh Williamson to *id.,* March 19, 1784, *ibid.,* 21–28; James Iredell to A. Neilson, June 15, 1784, in McRee, *Life of Iredell,* II, 104–105.

Bloodworth, in his avid Whiggism, seemed to want to "depopulate New Hanover county." [21]

As the battle progressed, the Conservatives, beaten, dropped from offense to defense. Their bills on confiscated property and the treaty were roundly defeated by the speculator-Radical team, and the counterproposals of the Radicals were only narrowly voted down in the senate. As in the cession fight, though now in alliance with the other party, the speculators' votes were decisive. [22]

For Blount personally, however, the most significant activity of the session concerned the West. Elijah Robertson sat in the assembly, and his father—Blount's agent, James Robertson—was an effective lobbyist. For their mutual benefit and for the Western settlers, Blount pushed several measures. At the elder Robertson's solicitation he introduced and secured passage of a law establishing the town of "Nash Ville," the former Nashboro or French Lick settlement, and providing for sales of lots. He obtained free pre-emption rights for a long list of settlers in Davidson County. He assisted in legislation to establish a court of oyer and terminer in the same county. He served on a committee which, despite the governor's protest, secured an amendment of his brother's 1783 bill by throwing open for sale even the Indians' Treaty Island in the Holston River. In the way of personal rewards, Blount's hand appeared in the grant of 960 acres to Elijah Robertson for official services, and the prize appointment as

[21] Archibald Maclaine to George Hooper, April 21, June 14, 1784, in Clark (ed.), *State Records,* XVII, 134–35, 144–47; Richard Caswell to William Caswell, May 3, 23, 1784, *ibid.,* 139–40, 142–44; Samuel Johnston to James Iredell, May 1, 1784, in McRee, *Life of Iredell,* II, 99; William Hooper to James Iredell, May 1, 1784, *ibid.,* 99–100; Samuel Johnston to Hannah Iredell, May 15, 1784, *ibid.,* 100–101; Benjamin Hawkins to George Washington, June 10, 1784, in Jared Sparks (ed.), *The Correspondence of the American Revolution* (Boston, 1853), IV, 69–71.

[22] Clark (ed.), *State Records,* XIX, 671–73, 674–75.

surveyor of the eastern district of the Tennessee country to Stockley Donelson.[23]

Seated on a committee to examine the surveyors' report on the military reserve, conferring daily with his grateful Western agents, and distributing largesse to such Western leaders as surveyor Daniel Smith and politician William Cocke, Blount was in an unparalleled position to know and to profit from the West. His holdings west of the mountains as well as those of John Gray & Thomas Blount, Merchants, rose by thousands of acres. He also made loans, entries, and arrangements with surveyors for friends, and himself entered an informal partnership with Congressman Hugh Williamson to buy lands for their joint account.[24]

Affairs of the Bend of Tennessee Company, too, prospered, though slowly. One hitch developed when the goods for the Indian Treaty were not delivered on schedule. Another was the commissioners' polite refusal to confer the desired colonelcy on Blount, since "some inconsistencey might appear in such appointment prior to His Visiting Said Lands or being possessed of an adequate knowledge that the measure was necessary." [25] On the other hand, the goods could still be forwarded, and the commissioners implied that the colonelcy was only delayed. Also, Congressional delegate Williamson wrote of the wishes of a Phila-

---

[23] *Ibid.*, XIX, 527–28, 569, 579; XXIV, 571, 599–600, 616–17, 629–30; Draper Collection, 32S369; Davidson County Deeds, Book A, 10.

[24] Bond of Joel Wall, August 4, 1784, in Pitt County Papers (North Carolina State Department of Archives and History); Hugh Williamson to John Gray Blount, December 6, 1784, in Blount Collection; warrants, grants, and lists of landholdings, *ibid.*, P.C. 881, 897; agreement of Elijah Robertson, William Blount, and Micajah Thomas (n.d.), *ibid.*, P.C. 881; William Blount to Abner Nash, December 2, 1784 (copy), in Keith (ed.), *Blount Papers*, I, 183–84; Abner Nash to William Blount, December 6, 1784, *ibid.*, 185–86.

[25] Extract of minutes of commissioners meeting (n.d.), in Blount Collection, P.C. 831; Lachlan McIntosh to William Blount (n.d.), *ibid.*; Martin Armstrong to Joseph Martin, August 11, 1784, in Draper Collection, 1XX75.

delphia Mennonite community to purchase lands in the
Bend. Blount sent an extract of the offer to his partners,
the North Carolina commissioners Donelson, Martin, and
Sevier, with instructions to use it to impress the Georgia
legislative commissioners, who were then on their way to
examine the Bend. The latter, he advised, should be made
members of the Bend Company and should not be allowed
to return from the West "without executing a Grant to the
Company as large as you can obtain" if not for the whole
Bend. He emphasized that the North Carolina cession to
Congress had greatly enhanced the value of Western lands
and as further business advice (and an unconscious illustration of his business ethics) added:

. . . . If you should think proper to open the . . . [office] to grant
Warrants at 1/8 of a dollar per Acre enter as much as you can and
make use of any Names fictitious ones will do I suppose, If not you
may use the Names of Blount, Williams Johnson Allen, Winnan,
Ogden and almost any other Name you please ading such Christian
Names to them as You please and You need not fear but I can find
the People to transfer their Rights to the Company. . . . May it
not be good Policy [to] Set some new Scheme on foot in Partnership
with the Gentlemen of Georgia to make further Purchases over the
Tenesee or on the Missisippi in on down near the Natches for they
must if possible be fixed [fired] with a thirst for back lands to effect
which no Pains must be spared. . . .[26]

At the same time the archpromoter wrote to the Georgia
commissioners offering them membership in the company
and urging that they be generous since the land would
probably be ceded to Congress by Georgia anyway. Further
arguments for liberality followed:

. . . . The Object of the Tenesee Company in purchasing the Bent
and (I suppose) your's in Accepting the appointment as commissioners must have been the same, *I mean private Emolument* and
in Order that we may both obtain our *purposes* it is Necessary, We
should understand each Other and that our Acts should tend to our

    [26] William Blount to John Donelson, Joseph Martin, and John Sevier, May
31, 1784 (copy), in Keith (ed.), *Blount Papers*, I, 167–69.

mutual advantage. . . . You have power, *to make the company such, compensation as may be deemed Adequate and satisfactory,* No Bond nor no Oath has been required nor no Instructions, given you . . . and if you accede to my Proposition of our Interest being the same you will have a share of your own liberty. . . . Such Another oppertunity may never present itself of Making a Spec and there's an old Proverb which says "make Hay while the sun shines," of which I wish you to be mindfull. . . . I wish you an agreeable Journey and greate Choice and Great plenty of Cheekamagga Squaws. . . .[27]

When the long assembly ended on June 3, 1784, Blount went home to carry on his multifarious enterprises in shipping, land-dealing, and merchandising. Meanwhile, he kept close watch on the Bend, where events slowly progressed. Despite the inducement of land and "Cheekamagga Squaws," only one of the Georgia commissioners, Stephen Heard, had appeared at Long Island to join his North Carolina conferees and, delayed by lack of wagons, the Indian goods arrived only after Heard's departure. Despite the fact that this precluded a purchase from the Indians, the four commissioners laid off a county on a map of the Bend and planned to open a land office at Muscle Shoals on March 15, 1785. They also selected seven officers, including Sevier as colonel and entrytaker, and Donelson as lieutenant colonel and county surveyor.[28] Thus, despite obstacles, Blount and his company kept the situation in hand.

However, at this point, the archmanipulator of men and legislatures met a check, for his cession act, so carefully designed to protect the Eastern speculators, proved to be a powder train leading to an unexpected and almost

[27] William Blount to James McIntosh, Stephen Heard, John Morrell, and William Downes, May 31, 1784 (copy), in Blount Collection. Italics are Blount's.

[28] Joseph Martin to William Blount, August 28, 1784, *ibid.*, 176; John Haywood, *The Civil and Political History of the State of Tennessee* (Nashville, 1891), 172–73.

ruinous explosion. From Western associates Blount knew something of Western unrest. He knew frontiersmen's anger over the burden of self defense, their irritation at the inconveniences of costly trips over the mountains to attend indifferent legislatures or courts. He had been told that the West resented the flow of scarce specie eastward to pay taxes and buy necessities. He understood the Western problem of transporting products over vast distances and rugged mountains. He knew the North Carolina constitution provided for statehood for the Western lands, and he must have been aware of the promise of Congress concerning equal statehood to the ceded territories, and of the aspirations it aroused in the Kentucky country.

Nevertheless, Blount underestimated the depth of Western irritation and aspiration. He failed to realize that the slighting remarks of easterners were carried back to Western ears and stung western pride. He understood the keen eastern competition for Western lands, but did not recognize some Westerners' anger over the seaboard gentlemen's disposal of the frontier's greatest asset.[29] Above all, he did not realize that in the West, ambitious men as avid as himself for land and power, were ready to seize upon the cession act as a means to bring about a revolution. Since 1780, Arthur Campbell of Washington County, Virginia, had agitated for a separation of the tramontane region. This active, resourceful leader, a colonel of the militia, was well known to the western Carolinians through their close association with southwestern Virginia. Ambitious and eager to secure both land and leadership in a frontier state, he had already worked hard in 1782 to pro-

---

[29] For causes of the state of Franklin, see Williams, *Franklin*, 5–8, 26–28, 31, 122–27; John D. Barnhart, "The Tennessee Constitution of 1796: a Product of the Old West," in *Journal of Southern History*, IX (1943), 536–37; Turner, "Western State-Making," *loc. cit.*, 251–61; and W. F. Cannon, "Four Interpretations of the History of the State of Franklin," in East Tennessee Historical Society's *Publications*, No. 22 (1950), 3–18.

mote such a state in southwest Virginia and western North Carolina. The cession act provided a new opening, the militia companies the machinery, and in August, 1784, the result was a convention at Jonesboro which voted for independence and called a constitutional convention for September.[30]

While these clouds gathered, Blount again prepared to attend the legislature, which was to meet in October, 1784, at New Bern. Here he faced a second storm. The months since the cession act had seen political upheaval in eastern Carolina paralleling that of the west. In July and August, state-first men, Radicals, and antispeculators campaigned over the state against cession. Led by Person, William R. Davie, and Alexander Mebane, they fiercely attacked motives and personalities with cries of bribery and corruption, appeals to state creditors to save their collateral, and charges of undue influence by Congress. A flank attack came from ex-delegate Hugh Williamson, himself a large landowner. Home from Congress in July, he attacked the act because it did not provide for the assumption by Congress of the cost of North Carolina's Indian wars. Usually Federal-minded, Williamson was now disgusted over the claims of other states to the West and the refusal of Georgia to cede her lands, and he pressed his attack on the cession, urging that North Carolina not give up the bargaining power with Congress furnished by her Western possessions.[31] Despite fierce opposition, the Blounts were elected, but of the Conservatives, Iredell and Hooper retired in pious anger, and Hawkins was defeated,

[30] John Sevier to Governor Caswell, October 17, 1785, in Clark (ed.), *State Records*, XVII, 545–46; Abernethy, *Frontier to Plantation*, 68–70; Williams, *Franklin*, 5–12, 44–47, 51, 53, 284–87; Palmer and McRae (eds.), *Virginia State Papers*, III, 414–15; IV, 3, 53–54; William Christian to Arthur Campbell, February 19, 1782, in Draper Collection, 9DD32.

[31] Hugh Williamson to Governor Martin, July 5, September 30, 1784, in Clark (ed.), *State Records*, XVII, 80–83, 94–105; Williams, *Franklin*, 35.

leaving only Maclaine to face the victors at New Bern.[32]

When the session convened October 22, Blount, seeking a post of maximum influence to stem the tide, succeeded in election to the house speakership, while Caswell presided in the senate. But the effort was in vain, for on November 18, after heavy skirmishing, the cession was repealed by a vote of 37–22, and two days later the house ordered the chagrined speaker to sign and ratify the act.[33] Meanwhile, with an eye for financial advantage, he sought the comptrollership, which, though he was nominated, he lost to Francis Childs; he did, however, receive the largest vote of any of the new delegates to Congress. Martin having reached the constitutional limit of three terms, Caswell won the governorship in a race with Nash.[34]

In the face of the gathering storm in the West, the assembly pursued its own policy. It rejected the bill of Westerner Alexander Outlaw, delegate from Greene County, to create a separate state which would use its land receipts to pay North Carolina's war debts. On the other hand, it created a judicial district of the four tramontane counties and named John Sevier a brigadier general and David Campbell superior court judge in a shrewd move to allay popular discontent and buy off potential leaders of the new state.

The cession repeal and the need for a Western policy also brought up the long delayed Indian treaty, belatedly provided for in 1783 in order to clear title for John Gray Blount's land act. Governor Martin, both as a partner in

---

[32] James Iredell to Henry E. McCulloch, June 15, 1784, in McRee, *Life of Iredell*, II, 103–104; William Hooper to James Iredell, July 8, 1784, *ibid.*, 105–108; Benjamin Hawkins to James Madison, September 4, 1784, in James Madison Papers (Division of Manuscripts, Library of Congress).

[33] Clark (ed.), *State Records*, XIX, 804–805, 814, 830–32; XXIV, 678–79.

[34] *Ibid.*, XIX, 774, 809, 813, 815; James Iredell to Hannah Iredell, November 18, 1784, in McRee, *Life of Iredell*, II, 113; Ashe, *History of North Carolina*, II, 37.

purchasing the necessary goods and officially, had attempted to negotiate such a treaty from late 1783 to the April session of 1784, but various delays had blocked it. The cession had caused the whole matter to be referred to Congress for action.[35] Now, with North Carolina still in possession of the West, the Indian problem was still hers, and the treaty delay was a cause of Western complaint; consequently, the governor resumed his plan. He named Caswell and Blount to act with himself and wrote in December to John Sevier sending the brigadier's commission and instructing him to attend the treaty meeting with soldiers. At the same time he wrote John Gray Blount to be ready to send merchandise in February for the treaty meeting to be held in late April.[36]

Across the mountains, however, events moved against both North Carolina's statesman and her speculators. After delays, the convention called in August organized on December 14, 1784, at Jonesboro with Sevier presiding. William Cocke, assisted by Joseph Hardin and David Campbell, directed events. Cocke, Arthur Campbell's mouthpiece, was similar to his mentor in physical size and fiery temperament, if not in breadth of spirit; Hardin was an influential and ambitious personality; and Campbell, brother of Arthur, was ever ready to offer advice and seek leadership. Attacking the land control and general selfishness of the east, and basing their case on the cession and the resolves of Congress looking to new states, these leaders carried on the move for the independence of the western

[35] Alexander Martin to John Gray & Thomas Blount, September 27, 1783, in Keith (ed.), *Blount Papers*, I, 113–14; *id.* to William Blount, January 2, 1784, *ibid.*, 148; *id.* to *id.*, October 20, 1783, in Blount Collection; *id.* to Hugh Williamson and Richard D. Spaight, June 4, 1784, in Clark (ed.), *State Records*, XVII, 78–80.

[36] Alexander Martin to John Sevier, December (n.d.), 1784, in Clark (ed.), *State Records*, XVII, 109–10; *id.* to John Gray Blount, December 4 1784, in Keith (ed.), *Blount Papers*, I, 185.

counties of Washington, Sullivan, and Greene. A temporary constitution, based on that of North Carolina and the
work of Cocke and Campbell, was adopted, and Sevier was
made temporary governor of the new state pending elections. Worst of all from Blount's viewpoint, the proposed
boundaries of the new state swept south to include the
Bend of Tennessee.[37]

Becoming slowly aware of the seriousness of these
threats, Blount strove to hold his company together. After
a conference with Caswell, he wrote to the Western associates urging that the opening of the company's land office
at the Bend be postponed as, "I purpose *certainly* to attend in the Character of a Commissioner the Indian Treaty
which is at present intended to be held between the 20th of
April and the 10th May and . . . Majr Genl Caswell
will attend as a Commissioner." However, if the opening
occurred in March, "We wish you to secure as much of
the Bent as may be in your Power." The worried speculator
also assured his associates that it was "the Opinion of
many well-informed People" that if Congress accepted
the original cession within the year allotted by the act,
that the repeal would be legally void.[38]

Sevier too, somewhat reassured and mollified by the
arrival of his general's commission, sought to stem the
Franklin tide by speeches and correspondence,[39] but as
the weeks passed, the movement became too strong even
for the Western hero. In the east his fellow speculators
realized that their operations were endangered by the new
state, but in the West "Nollachucky Jack" knew that his

[37] Williams, *Franklin*, 38–43; Haywood, *History of Tennessee*, 150–52;
Whitaker, "Muscle Shoals Speculation," *loc. cit.*, 372.

[38] William Blount to John Sevier, Joseph Martin, and John Donelson,
December 4, 1784, Draper Collection, 4XX18.

[39] Williams, *Franklin*, 55; John Sevier to Colonel Kennedy, January 2,
1785, in J. G. M. Ramsey, *The Annals of Tennessee* (reprint, Chattanooga,
1926), 291.

equally cherished popularity was imperiled by his opposition. Also, Cocke had interesting private proposals to
make concerning economic possibilities in a new state.[40]
The solution was not at once apparent, but once seen it
was easy. Sevier accepted the election as governor of the
state of Franklin; projects and popularity were saved.[41]

In the ensuing months, despite the opposition of such
leaders as the Blounts and Governor Martin, the men of
the new state continued their course. They replied firmly
to Martin's official thunders, passed laws to guide the infant commonwealth, appointed Sevier, Alexander Outlaw,
and Daniel Kennedy to negotiate a treaty and secure land
from the Indians, and sent William Cocke to Congress
with a petition for recognition. Easterners, including officials in Virginia, watched these events with increasing
dismay. To Blount the moves meant frustration unless
Sevier could and would secure their joint interests, and
even so, the settlement of the new state meant competition
with the Bend Company's plans.

On May 13, 1785, however, an event transpired which
was to affect profoundly the fortunes of the new state. As
late speaker, Blount invested his friend and mentor, Richard Caswell, with the insignia of the governor's office.
According to Caswell's wish the ceremony was "not done
in a corner" but included speeches, proclamations, and
artillery salutes.[42] These guns announced the inevitable
fall of Franklin. With an associate in each of the rival
governors, Blount and the other speculators felt growing
security. Caswell, more popular in the West than Martin,
spoke publicly in dulcet tones of separation on mutually

[40] Thomas Hutchins to General Shelby, April 22, 1787, in Clark (ed.),
State Records, XX, 679–80.

[41] Driver, *John Sevier,* 72–73, 87–88; Abernethy, *Frontier to Plantation,*
73.

[42] Richard Caswell to William Blount, April 27, 1785 (copy), in Rodman
Papers; Speaker Blount's address, May 13, 1785, in Governors' Papers.

satisfactory terms. But the old master of politics well knew that the assembly majority of Radicals and speculators, if they assented to separation at all, would take care that the terms protected both North Carolina and her business-men. Meanwhile, in private correspondence the two governors, ostensibly bitter enemies, gave mutual assurances of continued business co-operation.[43] In August, Sevier moved to aid the Bend Company and his state; his Franklin legislature passed an act to encourage an expedition to the Bend to occupy lands under Georgia title. Franklin-ites welcomed a Georgia alliance; the company welcomed settlers.

That the speculators held the key to independence was realized by Cocke and the true Franklinites. They therefore sought to arrange a division of spoils as the price of independence. Caswell and Blount counties appeared on the map of Franklin. As they had Sevier, so Campbell and Cocke now approached both Joseph Martin and Blount with prospects of "advancement," namely, a guarantee of enhanced land values.[44] This maneuver, however, was futile. Martin was the personal and official agent of Patrick Henry of Virginia, and, after a brief flirtation with the new state, he resisted temptation. As for Blount, with a foot in each camp and facing an uncertain future, it was inevitable that Cocke would entice in vain while the master speculator waited and watched.

Thus 1785 passed, and, while Franklin grew in num-

[43] Richard Caswell to John Sevier, July 12, 1786, Draper Collection, 4XX18 (2–4).

[44] Alexander Martin to John Gray Blount, February 26, 1785, in Keith (ed.), *Blount Papers*, I, 191–92; "Extract of a letter from a Gentleman living in the Western Territory . . . to his friend in Virginia," December 20, 1784, in *Gazette of the State of South Carolina*, November 8, 1784, *loc. cit.*, 373; Abernethy, *Frontier to Plantation*, 64–80; Joseph Martin to the Governor of Virginia, September 19, 1785, in Palmer and McRae (eds.), *Virginia State Papers*, IV, 53–54; Thomas Hutchins to General Shelby, April 22, 1787, in Clark (ed.), *State Records*, XX, 679–80.

bers, legislated, and made treaties with the Indians, and Caswell and Sevier kept up their mock hostilities, Blount busied himself at home. His brother Thomas again sailed for Europe to solicit trade for the flourishing firm, and Jacob Blount, Senior, traveled the countryside buying lands for himself and his sons.

William Blount was engaged in both mercantile and increasingly complex land matters. He joined Abner Nash and others in still further land purchases and employed Henry Rutherford and others to assist James Robertson in surveying greater tracts in the West.[45] Financing these growing purchases (Rutherford's party alone surveyed three hundred and sixty-five thousand acres) was made easier by strategic friendships. Besides Caswell, Blount's associations were friendly with his successful rival for the comptrollership, Francis Childs. This gentleman's occasional legal qualms brought Blount's epithet of "an obstinate Fool," but the comptroller agreed to "serve" the speculators by allowing the Blounts to pay their taxes illegally in notes from the entry-takers or in private credit notes in lieu of cash. John Gray Blount, therefore, had his brother's instructions to "attend to him and stand by him . . . at the next Assembly if He should be attacked." The entry-takers, too, were obliging and ignored the law by accepting Blount's entries on credit.[46] Thus assisted, the Blounts rapidly increased their holdings in both North Carolina and Tennessee.[47]

[45] Grant of October 23, 1783, Warrant Numbers 2533, 2597, 2598, 2817, in Tennessee County Deeds (State Land Office, Raleigh); Pitt County Entry Book, 110; Abner Nash to William Blount, December 6, 1784, in Keith (ed.), *Blount Papers*, I, 185–86; P. T. Glass, "Sketch of Henry Rutherford," in *American Historical Magazine*, V (1900), 227.

[46] William Blount to John Gray Blount, September 12, 1785, in Blount Collection.

[47] Craven County Entry Book, 18–23; Craven County Deeds, Book 12, p. 190; Book 26, p. 42; Elijah Robertson to William Blount, May 2, 1785, in Keith (ed.), *Blount Papers*, I, 196–97.

Affairs of the Bend Company progressed only slowly. In March, partner John Donelson took a company of prospective buyers to the Bend to meet the associates and open the land office there; but when none of the expected partners appeared and the Indians proved menacing, Donelson began a homeward trip on which he was killed by Indians.[48] This meant a delay in company affairs until Fall. Meanwhile the busy William kept in close touch both with the Franklinites in Jonesboro and with the Congress in New York. The latter body, while urging North Carolina to reconsider its cession repeal, had accepted that repeal as legal while it listened to the Franklin petition for statehood presented by agent Cocke.[49]

But developments in the West in 1785 compelled action even from the normally impotent Congress and plunged Blount into one of the last state rights battles of the Confederation. Since the collapse of the Revolutionary Anglo-Indian co-operation in 1781, waves of immigrants had swept into the upper Tennessee country. Pouring down the valleys of the Holston-French Broad system, the stream of settlers had by the Fall of 1782 pushed as far down as the Big Pigeon River, within a day's travel from a considerable number of Indian villages. Appeals by the Indians to Governor Alexander Martin were strengthened by Governor Harrison of Virginia, who warned Martin of Indian anger and suggested a boundary commission. Martin himself repeatedly ordered Colonel (and later General) Sevier to drive the white intruders from Indian lands, but even the governor insisted on a line beyond the 1777 treaty, and as for Sevier, the "Scourge of the Chero-

---

[48] *Report of the Select Committee to Whom was Referred the Petition of Andrew Jackson, of Thomas Carr, and of George W. Sevier . . .* , December 14, 1818, House Document Number 31, 15th Congress, 2nd Session, 5.

[49] Richard D. Spaight to Richard Caswell, June 5, 1785, in Clark (ed.), *State Records*, XVII, 464–66; Hugh Williamson to Richard Caswell, June 18, 1785, *ibid.*, 473.

kees" was not the man to antagonize white friends for the legal rights of the red enemy. Events, therefore, continued to accelerate the invasion. John Gray Blount's land act of 1783 had widened the area of exploration and thrown thousands of settlers, surveyors, and speculators into the westward push, in which enterprises such as William Blount's Bend Company further alarmed and enraged the red men. Into this dangerous situation the state of Franklin was projected, and Governor Sevier's extortions of land from the savages by means of farcical treaties drove the savages to desperation. As a result, on January 1, 1784, the Creek chieftain, Alexander McGillivray, had appealed to Governor Arthur O'Neill of Florida, proposing a Spanish-Indian alliance against the Americans, and this threat at length forced Congress to act.[50] That body entered a new field of authority by appointing a commission to negotiate a treaty with the Southern Indians, and on March 21, 1785, after the usual sectional quibbling, Andrew Pickens of South Carolina, Joseph Martin, Benjamin Hawkins, Daniel Carroll of Maryland, and William Perry of Delaware (later replaced by Lachlan McIntosh) were named Congressional commissioners. In the early summer a number of these men met in Charleston and decided to hold a treaty meeting in the Fall with all the major tribes of the southwest.[51]

[50] Randolph C. Downes, "Cherokee-American Relations in the Upper Tennessee Valley, 1776–1791," in East Tennessee Historical Society's *Publications,* VIII (1936), 39–42; S. B. Weeks, "General Joseph Martin and the War of the Revolution in the West," in American Historical Association *Annual Report,* 1893 (Washington, 1894), 442–45; correspondence of Governors Harrison and Martin, November, 1782, in Clark (ed.), *State Records,* XVI, 457–58, 460–62; Merritt B. Pound, *Benjamin Hawkins—Indian Agent* (Athens, 1951), 36–37.

[51] Clark (ed.), *State Records,* XVII, 429–31; Benjamin Hawkins, Andrew Pickens, and Joseph Martin to Richard Caswell, June 19, 1785, *ibid.,* 473–75; Ford *et al.* (eds.), *Journals of Congress,* XXVIII, 183, 184; Richard D. Spaight to William Blount, March 29, 1785, in Keith (ed.), *Blount Papers,* I, 194–95; John Sitgreaves to William Blount, March 9, 1785, in Blount Collection.

In North Carolina, the news of the Congressional appointments led to a revival of former Governor Martin's plans for a state treaty to clear title to the tramontane region. Blount, meanwhile, had planned to attend the Continental Congress in November according to his 1784 election, but upon receiving news of the Congressional commissioners' Charleston meeting, he perceived immediately an opportunity to combine a public office with private advantage. He still held the office of Indian agent, formerly bestowed on him for Martin's state treaty, and the Bend Company had taught him the possibilities of private purchases at public treaties. He therefore informed Governor Caswell of his plan to attend the treaty meeting instead of the Congress, and requested his salary. The governor's council approved, foreseeing, as did those of Georgia and South Carolina, a clash of state and central authority in the field of Indian relations.[52]

Firmly determined to protect both personal and state interests in the West, Blount set forth in September, 1785. Caswell furnished him with a new commission and £1,000 in warrants with which to buy goods which, with those already bought by the state and now in his brother's warehouses, were to secure Indian relinquishment of the Western areas desired by North Carolina. Stopping where convenient to transact his firm's business, the agent traveled via Fayetteville to Augusta, Georgia, arriving there September 17. He found that the Congressional commissioners had, because of delays in supplies and the dispersion of the Indians, postponed the intended meeting with the Creeks at Galphinton from September 19 until October 24. This meant that the subsequent Cherokee and Chicka-

[52] William Blount to Governor Caswell, July 3, 1785, in Clark (ed.), *State Records*, XVII, 479; Governor Caswell to the commissioners, July 23, 1785, *ibid.*, 487; Governor Caswell to William Blount, August 16, 1785, in Keith (ed.), *Blount Papers*, I, 205–206.

saw treaties would be delayed until mid-November; the delay, however, was satisfactory to the North Carolina agent, since it would afford more time for the arrival of the treaty goods from Charleston and for the arrival of the Georgia agents, whose undoubted support would strengthen Blount in case of a clash with the Congressional commissioners.[53]

The possibilities of such a conflict became more apparent as the days passed. Blount found that the Congressional commission, though containing two personal friends, was determined to regard the Indians "as Proprietors of the Soil and Sovereignty of all the Lands that they have not sold to the States." Furthermore, the commission planned to guarantee by treaty the Indian possession of such lands. This, of course, meant that the North Carolina Land Act of 1783 was void in the eyes of Congress, and hence the treaty would guarantee to the Indians the tens of thousands of acres already bought up by Blount and his fellow speculators. Under such a cloudy title the value of all Western lands would drop, and understandably the agent reported that the attitude of the "inflexibly determined" commissioners gave "much uneasiness to Georgia as well as to myself." [54] More bad news came from one Doctor Ramsey, *"immediately* from Congress," who reported it likely that Congress, then negotiating with Spanish envoy Gardoqui, would give up the navigation of the Mississippi to obtain in return commercial privileges from Spain. This, Blount at once reported to his brother, would further "much lessen the value of western Lands and may induce you to lessen our quantity in that quarter

[53] A. Vanderhorst to William Blount, October 4, November 5, 1785, in Clark (ed.), *State Records,* XVII, 536–37, 558–59; William Blount to Richard Caswell, October 8, 1785, *ibid.,* 538.

[54] William Blount to John Gray Blount, November 6, 1785, in Blount Collection.

so as to make it suit our convenience to pay fully for them." [55]

With respect to the decision of Congress on the Mississippi, Blount could do nothing until he reached Congress, but towards his immediate objective he did secure from the Congressional agents an agreement that he might negotiate the North Carolina Cherokee treaty prior to the Congressional treaty with that tribe in order to protect his and his state's claims despite the "inflexibly determined" commissioners.

At length agents and commissioners journeyed from the fur capital of Augusta to the yet smaller though well-known trading post of Galphinton on the Ogeechee. However, the Creeks, dismayed by rumors and held aloof by their chief, Alexander McGillivray, failed to respond to the treaty invitation, and since only about forty appeared after seventeen days of waiting, the commissioners left on November 9. Blount waited two days after the departure of the commissioners, partly to attempt a private purchase of more Indian land and partly to observe the Georgians, who, pleased by the commissioners' failure and by the arrival of a few more Indians, entered into a pseudo treaty to extort lands from the Creek nation by debauching those few Creeks present.[56]

Finally, on November 12, the North Carolina agent left Galphinton and followed the commissioners to Hopewell, General Pickens' plantation in South Carolina, about 120 miles above Augusta. Everything depended upon securing a Cherokee treaty for his state before any national treaty, and though he had heard nothing from Charleston, indirect reports had assured him that the

[55] *Ibid.*

[56] *Id.* to *id.,* November 6, 11, 1785, *ibid.;* William Blount to Richard Caswell, November 11, 1785, in Clark (ed.), *State Records,* XVII, 566–67.

goods were at the treaty ground. Upon reaching Hopewell, therefore, he was appalled to find that not only had the goods failed to arrive but that there was no report whatever of their progress. Since only five hundred Indians were present on November 18, the treaty was postponed four days, during which two Georgia agents arrived from Galphinton, but still no news came of the Carolina goods.

At length on November 21, the Congressional negotiations were ready to begin. The unhappy Blount displayed to the commissioners his credentials as North Carolina's agent; on the following day the treaty proceedings opened, and he began his painful vigil. As the little group of weary whites gathered daily with the chiefs under the "plane tree shelter" erected for the purpose, events became a land speculator's nightmare. Andrew Pickens, ignoring the highly questionable title to his own Hopewell farms, was most unfriendly to Blount's cause, opining that South Carolina had "behaved better to the Indians than North Carolina." Hawkins, with a vast contempt for the common white settler and an interest in Indian welfare which colored the whole of his later life, was scrupulous and legalistic, and he directed events.[57] The chiefs, after argument, relinquished claims to the area of the Henderson middle Tennessee purchase, and the commissioners refused to guarantee removal of the squatters on the French Broad River, referring this matter to Congress. Other than on these points, the Cherokee cause was entirely successful, and the commissioners, disregarding North Carolina's act of 1783, restored the principal areas of the whole Tennessee country to the natives.

Following the precedent of Georgia protests at Galphinton, the North Carolina agent now fought to establish a basis for subsequent nullification of the treaty. In order

[57] Pound, *Benjamin Hawkins,* 46, 51–52.

to establish the precedence of Carolina's Western jurisdiction over that of Congress, he submitted to the commissioners on November 22 a statement of the boundaries
of North Carolina as given in the 1776 constitution of
that state and based on the immense grant of Charles II.
Six days later he presented another letter defining the
Indian boundary as fixed by the 1783 land law, and pointing out the existence of the military reserve as well as
tens of thousands of grants sold by the state all the way
to the Mississippi. "Should you," he warned, "by treaty,
fix any other boundaries than the before mentioned, within
the limits of the said State of North Carolina . . . that
State will consider such a treaty a violation and infringe-
ment upon her legislative rights." [58] When the commissioners nevertheless proceeded to the completion of the
treaty, Blount entered a formal protest, claiming violation
of the state's "legislative rights."

To all this opposition, the Congressional delegation
replied with one polite letter promising to forward the
protests to Congress, enclosing articles of the completed
treaty, and calling on North Carolina for adherence to
and execution of them. "The local policy of some States,"
they concluded icily, "is certainly much opposed to federal
measures, which can only, in our opinion, make us respectable abroad and happy at home." [59]

Adding to the bitterness of defeat in this clash with
central authority, Blount now found that the long delayed
North Carolina Indian goods were at last to arrive that
evening, but the Indians, surprised and gratified by the

[58] Walter Lowrie and M. S. C. Clark (eds.), *American State Papers,
Class II, Indian Affairs* (Washington, 1832), I, 44 (hereinafter referred to as
State Papers, Indian); Charles C. Royce, "The Cherokee Nation of Indians," in Bureau of Ethnology, *Fifth Annual Report, 1883–1884* (Washington, 1887), 133–34, 153–59.

[59] Commissioners to William Blount, November 28, 1785, in Lowrie and
Clark (eds.), *State Papers, Indian*, I, 44.

commissioners' unheard-of sympathy, would no longer
consider a North Carolina treaty or a cession of land. The
only bright spot for the state's agent was the failure of the
Chickasaw and Choctaw to appear, and even this consola-
tion was soon denied. On the day before Blount's and
Hawkins' intended departure, runners from those tribes
arrived with news of the approach of their delegations,
presenting to Blount the nightmare that if the commissioners were as generous with these tribes as they had been
with the Cherokee, the speculators would lose the central
and west Tennessee lands as they had already lost the
eastern. Commissioner Martin having gone to Tugelo to
buy corn for the North Carolina agents, Blount wrote
him, beseeching that he use his influence to have the Chickasaw line drawn at the Tennessee "for across it they must
not come," if the Bend Company lands were to be saved.[60]

On December 26, 1785, 127 ragged, destitute Choctaw arrived after a 70-day trip, and on January 3, 1786,
the commissioners signed a treaty with them, Blount signing as a witness. Ten days later, a similar treaty with the
Chickasaw emerged, and the North Carolinian again entered the fray with a letter to the commissioners calling
attention to his former declaration of his state's rights. The
commissioners, however, continued as before, and the
agent's plan to draw a line on the Tennessee failed. Upon
the signing of the treaty, he therefore filed a protest similar to that on the Cherokee treaty. However, he did, as
before, sign the treaty as a witness, an act pregnant with
future difficulties.[61]

The negotiations over, the tired and disgusted agent
prepared to hasten home for "No Man was ever more tired

[60] William Blount to John Gray Blount, December 2, 23, 1785 (copies),
in Blount Collection; *id.* to Joseph Martin, December 23, 1785, in Draper
Collection, 2XX8.

[61] Clark (ed.), *State Records,* XVIII, 490, 491, 493–95, 799–802.

of laying on Blanketts and being in the Woods or more anxious to get Home than I am." [62] Nevertheless, it was necessary to go home by way of Augusta to dispose of the unused North Carolina goods, and affairs of the Bend Company also required further action by the master manipulator. Sevier, Downes, Heard, and Donelson, with Zachariah Cox and a considerable party, had descended the Tennessee to the Bend in December, opened a land office, and issued warrants, including generous grants to themselves.[63] However, despite the liberal attitude of the Georgia commissioners, opposition to the Company's plans was expected in the coming Georgia assembly. Worse still, attacks were to be anticipated there against the commissioners, and attempts made to reject their report and to replace them.[64] With his plans thus under fire, and realizing that his fight against the Hopewell treaties had made him popular in Georgia, Blount hurried to the assembly at Augusta to "try to put a finishing Hand to the Bent of Tenesee Business which at present seems to be on a bad way." [65]

In Augusta, though unable to put a "finishing Hand" to the company's business, Blount did well for himself. He knew that the Hopewell treaties if carried into effect, would depress land prices. On the other hand, he was realist enough to consider the contingency unlikely in view of Congress' usual impotence against state opposition, and the

[62] William Blount to John Gray Blount, December 29, 1785, in Keith (ed.), *Blount Papers*, I, 230–31.

[63] John Sevier to William Blount, October 7, 1785, *ibid.*, 221–22; Driver, *John Sevier*, 71–72; *Report of the Select Committee*, 2, 4–5, 11, 17, 19–20, 22, 23; Treat, *National Land System*, 366–67; Haywood, *History of Tennessee*, 172–73; Draper Collection, 11DD78a.

[64] Joseph Martin to Richard Caswell, May 15, 1786, in Governors' Papers; Wade Hampton to John Sevier, February 15, 1786, in Draper Collection, 11DD79a.

[65] William Blount to John Gray Blount, December 2, 1785 (copy), in Blount Collection.

"thirst for western lands" which he sought to instill in others was raging ever more fiercely in himself. He therefore bought *civilians'* warrants for nearly five thousand more Western acres and forwarded them to a western surveyor to be surveyed in the choicer *military* reservation, and passed into grants.[66] He then pushed on to Charleston and disposed of the unused North Carolina treaty supplies, after which he hurried home to Piney Grove, arriving in late February, 1786.

Almost six months in the wilderness had brought only public failure and would inevitably bring future censure. Yet, the experience had been valuable: Blount had seen the frontier. Around smoky fires, in rude shelters, in the wintry forests he had met, talked, and lived with its inhabitants, and, as he studied all men, he studied them. He observed the Indians, reserved in council or excited with rum; he noted the treaty protocol; he watched intently that key figure, the interpreter. He met chiefs, warriors, half-breeds, guides, and hunters. He talked land with surveyor Hay and speculator Martin, Indian goods with trader Ogg, legal principles with commissioner Hawkins. The information from these talks would powerfully influence Tennessee history. Yet, his immediate paramount aim and that of his state, to secure more land from the Indians, had been thwarted by agents of the central government. To retrieve this failure the defeated politician now bent his efforts.

[66] *Id.* to William Hay, January 27, 1786 (copy) in Keith (ed.), *Blount Papers*, I, 231–32.

CHAPTER V

FEDERALISM AND BUSINESS

ALMOST BEFORE his family could be resigned to another absence, Blount was again preparing to leave Piney Grove. The month of March had passed all too swiftly at home as he enjoyed his family life, conferred with John Gray Blount, sent official reports of the Hopewell meetings, and collected his salary warrants. Despite the restrictive terms of the treaties he bought lands heavily in the military reserve and in western Tennessee and planned with Governor Caswell concerning their speculative interests.[1]

Nevertheless, his situation and his state's called him northward. On December 12, 1785, in a special election, necessitated by the absence of North Carolina delegates at the Continental Congress, he had been again re-elected to Congress with a new delegation,[2] and, at the urgent request of that body, Governor Caswell was striving to get the state's representatives to New York, although with the

---

[1] William Blount to Richard Caswell, March 1, 2, 1786, in Clark (ed.), *State Records*, XVIII, 553–54, 554–56; *id.* to *id.*, March 23, 1786, in Governors' Papers; Grants of March 14, 1786, in Tennessee File (State Land Office, Raleigh); Davidson County Deeds, Book A, 192 (Tennessee State Library, Nashville); Beaufort County Deeds, Book 7, p. 496 (Washington, North Carolina).

[2] Governor Caswell to the assembly, November 21, 1785, in Clark (ed.), *State Records*, XVII, 272; *ibid.*, 330.

contrary purpose of preventing the ratification of the Indian treaties. Blount, personally and politically dedicated
to this same cause, agreed to go at once if he could return
as soon as relieved by another arrival, and he left by sea
in April, bearing letters and dispatches from Caswell.
These instructed the delegates "by all possible endeavors"
to "exert your powers to prevent a ratification of . . .
those Treaties which may have such pernicious tendency
to the injury of this State." [3]

On May 10, upon taking his seat, the delegate found
his state already represented by Dr. James White and
Timothy Bloodworth, seated a week earlier. To his disgust, he found also that on April 17 Congress had recorded
the treaties in its journal and that this in effect constituted
ratification. Though White and Bloodworth had awaited
his arrival before attempting to produce an answering
strategy, he was for the moment unable to devise any, and
the governor was so advised. [4]

The necessity of his tour being thus obviated, Blount
devoted his public services principally to a commercial
project of his state. From a new issue of paper money in
1785 the legislature had reserved £36,000 to purchase
tobacco, the receipts from the resale of which in the North
would be applied to the state's quota of the Continental
debt. Commissioners had easily purchased the tobacco at
the allowed price of fifty shillings per one hundred weight,
for this proved to be well above the current market value.
Much of it, when purchased, was stored by John Gray
Blount, who also bid on transporting it to the North. William and the other delegates were now to co-operate with

[3] Governor Caswell to the Delegates, April 3, 1786, *ibid.*, XVIII, 591–92;
id. to William Blount, April 4, 1786, *ibid.*, 594–95; William Blount to Governor Caswell, April 13, 1786, in Governors' Papers.

[4] Timothy Bloodworth to Governor Caswell, May 3, 1786, in Burnett
(ed.), *Letters*, VIII, 351–52; James White to *id.*, June 8, 1786, *ibid.*, 385.

the Congressional Board of the Treasury in securing good bids for the tobacco. Blount favored selling it to his friend Robert Morris, despite the financier's lack of interest and low bid, or to another friend, Dr. Nicholas Romayne, "a man of the most pointed punctuality in his contracts" and "of large property." [5] Yet, because of the characteristically divided authority to make the sale, negotiations dragged hopelessly.

In Congress the month of May passed amid furious debates over the Connecticut cession and the Western Reserve. The unexpected increase in delegates from all states also led to a flurry of speculation over possibilities of amendments to the Articles with a view to a stronger union, a possibility to which Blount gave close attention.

However, circumstances now called the delegate homeward. To manage Piney Grove and care for two daughters and an infant son, his wife needed her oft-absent husband. The Hopewell treaties were on the Congressional journals and could not easily be legally nullified; hence a conference with Caswell was indicated. Worse still, popular reaction to the restrictive treaties was dangerously high, for the Indian boundary therein guaranteed violated the interests of nearly every influential group in the state. The welfare of the state of Franklin was also drastically affected, for the land-minded citizens of the new commonwealth found their Indian treaties nullified, their area reduced by two thirds, and even their newly chosen capital, Greeneville, lying within Indian territory. At once their opposition to North Carolina intensified, and new settlers swept unchecked across the disregarded Indian boundary. On the Cumberland River, Robertson and his colony, although safely on the whites' side, found that their future

[5] William Blount to Richard Caswell, June 2, 1786, in Clark (ed.), *State Records,* XVIII, 642.

expansion was blocked and their homes dangerously close
to the territory guaranteed to their savage antagonists. In
eastern North Carolina every state-first leader was infuriated and every ambitious politician activated by this Congressional stroke. Most important, every actual or potential
landholder and speculator, great or small, saw his private
dream threatened.[6]

Amid this overwhelming condemnation of the treaties,
Blount's personal and political enemies found opportunities. The watchful Caswell wrote Blount from Kinston:

Some reports are propagated to your discredit respecting the disposition of the Indian Goods, 'tis said 'you took care they should
not be given to the Indians but reserved them to purchase Lands
from the Indians after the Treaty, for yourself and friends.' To
minds unprejudiced, this would easily be gotten over, but I appre-
hend some design in it, as from Hillsborough and Salisbury Districts, it seems to have taken its rise. On enquiry I hear Col. W.
Moore, late of Caswell, is the author given by persons of more consequence, but of this more at a future day, when things can be better investigated. I mention it now not to pain you but to apprise
you.[7]

To Sevier, partner in the Bend Company, Caswell wrote
more discreetly that he was "very glad the Attempt for
settling . . . [the Bend Company lands] was not made,
or rather that no attempt was made to Survey the Lands,
as a very great Clamour is making here respecting the
conduct of Col°. Blount at the Indian Treaty, tho' I am
satisfied he did every thing in his power to prevent the
same taking place, so much to the disadvantage of this

---

[6] Williams, *Franklin*, 95–96, 99–100; "Letters of Benjamin Hawkins,
1796–1806," in Georgia Historical Society *Collections*, IX (1916), 8–9;
James Phelan, *History of Tennessee* (Boston, 1888), 139–40; Alexander Outlaw to Richard Caswell, October 8, 1786, in Clark (ed.), *State Records*,
XVIII, 756–59; John Rogers to Governor Lee, January 10, 1792, in Palmer
and McRae (eds.), *Virginia State Papers*, V, 427–28.

[7] Richard Caswell to William Blount, June 7, 1786, in Clark (ed.), *State
Records*, XVIII, 646–47.

State if carried into effect. . . ." [8] Thus with political future and business ventures at stake, Blount in mid-June, 1786, left White and Bloodworth in Congress and hurried to Carolina to combat the "Clamour." [9]

In the following four months at home, he learned something of the antagonisms that racked the state. He noted the drop in the popularity of Martin and Hawkins as well as in his own. In late July he observed that the Franklinites, enraged at the Hopewell "betrayal," held another treaty with the Cherokee and demanded a second grant from those natives on threat of extirpation. The new state, meanwhile, was distracted by Indian attacks which were provoked by speculation and the expansion of white settlement. Disturbing rumors, fomented by agitators, declared that because of Hopewell the settlers' land titles were void.[10] Hence Sevier, blocked from independent status by the North Carolina assembly, renewed his negotiations with Georgia. To "Nollachucky Jack" and his fellow speculators these negotiations meant a settlement of the Bend in return for military aid to Georgia against the hostile Creeks, but to the majority of Westerners, the Franklin-Georgia entente meant securing a friend in Congress, where Cocke was renewing Franklin pleas for recognition.[11]

From the North came yet more disturbing news. On May 31, Secretary for Foreign Affairs John Jay had re-

[8] Richard Caswell to John Sevier, July 12, 1786, in Draper Collection, 4XX18 (2–4).

[9] Dr. James White to Richard Caswell, June 8, 1786, in Clark (ed.), *State Records*, XVIII, 648–49; John Pierce to Major Fenner, June 15, 1786, *ibid.*, 653; John Gray Blount to Richard Caswell, June 23, 1786, in Governors' Papers.

[10] Alexander Outlaw to Governor Caswell, October 8, 1786, in Clark (ed.), *State Records*, XVIII, 757–59.

[11] Williams, *Franklin*, 100–101, 102–10, 172–77; Whitaker, "Muscle Shoals Speculation," *loc. cit.*, 375–76.

quested of Congress specific instructions to guide him in his negotiations with Spanish chargé d'affaires Don Diego Gardoqui for a treaty. A committee had been appointed, and it became evident that, as Blount had learned at Galphinton, what was involved was a surrender of the rights of navigation on the Mississippi in return for commercial privileges in Spain. The constant sectional divergencies in the Confederation had thereupon flared dangerously, with some Southerners, such as Henry Lee, joining the East against the rest of the Southern states. During August the debate had raged fiercely and on August 29 the Eastern states, from Pennsylvania northward, by a 7–5 majority repealed the hitherto *sine qua non* of the treaty, the free navigation of the Mississippi.[12] North Carolina leaders were deeply alarmed by Bloodworth's gloomy letters from New York, and the news, as Blount had foreseen the year before, inflamed the West and caused land prices there to drop.[13]

This culmination of evils, added to a desire to sell lands to Northern speculators and the necessity of closing the still pending tobacco negotiations, induced Blount to prepare again for a trip northward. A further important motive was that Congressmen were talking of a Southern president of Congress, and Blount's ambition aroused him to seek the office.[14] At first he planned to take his wife and children, but the idea was abandoned. To climax his four months campaign for exoneration of Hopewell events, he

[12] Ford *et al.* (eds.), *Journals of Congress*, XXXI, 595–96; Burnett, *Continental Congress*, 654–59.

[13] Timothy Bloodworth to Governor Caswell, August 16, September 4, 29, 1786, in Clark (ed.), *State Records*, XVIII, 718–19, 724–25, 752–53; Arthur Campbell to Governor Randolph, February 16, 1787, in Palmer and McRae (eds.), *Virginia State Papers*, IV, 242–43; William Blount to John Gray Blount, November 6, 1785, in Blount Collection.

[14] William Blount to John Gray Blount, January 7, 10, 1787, in Blount Collection.

wrote Caswell, in a letter intended for the public, "As I find it generally believed that I purchased a large quantity of Land of the Indians, who attended the Treaties . . . last Winter, I think it necessary to declare upon my word & honor that I have not purchased any Land of any Indian, or Indians, nor been concerned in the purchase of any land of any Indian, or Indians, directly or indirectly, since the Month of June one thousand seven hundred and eighty-five." He went on to absolve from similar charge anyone at the treaty meeting and to call attention to his protests, defending himself in having signed the treaties as a witness: ". . . nothing more could be *fairly* understood by my subscribing as a Witness than that I saw the contracting parties sign the Treaties." [15]

Having sought to stop the attacks on his treaty role, the delegate sailed from North Carolina and arrived in New York November 5, 1786. He found, however, that Congress was paralyzed by lack of a quorum, and so it continued. North Carolina herself contributed to this situation, for Timothy Bloodworth had gone home, James White had resigned in October on being elected Southern Indian superintendent, and Abner Nash, who had arrived a few days before Blount, at once became very ill. Lack of adequate salary, inconvenience of service, and general disgust with Congress combined to make Blount the only delegate present from his state. So, as the winter weeks slipped by and the paralyzed Congress waited for further delegates, Blount busied himself outside its sessions. On December 2, Nash died. Blount as chairman of a committee to arrange the funeral expressed his fondness for the proprieties, and the result was an elaborate ceremony, graced by all the distinguished officials of the city. The

[15] William Blount to Richard Caswell, October 19, 1786, in Clark (ed.), *State Records*, XVIII, 767–68.

cares of an executor then fell upon the surviving dele-gate.[16]

The negotiations over the sale of North Carolina's tobacco had stalled when the council advised against ac-cepting Romayne's and Morris' offers to buy it. With tobacco prices rising, the firm of John Gray & Thomas Blount now entered bids, and William sought to start up negotiations again. One Edward Dowse, buyer for a syndi-cate, having appeared, Blount furnished him with a letter of introduction and sent him on to Carolina. There, too, he sent with approval the request of the French consul general for a list of exports of native products, for the firm of John Gray & Thomas Blount was preparing to enter the French market, as well as the Spanish, through the port of Cadiz. Watching with great alarm as the Shays uprisings in Massachusetts gathered in force, he conferred with Henry Knox and reported to Caswell on the "con-vulsed State of Massachusetts," where "much blood will be shed before they will submit to Government." [17]

In the international field, Blount cultivated a friend-ship with the French and Spanish ministers with a keen eye on the Floridas and the Mississippi. For additional pressure on Shays-frightened Easterners he had published a letter from Anthony Bledsoe describing the Western agi-tation over the prospect of a closed Mississippi. Bledsoe referred to assurances on Western navigation made by the Hopewell commissioners and promised that "you may de-pend on our exertions to keep all things quiet" but warned that tempers were rising over seizures and added, "we

[16] William Blount to Richard Caswell, December 7, 1786, *ibid.*, 793; Ford *et al.* (eds.), *Journals of Congress*, XXXI, 931; New York *Daily Ad-vertiser*, December 7, 1786; William Blount to Samuel Purviance, January 1, 1786 [1787], in Purviance-Courtenay Papers (Duke University).

[17] William Blount to Richard Caswell, November 16, 1786, in Burnett (ed.), *Letters*, VIII, 508–509; *id.* to *id.*, December 13, 1786, in Clark (ed.), *State Records*, XVIII, 793–94.

agree entirely with you that if our people are once let loose there will be no stopping them." [18]

As the year 1787 opened without prospect of a Congressional quorum the Carolinian was tempted to return to his home. Although successful in gathering Northern clients for his land partnership with Robertson and confident of the presidency of Congress, he was disturbed by Carolina events. The assembly had met at Fayetteville in November in a furious mood. The full force of resentment against the Hopewell treaties swept the commons. It resulted in a resolution expressing "utmost horror and indignation" at the treaty, and new directions to the state's delegates in Congress to secure exceptions or else protest the treaty. Maclaine's committee on the treaty refrained from censure of Blount and approved his protest; nevertheless, though nominated, he was not re-elected to Congress. Also, the newly elected Congressional Indian superintendent, Dr. James White, attended the legislature only to find his suggestions ignored and himself so coolly treated by his fellow Carolinians that he gave up his Indian plans in order to seek and obtain re-election to Congress from North Carolina. [19]

The angry legislators then fell upon the disposition of the public tobacco voted in 1785. Bought at exaggerated prices, it had wasted through shrinkage and transportation, and, while expenses mounted, no adequate avenue of disposal had appeared. Keen political noses scented public scandal, and again Blount was involved. [20]

Worst of all were the army-land scandals. For paying

[18] Representatives of Davidson County to William Blount and Benjamin Hawkins, December 29, 1786, in Papers of the Continental Congress.

[19] Clark (ed.), State Records, XVIII, 312, 337, 462–65, 483; Joseph Martin to Patrick Henry, January 20, 1787, in Henry, Patrick Henry, III, 382–85.

[20] William K. Boyd, Federal Period, Volume II of (no ed.), History of North Carolina (New York, 1919), 6; Richard Caswell to William Blount, June 21, 1786, in Clark (ed.), State Records, XVIII, 657–58.

soldiers' accounts it had been provided that a board of commissioners would pass upon certificates of service issued by commanding officers, and upon the commissioners' approval, the treasurer would pay the accounts. During 1786, frauds had been discovered, and the assembly in the Fall session conducted a fairly thorough investigation. The result rocked the state. False and forged certificates had been presented to and approved by the board, whose members received a part of the spoils. Twenty-three persons were arrested on the assembly's order. Griffith Rutherford and William Polk led a further investigation which resulted in Henry Montfort's expulsion from the house and the replacement of Memucan Hunt by John Haywood in the treasury. A special court was then created to meet at Warrenton in January, 1787, to try the other accused.[21]

These developments filled Blount with alarm—his friends and family were in danger, and possibly his land titles questioned. Only the continued lure of the presidency of Congress held him in New York. His letters to John Gray Blount contained anxiety and anger:

. . . many . . . are astonished to hear that The Constitution of the Country, [North Carolina] says the Judicial, legislative and Executive Powers shall be forever seprate and distinct. . . . Must not every thinking man view our Republican Government as the Most intolerable of all Tyranny? Can any Man be safe in his house while the Legislature are setting? . . . There [is] an old and common Exclaimation O Tempus O Moress! O Times O Manners Blessed Fruits of Independence. . . . Pray let me hear what the A [ssembly] has done I fear there has been the Devil to pay and you on the Weak Side . . . let me know the bad with the good if good there has been. . . .[22]

In February the delegate's perturbation increased when his half-brother Reading Blount was indicted by the grand jury at Warrenton for frauds. During the same

[21] Clark (ed.), *State Records*, XVIII, iv–vi; Boyd, *Federal Period*, 3–4.
[22] William Blount to John Gray Blount, January 13, 1787, in Keith (ed.), *Blount Papers*, I, 235–37.

month friends and associates were fined and imprisoned, and one, John Sheppard, subjected to the pillory.[23] The army fraud trials left Blount with a thorough dislike of all legislatures.

In addition to these abominations, the trials interfered with the plans of the still-cherished Bend Company. In January the glad tidings had come from Governor Telfair of Georgia to Sevier that the Georgia assembly had confirmed the Company's title to the Bend. Martin wrote happily, "the bend I hope is secure," and made plans for a gigantic private speculation to involve all lands from the Spanish line along the Tombigbee and Mobile rivers to the Bend. In the midst of the tumultuous assembly sessions in Carolina, John Gray Blount, Martin Armstrong, Joseph Martin, Stockley Donelson, Glasgow, Rutherford, and other company members met and agreed to obtain the legal conveyance by sending Glasgow to Georgia with Donelson, who was to perform his usual function—the overgenerous survey. The trials, however, drew Glasgow to Warrenton, from whence he returned too late for the Georgia trip, which was accordingly postponed until July.[24]

While family and business misfortune thus befell Blount at home, personal disappointment occurred in Congress. He had, especially since the death of Nash, been confident of election to the presidency. However, on January 17, when at last a quorum permitted balloting to begin "not more than two states could agree in any one Man," and as the voting continued, the disappointed delegate was

[23] John Haywood to John Gray Blount, March 14, 1787, *ibid.*, 263–64; Hugh Williamson to *id.*, February 16, 1787, *ibid.*, 249–50; Richard Caswell to William Blount, March 1, 1787, in Governors' Papers.

[24] Joseph Martin to Patrick Henry, January 20, 1787, in Henry, *Patrick Henry*, III, 382–85; Richard Caswell to John Sevier, February 27, 1787, in Governors' Papers; Joseph Martin to Richard Caswell, March 25, 1787, in Clark (ed.), *State Records*, XX, 653–54.

"unable to unravel the Mystery of this Business," nor could he even "form any Opinion who will be the Man." [25] A hiatus then occurred because of illnesses and the coming of a lately elected New York delegation, whom the disappointed Blount wrote were with one exception "antifederal Peasants notwithstanding the great Choice the state affords of Gentlemen of abilities and who are Candidates." [26] The "antifederal Peasants" probably hurt his candidacy, as did the reports of Edward Dowse, the tobacco buyer, lately from Carolina. That gentleman had felt the last assembly's wintry antifederalism and reported to Congressmen that the legislature there planned to direct that the receipts from the tobacco should be paid directly on the foreign debt instead of to the Continental Treasury —"a very antifederal Act." Dowse also maintained, according to Blount, that in Carolina "a Dissolution of the Union was publickly and openly spoke as a thing that would and ought to happen because the Northern states were injurious to the southern and that some Members said if a Dissolution was to take place that it would be best to hold on altogether upon the Tobacco." [27] Such reports fell coldly on the balloting delegates, and on February 2, Arthur St. Clair of Pennsylvania was elected president.

Infuriated again, Blount turned to the sole remaining reason for his Congressional service, the sale of the tobacco. Due partly to Virginia's decision to accept tobacco for taxes, the price of the commodity appreciated, and clearer instructions from North Carolina helped, whereupon after interminable negotiations a contract was made with the firm of Constable & Rucker, associated with

[25] William Blount to John Gray Blount, January 10, 1787, in Blount Collection; Burnett, *Continental Congress*, 673–74; William Blount to Richard Caswell, January 28, 1787, in Burnett (ed.), *Letters*, VIII, 532–34.

[26] William Blount to Richard Caswell, January 28, 1787, in Burnett (ed.), *Letters*, VIII, 532–34.

[27] *Ibid.*

Robert Morris, for the purchase of several thousand pounds, the receipts to be applied to the interest on the foreign loans.[28]

Blount's hours were also consumed in the usual varied duties of a public official. He sent official muster rolls ordered for the fraud trials and also Congressional journals to North Carolina, he directed a needed schoolmaster to the Hillsboro Academy, and, still smarting from criticism of his part at Hopewell, he invested the receipts from the sale of treaty goods in other products, compiling meticulous accounts in order that "the Tongue even of Malovence itself will be compeled to confess that I have no other interest in it than that of a Citizen in general." [29]

In the sessions of Congress, he received reinforcements in the arrival of Benjamin Hawkins in February and of Samuel Ashe in March, and he attended faithfully. From personal motives as well as those of state policy the delegates represented to Congress the growing dissatisfaction and anger of the West. On March 30, they transmitted papers relative to the seizure of a Westerner's property by the Spanish at Natchez and added the letter of Bledsoe with its threat of violence if the Mississippi were not opened. The matter was referred to the Secretary of Foreign Affairs. His report recommended either an enforceable treaty or war, and pointed out that a war would probably be lost unless the whole union supported it; whereupon the disappointed Southerners sought to recommit

28 Blount Collection, P.C. 833, 834, *passim*; Governor Caswell to the Delegates, January 12, 1787, in Governors' Papers; Clark (ed.), *State Records*, XX, *passim*; William Blount and Benjamin Hawkins to Governor Caswell, March 19, 1787, in Papers of the Continental Congress; Delegates to *id.*, April 18, 1787, in Charles McClung Papers.

29 William Blount to Richard Caswell, May 20, 1787, in Blount Collection; *id.* to Henry Toomer, May 20, 1787, *ibid.*; Ford *et al.* (eds.), *Journals of Congress*, XXXII, 242; Francis Nash, "History of Orange County," Pt. 1, in *North Carolina Booklet,* X (1910), 111; William Blount to Charles Thompson, February 12, 1787, in Papers of the Continental Congress.

the report. On April 25, Blount and Ashe presented their state's instructions denouncing the Hopewell treaties, and in conformity with these the delegates moved unsuccessfully that Congress disallow the treaties insofar as they conflicted with the state's policies. In another phase of the same fight, the Gardoqui negotiations, the Carolinians followed Virginia in seeking to replace Jay in New York with Jefferson at Madrid.[30]

Meanwhile, if business and public affairs were gloomy, the delegate's social life was of the polished variety he so cherished. The cultured drawing rooms of Dr. and Mrs. Romayne and other friends, including the French consul, welcomed the Congressman. Dinners, concerts, and balls afforded opportunities for meeting influential figures in finance and politics. The post of delegate, not politically potent, was socially rewarding, and in polite society Blount reveled all his life.

With the tobacco sold, however, his remaining objective in Congress was accomplished. Still smarting from his presidential defeat, he lingered only for an act of revenge, the removal of Congress to Philadelphia. "To do this act I owe myself, the Yankees, and the State of New York," he wrote his brother, and on April 10 he seconded Kearney's motion to this end, but the attempt failed.[31]

Like the other delegates, Blount was becoming increasingly intrigued by the prospect of the coming constitutional convention. By June, 1787, events had made him a moderate and pessimistic but distinct Federalist. A

---

[30] Benjamin Hawkins to Thomas Jefferson, March 8, 1787, in Burnett (ed.), *Letters*, VIII, 552–53; Protest of western citizens, March 29, 1787, in Draper Collection, 8CC5; Delegates to the Congress, (n.d.), in Papers of the Continental Congress; Delegates to Governor Caswell, April 18, 1787, in Clark (ed.), *State Records*, XX, 676–79; Ford *et al.* (eds.), *Journals of Congress*, XXXII, 147–48, 200–204, 216–20.

[31] William Blount to John Gray Blount, March 4, 1787, in Blount Collection; Ford *et al.* (eds.), *Journals of Congress*, XXXII, 167–69, 279–80; Burnett, *Continental Congress*, 690–91.

descendant of gentry, and never one who attributed much intelligence to the common man, he had been deeply alarmed by the social and economic threat of the Shays riots. At the same time in his own state the Radical-led legislature had fiercely attacked his family, his methods, and his associates, while, despite his efforts at Hopewell, he was popularly blamed for those treaties. His personal reputation was assailed, while his increasing wealth was envied, and Blount was ever extremely sensitive to criticism. Likewise, the storm over the tobacco contracts was still rising, along with ominous talk of the undesirable "Blount interest" in the legislature. Though North Carolina money was slowly appreciating in value, his difficulties in obtaining cash for his various warrants for salaries showed the inconvenience of a semiworthless currency. While association with the hares thus became more inconvenient, the goals of the hounds appeared increasingly desirable. If his own holdings could be guaranteed, Blount had always been in favor of Congressional control of the West in order to secure more aid against the Indians and to raise the value of Western lands. In April, 1787, travelers from across the mountains reported new Indian attacks had engulfed that area and stopped all surveying, along with "any probability of doing any while the war continues." [32] Furthermore, William Blount personally, and John Gray & Thomas Blount, Merchants, had grown financially. From essentially debtor, marginal enterprises of early years they were evolving by 1787 into creditor, big-scale operations. Increasing interstate and overseas commerce taught the value of sound money and international respect, while Blount's associations in Philadelphia and New York opened his eyes to ever larger pos-

[32] James Robertson to William Blount, April 7, 1787, in Keith (ed.), *Blount Papers*, I, 277.

sibilities. If a weak Congress could overrule two states at Hopewell, a strong Congress could enforce its will on a nation, and its will could be made Blount's advantage. To all Blounts at all times political power meant economic advantage and personal prestige. The family had successfully worked on this premise in an assembly of clashing economic and personal interests. Now a wider sphere beckoned. Granted rival sectional interests in the Confederation, a more powerful central government could confer on its agents far broader benefits and prestige. Under economic and social persuasion, therefore, Blount for the next six years served the cause of centralism.[33]

In the crowded closing days of the 1786 assembly, Conservatives Iredell and Davie, with the help of Caswell and John Gray Blount, had assured the participation of the state in the new convention to be held in Philadelphia. The hurried legislators had accepted a pro-Federal resolution but after "some maneuvering and jugling" named a left-center delegation made up of Willie Jones, Alexander Martin, Caswell, William R. Davie, and Richard D. Spaight.[34] The first two of these were known state-first men, the governor supposedly so, and the latter two partially or completely Conservative. As the new year opened, however, Jones declined to go, and Caswell himself, perhaps because half-ill, hesitated. Impressed with the need for personal unity and "respectability" in the state's delegation, the governor sought replacements. Williamson was available, and John Gray Blount assured the governor

[33] Clark (ed.), *State Records*, XVIII, *passim*.

[34] *Ibid.*, 462; Wagstaff, *States Rights and Political Parties*, 17; Trenholme, *Ratification of the Federal Constitution*, 63–66; A. R. Newsome, "North Carolina's Ratification of the Federal Constitution," in *North Carolina Historical Review*, XVII (1940), 288; Hugh Williamson to John Gray Blount, March 19, 1787, in Keith (ed.), *Blount Papers*, I, 270–71.

that his brother would go from New York to Philadelphia; these two, therefore, were named.[35]

Though suffering from an old illness, neuralgic pains, and a cold, Blount agreed to leave the Congress for the Convention, urging his brother to allay his wife's disappointment with "some good excuse for me." Spaight brought Blount's commission, and the latter planned to attend the convention early, but he was to know still another affliction—"blind piles . . . the most painful teasing Complaint that I have ever experienced and I have had great use for what I have none of when in pain namely Patience." The sufferer, therefore, stayed in New York, and as the days passed he became more reconciled, if not to pain, at least to delay, as the news from Philadelphia indicated that the Convention thus far had done "very little . . . and nothing definitive." [36]

At length on June 18, Blount, Hawkins, and William Pierce of Georgia left for Philadelphia, from whence Hawkins planned to sail for Petersburg, Virginia. They arrived June 19, and Blount took his seat on the following day. He found the business of the Convention not much advanced. Williamson was leading a very united delegation, "in Sentiment with Virginia who seemed to take the lead Madison at their Head tho Randolph and Mason are also great." [37] Calmly ignoring the Convention's secrecy pledge, Blount wrote to Caswell describing the Virginia plan. He doubted its utility, despite his colleagues' support of the plan, and declared, "for as I have before said, I still think we shall ultimately and not many Years

[35] Richard Caswell to William R. Davie, March 1, 1787, in Clark (ed.), *State Records*, XX, 627–28; Richard Caswell to William Blount, April 24, 1787, *ibid.*, 683–84; *ibid.*, 129.

[36] William Blount to John Gray Blount, April 4, May 22, June 15, 1787, in Blount Collection.

[37] William Blount to Richard Caswell, July 19, 1787 (copy) in Blount Collection.

hence be separated and distinct Governments perfectly independent of each other." [38] Blount's pessimism was the stronger since his arrival coincided with the report of the Committee of the Whole in favor of the Virginia over the New Jersey Plan. He was present therefore during the tense days of minor compromise leading up to the crucial vote on Monday, July 2, when the little states achieved a tie vote on the question of representation in the upper house. The Convention then named a committee of one from each state to work out a compromise, but before this committee reported on July 5, Blount had left the Convention.[39]

His departure was due to the receipt of a letter from Congressional secretary Charles Thompson stating that Congress had an important agenda, and that if North Carolina were represented, a quorum would be present. Blount at first wished to remain at Philadelphia as his departure might cost the state her vote in the Convention in case of an even division among her four remaining delegates. On the other hand, he and Hawkins strongly wished to be present in Congress to push for aid to the Indian-harassed Tennesseans and to continue the fight for an untrammeled navigation of the Mississippi, for which struggle the Southern delegations in Congress were now dangerously few. Observing that the state's convention delegation "were Generally unanimous and Competent to the Purposes of their Mission," he and Hawkins, with William Few of Georgia, left for New York, and on July 4 the Carolinians took their seats in Congress.[40]

[38] *Ibid.*

[39] Max Farrand, *The Framing of the Constitution of the United States* (New Haven, 1936), 91–99; Max Farrand (ed.), *The Records of the Federal Convention* (New Haven, 1911), III, 587.

[40] William Blount to Richard Caswell, July 10, 1787, in Clark (ed.), *State Records*, XX, 734; Benjamin Hawkins to *id.*, July 10, 1787, in Burnett (ed.), *Letters*, VIII, 618–19; Hugh Williamson to John Gray Blount, July 19, 1787, in Keith (ed.), *Blount Papers*, I, 324–25.

The proceedings which followed were of great interest to Blount and of considerable significance to his later career. On the day of his arrival a committee on which Hawkins formerly sat reported in favor of a firm stand with Spain for the free navigation of the Mississippi. Blount was also present for the debate on and passage of the ordinance for the government of the Northwest Territory. On July 18 he heard Secretary Knox's report recommending further pressure on North Carolina for a Western land cession and excoriating the flagrant violation of the Hopewell treaties by the whites. To this attack Blount replied on August 3 by sponsoring with Few a motion for a three-power treaty between the Southern Indian Superintendent, Georgia, and the Creeks; but this attempt to secure more lands was countered by Nathan Dane of Massachusetts, who, representing Northern and Western interests, produced a long denunciatory committee report. This stated that "the principal source of difficulties with the Indians" was "an avaricious disposition in some of our people to acquire large tracts of land and often by unfair means." It announced that "there can be no doubt that settlements are made by our people" on lands given the Cherokee by the Hopewell treaties as well as on Creek lands in Georgia. It criticized North Carolina and Georgia for usurping Congressional powers in making Indian treaties, and flatly denied Blount's Hopewell protest that Congressional Indian treaties violated state legislative rights. The report then continued with an urgent request for North Carolina and Georgia to cede their Western lands as a solution to the Indian problem, and with assurance to both Indians and whites that Congress would see justice done. This report, so antipathetic (except for the cession plea) to Blount's views, was supported by the legalistic Hawkins, but it was narrowly defeated. Action

on a treaty was delayed until October, possibly as a compromise.[41]

Meanwhile, the speculator continued his incessant
undercover efforts both to defeat Spanish control of the
Mississippi and to people the West. In his Spanish campaign he adopted a typical bit of strategy. On his suggestion, he and Williamson, with Hawkins' knowledge,
composed an unsigned "Extract of a letter" addressed to
the "Hon B[enjamin] H[awkins]" and dated "Nashville
May 1, 1787," which Blount had printed in the New York
Journal and Weekly Register of July 19 as well as in
foreign newspapers. In the extract the writer repeated the
"reports" of which he wrote "last October" in which Spain
claimed not only exclusive Mississippi navigation, but also
everything west of the Appalachians north of a Kanawha-
to-Great Lakes line. He continued: "Their perseverance
in such claims does not well accord with the flattering
hopes you gave us last Summer when you said all would
go well in the course of a year." The writer demanded an
explanation and, using this as a point of departure, re-
futed Spain's claim by the Carolina charter and the treaties
of 1763 and 1783. He stated that the true basis of Spain's
claim was the "longest sword" but that this, due to the
West's growth, would "soon be in our favor, whereupon,
profiting by her example . . . we shall not fail to use it."
He prophesied that at that time as a result of Western
seizures of Spanish goods, war would result in which the
East would bear the brunt, since the West had nothing to
lose but cattle, lands, and "a considerable number of un-
polished citizens," whom Spain would ignore. Or, he
said, if Spain should try to establish Western posts there
would be Western war, "or as you may rather be pleased

[41] Ford *et al.* (eds.), *Journals of Congress*, XXXII, 299–300, 334–43,
365–69; XXXIII, 454–63, 706–10.

to call it an experimental inquiry concerning the meaning of treaties and the rights of men." The writer concluded by expressing his amazement that Spain would hazard so much "for the mere pleasure of distressing a few honest planters who are only desirous to paddle their canoes up and down the River Mississippi." [42]

This curious mixture of irony, resentment, and threat displayed, as Blount remarked to Caswell, that "it was fabricated by a Person better informed [than] any inhabitant of Davidson County can be." It was, according to the Congressman, "here much applauded as well written and . . . certainly is well timed." [43]

Continuing his campaign for his own lands in the West, Blount wrote another propaganda letter, to his brother Thomas in London. In it he pretended that Thomas had "an Inclination to make a Purchase of a large Body of Land from the United States on the North West of the River Ohio." He informed him that "the Door is now open to such a Speculation" due to the Scioto purchase, by which "the Precedent is established of selling the back Lands in large quantities." The Scioto Company, according to the writer, planned to settle their lands without delay, and, in addition to this "certain Prospect," Western immigration (according to the account of Colonel Harmar in the Northwest) was proven to be "very great"; "a great part" of this immigration, moreover, had settled "in Davidson County on the rivers Tennessee and Cumberland." To this advertisement was added a copy of the spurious "letter" to Hawkins, "shewing the undoubted Right of the United States" to free navigation of the Mississippi. Blount's

[42] New York *Journal and Weekly Register,* July 19, 1787; William Blount to Richard Caswell, July 19, 1787 (copy) in Keith (ed.), *Blount Papers,* I, 321–23.

[43] William Blount to Richard Caswell, July 19, 1787 (copy) in Keith (ed.), *Blount Papers,* I, 321–23.

letter to his brother closed with the significant postscript: "P.S. The Writer of this Letter conceives if it should be published in the english News Papers He means several, that it will be beneficial to himself and associates holding Lands in Davidson County, therefore begs the favour of those to whom it is addressed to cause it to be accordingly published by Way of Extract of a Letter from a Gentleman in Newyork to his Frind in London concealing the name of the Writer and that of the Person to whom it is addressed." [44]

Blount would gladly have continued in Congress for his state's interests and his own; but Sam Ashe arrived in August and Robert Burton was expected soon. The two of them would complete a Congressional delegation, while the departure of Davie and Martin from the Philadelphia Convention would destroy a North Carolina quorum. Therefore, Hawkins and Blount left Congress again, the former to go home, the latter to the Convention.

At Trenton Blount broke his journey for a minute examination of Robert Morris' ironworks and nail factory, where, he wrote his brother, "it appears to me that Nail Rod enough is or might be Slit to supply all Christemdom with Nails." His careful examination of methods and costs convinced the slaveowner that such a factory was desirable as a Blount enterprise, since "of all Works that I have seen I have seen none more easily done nor none so proper for the employment of Negroes because they may always be kept at the same spot and at the same Work and there's no rainey days & they may be [tasked] and I conceive one Week is quite long enough for any person black or white to learn to make a good Nail." [45]

[44] William Blount to Thomas Blount, July 30, 1787 (copy) in Keith (ed.), *Blount Papers*, I, 327–28.

[45] William Blount to John Gray Blount, August 9, 1787, in Keith (ed.), *Blount Papers*, I, 331–33.

Arriving in Philadelphia on August 7, Blount found that the Convention's committee of detail had reported on the previous day, and the Convention had settled down to filling out the particulars of a general outline whose main form had been determined. Every day from ten in the morning until four in the afternoon the Convention labored at its task of detail and compromise. The unanimity of the North Carolina delegation continued, although Martin at times called forth Hugh Williamson's ironic private comment, and the ex-governor's departure was much less regretted than that of Davie.[46] The state delegation's work, like its personnel, was not nationally outstanding; the members played a "creditable and important but not a leading or conspicuous role." [47] Williamson continued to be its major figure, and Blount's work, as he ever sought to make it, was completely hidden. His influence, which may have been considerable on his delegation, was exerted in social relationships in which he impressed one delegate as "a character strongly marked for integrity and honor . . . plain, honest, and sincere." [48]

As the Convention drew to its close, the delegates' thoughts turned to the country's reception of their labors. Hawkins and Martin, before their respective departures from Congress and the Convention, had urged that the state be represented in Congress when the Convention reported to that body. Blount felt so strongly the advisability of this that he planned to defer his homeward trip, if necessary, to give the state a Congressional representation. Wil-

---

[46] William Blount to Richard Caswell, August 20, 1787, in Clark (ed.), *State Records*, XX, 764–65; Hugh Williamson to *id.*, August 20, 1787, *ibid.*, 765–66; *id.* to James Iredell, July 8, 1787, in McRee, *Life of Iredell*, II, 163; *id.* to John Gray Blount, July 19, 1787, in Keith (ed.), *Blount Papers*, I, 324–25.

[47] Newsome, "North Carolina's Ratification," *loc. cit.*, 288; Pound, *Benjamin Hawkins*, 61; Boyd, *Federal Period*, 26–30.

[48] Farrand (ed.), *Records of the Federal Convention*, III, 95.

liamson, meanwhile, urged upon James Iredell the necessity for a Conservative legislature, including Samuel
Johnston, whom the delegate favored to succeed the retir-
ing Governor Caswell.[49]

At length, on September 17, the delegates gathered for
the signing. Blount, like all the rest, was not entirely satisfied with their labors; but the weeks of compromise had
modified his earlier pessimism over the instrument. He
ventured to assure Caswell that the Constitution would
"be such a form of Government as I believe will be readily
adopted by the several States because I believe it will be
such as will be their respective interest to adopt." [50] On the
other hand, the memory of the storm over Hopewell flashed
a warning to the politician, and he at first refused to sign
the instrument, relenting only on Gouverneur Morris' explanation that his signature attested merely the unanimity
of the states present. He then agreed to sign "without committing himself." [51]

On the following day, Blount, Spaight, and Williamson enclosed a copy of the work in a letter to Caswell, urging
that the state had gained more than she gave up. With this
opening defensive barrage, Spaight and Williamson left
for Carolina. Blount, finding Burton to be temporarily
alone in Congress, returned there before departing on the
twenty-fifth for his wife and his long-neglected home.

Life at Piney Grove was pleasant to the weary statesman. With the influence of wealth, he now carried the

[49] Benjamin Hawkins to Richard Caswell, August 14, 1787, in Burnett
(ed.), Letters, VIII, 639; Alexander Martin to id., August 20, 1787, in Clark
(ed.), State Records, XX, 763–64; William Blount to id., August 20, 1787,
ibid., 764–65; Hugh Williamson to James Iredell, July 8, 22, 1787, in McRee,
Life of Iredell, II, 163, 167.

[50] William Blount to Richard Caswell, August 20, 1787, in Clark (ed.),
State Records, XX, 764–65.

[51] Farrand (ed.), Records of the Federal Convention, II, 646.

prestige of association with the country's famous. The opinions of Washington, the arguments of Madison, Lee, and Randolph, the mannerisms and small talk of famous men were recounted for admiring family and friends. With his wife he visited New Bern's theater or drove about the country visiting his friends and numerous relatives. Reading's release from fraud charges and Willie's return from Princeton gladdened the family, and the arrival of his brother John Gray's first daughter called for visits and celebration. The sensitive Thomas, still in Europe for the firm, wrote of being torn between tender sentiment and practicality. He had "by singular instance of female candour" discovered that a young lady at The Hague was "desperately in Love with me. . . . Her fortune is said to be about £6000. Sterling—Her character without blemish, her person handsome, her manners agreeable, her age 22." [52] Disturbed because she was a foreigner, he had asked the family consensus on marriage, and William from New York had given the inevitable answer. Now, in October, came the lover's reaction to the advice: "W. Blount . . . says he has heard that a Lady at the Hague & myself have formed a mutual attachment for each other &, because she has much Money, he advises me to marry her—tell him that, *for that very reason,* I will not—Sooner than marry any woman on earth that has Dutch blood in her veins, either for Love or Money or both united, I would ravish my grand Mother, live a Beggar, & die of famine in a ditch." [53]

The pursuit of gain, in one form so repugnant to Thomas Blount, attracted his father and brothers deeply during the Fall months. Jacob, Senior, and John Gray

[52] Thomas Blount to John Gray & Thomas Blount, July 7, 1787, in Keith (ed.), *Blount Papers,* I, 316–19. Thomas Blount's first wife had died in March, 1783.

[53] Thomas Blount to John Gray & Thomas Blount, October 4, 1787, *ibid.,* 347–49.

THOMAS BLOUNT

Blount continued their heavy land purchases, and William wrote to Thomas about soliciting mercantile connections in England. However, the calm progress which existed in the family's personal and economic affairs was not reflected in the state's politics, in which the family was now deeply concerned.

Well before the Philadelphia Convention adjourned, the reaction to its labors agitated Carolina. Elections for the assembly of 1787 were fought out with utmost violence on the issue of the new government, for Caswell's handpicked delegation, while "respectable," cohesive, and Federal, by no means represented the isolationist, debtor, small-farmer attitude of the state. The Radical leadership realized this. Eyeing the Conservative-minded group at Philadelphia and hearing rumors of the nature of their work, Tom Person, Willie Jones, David Caldwell, and other voices of the people prepared to do battle for their position on the grounds of "tyranny" and "heavy taxes." Conservatives, besides generally favoring any form of stronger union, saw a chance to shift from old battlefields to new ground, and charged the opposition with an attempt to condemn the instrument before seeing it. A violent campaign ensued on paper and public platform.[54] Johnston, sensing defeat, refused to run; in Edenton, through mismanagement, Federalist James Iredell was defeated by equally Federalist Stephen Cabarrus, against the wishes of both. In Orange County, Hooper "had an engagement" with a certain McCauley "in which he came off second best, with his eyes blacked." In Wilmington, Archibald Maclaine declined to run and attempted to name his successor; but a rival stirred up "the lowest of the people,"

[54] Nevins, *American States,* 406–407; Trenholme, *Ratification of the Federal Constitution,* 100–102; H. M. Wagstaff, "Federalism in North Carolina," in *The James Sprunt Historical Publications,* IX (1910), No. 2, 10–11.

and by "misrepresentations" and "a number of illegal votes" came within one vote of upsetting the accustomed favorite.[55] In Craven County, as canoe and skiff and horse brought voters to New Bern, the town buzzed with charges against the "Blount Interest." Blount's cousin Abner Neale was defeated, though family lawyer John Sitgreaves, after a battle, secured election to the senate.[56]

On November 19, 1787, the assembly jammed the tiny hamlet of Tarboro. Blount rode over to watch the session from Thomas' home. The comforts he enjoyed there seemed lavish to the miserably lodged legislators. Each day the solons packed themselves into the tiny courthouse for the sessions. The senators assembled in the small upper room behind their house's bar (a board laid between two trunks) beyond which the curious countryman might stand uncovered to watch the august group. In the larger lower room, the county courtroom, the commons gathered to deliberate, heads covered also in imitation of their British models.[57]

Despite the heat of the campaign and the discomforts of the session, the legislators' mood was moderate. Two days after the opening, Caswell submitted the Constitution and its accompanying papers. Ignoring Person's attempted filibuster, the assembly agreed to set December 5 for a joint session of committees of the whole house to consider the proposed fundamental law. On that date, therefore, the discussions took place and resolutions were framed, which

[55] McRee, *Life of Iredell*, II, 170; Archibald Maclaine to James Iredell, August 29, 1787, *ibid.*, 178–79; Trenholme, *Ratification of the Federal Constitution*, 101–102; John W. Moore, *History of North Carolina from the Earliest Discoveries to the Present Time* (Raleigh, 1880), 382.

[56] John Sitgreaves to John Gray Blount, August 12, 24, 1787, in Keith (ed.), *Blount Papers*, I, 336–39, 340–41; Abner Neale to *id.*, August 15, 1787, *ibid.*, 339–40.

[57] Lida T. Rodman (ed.), "Journal of a Tour to North Carolina in 1787 by William Attmore," in *The James Sprunt Historical Publications*, XVII (1922), No. 2, 38.

on the following day were adopted by both houses. These set elections in late March for a convention to be held at Hillsboro on July 21, 1788. Qualifications for both voters and members were established, and fifteen hundred copies of the Constitution ordered printed for public distribution. This Federalist victory, opposed to the end by Person, was achieved by a coalition of Conservatives, Federal-minded businessmen such as the Blounts, and moderate Radicals. The latter group was moved by several considerations: curiosity over public reaction to the Constitution; the ever-potent influence of Virginia, whose convention proceedings were carried in Carolina newspapers and in much correspondence; and fear of popular disapproval of a too hasty rejection without examination.[58]

Through the influence of the same coalition, Blount, Hawkins, and Burton were asked by the assembly to report on "the present State and Circumstance of the Union." They complied on December 15 with a strongly pro-Federal report to prove that "we are at the Eave of a Bankruptcy and of a total dissolution of Government." They reviewed the poverty of the national revenues and showed that, though the domestic debt could be handled by land sales, the growing foreign debt, judged by North Carolina's own resistance to requisition, was hopeless. On the Spanish treaty, they touched but lightly and with ominous implication. They closed with remarks on the unpopularity of North Carolina and Georgia because of their failure to make land cessions, and with implied approval of the Constitution as a solution of the country's ills.[59]

Meanwhile, on December 8, Blount's name, along with those of Samuel Johnston, Alexander Martin, John Wil-

[58] Clark (ed.), *State Records,* XX, 194, 196–97, 369–72; *State Gazette of North Carolina,* November 15, 1787.
[59] Clark (ed.), *State Records,* XX, 228, 240–43.

liams, and W. R. Davie, was placed in nomination for governor. The strongly Conservative cast of the nomination reflected a Radical dearth of candidates as well as the same feeling for the proprieties that dominated this session. Spaight was later added but was regarded by most as too young. Alexander Martin was declared ineligible, and Blount and Davie, partly perhaps to strengthen the Conservatives' candidate, withdrew their names. To the former, at least, a low-salaried and impotent governorship was no particular lure, and strong opposition indicated that strategic retreat would be better than defeat. On December 12, Johnston was chosen over Williams.[60]

While thus working publicly and privately for the Constitution, Blount labored likewise for himself. Through Davie he petitioned that the comptroller's account against him as Indian agent at Hopewell be charged off as "Money received for Services actually performed & done," and a friendly committee stayed the comptroller's hand until more evidence could be brought up. On the other hand, Person's committee reviewed his entire transactions with the Hopewell goods and recommended—since his sale of the goods was not justified by law—that he therefore account for the same by the next session. The house adjourned before acting on this report, but its temper boded ill for the ex-agent.[61] Through his influence, meanwhile, John Skinner in the senate moved to rescind the repeal of the cession act. After a bitter battle this motion passed the senate by a vote of 23–22, but the house on receiving it killed it on the first reading without even a recorded vote. On the other hand, a state-first move to reopen the state's office for Western land sales also failed. On the Western

[60] "Extract of a Letter from Tarboro, December 12, 1787," in North Carolina *Gazette*, December 19, 1787.

[61] Clark (ed.), *State Records*, XX, 273, 285–86, 402–406.

land question, the political forces were on a dead center.[62]

Towards the dying but defiant state of Franklin, how-ever, the legislators united in a continuation of their con-ciliatory but firm policy. The Franklinites, disappointed in the Philadelphia Convention, were badly divided. Gov-ernor Sevier's term was expiring with no successor in view, and the legislature was split over Sevier's plan for a Georgia alliance, which still failed to produce results. In the 1786 assembly pro- and anti-Franklin delegations had arrived from Washington County, each claiming legal election, and the anti-Franklinites had been seated.[63] Now, in 1787, a Franklin commissioner appeared authorized to offer Franklin's assumption of North Carolina's Con-tinental debt quota as the price of independence,[64] but the assembly merely extended the acts of pardon and tax-remission and elected Joseph Martin to the generalcy of Washington district. The divide and rule policy of the parent state was succeeding, and neither the state-first group nor the speculators of North Carolina proposed to allow control of the Western lands to pass to rivals. On the other hand, roads to the West always pleased the frontiersmen and encouraged immigration thither, and road legislation was accordingly passed.[65]

Meanwhile, from the middle Tennessee counties of Sumner and Davidson came a delegation of Western lead-ers that included James Robertson, Robert Hays, and Anthony Bledsoe. These representatives of a people frantic

[62] Ashe, *History of North Carolina*, II, 81; James Sanders to Daniel Smith, December 23, 1787, in Draper Collection, 4XX54. See also Williams, *Franklin*, 190–91, and Clark (ed.), *State Records*, XX, 202.

[63] Williams, *Franklin*, 144, 156–58, 178, 182, 186–87; Ashe, *History of North Carolina*, II, 64; Posey, "William Blount," 50; Haywood, *History of Tennessee*, 181–87; Clark (ed.), *State Records*, XVIII, 230, 243–45.

[64] Williams, *Franklin*, 190.

[65] *Ibid.*, 192; James Sanders to Daniel Smith, December 23, 1787, in Draper Collection, 4XX54; Clark (ed.), *State Records*, XX, 225, 255.

over the flame of Indian war sought out business-partner Blount for his influence. Together the associates composed a pitiful address to the assembly setting forth the tribulations of the Westerners and recommending cession of the West to Congress as the solution.[66]

The newly elected Governor Johnston was greeted by the Conservatives somewhat ostentatiously in order to embarrass Caswell, and the assembly then concluded its labors. The results of these to "the Blount Interest" were of mixed value. Though the Hopewell cloud still remained, the prospect of a stronger national regime, the still existent cession issue, and the impending collapse of Franklin all were hopeful portents.

The prizes which made these portents important grew ever larger. Despite the calls of official duty in 1786 and 1787, Blount, both personally and in the firm, had followed persistently an ever expanding pattern of land acquisition. His brother John Gray bought and sold lots in New Bern and Washington. In Georgia, Blount agent George Ogg acquired lands in the Bend and transferred them to agent Edward Hall. From Tennessee, in three days, Edward Harris and Henry Rutherford recorded surveys of 116,000 acres.[67] Blount entries grew into hundreds, Blount acreage rose to dizzying figures, and the Blount name became a byword for princely land proprietorship. Stirred by the vast purchases north of the Ohio, the Blounts, as patrons and benefactors of such officials

[66] Ramsey, *Annals*, 502–503.

[67] Beaufort County Deeds, Book 6, pp. 317, 338; Craven County Deeds, Book 28, p. 248, and Book 26, p. 105; Blount Collection, P.C. 834, *passim*; Absolom Tatum to John Gray Blount, July (n.d.), 1787, *ibid.*; Charles Gerrard to *id.*, June 23, 1787, *ibid.*; Griffith Rutherford's receipts and certificates, December 22, 23, 1786, *ibid.*, P.C. 881; E. Harris to John Gray Blount, April 10, 1787, in Keith (ed.), *Blount Papers*, I, 279–80; Keith, "Three North Carolina Blount Brothers," 267–68.

as John Haywood, the new treasurer, played for higher and yet higher stakes.[68]

Under the pressure of hundreds of such speculators, the cumbersome machinery of legal land acquisition had already broken down completely, and entries, warrants, and grants, both real and spurious, floated through the business world like the wildest inflated paper currency. Venal officials added both to the chaos and to the chance for gain. With warrants passing as currency, the Blounts employed perhaps a half dozen agents, all armed with powers of attorney. In such a situation, William Blount and the firm entered, consciously or not, into the far-flung net of frauds. The firm's name appeared on fraudulent endorsements and illegal duplicate warrants. By 1798, "upwards of 100,000 acres" of forged duplicate warrants were discovered in their account.[69]

These slips or sins had begun earlier; but—if in 1787 occasional complaints began to arise—the larger storms lay in the future, and in that the Blounts were ever willing to gamble. Not with cautious examination of the day but with yet more expansive plans for the morrow, William Blount and his family awaited the establishment of the new nation.

[68] Keith, "Three North Carolina Blount Brothers," 270; John Haywood to John Gray Blount, March 14, 16, 1787, in Keith (ed.), *Blount Papers,* I, 263–64, 266–67; Thomas Blount to *id.,* February 15, March 4, 1789, in Blount Collection.

[69] Michail Rogers to John Gray Blount, December 24, 1787, in Keith (ed.), *Blount Papers,* I, 364; *North Carolina Minerva and Fayetteville Advertiser,* December 15, 1798; Land Fraud Commission Report, IV (North Carolina State Department of Archives and History); Fraud Commissioners' Report to Governor Ashe, March 24, 1798, in Governors' Papers.

CHAPTER VI

FEDERAL SERVICE AND REWARD

THE NOISE OF POLITICAL BATTLE filled the state. On market day, at militia muster, in tavern, street, and churchyard, words flew and often fists followed. Editors and tract-writers enjoyed an unprecedented interest. Thunderous warnings of "Honestus" and polished logic from "Marcus," "Publicola," and "Sylvius" was elegantly recited in polite Wilmington drawing rooms and laboriously spelled out in western piney woods cabins. In Edenton successful candidate Iredell announced that "the security of everything dear to us depends on our adoption of the proposed constitution," and admonished of "the respect and deference which we owe the great characters who formed it." In Hertford County the Reverend Burkitt warned his Baptist flock of the proposed federal walled city from whence would issue a licentious federal army to ravage honest farmers' homes. Letters carried more hopes than facts: from Hawkins to Madison, "the honest part of the community whether merchants or planters are for it"; from Person to John Lamb, "nine tenths of the people of this State are opposed to the adoption of the New System, without very considerable Amendments." With riots, fist fights, argument, and invective, the Carolinians reveled in their first clear-cut election issue, their Armageddon of state and Federal loyalties.[1]

Amid such scenes of excitement it was a Blount trait to become inconspicuous. Only the excitable brother Thomas really enjoyed politics on the lower levels of open combat. William and John Gray Blount, feeling no less intensely, worked by influence and suggestion, seeking to "stand behind the Curtain & give the Necessary Directions." In the fierce ratification contests of March and April, 1788, the blatant appeals to the populace and the open attacks on motive and personality were especially unsuited to Blount talents. So, while Judge Samuel Spencer and Willie Jones conjured visions of an all-powerful and creditor-minded judiciary; while Thomas Person and Timothy Bloodworth depicted a ravenous hoard of tax collectors; while learned clergymen David Caldwell and James Tate deplored the absence of bills of rights and described a ruinous northward exodus of specie, the Blounts were publicly silent. Unlike Hooper or Maclaine, they engaged in no acidulous tournament of personalities; unlike Iredell or Spaight, they wrote no disquisitions on the virtues of conservatism; unlike Williamson, they addressed no audiences; and unlike Ben Sheppard, they led no election riots. Instead, the influence of family and wealth were brought to bear. Blount's lawyer and kinsman John Sitgreaves, his cousin Abner Neale, his brother John Gray, and he himself all sought seats in the coming ratifying body. Long

---

[1] Trenholme, *Ratification of the Federal Constitution*, 107–10, 116, 121–22, 131–32; Wagstaff, *States Rights and Political Parties*, 21–23; Thomas Person to John Lamb, August 6, 1788, in William K. Boyd (ed.), "News, Letters, and Documents Concerning North Carolina and the Federal Constitution," in *Trinity College Historical Papers*, XIV (1922), 79–81; *ibid.*, 75–79, 82–95; Newsome, "North Carolina's Ratification," *loc. cit.*, 289–91; *North Carolina Historical Review*, XVI (1939), 36–37; *ibid.*, VII (1930), 410; *ibid.*, VIII (1931), 117–25; McRee, *Life of Iredell*, II, 220; Benjamin Hawkins to James Madison, February 14, 1788, in McPherson (ed.), "Unpublished Letters from North Carolinians to James Madison and James Monroe," *loc. cit.*, 159–60.

and earnest conference took place; much visiting occurred.

As the political thermometer rose steadily during the first six months of 1788, William Blount was also engrossed in private affairs. Family and dependents claimed much attention. His sister Louisa, married but a short time to Richard Blackledge, died. The marriage settlement directed property to William and her husband, but other claimants invoked law suits. The death of his brother-in-law Will Grainger meant that Blount, as executor, had duties in the county courts. The eldest son also determined that his youngest half-brother, Willie, should study law with Sitgreaves—thus involving argument with Jacob, Senior, who sought to hold his younger ones at home, and arrangements with John Gray for materials to build the new office.

More troublesome problems arose in connection with Blount's ward, young Abner Nash. The widow Nash could keep her brash, incompetent son no longer, and "no Merchant, Lawyer nor in short no decent Person here will take him on any Terms." With a growing family and young apprentice Titus Ogden already crowding Piney Grove, Mrs. Blount flatly refused another permanent guest. William rented the youth's slaves and wrote persuasively to John Gray Blount that he would pay one half the proceeds to anyone to employ the boy in "ostensible" business, "for he is really incapable of any other . . . or if you will keep him a few Weekes or Months and imploy him occasionally about any thing so as to show him he is a Boy you will much oblige me. This last I presume you may do without much Inconveniency as he may be generally engaged either in Business or Amusements out of the House and I am sure your Presence will sufficiently awe him when in it." [2]

---

[2] William Blount to John Gray Blount, February 8, 1788, in Keith (ed.), *Blount Papers*, I, 370–72.

Young Dick Blackledge, widower of Blount's sister Louisa, like Reading Blount, was both openhanded and impulsive. These traits, regarded by the elder Blounts with something less than tolerance, had brought him to the verge of bankruptcy, and the older brothers sought to save him.

Outside of the family, society made its demands. "Recommended" business visitors had to be entertained. Rising prominence had brought trusteeships at the three leading academies—New Bern, Dobbs, and Pitt—all three honors entailing financial responsibilities.[3] The demands of business, too, were engrossing. The nail factory was established with much difficulty near Washington, but supplies of bar iron were difficult to get on credit. The search for corn, salt, and naval stores went on, as did that for the better class of currencies. There were runaway slaves to be negotiated for, suits to be averted, debts to be collected, and Thomas Blount—soon to return from Europe—advised and financed.

All the while the expanding game of land went on. Reports came from the Blount firm's purchasing agents in western Georgia and from surveyors in Kentucky. The growing amounts of Blount land in Tennessee necessitated a resident agent there, and the brothers conferred on candidates. One sales agent, Andrew Connor, reported unfavorably from Ireland and asked for more prospectuses and information on the location of the firm's Tennessee lands, and on transportation methods for European purchasers. Meanwhile, at home growing public prosperity made for remunerative sales in New Bern and Warrenton.[4]

[3] William Blount to John Gray Blount, June 22, 1788, *ibid.*, 405; Clark (ed.), *State Records,* XXIV, 607, 754, 867.

[4] Letters of John Trippe, Charles Gerrard, George Nicolson, and Andrew Connor to John Gray Blount, July–October, 1788, in Blount Collection, P.C. 837; William Blount to *id.*, October 24, 1788, in Keith (ed.),

In late March and April riot-marred elections were held, and on July 21, 1788, the 280 convention members met in the Presbyterian Church at Hillsboro. John Gray Blount, John Sitgreaves, and Abner Neale represented the Blounts, for William Blount, with a great number of other Federalists, had tasted the mortification of defeat by political unknowns. Alexander Martin had been chastised for his desertion of the state-first camp. Richard Caswell, seven times governor, was rejected by the voters in favor of an unknown but vociferous state-firster, and Ben Sheppard's riot had not kept the victors from taking their seats. Experienced politicoes Allan Jones, William Hooper, James Glasgow, and others also fell before the Antifederalist onslaught. It was from family and friends, therefore, that Blount learned of the lost cause at Hillsboro, of how the tireless debates of Iredell, the angry logic of Maclaine, the stout defenses of Davie, Spaight, and Johnston were impotent before the onslaught of Thomas Person, David Caldwell, Timothy Bloodworth, Samuel Spencer, and Joseph McDowell. Especially deadly was the lobbying of the aristocratic democrat, Willie Jones, who spoke so seldom but managed so well. If, as the Conservatives sneered, that patrician individualist felt "mortification in finding himself in the company of Bloodworth and Persons" and in Virginia's adoption of the Constitution, he never lost his skillful touch. Following the ideas of his mentor, Jefferson, he guided the convention into actual rejection through the technicality of a number of proposed amendments.[5]

Blount Papers, I, 429–30; Thomas Blount to *id.,* November 7, 1788, *ibid.,* 434; Beaufort County Deeds, Book 27, p. 66.

[5] William R. Davie to James Iredell, July 9, 1788, in McRee, *Life of Iredell,* II, 230–31; Clark (ed.), *State Records,* XXII, 16–28; Wagstaff, *States Rights and Political Parties,* 23–27; Trenholme, *Ratification of the Federal Constitution,* 150–91.

However disappointed with the convention and its decision, Blount, well-accustomed to the vagaries of North Carolina radicalism, did not fall into the despair that afflicted Hugh Williamson. Like his friend, Blount was "fully persuaded that the Value of those Lands [in the Western country] must be increased by an efficient federal Gov^t." [6] Furthermore, the full popular effect of Virginia's adoption, followed by that of New York, lightened prospects in that direction. Desperately, the Federalists began the most intensive campaign of education in the state's history. With great care for unanimity of aim, petitions were circulated in almost every county calling for a new convention. Iredell and Davie financed the printing of the convention journal. Efforts were made to circulate *The Federalist* yet more widely. Public letters and tracts redoubled; "A Citizen and a Soldier," "An Honest Man," and "Antifed, Sr." belabored the past convention and each other with zeal. Williamson in New York contributed to the other states an apologia and explanation of the convention's decision. Slowly, encouraging reports circulated of a popular Federalist reaction; the effigies now burning were those of Willie Jones and Person. Deriving full advantage from this turn of affairs, Blount shifted his ground to candidacy for the senate and applied the full pressure of "the Blount interest." As a result the lately rejected politician in November represented Pitt County in the senate of the Fayetteville assembly.[7]

[6] Hugh Williamson to James Madison, June 2, 1788, in McPherson (ed.), "Unpublished Letters from North Carolinians to James Madison and James Monroe," *loc. cit.*, 160–61.

[7] William Hooper to James Iredell, September 2, 1788, in McRee, *Life of Iredell*, II, 238–39; William R. Davie to *id.*, July 9, September 8, 1788, *ibid.*, 230–31, 239; Archibald Maclaine to *id.*, September 13, October 27, 1788, *ibid.*, 239–40, 243–44; Hugh Williamson to *id.*, September 22, 1788, *ibid.*, 241–42; Clark (ed.), *State Records*, XX, 477; Wagstaff, *States Rights and Political Parties*, 27–29; Newsome, "North Carolina's Ratification," *loc. cit.*, 296–99.

Yet the tide, though turning, was not entirely in, and leaders of both factions would have to proceed with caution. Blount held careful caucuses with his aides at the Pitt County court, then left for Fayetteville, where he lodged with John Williams in a room at Dickinson's tavern, and surveyed the scene of battle. The Federalist efforts, he found, had resulted in their control of the senate, led by Caswell, Allan Jones, Blount, and Alexander Martin. In the house, Person, deprived of the assistance of cohorts Bloodworth and Rutherford, led a reduced majority. The portents were favorable.

The senate organized on November 3, 1788, when Alexander Martin, on nomination by Caswell, was elected speaker. Blount was named to the steering committee, to another committee to audit the comptroller's account, and to a third to examine the complaints and communications from the distracted West. Despite his influential posts, he was pessimistic over the chances for a new ratifying convention, for, although he reported "Party Spirit" slow in appearing, he still considered Willie Jones "inflexible," and, hence, ratification chances poor.[8] However, the Federalists were heartened when, on the day of the session, a secret caucus revealed their small senatorial majority, and at once, in order to bring maximum pressure on the commons, Caswell was selected to introduce a resolution for a second convention. Willie Jones was not one to be thus trapped. Depending on the commons to outvote the senate, he immediately proposed a joint session of the present houses to consider the question, and called "for the previous question." Jones' motion won, thereby killing Caswell's proposal, but in the house, Person and his ultra-

---

[8] William Blount to John Gray Blount, November 6, 1788, in Keith (ed.), *Blount Papers*, I, 433–34.

Radicals either failed to grasp or to appreciate Jones' strategy, and they refused his resolution.[9]

The Federalists now applied intense pressure. Petitions from nineteen counties had been received, and more were added. Blount, Caswell, and Johnston conferred with leaders of east and west. To conservative eastern Carolinians they pictured a revived currency and assistance with the staggering debt. On the other hand, they urged that without union danger threatened in commercial exclusion and retaliation by the other states. Also, ratification followed by a Western cession would relieve the state of the burden of the impending Indian wars. To southern county members, hopes were held out of a reconsideration of the site of the state capital. To far westerners, they urged that ratification would certainly bring a Carolina cession and speedy statehood as well as military aid. In east and west such advantageous prospects outweighed the once decisive fears of Federal relinquishment of the Mississippi to the Spanish.[10] Besides, membership in the Union meant a stronger "southern interest" in Congress to oppose such Northern designs.

The result of this pressure, combined with news of ratification by other states, was a strengthening of ratification sentiment, and a Caswell-Blount resolution for a new convention easily passed the senate. Jones, foreseeing the inevitable, sought to play for time. The shrewd Antifederalist, therefore, struck first, and moved a resolution for the election in August, 1789, of a second convention to meet in October, a whole year hence. To capitalize on

[9] Charles Johnson to James Iredell, November 14, 1788, in McRee, *Life of Iredell*, II, 600–601.

[10] Hugh Williamson to James Madison, June 2, 1788, in McPherson (ed.), "Unpublished Letters from North Carolinians to James Madison and James Monroe," *loc. cit.*, 160–61.

current sentiment, Caswell and Blount sought to advance the election, but their amendment failed; the house this time accepted Jones' bill, which, despite Person's efforts and a few amendments, prevailed. Radical Antifederalists were appeased with the election of their leaders to a proposed second constitutional convention.

Blount's chief preoccupations in the short course of the assembly were with the Constitution and the West. He did, however, give his usual attention to the interests of his constituents and his family and friends. He moved a bill to allow faster foreclosures on absentee Loyalists; he upheld the more northern over the Fayetteville forces in the continuing fight to locate the capital and opposed representation for ambitious Fayetteville; he voted against a canal bill which would divert traffic from eastern Carolina seaports; he sought to improve the ferry at Edenton; he introduced and forced through a bill extending the time to register land grants; he fought for a redistricting bill to increase the power of the eastern counties; he assisted in securing time for Henderson associates to complete their surveys; and he supported the continuation of his friends Hodge and Wills as state printers. In short, he upheld consistently the interests of the Neuse and Albemarle sections against the southern counties, of the seacoast against the Piedmont, and of himself and associates against all others.[11]

However, the statesman-speculator's primary interest, dictated by the ownership of many thousand acres, was ever in the tramontane West, and this area received his most devoted attention. A strong delegation from across the mountains included James and Elijah Robertson, John Tipton, James Roddy, Joseph Hardin, and Alexander

[11] Clark (ed.), *State Records*, XX, 502, 523, 527, 530, 544, 547, 561, 567, 571, 594; *ibid.*, XXIV, 991.

Outlaw. Blount, associated closely with some of these in business and even now arranging further land purchases from Elijah Robertson, prepared to champion his Western associates' wishes in the assembly. He had long been aware of the desperation of the frontiersmen without being very closely identified with the separatist movement thereby initiated. As a colleague of Dr. James White's in Philadelphia in 1786 when the latter began his intrigue with the Spanish chargé, Don Diego Gardoqui, for a Western-Spanish alliance, he probably knew of it, although he was not present when it began nor when White was elected Indian agent. During 1788, upon the revival of the so-called Spanish conspiracy, Blount was also undoubtedly in touch with the endeavors of James Robertson and Daniel Smith in Cumberland to interest Spanish Governor Miró in their suggestions. Furthermore, when Sevier, approached by White, began his correspondence with Gardoqui in the hope of salvaging the Muscle Shoals project, Blount unquestionably followed these plans to advance their mutual interest. On the other hand, the Eastern speculator probably saw earlier than some of his Western associates that, while the intrigue could be well used as a threat to extort a cession from Carolina, yet the essential incompatibility of the aims of the Westerners and of Spain precluded carrying separatist ideas to any radical conclusion. With Robertson and the Cumberland leaders, therefore, he encouraged the threat, but primarily worked for Western appeasement and for cession to the central government.[12]

In this campaign for appeasement and cession, he

[12] Whitaker, "Muscle Shoals Speculation," *loc. cit.,* 378. For the Spanish intrigue, see Whitaker, *Spanish-American Frontier,* 108–15; Abernethy, *Frontier to Plantation,* 90–102; and Archibald Henderson, "The Spanish Conspiracy in Tennessee," in *Tennessee Historical Magazine,* III (1920), 229–43.

again found an unexpected ally in Willie Jones. For that supreme politician, appearing for the last time in the assemblage he had so long dominated, pursued a course of neo-Federalism that must have amazed his friends as it did his enemies. Perhaps the shift in popular sentiment which so decimated his ranks disgusted him. Perhaps he felt that the strength of the Conservative-speculator bloc was too great to combat further. Perhaps he sought to defeat ratification of the Constitution by dividing its adherents, or, impressed by the strength of Federalism in the sister states, especially Virginia, he felt the Radical program was doomed. Perhaps he was merely bored with politics. At any rate, he worked with Blount in finance and tax measures, in support of Hodge and Wills, and in unparalleled attention to Western interests. On November 17, soon after introducing a measure to extend pardon to ex-Franklinites, he moved a bill to cede the tramontane area to the central government, and his forces, including Blount, beat off an amendment to make the Cumberland River the dividing line. Seconded by Blount, he moved that a message be sent to the half-breed chief Alexander McGillivray, with whom, as the state's agent, he had dealt in Revolutionary days, to inform that Creek leader of a proposed treaty and to ask for a truce in the incessant attacks.[13]

Despite the efforts of the two leaders, the cession bill was deferred to the next session; Blount, however, was already at work on other Western aims. His committee on the Western territory secured the adoption of a resolution accepting a Congressional offer to participate with Congress, South Carolina, and Georgia in a new treaty meeting with the Southern Indians; and Blount's friend Federalist John Steele was named the state's representative.[14]

13 Clark (ed.), *State Records*, XX, 513, 535–36, 552–53.
14 *Ibid.*, 551, 568.

In order that this treaty should be no repetition of Hopewell, Jones, Blount, and their associates drew up careful instructions for Steele, who was ordered not to cede any lands to the Indians beyond those small areas set aside in the 1783 act, to seek further cession from the savages if possible, and to guard the Henderson claims, now appropriated by the state.[15] To assist further the angry and faction-ridden people of the Tennessee country,[16] Blount sponsored the creation of a new county, created from Davidson, and the formation of a new judicial district. The latter, despite criticism of Robertson's appeasement policy, was named Mero in an attempt to honor Don Esteban Miró, Spanish governor and intendant of Louisiana and West Florida. The popular and influential Daniel Smith of Davidson County was appointed Brigadier General of the new district.[17]

In Blount's program of assistance to the West, one circumstance made careful diplomacy necessary. This was the collapse of the Franklin movement. Although its aim of independence from Carolina was still the wish of a majority of Westerners, by 1788 the new state was in dissolution. The success of Carolina's divide-and-rule policy coupled with Georgia's decision to postpone the contemplated attack on the Creeks pending Congressional action had brought Sevier's commonwealth to its knees. The ex-governor himself, in an effort to salvage his fallen Western popularity, fled to the farthest frontiers to carry on attacks against the Indians. Meanwhile, he looked to his business associates in the assembly to save his name in the

[15] *Ibid.*, 562, 582–83; H. M. Wagstaff (ed.), *The Papers of John Steele* (Raleigh, 1924), I, 21–24.

[16] Haywood, *History of Tennessee*, 244–50; Clark (ed.), *State Records,* XXII, 722–25.

[17] Clark (ed.), *State Records*, XX, 554–55, 568; XXIV, 975; John Allison, "The Mero District," in *American Historical Magazine,* I (1896), 116–17; Haywood, *History of Tennessee*, 250–51.

East. To do this in the presence of an unfriendly governor and such of Sevier's mortal enemies as John Tipton required address, for the latter had already managed to exclude the Franklin chief from the amnesty extended to his followers. In such an atmosphere the best that could be done was to prevent further reprisal, elect Sevier followers to Western offices, and hope for better times. Thus, Thomas King, Landon Carter, Francis Ramsey, and William Cocke, all Sevier followers, were given offices.[18]

Despite such successes and the fulfillment of much of his own program, Blount felt as keenly as ever the personal animosity of his fellow legislators, led by James Galloway and Joseph McDowell and his son. "This General Assembly," he wrote to his brother, "would be supremely happy in my Opinion if they could see with certainty the Ruin of Caswell you and myself and with us our Friends." [19] The resentment against the speculator arose from his prestige, derived from long public service, his ambition, his business ethics, his wealth and financial power, and his continued political influence, which, despite the Hopewell fiasco, appeared greater than ever.

Those obnoxious treaties had been continuously ignored by the whites, and the North Carolina delegation in Congress had finally succeeded, at least to their own satisfaction, in obtaining "such amendments as seem to render the Treaty very harmless." [20] Nevertheless, Blount's 1786 transactions with the state's goods offered a target to his enemies, and they attacked. Taking up the last assembly's committee report, they forced the ex-agent to pay part of his still unsettled Hopewell account at once and threatened

18 Abernethy, *Frontier to Plantation*, 86–88; Williams, *Franklin*, 241; Clark (ed.), *State Records*, XX, 326.
19 William Blount to John Gray Blount, December 4, 1788, in Keith (ed.), *Blount Papers*, I, 438–40.
20 Hugh Williamson to Governor Johnston, September 6, 1788, in Clark (ed.), *State Records*, XXI, 497–98.

suit for the rest. They also refused to agree to a charge for services by Blackledge, one of the "Blount interest," which dated from the Revolution.[21]

As the session closed, Blount regarded this animosity with deep resentment. "The Spirit of Persecution still prevails against me," he wrote his brother, and added the typical reaction: "Pray keep in view the Election of as many Blounts as possible for the next year." [22] On December 6, he planned to leave the legislature in its final day to travel to Wilmington on business affairs. He asked his brother to satisfy his wife's household needs—"for I suppose She will be enough dissatisfied at my Absence"— and then prepared to leave with Hawkins. On the day intended for departure ill fortune struck again. Through the carelessness of his host's servants, a fire nearly consumed the lodging house, destroying part of Blount's clothes. The next evening, as he rode in a borrowed chaise, the horse took fright, bolted, and dashed the chaise over a high stump, tossing the assemblyman "full ten feet." With no injuries save bruises, but sore and angry, he finally proceeded on his journey and arrived at Wilmington on December 10. This done, he forewent a contemplated trip to Georgia to see "about this damned Indian Treaty [Hopewell] Affair," and on December 29, was back home to defend his interest in Blackledge property about to be sold for debt.[23]

These demands of business continued to absorb Blount's time as the new Federal government began its

[21] William Blount to John Gray Blount, December 4, 5, 1788, in Keith (ed.), *Blount Papers,* I, 438–41; receipt of John Haywood, December 4, 1788, in Blount Collection, P.C. 898.

[22] William Blount to John Gray Blount, December 5, 1788, in Keith (ed.), *Blount Papers,* I, 440–41.

[23] William Blount to John Gray Blount, December 4, 5, 11, 1788, *ibid.,* 438–41, 442–44; notice of William Blount, January 1, 1789, *ibid.,* 556–57; William Blount to John Gray Blount, December 28, 1788, in Blount Collection.

function in early 1789. There were, of course, family visits, trips with his wife to New Bern for the theater, dances, and musicals, or to Washington for the races. Occasionally "Parson Blount," an Episcopal rector and cousin of Jacob, Senior, visited at Greenville and held formal services, which the family preferred to the more prevalent Baptist and Methodist zeal. In May, Blount's third son was born and named for Richard Blackledge. Piney Grove with his wife, her mother, and the children, along with wards and apprentices, was filled with the ceaseless liveliness of an active family.

Varied enterprise, however, kept the head of the family frequently on the roads. He sought to recover estates for business clients, dunned for debt collections, sold cargoes from the West Indies, and found farms and positions for the numerous Harvey family connections. In March, he traveled to Wilmington for a lawsuit and thence to Charleston to enter negotiations with "an old Rake of Fortune," who, though "the damndest Rascal in the World," wanted oil of turpentine, tar, shingles, and lumber for Jamaica plantations.[24] The Carolinian then moved on to Georgia seeking a contract to furnish the Spanish garrison on Amelia Island. There he discovered the tavernkeeper to be a lady whose maiden name was Blount and who claimed kinship. This amiable soul was the mistress of the Spanish governor's son who commanded the garrison and who was "himself much attached to the Americans." Blount, therefore, recommended to his brother that their ship captain should "let her understand that his Vessel belongs partly to me." Furthermore, as to the Georgians, the captain "had best be very particular how he lets any part of his Cargo out of his Hands to the Citizens of Georgia without

24 William Blount to John Gray Blount, March 25, 1789, in Keith (ed.), *Blount Papers,* I, 468–70.

Payment in hand and . . . he had best consult Owens & Thompson before he trusts any Man an hour for there are many [more] people in Georgia who live by there Wits & Roguary than any where on Earth beside in proportion to the Number of People." [25]

So, shrewdly and minutely Blount performed his business reconnaissance as far as Augusta. After an unsuccessful attempt there to revive the moribund Bend scheme, he returned to make his report to his partner, for as contact man and lobbyist William Blount had few peers, but final decisions were left to the better mercantile judgment of his brother.[26]

Despite the demands of the firm and of such civic and educational duties as those of town commissioner of Greenville and trustee of the new state university, Blount still devoted primary attention to his first love—land.[27] While he bought and sold in the Eastern counties, his major interest remained in the West. In the Bend country, though Houston County had been laid off on a map of the Tennessee bend and grants had been issued, the Bend Company remained inactive because of the opposition of Georgia legislators and governor; but there were other Western prospects. In that entire area land speculation in 1788 had run to fever heat, induced by the organization of the new central government. The new regime was evidently more powerful, and already carried more prestige, than the old Congress. Hence, some operators regarded the rise of Western land values as inevitable. Others sought

<hr />

[25] William Blount to John Gray Blount, August 7, 1789, *ibid.*, 498–99.

[26] William Blount to John Gray Blount, December 4, 1788, June 12, 1789, *ibid.*, 438–40, 486–87; Richard Caswell to William Blount, February 18, 1789, in "An Outline of the Life of Governor Caswell with a Selection of His Letters," in *University of North Carolina Magazine* (March, 1855), 84.

[27] Pitt County Deeds, Book M, 122, 154–55; Pitt County Entry Book, Books 1–2, June 25, 1789; William Blount to John Gray Blount, June 6, 1789, in Keith (ed.), *Blount Papers*, I, 485–86; Clark (ed.), *State Records*, XXIV, 867; XXV, 22.

feverishly to acquire vast empires from the state before such acquisition was made more difficult by Federal ownership. The result was an avalanche of Western enterprise. In the 1788 assembly a committee investigating Armstrong's office had reported 4,393,945 acres entered in the Tennessee country exclusive of the military grants, which amounted to nearly 3,000,000 more acres.[28] To the southward, the three Yazoo companies, despite the earlier Bourbon and the Houston County failures, were preparing to launch a campaign in the Georgia legislature which was to result in grants totaling 25,400,000 acres.[29]

This renewed interest in the Western lands focused attention on those who had long been active in acquiring them. Charges were made openly against the Blount firm for obtaining grants by spurious military claims. Political enemies, notably ex-Tories and politicians of Fayetteville who were angered by Blount's opposition in the capital fight, took up the attack, and caricatures and denunciation of the family appeared in William Boylan's North Carolina *Minerva and Fayetteville Gazette*.[30]

Little intimidated by talk when gains offered, the Blount firm and its friends worked steadily to enlarge their operations. Hawkins kept up contact with the Romaynes in the East and wrote letters to Gardoqui to strengthen the Cumberland flirtation with Governor Miró. The French consul's friendship was evinced in the name of his natural son, Blount Hawkins de la Forest. In New

[28] Clark (ed.), *State Records*, XXI, 133; Goodpasture, "Education and the Public Lands," *loc. cit.*, 216; Walter Lowrie and M. S. C. Clark (eds.), *American State Papers, Class VIII, Public Lands* (Washington, 1834), I, 18. (Hereinafter referred to as *State Papers, Public Lands*.)

[29] Treat, *National Land System*, 356; Whitaker, *Spanish-American Frontier*, 126–33; C. H. Haskins, "The Yazoo Land Companies," in American Historical Association *Papers*, V, Part 4, 61–71; Sakolski, *Great American Land Bubble*, 125–27.

[30] George Ogg to William Blount, May 10, 1789, in Keith (ed.), *Blount Papers*, I, 478–79.

York, Hugh Williamson used the familiar "extract of a letter" method to propagandize the Tennessee country, seizing upon Robertson's customary newspaper notice of the departure of an armed convoy for middle Tennessee and transforming the somber bulletin into a glowing description of a Western paradise where peace, law, and order reigned, and immigrants responded to fostering care by increasing in thousands.[31]

Meanwhile the firm of John Gray & Thomas Blount, through William, was busy in its land projects. A suitable agent, Charles Gerrard, was sent to Hillsboro to check on Blount land entries and those of their surveyor Stockley Donelson. The latter held the Blounts' power of attorney, and his gargantuan frauds, though only beginning, were half suspected. A map of the West was drawn up to be sold cheaply in Maryland, Pennsylvania, and New Jersey, accompanied by a glowing prospectus drawn by Hugh Williamson. Micajah Thomas, an old partner in the Bend and other plans, died and was replaced by Abishai Thomas, whose official task of settling North Carolina military claims against Congress gave him splendid opportunities of buying military warrants. Other partners were speculators James Porterfield and Wilson Blount, a very distant relative, whom William Blount despised as "the most trifling damned Creature in the world" but whose financial position required that he be paid "the necessary attentions &c." His utility, however, did not prevent the brothers from giving him invalid deeds for his share until the firm members could locate and secure the choicer parts of their joint purchase, which totaled 118,000 acres west of the Tennessee River in Chickasaw country.[32]

---

[31] Benjamin Hawkins to William Blount, January 30, 1789, in Blount Collection; Hugh Williamson to *id.*; February 22, 1789, *ibid.*; New York *Daily Advertiser*, February 17, 1789.

[32] Thomas Blount to John Gray Blount, November 7, 1788, in Keith (ed.),

Meanwhile, as had the Confederation Congress, the new Federal legislature was showing a strong aversion to purchasing more land from the Indians.[33] This meant to the heavily invested Blount that it was essential for North Carolina, while she still could make Indian treaties, to secure clear title to lands which she had so lightheartedly opened for exploitation in 1783 and which he and thousands of others had so eagerly bought. Both before and during his trip to Georgia, therefore, he wrote carefully to Commissioner Steele, who was now preparing for this Carolina-Georgia-Congress treaty with the Southern Indians. Since Blount lands were threatened mainly by the Cherokee, the speculator lengthily urged the new commissioner that a Cherokee treaty was North Carolina's *"only* object . . . and as you effect this upon good or bad terms so will you be applauded or censured by her citizens. . . ." For Steele's guidance the politician outlined strategy and estimated the other commissioners: Pickens "a cunning and artful Man," Matthews "not so much so." Making a Cherokee treaty first would appeal to Pickens through self-interest, to Matthews after "talking much to him privately" on the similar status of Georgia and North Carolina as victims of a Federal government greedy for Western land control.[34] He ironically flayed Pickens' pro-Indian stand at Hopewell, though he did "not wish to be given as the Author" since "it may sour his disposition and make him obstinate and it will be your

Blount Papers, I, 434; Charles Gerrard to *id.,* March 10, 1789, *ibid.,* 464–65; William Blount to Wilson Blount, January 20, 1789 (copy), *ibid.,* 455–57; Thomas Blount to John Gray Blount, February 14, 1789, in Blount Collection; Abishai Thomas to *id.,* November 18, 1789, *ibid.;* William Blount to *id.,* March 2, 1789, *ibid.; id. to id.,* (n.d.) [1789], *ibid.,* P.C. 840.

[33] Ford *et al.* (eds.), *Journals of Congress,* XXXIII, 710; Hugh Williamson to John Gray Blount, August 8, 1789, in Keith (ed.), *Blount Papers,* I, 499–501.

[34] William Blount to John Steele, January 17, 1789, in Wagstaff (ed.), *Papers of John Steele,* I, 27–30.

Business good humouredly to bring him to your purposes." [35] How the commissioner was to comply with the conflicting Congressional and state instructions not even Blount sought to explain; he merely emphasized the dangers of not upholding the terms of the 1783 land law.

While the busy Blount traveled, traded, bought, sold, and advised, he kept an alert eye on the political scene. Federalist prospects brightened with the passing months. The ratification by Virginia was influential. In the Federalist camp, John Gray Blount joined the arch-Conservatives in propagandizing. The auspicious start of the new government, with Washington presiding and Congress adopting constitutional amendments in the form of guarantees of private citizens' rights, destroyed Antifederal arguments. The advancing threat of commercial exclusion from sister states, the unwelcome association with Rhode Island, the prospect of political largesse from membership in the Union all worked powerfully for ratification sentiment. With those more sectional than state-minded, the plea to strengthen the "southern Interest" in Congress had weight. Western citizens hoped for a ratification followed by a cession and statehood, and when Steele's mission failed this disappointing circumstance was attributed to the state's first refusal to ratify.[36]

[35] William Blount to John Steele, May 5, 1789, *ibid.*, 38–44.

[36] William R. Davie to James Iredell, June 4, 1789, in McRee, *Life of Iredell*, II, 260; Benjamin Hawkins to James Madison, June 1, 1789, in Madison Papers; William R. Davie to *id.*, June 10, 1789, in McPherson (ed.), "Unpublished Letters of North Carolinians to James Madison and James Monroe," *loc. cit.*, 166–67; D. L. Corbitt (ed.), "Historical Notes," in *North Carolina Historical Review*, V (1928), 224–44 *passim*; J. F. Grimke to General Harrington, January 16, 1789, in Clark (ed.), *State Records*, XXI, 521–22; "Extract of a letter from . . . Edenton to . . . Boston," in *State Gazette of North Carolina*, October 1, 1789; James Iredell to John Gray Blount, July 1, 1789, in Keith (ed.), *Blount Papers*, I, 490–91; John Reid to Daniel Smith, September 14, 1789, in "Papers of Gen. Daniel Smith," *American Historical Magazine*, VI (1901), 217; Trenholme, *Ratification of the Federal Constitution*, 207–12, 214–32; Wagstaff, *States Rights and Political Parties*, 29–31.

These various circumstances produced changes. Surveyor Will Polk reported the West "fast settling," and that "the Constitution will go down with the back Country *Now.*" In the eastern Tennessee country partner Sevier's pro-cession group was gaining strength over his arch-rival, John Tipton. In middle Tennessee Daniel Smith was equally optimistic as, in the East, were Hawkins, Davie, and, at times, Williamson. Blount's spirits rose. He talked of Abner Neale being made admiralty judge after ratification; for the next assembly he planned hopefully for his cohorts "to be very Strong," and was led to believe there would be "no Tiptonians to oppose us but the followers of Severe to aid us." [37] Blount was now in fact the recognized champion of Western speculators and of the West. Through agent Robertson, the founder (and boss) of middle Tennessee, he was building there a political following, while getting the best of advice on land investment from across the mountains. With ratification he could count on Western support for Congress.[38]

Only a few clouds darkened family horizons. On August 17, Jacob Blount, Senior, succumbed at sixty-three to the malarial fevers so often deadly to the lowlanders. He had remained active to his last days and from their earliest childhood had profoundly influenced his successful sons. From him they had acquired the dominant traits of their natures, and the two eldest sons respected his wishes and felt his death.

Blount public careers, too, had shadows. The exposures and complaints in land frauds had turned investi-

[37] William Polk to John Gray Blount, July 27, 1789, in Keith (ed.), *Blount Papers,* I, 494–95; William Blount to *id.,* March 3, 1789, *ibid.,* 463–64; Daniel Smith to Governor Johnston, July 24, 1789, in Clark (ed.), *State Records,* XXI, 558–59; William Blount to John Steele, January 17, 1789, in Wagstaff (ed.), *Papers of John Steele,* I, 27–30.

[38] James Robertson to William Blount, September 21, 1789, in Keith (ed.), *Blount Papers,* I, 506–507.

gators on the entry-taker. This officer, John Armstrong, puppet and creature of Blount and the other speculators who gave him office, now felt the "bite of benefits forgot." His property under execution, he pleaded with William, "if You will be kin Enough to Stand my friend at the time, Nothing But death Shall Ever stop me from doing Every good office that lys in my power toward You." [39] Blount political enemies were also compelling Treasurer Haywood, to his extreme pain, to sue his friend John Gray Blount for unpaid accounts. [40]

Despite these attacks on the "Blount Interest," William Blount was elected to the 1789 senate from Pitt County and John Gray to the commons from Beaufort County. The former at once left for Fayetteville, though his brother was delayed by a severe illness among his slaves and the necessity of supervising the loading of four vessels. William Blount took his usual place on the steering committee, while both brothers sat on committees to consider Western affairs. Assembly membership augured well for the Federalists in the coming convention. Nearly one half of the members were new men, and, despite the presence of Thomas Person, Timothy Bloodworth, Matthew Locke, and William Lenoir, it was the most moderate such gathering for many years, the senate having only ten Antifederalists and the house, twenty-nine. [41]

On November 7, the uninitiated were much surprised when the senator from Greene, John Sevier, appeared and took his seat. This move, made after several days of strategic planning with the Blounts, was carefully timed to follow convincing argument: Franklin was dissolved, and

[39] John Armstrong to William Blount, October 6, 1789, *ibid.*, 507–508.

[40] John Haywood to John Gray Blount, October 13, 1789, *ibid.*, 508–10; Archibald Maclaine to James Iredell, November 26, 1789, in McRee, *Life of Iredell*, II, 273–74.

[41] Archibald Maclaine to James Iredell, November 26, 1789, in McRee, *Life of Iredell*, II, 273–74; Gilpatrick, *Jeffersonian Democracy*, 37–38.

Sevier was a strong Federalist and the associate of Federalists. With ratification plans in need of support and a new cession pending, why re-open healed wounds? The assembly was convinced, and Davie's motion for an inquiry was tabled despite furious objection by McDowell and other Radicals. The "Scourge of the Cherokees" then received his old brigadier generalship and absolution for his political sins. Along with friends, the present brigadier, Joseph Martin, was enraged by this about-face; but the ambitious Martin was himself under attack for military failures against the Cherokee and for suspected correspondence with McGillivray. By securing both his exoneration from attacks and the payment of his soldiers in the late campaign, the Blounts somewhat appeased the sensitive Westerner and kept peace among the associates.[42]

An irreparable loss to Blount's personal and political strength, however, came on November 5, when Caswell, long ill and saddened by the loss of his two sons, collapsed in the speaker's chair. After five days of coma, the master strategist of so many campaigns died. Blount, deeply moved, helped direct the state funeral and carried out the last arrangements for his mentor, partner, and friend.

Six days later the senator attended the opening of the ratification convention which he and Caswell had so effectively promoted. In this assemblage the Blounts were well represented, with John Gray from Beaufort, Thomas from Edgecombe, and William representing both Pitt and Tennessee counties. His selection in the far Western country, where he had never been, in the face of local favorites clearly showed both his position as a Western spokesman and the ability of Western leaders such as Robertson to

---

[42] Haywood, *History of Tennessee,* 211–12; Clark (ed.), *State Records,* XXI, 213, 581, 584–85, 594, 691, 725–26, 728.

deliver the vote for a pre-chosen candidate.[43] As the still-apprehensive Federalists counted forces, it was soon evident that, despite many hostile figures from the Hillsboro defeat, the result was no longer in doubt.[44] Willie Jones, mainspring of opposition, had declined to campaign, and through the work of Conservatives and businessmen the complexions of the Western delegations had radically changed. A few Antifederalists such as Bloodworth, Spencer, Lenoir, and Person held their constituents in the opposition by personal prestige, but, like a later band, they were "noisey but not numerous." Their attempt to name Spencer chairman was easily defeated; their delaying tactics were beaten down; and their efforts to precede ratification with proposed amendments were swept aside. In seven days the Constitution was debated and reported favorably by the committee of the whole, and the report, on John Gray Blount's motion and Williamson's second, was adopted by the convention. To mollify Antifederalists, proposed amendments were transmitted to Congress, but the ratification was not made contingent upon their adoption. Ironically for Blount's future, the last of these amendments proposed that some tribunal other than the United States Senate should try cases of impeachment of Senators.[45] Then, having given Fayetteville borough representation and denied the same to Tarboro, the delegates adjourned, and Blount and about one half of the members

[43] Elijah Robertson to William Blount, December 25, 1788, in Keith (ed.), *Blount Papers*, I, 448; Papers of the Convention of 1789 (North Carolina State Department of Archives and History).

[44] Benjamin Hawkins to James Madison, August 27, 1789, in Madison Papers; Archibald Maclaine to James Iredell, September 15, 1789, in McRee, *Life of Iredell*, II, 266–67.

[45] Archibald Maclaine to James Iredell, September 15, 1789, in McRee, *Life of Iredell*, II, 266–67; William J. Dawson to *id.*, November 22, 1789, *ibid.*, 272; William R. Davie to *id.*, November 16, 1789, *ibid.*, 271; *State Gazette of North Carolina*, December 3, 1789; Clark (ed.), *State Records*, XXII, 42–53.

returned to the assembly, which had stood adjourned until the close of the convention.

While Federalists rejoiced, Blount, though racked by fever and ague, now prepared to battle for his climactic goals—cession and Federal office. On November 26, three days after the adoption of the Constitution, a bill was introduced in the commons for the cession of the trans-Allegheny lands to the Federal government. Person countered with a bill to create a separate state in the West and to open the land office, followed by the usual attempt to halve the ceded area, but these enticements failed.[46] The Western representatives, through the combined influence of Blount, Sevier, and Robertson, were almost solidly pro-cession. The Eastern members, always reluctant to spend money on the West, had been appalled by the cost of Joseph Martin's 1788 campaign against the Chickamauga. Conservatives had always sought riddance "of a people who were a pest and burthen to us." Federalists were anxious for an expression of their state's delayed Federal sentiment. Even state-first men realized the inutility of an area whose available Indian-free land was already claimed to an amount of over seven million acres, especially since the settlers, claiming the illegality of the first cession repeal, were refusing to pay state taxes. Hence, on December 12, 1789, tramontane North Carolina was again offered to the central government under strong guarantees to the parent state and the speculators. Though largely a speculator-inspired measure, this cession enraged two speculator groups: those who, like Patrick Henry, had unfulfilled plans for the area, and those in the West whose prospects appeared to be brighter in a new state under their own control. Nevertheless the cession act was well received in

[46] Clark (ed.), *State Records,* XXI, 270, 271, 648–49; Abernethy, *Frontier to Plantation,* 112–13.

general, and the assembly accepted Blount's resolution to forward the act to Congress at once, with instructions to the state's new Senators to hasten its acceptance.[47]

While his foes watched angrily, Blount then turned to his other objective—Federal office. The politicians talked of him for governor, but this was not his aim. Concern for his Western interest, love of prestige, sense of opportunity, all pointed to the national Senate, to which, on November 24, he was nominated, with a group of varied political complexion.[48] In this Federalist field day, Samuel Johnston, governor, ex-president of the convention, and at the apogee of popular strength, easily won a seat on the first ballot; but no other candidate received a majority. Postponed until December 2, the second ballot then showed Lenoir with sixty-six votes, leading Blount by six, and Hawkins third with forty, but no majority.[49] Daily the balloting continued as contenders' followers jockeyed for advantage. To help Lenoir, John Stokes and Joseph McDowell withdrew from the race. To assist Blount and Hawkins, Spaight and James White did likewise. The brothers of the two candidates managed their campaigns: Philemon for Benjamin Hawkins, John Gray for William Blount.[50] To embarrass his foe's candidacy, a petition for inquiry into the Blount firm's transactions for the state

[47] Abernethy, *Frontier to Plantation*, 113–14; Bramlett, "North Carolina's Western Lands," 104; Clark (ed.), *State Records*, XXI, 345–46, 376, 679, 697; Williams, *Franklin*, 242–43; Archibald Maclaine to James Iredell, December 22, 1789, in McRee, *Life of Iredell*, II, 275–76; Haywood, *History of Tennessee*, 212–15; Patrick Henry to Joseph Martin, March 10, 1790, in Draper Collection, 11DD87a; David Ross to John Sevier, February 20, 1790, *ibid.*, 11DD86a; Theodorick Bland to Patrick Henry, March 9, 1790, in Henry, *Patrick Henry*, III, 417–20.

[48] Samuel Johnston to James Iredell, November 23, 1789, in McRee, *Life of Iredell*, II, 272; Clark (ed.), *State Records*, XXI, 253, 282, 614.

[49] Clark (ed.), *State Records*, XXI, 282, 628; North Carolina Legislative Papers, 1789 (North Carolina State Department of Archives and History).

[50] Clark (ed.), *State Records*, XXI, 623, 627, 647, 652; John H. Wheeler, *Historical Sketches of North Carolina* (Philadelphia, 1851), II, 428.

was drawn up by the Radical anti-Blount Joseph Mc-
Dowell and presented by James Spiller. Most important,
however, was the fact that the assembly majority was
Conservative, and Conservative votes, unfortunately for
Blount, determined the election. He had, of late, acted
more often with Federalist forces; but the memory of his
Radical dalliance, of high prices charged and of Loyalists
hounded, were too fresh in Conservative minds, and even
now the Blount interests were pressing for more of that
anathema of conservatism, paper money. On December 9,
therefore, Hawkins was elected and the chagrined Blount
delegated to apprise his rival of his victory, a victory which
sowed bitterness in Blount's mind.[51]

This personal defeat reoriented Blount's primary interest to its usual subjects—the business affairs of himself
and his associates and the aims of the West. He petitioned
for relief from liability from the Hopewell accounts, and
with his brother John Gray, for confirmation of disputed
titles to confiscated property. For his fellow speculators he
secured a still longer period for registering land claims.
For the harassed entry-taker John Armstrong he secured
a commission on the sale of confiscated land. For Timothy
Bloodworth he secured the closing of the Radical's public
accounts. He assisted in raising the salary of his partner,
the secretary of state (James Glasgow), and in securing
election and a salary for his own newest protégé, the attorney general of Mero (Andrew Jackson). He sustained
William Lenoir's report approving of John Steele's transactions in the futile attempt for a treaty, and he approved
payment for his friend and agent James Robertson for

[51] *State Gazette of North Carolina,* December 17, 1789; Abernethy, *Frontier to Plantation,* 114; Archibald Maclaine to James Iredell, November 26,
1789, in McRee, *Life of Iredell,* II, 273–74; Clark (ed.), *State Records,*
XXI, 666, 669.

the presents with which the Cumberland leader secured Indian friendships.[52]

In fact, in this last assembly of Blount's, a Western delegation that, in addition to Sevier, included Landon Carter, James White, Alexander Outlaw, and John Rhea, and was backed by Blount influence, secured considerable attention to its wishes. Forts, provision posts, and tobacco warehouses were established; a county seat was incorporated for Hawkins County. Medical care was provided at public expense for those wounded by Indians, and physicians were exempted from military duty. The jurisdiction of the Mero superior court was enlarged and its judge's salary increased. A senate resolution declared Franklin's treaty with some Cherokee chiefs in May, 1785, valid, and the Indians were ordered to be paid for the lands there obtained; the lands were to be sold at eight shillings per one hundred acres with pre-emption to settlers.[53] Further bills to make administrative changes were laid by only because of the impending change of ownership of the area. The Western politicians had little cause to question Blount's influence for their section.

On December 22, the assembly adjourned, and most members hurried homeward. Blount lingered for the utterly characteristic attempt to collect mileage as delegate to the ratification convention from the frontier Tennessee County, seeking fees for 750 miles coming and going. The clerk, however, refused to issue such a certificate, as Blount "in fact . . . did not travel . . . the miles he charges," [54] and the delegate turned homeward over the

[52] Petition of William Blount, December 2, 1789, in North Carolina Legislative Papers; Clark (ed.), *State Records*, XXI, 300, 607, 637, 639–40, 644, 670, 676, 695–96, 717; XXV, 58–59, 62.

[53] Clark (ed.), *State Records*, XXI, 635–36; XXV, 44–45, 49, 58–59, 60.

[54] William Blount to John Hunt, December 24, 1789, in Papers of the Convention of 1789; Clark (ed.), *State Records*, XXI, 1007.

icy roads, meditating accomplishments and prospects. Though bitter at personal opposition and defeats, he had in fact no little cause for satisfaction. His enemies were virulent and active, and he had lost his old political guide. But his program had been made state policy, and his position, especially in the West, was foremost among men whose friendship and guidance was to be sought.

Outstanding among Blount characteristics was that of the close observation of public events with a view to private advantage therefrom. No event was too large or too small to escape that unceasing vigilance, just as no transaction was too insignificant to be deemed unimportant. It was this vigilance and this absorption, termed "his unvaried attention to two-penny matters" by the irascible Maclaine, that absorbed the speculator in the winter of 1789–90. With a new central government in motion and decisions pending in the state administration, the businessman engrossed himself in an even greater than usual variety of affairs.

He was by now frequently shaken by a "big Ague" and a "little one," contracted from years of lowland residence; also, his travel and exposure in the unusually severe winter of 1790 brought a racking cough. But no illness could slow down ambition-driven activity. Convinced that the Fayetteville interests would at length secure the state capital, he made plans to trade Tar River lands for plantations on the Cape Fear, and since Augustus Harvey, brother-in-law of the Blounts, was possessed of such desiderata, he was therefore selected as an object of attention. Jacob's estate had to be divided among the children, a Blount cargo sent off to Ireland, plans made with John Gray to build a warehouse and pilotage platform at Ocracoke Inlet, a defense planned in suits against the firm, and care taken to have the trial before friendly judge and sheriff. Blount covered counties on horseback or in carriage to collect debts, to buy corn (the crop selected by the firm for an attempted local monopoly), to attend surveys at Wilmington, to inquire for runaway slaves, or to explore market prices. He suggested another voyage to smuggle turpentine into Jamaica and speculated in futures in alum, salt, and coffee.[55]

Also, with the West soon to be securely in Federal hands, Blount's activity in the land market continued at its high rate. From information furnished by Robertson, Western agent Gerrard reported "But one killed Since I left there, and the immigrants upwards of 800. the price of Land rising." From Williamson in New York came word that their long-planned new map and prospectus of the West was nearly ready and that the bill for the government of the ceded territory was halfway through Congress. These two events occurring together, he wrote John Gray Blount, "must affect the public Mind and turn the Current of migrations toward Tenessee." [56]

At this stage, Blount's land transactions were of two kinds. The first was regrouping and accounting. After some search, a buyer was found for all Blount holdings in Georgia. Also, Blount traveled to the land office at Hillsboro to find 2,760 entries in the family's name, for which he made arrangements to pay. He also obtained warrants of survey (orders to the surveyor) for 97,000 acres which the Blounts had already entered in partnership with John Donelson, and he now gave orders to Stockley Donelson for the surveying.[57]

At the same time, Blount was absorbed in constant new acquisitions and sales. Alone or for the firm, in his own

[55] Blount Collection, P.C. 840, 841, 842, *passim.*

[56] Charles Gerrard to William Blount, March 1, 1790, in Blount Collection; Hugh Williamson to John Gray Blount, April 16, 1790, *ibid.*

[57] Memorandum of William Blount, April 9, 1790, *ibid.*; William Blount to John Gray Blount, April 17, 1790, *ibid.*

name or others' names, in North Carolina or the Western country, buying, renting, and selling, he lengthened the record of his involved and often tortuous dealings. Although North Carolina had closed her western land office at Hillsboro in 1784 and never reopened it, legal provisions for transfers and generous grants by the legislature kept the land officials busy. Also, enormous tracts had been surveyed before 1784, and these were now for sale; for example, Blount wrote to his brother in April, 1790, that there remained in the land office warrants in five thousand acre tracts to the amount of 250,000 to 300,000 acres, of which Donelson had offered the Blounts 15,000 acres.[58] As usual the "friendly services" of officials were most helpful. State Treasurer John Haywood loaned money and certificates from the treasury and delayed tax collection. Secretary of State James Glasgow, a close personal friend as well as business associate, issued warrants generously without caviling scrutiny. Reports of friends in Congress were informative. In turn, Blount, observing that entry-taker Armstrong was still under a public scrutiny which might discover the Blount accounts unpaid and that "we had drawn money from the Treasury," protected himself and friends by paying up the Blount debts. He did so in certificates, however, with the understanding that if the national assumption bill should be passed he might redeem the paid-in certificates at their depreciated value in order to cash them in for his own profit.[59]

[58] William Blount to John Gray Blount, April 17, 1790, in Blount Collection; John Gray Blount to John Strother (n.d.), *ibid.*, P.C. 905; certificate of George Doherty, April 9, 1790, *ibid.*, P.C. 883; land warrant of May 1, 1790, *ibid.*; Pitt County Deeds, Book M, 341; Craven County Deeds, Book 27, pp. 338, 339; Davidson County Deeds, Book E, 125, and Book 73, pp. 386, 429; Beaufort County Deeds, Book 6, p. 138, and Book 14, p. 134.

[59] William Blount to John Gray Blount, March 22, 26, April 17, 1790, in Blount Collection; Haywood–Glasgow–Hawkins–Blount correspondence, February–April, 1790, *ibid.*; Comptroller's Office Vouchers, *passim* (North Carolina State Department of Archives and History).

In early 1790, still another interest rivaled the land lure to the Blounts. This was speculation in money. The proposal for national assumption of state debts had filled North Carolina with swarms of money speculators, and upon meeting one of these—a buyer for a Northeastern syndicate—Blount at once conceived that "some advantageous Scheme of Certificate speculation might be fallen on." With state certificates selling for credit at two shillings to the pound and the possibility of redemption at eight shillings, or 300 per cent profit, Blount was intrigued. It was a complicated subject for speculation. Certificates issued for wartime supplies differed from those issued for soldiers' pay; certain issues, because of fraud, had been superseded by others; and selling price, of course, depended on whether or not the issue in question bore interest. The inevitable use of credit still further complicated the transactions. Nevertheless, despite conflicting reports, Blount was sure that a national assumption bill would pass, and he entered a partnership with Ben Sheppard in which the Blount firm would buy £10,000 worth of military certificates at two shillings per pound and instructed Congressman Williamson that "they must be included in the [assumption] Bill." From Cumberland, agent Robertson sent certificates collected on credit from the frontiersmen. The speculator also joined the Eastern syndicate's buyer in an arrangement in which "my Credit & his Money" were "equally and mutually beneficial to each other." [60] Thus William, John Gray, and the Blount firm were plunged into the craze of paper buying which was sweeping the nation in 1790. Their agent Gerrard traveled constantly collecting paper money. In the West, speculator

[60] Abishai Thomas to John Gray Blount, January 31, 1790, in Blount Collection; William Blount to *id.*, March 22, 26, 29, June 8, 1790, *ibid.*; Ben Sheppard to William Blount, April 25, 1790, *ibid.*; Thomas Stewart to John Gray Blount, March 30, 1790, *ibid.*

Absalom Tatum purchased paper from the uninformed frontiersmen for the well-informed Blounts. From New York Abishai Thomas and Hugh Williamson sent a stream of advice on Congressional trends and sold paper for the firm in the East.[61]

However absorbing were these multitudinous business affairs, Blount's keen interest in political events never lessened. Immediately after the state's adoption of the new government his attention was fixed on the elections to Congress. He observed with keen pleasure the success of his friends John Ashe, John Steele, Hugh Williamson, and John Sevier, who were among the state's first Congressmen, and his own defeat by Hawkins did not lessen —on Hawkins' part at least—their friendship. Indeed, it would seem that the possibility of a coveted Federal appointment in the West for his friend was early in the new Senator's mind. Immediately after laying the cession before Congress, he asked Blount to "write me freely and confidentially on any of your prospects, I have had occasion to name you once or twice in a manner as you deserve. We shall be embarrassed with the Indian business and shall want some very confidential man in that quarter." [62] Williamson too kept his friend informed on the progress of legislation on the new cession, and on possibilities for personal advancement. Therefore, by the end of March, Blount announced himself *"assured"* that he would be appointed governor of the ceded territory.[63]

[61] Thomas Blount to John Gray Blount, February 22, March 27, 1790, in Blount Collection; Abishai Thomas to id., March 12, May 5, 17, 1790, ibid.; Hugh Williamson to id., February 24, March 12, April 16, 1790, ibid.

[62] Benjamin Hawkins to William Blount, February 6, 1790, in Blount Collection.

[63] Hugh Williamson to John Gray Blount, April 6, 1790, ibid.; Archibald Maclaine to James Iredell, March 31, 1790, in McRee, *Life of Iredell*, II, 285–86.

This post had been in the speculator's mind at least since the state's cession in November, and, with his defeat for the national Senate, it became his principal ambition. The vast extent of the Western land he held for sale, the power of treaty-making vested in Federal officials, and the need to keep Western taxation low in his own interest, as well as a real interest in the West, were powerful motives in fixing his attention on the new post. Too, having been in the old Congress when the Ordinance of 1787 passed, he was familiar with the power and prestige conferred on a territorial governor, and Blount loved power. He had therefore watched with keen interest as Congress accepted the cession on April 2, 1790, and on May 26 established a government for the ceded area, cumbersomely termed "The Territory of the United States South of the River Ohio." [64]

The coveted prize, however, was not to be his without a struggle. Patrick Henry of Virginia, deep in land speculation, urged his own candidates. One of these was George Mason, the other, Henry's agent and friend, Joseph Martin. Mason, however, had no arresting military record and no connection with North Carolina. Martin had spent his adult life in the West and had given his best service for the preservation of peace and good relations with the Indians, but this very activity hurt his cause. With the approval of Henry, he had corresponded with the ominous Alexander McGillivray to placate that potent chieftain. These letters were now produced by his enemies and rivals, especially George Matthews of Georgia and Sevier, to support charges of treason. Furthermore, though a speculator himself, his efforts to bring peace to the West had

---

[64] Clarence E. Carter (ed. and comp.), *The Territorial Papers of the United States* (Washington, 1936), IV (*Southwest Territory*), 13–17, 18–19. (Hereinafter referred to as *Territorial Papers*.)

shown a regard for the Indians intolerable to many settlers and speculators. Hence, in spite of strenuous efforts
in his behalf by Edmund Randolph, R. H. Lee, William
Grayson, Theodorick Bland, and even Jefferson, the ex-
Indian agent was passed over.[65]

Two other formidable names appeared in opposition.
Anthony Wayne hungrily eyed "this immense and valuable country" as a "vastly superior" field for national
speculation and sought Congressman Edanus Burke's aid
in securing the appointment.[66] Meanwhile in the Territory,
one name led all the rest in popular appeal. A convention
called for the purpose besought Samuel Johnston's influence in securing the Western governorship for "the
Honorable John Severe." They assured the Senator "in
the Name of the People . . . that no other man upon the
Continante the Presidente of the United States (not excepted)—can give as general satisfaction to the People of
this Country in that office. . . ." [67] So likely did Sevier's
success seem that even North Carolina's Judge Spencer,
seeking appointment to a territorial bench, applied to him
for patronage.

To combat these rivals Blount mustered every resource.
He wrote Congressman Steele and frankly solicited aid.
From the Western country influential General Daniel
Smith also wrote to Congressmen in Blount's behalf. In

[65] Phelan, *History of Tennessee,* 148; Ramsey, *Annals,* 541; correspondence
of Grayson, Lee, Martin, and Henry, September, 1789–June, 1790, in Henry,
Patrick Henry, III, 387–95, 407–17, 420–22; Weeks, "Joseph Martin," *loc.
cit.,* 456–60, 465–69; Henry Knox to Joseph Martin, September 11, 1790, in
Draper Collection, 2XX36; Lyman Draper–William Martin correspondence,
May–July, 1846, *ibid.,* 3XX54 (2), 3XX55 (1), 3XX56 (2); Oliver Taylor,
Historic Sullivan (Bristol, 1909), 18.

[66] Anthony Wayne to Edanus Burke, June 4, 1789, in Wayne Manuscripts
(Pennsylvania Historical Society).

[67] Memorial of citizens of the ceded area, May 5, 1790, in Johnston Collection (Hayes Library, Edenton). A typed copy is in North Carolina State
Department of Archives and History.

the national capital, Ashe, Timothy Bloodworth, Hawkins, and Williamson united on his candidacy.[68] To meet charges of land speculation, Williamson wrote disarmingly to President Washington in his friend's behalf that "it is true that Mr. Blount has a considerable Quantity of Land within the ceded Territory, but he has none to the Southward of it, and he must be the more deeply interested in the Peace and Prosperity of the new Government. Perhaps it is because I have many Relations and some Land there, given me by the State, that I am the more anxious to see it prosper." [69]

Unlike Wayne, Blount was a native of the state which had ceded the land. Unlike Sevier, he was untainted by Franklinism and by Indian massacre. He had a military and a Federalist record, and he knew President Washington from Convention days, if not earlier. He was thoroughly familiar with Western affairs and leaders, and among the latter he was respected for his pro-Western activities in the assembly. His influence, therefore, in calming a turbulent and possibly Antifederal West would be considerable. Except for Johnston, who was silent, and Sevier, who was absent, he had the unanimous recommendation of his state's representatives in Congress. In short, his qualifications were impressive to the Administration, and he was on June 8, 1790, appointed governor of the Territory and superintendent of Indian affairs for the Southern department.[70] Named with him were surveyor Daniel

[68] William Blount to John Steele, April 18, 1790, in Wagstaff (ed.), *Papers of John Steele*, I, 57–58; *id.* to Daniel Smith, September 6, 1790, in Miscellaneous Manuscripts (Tennessee State Archives); Timothy Bloodworth to the President, June 5, 1790, in Carter (ed.), *Territorial Papers*, IV, 20–21; John B. Ashe to *id.*, June 5, 1790, *ibid.*, 22–23; Jefferson's memorandum [1790], *ibid.*, 23.

[69] Hugh Williamson to the President, May 28, 1790, in Carter (ed.), *Territorial Papers*, IV, 19–20.

[70] Whitaker, *Spanish-American Frontier*, 120–21; Ramsey, *Annals*, 541, 545–46.

Smith to be secretary, and David Campbell and John Mc-
Nairy to be judges. With both Smith and McNairy, especially the latter, Blount's relations had been close and
cordial.

The eagerly anticipated news of his appointment
reached the businessman at home about June 26, and he
and his friends rejoiced for various reasons. Steele was
happy, "not that I suppose the Office a great acquisition,
or that it will add any dignity to his character more than
he is otherwise entitled to, but that it will put him out of
the reach of, and raise him above his enemies. . . . I
conceive it a great point gained to our landholders, that
the business of an Indian boundary will fall into the hands
of a man, of all others the most proper." [71] Williamson's
mind was "relieved from any anxiety respecting our Western Territory . . . I am now only to consider how the
current of Migration shall best be turned towards the
Tennessee Government so . . . the value of our land may
be improved or increased." [72] Blount rejoiced "at it myself for I think it of great Importance to our Western
Speculations." [73] Apart from "being delivered from my
State Enemies," he regarded "the appointment *itself*" as
"truly important to me more so in my opinion than any
other in the Gift of the President could have been, the
Salary is handsome, and my Western Lands had become
so great an object to me that it had become absolutely necessary that I should go to the Western Country, to secure
them and perhaps my Presence might have enhanced there
Value.—I am sure my present appointment will." Even
his Senatorial defeat brightened in retrospect. "May it

[71] John Steele to John Gray Blount, July 10, 1790, in Blount Collection.
[72] Hugh Williamson to John Gray Blount, June 15, 1790, *ibid*.
[73] William Blount to John Gray Blount, June 6, 1790, *ibid*.

not be said that Jo. McDowell and his Friends have rendered me essential Service?" [74]

Exultantly, then, the speculator prepared to assume his new post and to develop its opportunities. His pride was justified; he had played his hand well to win his prize. At forty-one years of age, he found place, power, and profit —the credo of his life—at hand. The future was unlimited.

[74] William Blount to John Steele, July 10, 1790, in Wagstaff (ed.), *Papers of John Steele*, I, 67–70.

CHAPTER VII

APPRAISAL
AND ACCOMPLISHMENT

DESPITE FAIR PROSPECTS, the new appointee had problems to overcome before duties could be met. At home his wife wept and spoke of Indian perils and of the desolation of his absence, for she refused to take the children to the new and dangerous frontier. A dozen business deals required closing transactions. Money would be needed for the trip and to support his new dignity. Two good horses, saddles, bridles, portmanteau, clothing for himself and slave, and traveling money, all had to be acquired, and he, like most businessmen of that specie-scarce era, was "without a copper." Of knowledge of the legal necessities and procedures he was equally destitute, for although his commission arrived July 6, there was not a copy of the territorial act or of the Ordinance of 1787 to be had, nor advice on the procedure of qualifying or setting his government in motion.

Fearful lest he be ordered West too soon, and still shaken by recurring chills and fever, Blount attacked his problems energetically. To John Gray Blount went orders, backed by the prospect of a hard money salary, for a portmanteau to be ordered from Philadelphia, broadcloth and nankeen for his wardrobe, and "Toe cloth" and "milled drab" for his slave's. The horses and their equipage were also ordered, and elaborate plans made to raise cash for the trip. To close his varied accounts, Blount followed the judges on circuit to Hillsboro, Edenton, New Bern, and Wilmington, for although his legal business was small, the court sessions brought together the businessmen of the neighborhoods. He collected credits due and sold slaves to pay for his most pressing obligations, including those to state officials. He attempted by various means, including alterations in the map, to induce Wilson Blount to select his part of their joint Western land holdings so as to leave William Blount's clear for future operations; and for the same purpose he balanced the Blount land and financial accounts with other partners. The persuasive powers of John Gray were invoked to reconcile his wife to her husband's absence "so absolutely necessary to her Interest as well as her Friends." [1] With all these hurried preparations the speculator found time for another plunge in the certificate market, selling to other investors a part of those certificates sent to him by Robertson from Mero District, and exchanging the rest for paper likely to be assumed by the national government and therefore of greater potential value.[2]

During these busy weeks the new appointee, through Williamson in Congress, kept in contact with the Administration's New York negotiations with McGillivray. By the same means in August he obtained copies of the Congressional acts on his Territory and information on procedure for establishing his government. At Hillsboro he found time to engage the services of printer Robert Ferguson, who with George Roulstone, editor of the Fayetteville

---

[1] William Blount to John Gray Blount, September 5, 20, 1790, in Blount Collection; id. to Wilson Blount, July 30, 1790, ibid.

[2] Blount–Hogg correspondence, August–September, 1790, in Blount Collection.

Gazette, agreed to cross the mountains as soon as possible with their press.[3]

At length in early September, Blount began his trip westward, stopping at Governor Martin's Guilford County home in order to secure final confirmation of all his land titles in the form of grants signed by the governor. Here, however, he found that his oath of office would have to be taken before Federal officials and that instructions on territorial policy were needed from the Executive branch. The President, he learned from newspapers, was at Mount Vernon, so he turned northward,[4] first, however, sending his friend and aide Major George Farragut to Secretary Smith in the Territory with the latter's commission, and to Judge McNairy with a long-sought copy of the Ordinance of 1787. Farragut also carried a large sum of money to buy military certificates collected by James Robertson before the inauguration of the new government should raise their price.[5]

Meanwhile, Blount hurried northward down the long valleys of the Dan and the Staunton where record crops were moving, and the roads were crowded with cattle and wagonloads of corn, tobacco, and wheat on their way to Eastern markets. The businessman's eye noted all, and his pen duly reported crops and prices to his brother John Gray at Washington.

On September 17 the governor-designate arrived at Alexandria and spent the following day and night at Mount Vernon. His aristocratic tastes were charmed with the famous household. It was, he reported, "the most agreeable

[3] George F. Bentley, "Printers and Printing in the Southwest Territory, 1790–1796," in *Tennessee Historical Quarterly,* VIII (1949), 333–34.

[4] William Blount to John Gray Blount, November 10, 1790, in Blount Collection.

[5] William Blount to Daniel Smith, September 6, 1790, in Miscellaneous Manuscripts.

Place I ever saw," though the General himself somewhat
daunted the businessman, who found him "too awful, for
I verily believe he is awful as a God," although "great
and amiable indeed admirable." The approving visitor
found Mrs. Washington "certainly one of the most agreeable Ladies of the whole World," Major Bushrod Washington "handsome genteel, attentive," his wife "handsome
and elegant," and even Martha's grandchildren "very
promising." For the house, crops, and tree-shaded grounds
he had warm praise, especially for "the Poplar of the
Poe of which Ovid sings many hundred years past." The
deeply impressed but still inquisitive taxpayer confessed
that the "Style and Manner of his living surpasses what
I have before seen particularly in Dignity and I suppose
I saw him living on his own Funds, not those of the
United States in fact Major Jackson so informed me."
Blount also reported on the probability of the President's
trip to the South and the most likely route, adding "I
want that Molsey and my Children should see him for
certainly such another Man will not again appear in there
day." [6]

Referred by the President to Attorney General Randolph for induction into office, Blount returned from
Mount Vernon to Alexandria, where he met James Iredell,
now a member of the Supreme Court, and from him took
the oath of office on September 20, 1790. Thus relieved
of the necessity of seeking Randolph in Philadelphia, the
governor paid a second visit to the President, and on September 22 took up his journey to the seat of his government. [7] As he traveled the long road following the Great
Trading Path of colonial days through Winchester, Staun-

6 William Blount to John Gray Blount, September 20, 1790, in Blount Collection.
7 William Blount to John Gray Blount, September 22, 1790, ibid.; Carter
(ed.), Territorial Papers, IV, 24.

ton, Botetourt Court House, and Chiswell's Mines, Blount reviewed the results of his Northern detour. Besides incurring further expense, this northward swing had changed his plans, for he could no longer hope to carry out his earlier program of returning from the Territory to attend the Carolina November assembly and to visit his family. On the other hand, he had learned that his powers were greater than he had anticipated. As Indian superintendent he was responsible for all Indian affairs in the Southwest. He was to name and commission all civil officers from constable up, and all military officers except generals, whom he would nominate to the President. Overall direction of civil and military affairs was his; he licensed the politically potent lawyers, and he was answerable only to the President, whose instructions as to policy left the governor wide latitude. Never in his palmiest days in the assembly had he wielded such power.

The tedious journey, made five days longer by his slave's illness, was at last ended on October 10, when the new governor arrived at William Yancey's house on the upper Holston. Then, after a brief pause to rest and forward word of his arrival, he moved south to the home of William Cobb, in the fork of the Holston and Watauga rivers, which was to constitute his temporary capital, and here his administration began. Cobb was a well-to-do North Carolina immigrant of the late 1760's, of considerable influence and great hospitality. A leader since King's Mountain days, he had formerly been a close associate of Richard Caswell's, and, until the Franklin episode, a friend of Sevier's. His white-oak log home contained nine rooms, and the governor, made comfortable in a chamber with glass windows and fireplace, conducted state business, entertained, or read Reverend John Trusler's *Principles of Politeness* in the atmosphere of dignified affluence which he always sought to maintain.[8]

He learned much as he moved through the formalities of establishing his government, as he met the citizenry, studied the country, and heard from first hand of conditions formerly only reported by hearsay. Ever quick in appraising situations, he discovered in his new realm that variance of theory and fact, that contrast of the potential and the actual which pervaded the Territory. In theory his government ruled from the mountain crests to the Mississippi and from the thirty-fifth to the thirty-sixth-and-a-half degrees of latitude—an area comprising nearly 43,000 square miles of territory; and as Indian superintendent his authority presumably extended southward to the thirty-first parallel. In practice, however, the crown of Spain had excellent claims up to 32°28′ and others, less solid but far more ambitious, extending to the Tennessee River; and one of His Catholic Majesty's servants was making extensive plans to enforce all these claims. The Spaniard's concern was, however, in 1790 largely anticipatory, for the new governor's writ ran chiefly in a narrow strip of country from the Virginia line some 150 miles southwest to the Little Tennessee. This settled area, extending in breadth from 25 to 60 miles, was bounded on the south by high and Indian-claimed mountains, on the west by the savages' hunting grounds, on the north and northwest by the Clinch and Cumberland mountains. In the narrow valleys of the Holston, Nolichucky, French Broad, and Little rivers dwelt the majority of the Territory's population, about 28,000 people. Over 100 wilderness miles to the west lay the other settlements, a population

[8] Reverend P. L. Cobb, "William Cobb—Host of Governor Blount," in *Tennessee Historical Magazine*, IX (1926), 241–63, *passim*; Samuel C. Williams (ed.), *Early Travels in the Tennessee Country* (Johnson City, 1928), 299; William Blount to John Gray Blount, October 20, 1790, in Blount Collection.

of between 6,000 and 7,000 more, strung out along the
Cumberland for a distance of about 30 miles.[9] Between
these settlements, and indeed throughout the remainder
of the Territory, stretched wilderness pervaded by and
legally guaranteed to a savage enemy.

Moreover, even this restricted settlement overran its
authorized boundary. The legally just but practically in-
judicious treaty line of Hopewell in the east ran a few miles
east of Greeneville, and in the west followed in general the
watershed south of the Cumberland River, thereby slash-
ing deeply through the areas of habitation. By its terms,
towns, farms, forts, whole counties lay in Indian territory, and even the cession extorted from the Indians by
Franklinites could not contain the ever-widening rivulets
of settlement. To the westward, fairly compact habitation
extended to the Clinch, and more than a few intrepid homeseekers had pushed beyond this stream to make their clearings between it and Cumberland Mountain. To the south,
although denied to white settlement by the 1783 land act,
the rich acres south of the French Broad had drawn land
seekers since that act had opened western North Carolina.
By 1790 these settlers had pushed all the way to the Little
Tennessee, the now-repudiated Franklin-Cherokee line of
1786, and their cabins rose but five short miles from the
Cherokee's "Beloved Town" of Chota. To the Cumberland settlements the Hopewell agreements had been more
generous, but here too the lengthening string of cabins
along the Duck and its tributary creeks invited savage
wrath.[10] For Blount the heavily invested speculator, such
expansion of settlement was the life of all his hopes. For
Blount the governor, it was a challenge to his powers and a
never-ending source of Indian warfare. That distant au-

[9] Ramsey, *Annals*, 544, 545, 547–48; Williams, *Franklin*, 268–69; Williams
(ed.), *Early Travels*, 412; Carter (ed.), *Territorial Papers*, IV, 81.
[10] Haywood, *History of Tennessee*, 263–65; Ramsey, *Annals*, 549.

thority which had drawn and guaranteed the restrictive if oft-ignored line of Hopewell now sent the speculator-governor to enforce it.

The same antithesis of fact and theory occurred in the Territory's economy. The fertile valleys, gentle hills, and enriching streams bespoke a thriving agrarian economy. But in the east the towering mountains from which the streams flowed defied most efforts at transport to Eastern buyers, while the westward-flowing Tennessee slipped between miles of Indian-infested banks before it could lead to any market. Boxed in their valleys, the eastern farmers of the Territory looked to the Shenandoah Valley as the export route for their wheat, corn, hemp, pork, beef, or tobacco. Even so, the route was long, tedious, and costly. The same heavy expense of transport added perhaps a third to the cost of their imports of manufactured goods from Baltimore or Philadelphia. Similarly, in isolated Mero the inviting Cumberland River led but to a Spanish Mississippi and a precarious market at Natchez or New Orleans. The dry goods, ironmongery, glassware, saddlery, and spices that stocked the shelves of Lardner Clark and other merchants of the Nashville settlement had traversed an even longer route. From Baltimore or Philadelphia they had been packed overland to Pittsburgh, thence down the barge-laden Ohio to the Cumberland, up which they were laboriously moved by oar or pole to the little settlement on the bluffs. Thus, blocked in the east by mountains which roadbuilders had not yet conquered, and in the west by distance and the jealous Spaniard, the territorial farmer lacked an easy means of export, a reasonable source of supplies, or a currency with which to traffic. His demands for all three were not the least of his plaints to the new governor.[11]

[11] A. P. Whitaker, *The Mississippi Question, 1795–1803* (New York, 1934), 9–14.

Likewise, divergence marked the Territory's political scene. According to their leaders' votes at Fayetteville, these Westerners had sought cession to the United States; a national governor, then, should find abundant welcome. But to many whose voices were not heard at Fayetteville the United States meant a Hopewell; it meant surrender to the Indians; it meant subserviency to the Spanish on the Mississippi. It meant taxation without defence or self-determination, a proconsul's rule in the interest of the Indian. Inflamed by constant Indian threat, the wounds of Franklin, covered but fresh, yet racked the Territory. In Washington District resentment kindled against Mero; in the latter area, jealousy burned against the older, larger, dominant settlements to the east. On the Cumberland Robertson led unchallenged, at least on the surface, but on the Holston and French Broad the Sevier and John Tipton forces vied for control, and neither sought the leadership of Blount. For the Tiptonians, beaten in the fight for cession, well knew of the old Sevier-Blount entente, while Sevierites, whose hopes had risen after 1789, chafed under any leadership other than that of their "Nollachucky Jack." [12]

Resentful, Indian-harassed, factional, suspicious—the territorial citizenry heard of their new governor's arrival, and they awaited with cold and pragmatic judgment his first decisions.

The object of this scrutiny found his first weeks both busy and unexpectedly harmonious. He had apprehended, and even more than once been warned of, the probable

[12] Roosevelt, *Winning of the West,* III, Pt. 1, 93; Whitaker, *Spanish-American Frontier,* 124–26; Williams, *Franklin,* 346–48; memorial of citizens of the ceded area, May 5, 1790, in Johnston Collection.

hostility of a jealous Sevier and his followers. But the ex-governor of Franklin proved a good politician. Though feeling some resentment at Blount's neutral Franklin attitude and keenly desiring the territorial governorship, he yet realized the necessities of the situation. On his part, Blount soon recognized the vast personal popularity of the Indian-fighter, and also the fact that the majority of Western leaders were ex-Franklinites. A political alliance thus developed to supplement the older economic connection, and Sevier, according to Blount, became "open and clear in his Declarations in my favour." [13]

As the governor proceeded to organize his administration the effects of the alliance became evident. Though old officeholders under North Carolina, especially those of long service, were generally retained regardless of faction, the majority of appointees were Sevierites. For the important colonelcies in the militia Blount named three Franklinites: Landon Carter, Gilbert Christian, and Stockley Donelson. He had suspected the influential Carter of enmity, but, finding him reported as "much my friend and perfectly pleased with my appointment," the governor chose him for the Washington colonelcy over Tipton. This blow the fiery Tipton appeared to accept, but he declined appointment as senior justice of the peace and bided his time.

Meanwhile, the governor and Judge Campbell traveled through the four counties (Washington, Sullivan, Greene, and Hawkins) which constituted Washington District. Stopping at each county seat, Blount reconstituted the county under the new authority, read North Carolina's cession act and proclamation, his commission, and Congress' organic laws for the Territory. He then named officers,

<hr />

[13] William Blount to John Gray Blount, October 20, November 7, 10, 1790, in Blount Collection.

who took their oaths before Campbell. Amid addresses of welcome and polished replies the governor was delighted with "the Honors, Respect and Attention" shown him, accounts of which were duly relayed to Carolina.[14] True, there were disappointed office seekers and some dissatisfaction, and a petition appeared protesting his appointments. But the governor disdained the "Whisper of Dissatisfaction from . . . some contemptable Tiptonites and only the most contemptable Part of his Party remain attached to him the more sensible having entirely abandoned the Party." The politically orthodox, on the other hand, continued to be rewarded. Sevier, Carter, Charles Robertson, John Chisholm, William Cobb, Joseph Hardin, James Hays, Thomas Amis, James White, Francis Ramsey, and George Farragut were among the many appointed whose fame had long rested upon or would soon overspread the land. One young protégé, Archibald Roane, was named county attorney (in Greene County), and his fellow attorney, Andrew Jackson, was soon to receive even more in Mero District.[15]

At the same time there were other interesting decisions to be made. The location of the capital, a prerogative of the governor, was arousing the liveliest interest, not only among large speculators in both East and West, but also among the humbler woodsmen, whom some of their descendants were to regard as unsophisticated in such complexities. Through their associate, Secretary Daniel Smith, speculator James Mountflorence and others brought heavy pressure for the selection of a site in Mero District. On the other hand, the Indians whose land claims chiefly

[14] William Blount to John Gray Blount, October 20, 1790, *ibid.*; *State Gazette of North Carolina*, December 17, 1790; William Blount to John Sevier and others, November 8, 1790, in Draper Collection, 4XX20; *ibid.*, 11DD89a.

[15] William Blount to John Gray Blount, November 10, 1790, in Blount Collection; Ramsey, *Annals*, 553; Carter (ed.), *Territorial Papers*, IV, 432–38.

clashed with white settlement were the Cherokee, and their principal towns lay closer to Washington District. In addition to this, the governor's own land on Emory River held a strong attraction for him. His decision was delayed, however, pending the arrival of his instructions from Philadelphia along with an Administration decision on the location of Federal troops in the Territory. Meanwhile, the advantages to be expected from landholdings at the capital and Indian trading center caused a wild inflation of land prices at likely sites.[16]

Sevier, Robertson, and their chief at this time began to plan for the financial rewards of co-operation. Landon Carter, Edmond Williams, and Sevier had been named in 1783 to a board to issue Carolina Revolutionary military certificates. These had not been issued, and Sevier and the governor now planned to issue them as of the date they were originally supposed to have been issued, and thus accrue seven years' interest. In addition, the certificates would be so worded as to assure assumption by the United States at their face value according to the Assumption Act of 1790. Sevier's son was to hold them until John Gray Blount sent paper from North Carolina to buy them at the depreciated price of four shillings on the dollar, thus both satisfying the uninformed claimants and affording a handsome profit to the speculators. With North Carolina's querulous assembly over, John Gray Blount could easily borrow the cash from his friends the collectors of taxes or from the treasurer.[17]

General Sevier presented other alluring prospects to the governor. Landon Carter, as entry-taker for Washing-

[16] Hugh Williamson to John Gray Blount, August 3, 1790, in Blount Collection; William Blount to *id.*, November 10, 1790, *ibid.*; James C. Mountflorence to Daniel Smith, August 16, 1790, in "Papers of Daniel Smith," in *American Historical Magazine,* VI (1901), 217–18.

[17] William Blount to John Gray Blount, November 10, 1790, in Blount Collection.

ton County under a 1779 act, had in his office unlocated entries by Sevier for some 30,000 acres of land, entered at fifty shillings per one hundred acres. If grants could be obtained for these from North Carolina, they could be located on the rich lands south of the French Broad and sold for ten pounds per one hundred acres, a handsome profit. The only difficulty was that of obtaining the Carolina governor's assent, inasmuch as the entries were legally limited to Washington County.[18] On the other hand, there were advantages to this scheme, as there was no money to advance and Blount's name was not to appear.

At the same time, official duties were insistent. Blount realized the necessity of formally commencing Indian relations, but could do nothing before the arrival of his instructions, and these, sent via Virginia, had miscarried. Meanwhile, the establishment of the Mero counties was imperative. Sevier had returned to Congress, and Judge Campbell had crossed the mountains for judicial conferences in the East, but despite these absences and bitter snowy weather the governor on November 27 took up his journey to the Cumberland settlements. His retinue of friendly Indians, twenty-five mounted riflemen, and as many prominent citizens was impressive.[19]

The entourage was hampered by weather and the precautions necessary in crossing the Indian country, but mid-December found the governor in Nashville. Here, with the same ceremony as in the eastern district, he reconstituted Mero District and its counties (Davidson, Sumner, and Tennessee), named civil and military officers, and swore

[18] *Ibid.*; Abernethy, *Frontier to Plantation,* 173–78.
[19] William Blount to John Gray Blount, November 27, 1790, in Blount Collection; Henry Knox to Edmund Randolph, September 6, 1790, in Palmer and McRae (eds.), *Virginia State Papers,* V, 206; *id.* to Richard Henry Lee, December 20, 1790, *ibid.,* 232–33; William Blount to James Iredell, November 17, 1790, in Charles E. Johnson Collection (North Carolina State Department of Archives and History).

Daniel Smith and John McNairy into office, after which the latter gave the necessary oaths to the other appointees. As in the eastern counties, these officers represented the past and future leaders of their region. Without the complication of a Tipton faction, the governor was able to follow unhampered his own and Robertson's selections. Stockley Donelson, Sampson Williams, the two Robertsons, the Winchesters, William Cage, and Robert Hays were only a few of the many associates rewarded. Andrew Jackson, David Allison, Howell Tatum, J. C. Mountflorence, and Dr. James White, all close associates, received the coveted attorneys' licenses.[20]

The governor's visit was short. He did not travel in Sumner or Tennessee counties but performed all the ceremonies at Nashville. Yet his eight-day stay allowed time for contacts and observation. He visited James Robertson's nearby estate of four thousand rich acres in the Cumberland Bend and observed the general's grist and saw mills and blooded stock. In Nashville itself he inspected Lardner Clark's store and with him discussed merchandising problems; also his attention was drawn to Robertson's town lots and the other rich, black Cumberland lands with their limestone outcroppings.

The inhabitants of this fertile and undeveloped country likewise received a close inspection as Blount and the citizens regarded each other with great interest and considerable curiosity. The inhabitants beheld a courteous and dignified figure. The well-cut coat, the lace, the buckled shoes, the polished phrase and manner bespoke a foreigner; but the polite attention, optimism, and affability denoted a real interest in them and their country. The more discerning noted a reserve, a limit to conversational topics, assurances given but not promises, acquiescence made but

[20] Carter (ed.), *Territorial Papers*, IV, 438–42.

not commitment. The frank bonhomie of a Sevier was notably absent.

The governor on his part saw a society in transition. The inhabitants, who but lately had borne an unfavorable reputation for drunkenness, brawling, and the cropping of official ears, were now evolving a society much like that of the envied Eastern district. Fights and brawls occurred less often. Buckskin clothes were disappearing in favor of Eastern dress and clubbed hair, once seen only at the inns. Religion and education were beginning to soften social mores. The Presbyterians' stern, learned, and precise Thomas Craighead, a graduate of Princeton, was well established by now in Spring Hill meeting house. The Methodists, after using the jail as a meeting place, had recently built their new church, and a scattering of Baptists, Quakers, and Moravians gave further depth to the ranks of religion.

As yet, of course, the classroom but indifferently complemented the pulpit. Pastor Craighead conducted classes in addition to his ministerial duties, and a few other individuals somewhat more learned than the average kept more or less desultory classes, but the average child's education was the familiar fireside learning. Of higher educational aims, intent still substituted for achievement despite North Carolina's legal establishment of Davidson Academy, presided over by Craighead; and those who dreamed of advanced learning envisioned the Reverend Samuel Doak's Martin Academy in Washington County, or, in wilder flights of fancy, sojourns in Philadelphia or Princeton.

Concurrently with social change ran economic diversity. The increasing number of saw- and gristmills and iron works presaged a diversion from the all-pervading agriculture and hunting. The mounting population, the increasing number of stores and the growing variety of merchandise in them, the plans and speculations concerning a livelihood gained through special services or artisanship—all these foretold a more varied and more complex economic future.[21] In short, the observant governor saw a frontier society on the eve of transformation.

Nevertheless, it was in 1790 a rude society, a far outpost of civilization. Each week brought accounts of violence and death, ravishment and pillage on the Kentucky Road or on the thin line of communication with the lower Holston country. Fire and the tomahawk were constant visitors to the scattered homesteads along the Cumberland and its tributaries. The "station" or half-forted cabin was the rule, and Nashville itself boasted of but two formal "houses." The grim days of '81 and '82 were over; but the peril was still omnipresent, and no man knew how soon would come the blow. Many were discouraged and took the road for the East; more were hopeful for better days. A few, the leaders, planned for those days, and with these few the speculator-governor, the owner of thousands of acres of Cumberland and western Tennessee lands, was often in conference. In eight short days he sampled thoroughly the far-Western mind.

Circumstances, however, now called the executive to the East. The long-awaited Indian instructions surely must have arrived, and the Indian problem was, as it remained, the keystone of all policy. With his party, therefore, Blount left Mero District and took the cold and dangerous road to the East, arriving at Cobb's on December 29, 1790.

Several disappointments met him on his return. The complete absence of letters from home was disheartening. A protégé sent to North Carolina to obtain the strategic

[21] Whitaker, *Mississippi Question*, 10–22, *passim*; Abernethy, *Frontier to Plantation*, 144–63.

surveyor's position had fallen ill and failed in his mission. A quarrel was brewing with Virginia over the Territory's northern border. Complaints were rising over the persistent practice of the North Carolina land office of issuing grants for land south of the French Broad.[22] William Peery of Maryland, third of the territorial judges, had not appeared, nor was his whereabouts known. Orders from Philadelphia instructed the governor to hold a treaty with the Cherokee, but only within the framework of the Hopewell agreements and for the principal purpose of checking the Tennessee Yazoo Company's project for settlement at Muscle Shoals.[23]

Some Indian agreement was, however, indispensable. Although trouble was brewing in their quarter, the Creeks were as yet quiescent under McGillivray's New York treaty of 1790; likewise the usually friendly Chickasaw and Choctaw were no immediate problem. The Cherokee, however, posed an imminent threat. This tribe of some two or three thousand warriors had been divided since the Revolution, and the seceding band, the Chickamauga, proved the most vigorous and incessant enemies of the advancing whites. Attacks from their five towns, located about one hundred miles below the mouth of the Holston River, had been fierce and incessant since 1782. By 1791 the enmity of both of these Cherokee factions was increased. The flood of immigration following the 1783 land law carried white cabins deep into Indian hunting lands. The Franklin treaties excited the savages further, especially when coupled with the appearance of speculators on the Bend of the Tennessee River. Reassured somewhat

[22] William Blount to Governor Martin, January 22, 1791, in Governors' Papers; Blount–Martin–Jefferson correspondence, April–October, 1792, in Carter (ed.), *Territorial Papers*, IV, 142–43, 155–56, 164–66, 191–93.

[23] John McNairy to Thomas Jefferson, March 7, 1791, in Carter (ed.), *Territorial Papers*, IV, 49; Henry Knox to the President, March 10, 1791, *ibid.*, 50–52.

by the Congressional commissioners at Hopewell, the Cherokee were dismayed the more by the complete negation of that treaty by the rising white tide. In addition, the Georgia grants to the three Yazoo companies in 1789 and the activities of James O'Fallon, the South Carolina Company's agent, throughout 1790 had deeply disturbed the Federal government, the Spanish, and the savages. Therefore, the Indian defeat of General Josiah Harmar's expedition in the Northwest in October presented to the resentful Cherokee an inducement to chastise and restrain the invader in the Southwest as well. Already sporadic Indian harassment was increasing, and informed people both within and outside the Territory anticipated a general attack.[24]

Blount, therefore, hastened to prepare for a treaty. He dispatched Major Robert King, United States agent to the Cherokee, to that nation requesting a meeting on May 31, 1791, at the mouth of the French Broad, then busied himself in preparations for the treaty. To Secretary of War Henry Knox he wrote a detailed argument in favor of scrapping the Hopewell agreements altogether and of obtaining further Indian cessions, to be paid for by the annuity of one thousand dollars which Knox had proposed merely as a gift to insure Indian favor. The lands he suggested for purchase were in the Muscle Shoals area, the object of both Zachariah Cox's Tennessee Yazoo company and his own earlier project.[25] His careful estimates of the expenses of the treaty meeting and the method of payment were at once accepted by the Administration. Meanwhile, Major King returned with a report that both

[24] Mary Mitchell to Governor Shelby, May 1, 1793, in Draper Collection, 11DD19c; Ramsey, *Annals*, 552, 557, 561, 562; Haywood, *History of Tennessee*, 269–70; Weeks, "Joseph Martin," *loc. cit.*, 432–36, 442–65.

[25] Henry Knox to the President, March 10, 1791, in Carter (ed.), *Territorial Papers*, IV, 50–52; Haskins, "Yazoo Land Companies," *loc. cit.*, 80.

the Upper Towns led by Hanging Maw and the Lower Towns under Little Turkey were disposed to negotiate. As the weeks passed, however, problems increased. Andrew Pickens of South Carolina, angry with Blount over their clashes at Hopewell, warned the Cherokee against him as the worst governor possible, pointing out "that he loved land, and would have all their lands." [26] At the same time, hostile Indian traders worked against the governor's aims so that rumors swept the tribes that he was luring them to be massacred, and Blount found it necessary to send Robertson into the nation with assurances of benevolence.[27]

While working for the treaty, Blount by no means abandoned his many business interests either in his old home or his new. He followed the certificate market closely through his brother John Gray and through Ashe and Steele in Congress. In land operations, Robertson was sent forth on a surveying expedition, and the governor, deeply impressed with the richness of Cumberland soil, but acting more and more often through intermediaries to escape criticism, continued to purchase military warrants and otherwise to acquire acreage.[28] He also returned to an earlier enthusiasm by buying an interest in the well-established and profitable ironworks of Colonel James King and John Sevier.[29] He continued to give thought to the location of his capital and about this time decided in favor of White's Fort near the junction of the Holston and the French Broad, provided that, on examination, the treaty site proved satisfactory. The advantages of this

---

[26] Ramsey, *Annals*, 544; "General Lincoln's Journal," in Massachusetts Historical Society *Collections*, 3d ser. (Boston and Cambridge, 1825–49), V, 171–72; Pickering Papers, LIX, 15 (Massachusetts Historical Society).

[27] Ramsey, *Annals*, 554; Haywood, *History of Tennessee*, 269.

[28] Draper Collection, 32S374; Tennessee County Deeds, *passim*; Sumner County Deeds, *passim*; Knox County Deeds, Book A, I, *passim*.

[29] Taylor, *Historic Sullivan*, 153; *American Historical Magazine*, V (1900), 204; Whitaker, *Mississippi Question*, 18.

site were several, both in public utility and in the governor's ownership of land in the neighborhood.[30]

Too, there were official duties besides preparations for the treaty. Elijah Robertson, pursuing a fugitive debtor into West Florida, was furnished with a letter of introduction to Governor Gayoso. In February, Blount named Andrew Jackson attorney general of Mero District and William Cocke to the same office in Washington District. He also recommended Robertson and Sevier for the brigadier generalships of the two districts, which posts they received from the President. A long list of minor appointments consumed time but contributed political strength.[31]

More difficult tasks than patronage also pressed. Congress had not provided for the 1790 census-taking in the Territory, and a system had to be worked out through the sheriffs. Also, Secretary of State Thomas Jefferson, in compliance with a resolution of Congress, was determining the amount of unallocated land within the Territory. Blount and Governor Martin in Carolina were both enlisted for this task, and the former ordered returns made from the old land offices of Washington and Sullivan counties as well as from the two Armstrong offices.[32]

At the same time, the perseverance of Zachariah Cox and his associates continued to cause at least official concern. Despite three warning proclamations by Washington, the promoter and thirty-one others on March 26 left the

[30] Abernethy, *Frontier to Plantation,* 53; deed of James White and William Blount, September 6, 1791, in Tennessee File (State Land Office, Raleigh); William Blount to John Gray Blount, November 10, 1790, in Blount Collection.

[31] Carter (ed.), *Territorial Papers,* IV, 442–44; William Blount to Governor Gayoso, March 8, 1791, in Papeles de Cuba (translated, typed copy in Lawson McGhee Library); Ramsey, *Annals,* 543–44.

[32] Thomas Jefferson to William Blount, March 12, 26, 1791, in Thomas Jefferson Papers (Division of Manuscripts, Library of Congress); Blount circular, March 7, 1791, in Carter (ed.), *Territorial Papers,* IV, 49–50; William Blount to Thomas Jefferson, July 17, 1791, *ibid.,* 69–70.

mouth of the French Broad to make their attempt at settlement at the Shoals. Though Blount knew of but three of his citizens being in the party, two of these were ex-Franklinites, of whom one, James Hubbard, had a most violent and unsavory record in dealing with Indians. The governor was therefore deeply concerned over the effect of the expedition on the forthcoming treaty negotiations and willingly followed instructions to discourage the prospective settlements and to bring legal action if necessary. Sentiment in the Territory, however, was strongly in favor of Cox's project, and Blount, purposely or otherwise, failed to use effective legal restraint on the settlers in time to prevent their departure.[33]

Caution was the more necessary since another battle with popular feeling was simultaneously in progress. The Administration having decided to mount another expedition against the Indians in the Northwest, Blount was instructed to raise men under Sevier to join General Arthur St. Clair at Fort Washington in June or July. The governor was much interested in the success of this Northwestern expedition since if all went well a fort was to be established at the Muscle Shoals, and after the expected victory in the North he was sure of a sizeable diversion of troops to his Territory.[34] Most Southwesterners, however, felt that excessive attention was devoted to their favored brethren to the northward while they themselves were ignored in their Indian-infested misery. The savage threat

[33] William Blount to Daniel Smith, April 17, 1791, in Philip M. Hamer (ed.), "Letters of Governor William Blount," East Tennessee Historical Society's *Publications*, IV (1932), 123–25; *id.* to James Robertson, September 3, 1791, in "Robertson Correspondence," *loc. cit.*, I, 192–93; Lowrie and Clark (eds.), *State Papers, Indian*, I, 112–13, 114–17; Haskins, "Yazoo Land Companies," *loc. cit.*, 80.

[34] Randolph C. Downes, "Indian Affairs in the Southwest Territory, 1790–1796," in *Tennessee Historical Magazine*, 2d ser., III (1937), 240, 242–43; William Blount to James Robertson, September 21, 1791, in Carter (ed.), *Territorial Papers*, IV, 82.

at home brought constant anxiety, increased by the distasteful militia service and the memory of the disaster of Harmar, in which a number of Tennesseans had been involved. The governor therefore found himself hard put to raise the men. His orders were, perforce, mingled with moral and economic appeals:

It is hoped that this Requisition of three hundred and thirty two Men will not be thought oppressive when it is recollected that the people of this territory pay no Public Taxes, when it is recollected that they are exempt from paying the Opperation of the Act imposing a duty of nine Cents per Gallon on Whiskey and other distilled Spirits and I have not the least doubt but the President believed when he gave the Order that the Men in so remote a back Country would readily turn out voluntarily for the Bounty, Pay & Clothing which are offered and well he might so believe since the Price offered is much more than can be obtained in Money for hard labour for that Space of Time. These Troops are to go to the relief and aid of our neighbors of Kentucky and to love your neighbors as yourself is one of the first of the Christian virtues. What is promised on the part of the United States will be faithfully performed. There will be no putting soldiers off with paper money or certificates for the United States are in Cash and want not Credit.[35]

However, the response to these arguments, even when they had been reinforced by a draft of men, continued to be reluctant, and the governor willingly turned over to Sevier the unpopular tasks of enlistment and equipment. His excuse for this—that preparations for the treaty absorbed his own time—was by no means unjustified. Small parties of savages appeared at Cobb's to confer, and policy dictated that they be given attention and presents. The Chickamauga were relatively quiet at the moment, although carrying on attacks against the pro-white Chickasaw; however, the Cherokee were alarmed and uneasy over the proposed treaty and still delayed coming. The Creeks, now torn by the rival leadership of William Augustus

[35] William Blount to Colonel Kennedy, May 21, 1791 (Blount Mansion, Knoxville, Tennessee). A photostatic copy is in the Lawson McGhee Library.

Bowles and McGillivray and instigated by the Spanish, repudiated the New York treaty and recommenced attacks, especially on the exposed Cumberland settlers.[36]

As the treaty time approached, therefore, Blount devoted more and more time to preparations for obtaining the best possible terms. Joseph Martin, despite the suspicions of the settlers, joined Robertson in "endeavors to put the Indians in the proper way of Thinking" preliminary to the negotiations. From the East Hawkins warned the governor that the principal aggressors since Hopewell had been the whites, and urged that he not seek too great a cession. Williamson likewise felt that the Administration would be satisfied with a moderate acquisition. McGillivray, in accordance with his promise at New York, advised the Cherokee to treat, provided the whites would promise to cease their speculative purchases. On the other hand, speculators and Western officials argued that if possible the three hundred squatter families south of the French Broad should have their holdings legalized and that sufficient further land should be obtained, if at all possible, to include the routes between Cumberland and East Tennessee. Knox, in response to Blount's suggestions along this line, appears to have written new instructions allowing more latitude to the negotiator.[37]

At length, charged with various advice and instructions

[36] Henry Knox to Arthur St. Clair, August 11, 1791, in Lowrie and Clark (eds.), *State Papers, Indian,* I, 181; William Blount to Daniel Smith, April 17, 1791, in Hamer (ed.), "Letters," *loc. cit.,* 123–25; A. V. Goodpasture, "Indian Wars and Warriors of the Old Southwest, 1730–1807," in *Tennessee Historical Magazine,* IV (1918), 178; Ramsey, *Annals,* 552, 553, 557.

[37] William Blount to Joseph Martin, June 6, 1791, in Hamer (ed.), "Letters," *loc. cit.,* 125; Benjamin Hawkins to William Blount, March 10, 1791, in Roosevelt, *Winning of the West,* III, Part 1, 255–56; Hugh Williamson to John Gray Blount, August 15, 22, 1790, in Blount Collection; Alexander McGillivray to Governor Miró, August 28, 1791, in Papeles de Cuba; Henry Knox to the President, March 10, 1791, in Carter (ed.), *Territorial Papers,* IV, 50–52; William Blount to Secretary Knox, July 2, 1791 (excerpt), in Lowrie and Clark (eds.), *State Papers, Indian,* I, 628.

and balanced between ambition and anxiety, the governor
departed in June, 1791, for the treaty ground at White's
Fort. Here again delay paralyzed affairs as John Watts
and the Bloody Fellow, perhaps the most influential Cherokee chiefs, still held back, and Martin's utmost exertions
were necessary to urge them on. Meanwhile, Colonels Isaac
Shelby and Thomas Kennedy arrived from Kentucky with
such harrowing tales of Cherokee atrocities and such demands for action that a volunteer retaliatory force rose
and only with great difficulty was restrained, not by
the governor, who lacked the influence, but by the all-
important militia officers.[38]

But at last the many difficulties were overcome and
some twelve hundred Indians had arrived at the treaty
ground. Disappointed by the absence of the Chickamauga,
Blount nevertheless realized that enough Cherokee were
present to formulate a binding treaty. His love of ceremony and ritual was in keeping with Indian tastes, and
it was given free rein. On a bank of the Tennessee (then
called the Holston) and shaded by giant trees, a marquee
was erected. Under it sat the governor in full dress with
sword and military hat, flanked by his uncovered civil and
military officers. Behind these stood the knots of curious
citizenry whose homes lay about the neighborhood of the
fort. Before the marquee were grouped the Indian braves,
resplendent in eagle feathers and other finery. In the front
rank the older chiefs and the medicine men, in more somber dress, eyed the splendor of the governor-superintendent.
James Armstrong, who claimed familiarity with the eti-
quette of European courts, acted as master of ceremonies.
One by one in order of age the chiefs were introduced to
Armstrong by an interpreter, and Armstrong then pre-

---

[38] William Blount to Joseph Martin, June 16, 1791, in Hamer (ed.),
"Letters," *loc. cit.*, 126; James Robertson to Daniel Smith, June 6, 1791, in
Carter (ed.), *Territorial Papers*, IV, 59.

sented them by their Indian names to the seated governor.[39]

After this ceremonial opening, the negotiations began and were carried on in the style of the Indian council. Blount opened his attack at once with the announcement that the purpose of the meeting was to obtain a cession of land from the Indians. The latter, who professed to believe that the negotiations were to have dealt chiefly with procedural difficulties in the Hopewell treaties, appeared deeply chagrined, but the governor pressed the attack. He sought to begin the new boundary line in the Cumberland area, but the chiefs insisted on beginning it in the east where the major collisions were occurring. Blount therefore recommenced with a proposal that the new line be from the Tennessee River to a ridge between the Little Tennessee (then called the Tennessee) and Little rivers, thus to include the settlers south of the French Broad. The Indians rejected this, so the governor proposed a yet larger cession, coupled with an offer to settle himself on the new line in order to enforce it. By now the Indians knew something of the man with whom they were dealing, and this last suggestion was hastily rejected, whereupon Blount returned to his first proposal, to which the Indians replied with a counterproposal that the line be run down the Holston from the Great Island. This would involve a smaller cession and in addition leave out land along the route of the Mero-Washington road which the governor was intent on securing, and he therefore refused it.[40]

Day after day thus passed with both sides becoming angrier and the debate more acrimonious. Indian complaints of white encroachments grew bitter. Chief John Watts denounced North Carolinians as treaty-breakers with whom all negotiations were useless and expressed sur-

[39] Ramsey, *Annals*, 555–56.

[40] For accounts of the treaty proceedings, see Lowrie and Clark (eds.), *State Papers, Indian*, I, 204–205, 628–29.

prise that the governor, a Carolinian, should have been sent to treat; Blount's desire for a boundary on the winding ridge was declared to be evidence of his crooked heart. On his side, the governor brutally told the chiefs that they could not appeal to the President for they had no money to make the trip. Also, in reply to the charge of white encroachment, he flatly ignored the policy of the United States by claiming all the disputed lands by right of conquest in the Revolution.

At length the Indians yielded to the main contention of the inexorable governor, but they remained adamant that the line should be drawn straight from the point where the ridge between the Little and the Little Tennessee rivers struck the Holston eastward to the North Carolina line and westward to the mouth of the Clinch, instead of following the meanderings of the natural boundary as he desired. The Clinch River became the western boundary of the cession in East Tennessee. The argument then turned to compensation. The chiefs scornfully remarked that the one thousand dollars offered would not buy a breech cloth for each of their nation, and only with difficulty were they persuaded to settle temporarily on that annual sum, provided Congress on application should raise the figure.[41]

After these main contentions were settled, other provisions were inserted in the treaty. One of these placed the Cherokee and their trade under the protection of the United States. Another provided for a mutual exchange of prisoners by the following April. The boundary, guaranteed by the United States, was to be marked by a joint commission of whites and Indians, and intruders on Indian lands would be left to the mercy of the savages. Passports were required to enter Indian territory, and horse

41 *Ibid.,* 204–205.

thieves and other felonious fugitives were to be given up by the Indians to the whites. Likewise, crimes committed by whites in Indian territory were to be punished by the criminal's home government, and acts of retaliation were renounced. Other stipulations concerned agricultural tools and interpreters for the Indians and unhindered use of the Washington-Mero road and the Tennessee River by the whites.[42]

As the provisions were discussed and agreed to, the traditional double transition from oral agreement in the Indian tongue to written English in the treaty gave opportunity for both honest misunderstanding and deliberate chicanery. The Indians later flatly denied knowledge of or consent to the clause on the free navigation of the Tennessee, and they further charged that as to the white area on the western end of the dividing line they had agreed to an area ten miles above Nashville, whereas the interpreter had been bribed and the treaty provided for forty miles. They also maintained that they had been promised two thousand dollars at once, but that "one thousand" dollars had been secretly inserted in the treaty.[43]

In any event, Blount did not forget his personal interests. Early in the meeting, according to the Indian account, he approached the chiefs to obtain a sale of the Muscle Shoals lands, since, he told the Indians, "he had already purchased these lands of the State of Georgia, but was desirous of making a fuller purchase of our nation." Yet despite his promises to erect storehouses and gunsmiths' shops for the use of the Indians, the chiefs refused

---

[42] For the text of the treaty, see Carter (ed.), *Territorial Papers,* IV, 60–67.

[43] "Diary of Jacob Lindley," in *Michigan Pioneer and Historical Collections,* XVII (1890), 611; "General Lincoln's Journal," *loc. cit.,* 171; George Welbank to Colonel Alexander McKee, January 16, 1793, in Philip Hamer, "The British in Canada and the Southern Indians, 1790–1794," in East Tennessee Historical Society's *Publications,* No. 2 (1930), 115–18; Pickering Papers, LIX, 15.

to sell the lands, saying that they were the common hunting grounds of four nations.[44]

Notwithstanding this defeat, the governor had made a treaty successful both from a public and a private point of view. He had, at least on paper, regularized Indian-white relations on critical points, legalized the settlements south of the French Broad, obtained a considerable cession of territory (including some of his own lands), and had included in the treaty certain indefinite terminology, favorable construction of which might bring yet more land and squatters within white territory.[45] Hence, convinced that no more land could have been obtained, he expressed himself as well satisfied. An express was sent off to Philadelphia with the treaty, and diplomatically worded reports were directed to frontier leaders in Kentucky and South Carolina.[46]

His sojourn on the lower Holston had confirmed the governor's decision to locate his capital at White's Fort; he therefore arranged for the construction of a weatherboarded log cabin on a little hill near the Tennessee River to serve as a temporary home for his family until a more fitting mansion could be built. The selection of this site for the capital had been anticipated for some time now, and the heavily forested hills and plateaus about White's Fort were increasingly dotted with clearings. The two-storied fort itself was the only building of any size, but General James White now planned to lay off streets and lots, and owners of surrounding lands, including the gov-

[44] Lowrie and Clark (eds.), *State Papers, Indian*, I, 203–204.

[45] Bramlett, "North Carolina's Western Lands," 80–81; Hugh Williamson to John Gray Blount, August 15, 1790, in Blount Collection; Lowrie and Clark (eds.), *State Papers, Indian*, I, 629.

[46] Lowrie and Clark (eds.), *State Papers, Indian*, I, 628–29; William Blount to Harry Innes and others, July 2, 1791, in Innes Papers (Division of Manuscripts, Library of Congress); *id.* to Governor Charles Pinckney, July 8, 1791, in "Correspondence of William Blount, 1777–1797" (typed copies in Lawson McGhee Library), 25.

ernor, anticipated sizeable profits. In honor of his superior officer, Secretary of War Knox, Blount named the place "Knox-Ville." [47]

Meanwhile, with his most immediate objective accomplished, the weary governor now planned his delayed trip to North Carolina. His wife had at length agreed to come to the frontier, and, in addition to bringing his family to the West, he had both old and new business demands to answer. James Mountflorence, a lawyer and speculator of Nashville whom Blount had known in North Carolina, had proposed to use his connections in France to sell Blount lands abroad, and this and certificate transactions required conferences with John Gray Blount. In addition, Blount's foes in the December Carolina assembly had secured a resolution directing the attorney general to sue for the unpaid Hopewell accounts of the ex-agent, whose personal attention was now required for his defense. He therefore requested of Knox a leave of absence from September 15 to November 20.[48]

He did not, however, idly await permission for his trip East. Mountflorence was sent to Philadelphia and Titus Ogden to Carolina to settle accounts and speculate further in certificates, Mountflorence being charged also with the reports on land occupation and geography that had been requested by the Secretary of State.[49] Also the governor was again plagued by frontier enterprise. The expedition to the Muscle Shoals under Zachariah Cox had

[47] For a description of the site, see Ramsey, *Annals*, 558–60.

[48] William Blount to Secretary Knox, July 17, 1791, in Carter (ed.), *Territorial Papers*, IV, 70–71; Alice B. Keith (ed.), "Letters from James Cole Mountflorence to Members of the Blount Family," in *North Carolina Historical Review*, XIV (1937), 253–54.

[49] James Mountflorence to William Blount, November 17, 1791, in Blount Collection; William Blount to John Steele, July 22, 1791, in Wagstaff (ed.), *Papers of John Steele*, I, 79–80; Blount–Jefferson correspondence, July–August, 1791, in Carter (ed.), *Territorial Papers*, IV, 71–72, 74–75.

failed, due to the warnings of a party of Cherokee, but popular sympathy was so strongly in favor of the trespassers that to Blount's chagrin a grand jury impaneled in Washington District refused to indict them. The Spanish, however, had taken a more serious view of the effort, and, by Miró's orders, had raised a fort at Walnut Hills (the present Memphis) to prevent the success of this or any other such enterprise. This Spanish stroke was observed by Secretary Daniel Smith on a surveying expedition, and he reported it to Blount, who, deeply alarmed, informed the Secretary of War.[50] Finally, the routine and tedious tasks of passing on commissary accounts, filling militia offices, and collecting information on Indian troubles absorbed much time. In July, Joseph Anderson of Delaware, named by Washington as the third territorial judge after Peery had declined the post, arrived and was sworn in. The governor had not formerly known him, but found him "a genteel man . . . a learned Judge and a very agreeable open Companion," and sent him to Robertson with warm recommendations.[51]

The census-taking of the Territory was delayed both by the difficulties of communication and by the reluctance of the citizens to be counted, since they feared, so the governor alleged, that ascertaining their number would result in the establishment of a legislature. Whether or not this was a true cause of reluctance, it was entirely in accord with the governor's own distaste for a division of his authority. Therefore, although even incomplete figures

[50] William Blount to Secretary Knox, July 29, 1791 (extract), in Thomas Jefferson Papers; *id.* to James Robertson, September 3, 1791, in "Robertson Correspondence," *loc. cit.*, I, 192–93; Ramsey, *Annals,* 550–51; Whitaker, *Spanish-American Frontier,* 148, 214.

[51] William Blount to James Robertson, September 3, 21, 1791, in "Robertson Correspondence," *loc. cit.*, I, 192–94; Carter (ed.), *Territorial Papers,* IV, 49, 446.

totaled 35,691 persons as of late July, the governor made no plans for this next step in territorial administration.[52]

His principal concern, however, in the late summer of 1791, was the mounting tempo of Indian attacks. The businessman-governor naturally attached great importance to written agreement. He regarded treaty-making and treaties in much the same manner as he did the clever maneuvering for binding advantage with which he was familiar in the mercantile world. Several years of crushing disillusionment would yet be required to instruct him in the real weaknesses of the treaty process between equally dissatisfied whites and savages. It was with deep concern, therefore, that in the face of his new treaty he heard of the increasing violence which beset his citizens. With the aid of the militia officers, he had drawn up and forwarded by Mountflorence a plan of defense for the Cumberland area, which called for the stationing of regular troops in the Territory. This was seconded by a respectful but plain-spoken memorial to the President from the civil and military officers of the Mero District. But, while the national Administration gave languid attention to the "depredations" of "a few rascally Indians," the settlers were growing increasingly restive under the mounting attacks of Chickamauga, Creeks, and even Cherokee recalcitrants.[53]

Knox, straining to equip St. Clair's expedition and anxious for the assistance or at least the neutrality of the

[52] William Blount to Thomas Jefferson, September 19, 1791, in Carter (ed.), *Territorial Papers,* IV, 80–81; *id.* to John Sevier, May 31, 1793, in Draper Collection, 4XX35. See also A. V. Goodpasture, "William Blount and the Old Southwest Territory," in *American Historical Magazine,* VIII (1903), 9, and Abernethy, *Frontier to Plantation,* 133.

[53] James Robertson to William Blount, August 25, 1791, in "Robertson Correspondence," *loc. cit.,* I, 191; William Blount to James Robertson, September 3, 1791, *ibid.,* 191–93; memorial of Mero officers, August 1, 1791, in Carter (ed.), *Territorial Papers,* IV, 72–73; James Winchester to Daniel Smith, June 20, 1791, in Draper Collection, 7ZZ32–33; Haywood, *History of Tennessee,* 269–70, 341; Henry Knox to Arthur St. Clair, August 11, 1791, in Lowrie and Clark (eds.), *State Papers, Indian,* I, 181.

Southern Indians in the coming campaign, could authorize nothing more than calling out two companies of militia who, already tired of too constant calls, showed marked reluctance to leave their homes unguarded. The governor, therefore, could do little but remind the militia officers that they were sworn to support the Constitution and the government and to urge that the treaty be observed.[54] Blount, in fact, now faced the problem which beset his entire administration—that of making palatable to the harried and resentful frontiersmen policies of the national government which, however intrinsically sound, appeared callous to the interests of his citizens.

For the present, however, escape from the problem was possible, since Secretary of State Jefferson informed him that his request for a leave of absence had been approved by the President. Hence with a sense of both accomplishment and relief, Blount turned eastward on September 15, 1791, to take the winding road for home, his wife, and his family.

[54] Henry Knox to William Blount, August 18, 1791 (extract), in George Washington Papers (Division of Manuscripts, Library of Congress) ; William Blount to James Robertson, September 3, 21, 1791, in "Robertson Correspondence," *loc. cit.*, I, 192–94.

CHAPTER VIII

FEDERALIST ON THE FRONTIER

To be home again was pleasant. The comforts of Piney Grove and of John Gray's Washington residence seemed real luxury to the frontier governor. To be surrounded by an understanding family, to drop diplomacy and tact and make decisions regardless of official circumstance, to visit friends in comfort and leisure, to be received with deference and to speak of the West with the authority of experience and office, all these refreshed him.

There were, of course, many things to be done, much planning and many decisions. To prepare a large and well-equipped household for the long journey to the edge of civilization involved a thousand details. His wife needed constant reassurance. With half brother Willie Blount, chosen to be his brother's private secretary, there were briefing sessions on Western affairs. Brothers John Gray and Thomas assembled for consultation on present problems and future prospects. The Hopewell accounts had to be redrawn, and arrangements made to meet the suit of the solicitor general. In Philadelphia, associate David Allison speculated in certificates and negotiated with wholesale merchants to furnish territorial stores with goods for the convenience of the citizens and the financial advantage of the governor.[1] The latter, meanwhile, busied himself with the resuscitation of his old Bend Company, whose pretensions were now threatened by the Indians, Zachariah Cox's company, and the refusal of the Georgia governor to sign land grants there.[2] Other land affairs also occupied him, since after personal observation he had chosen more tracts in the Territory now to be purchased from Carolina owners.

Much of the three brothers' time was spent in discussing a new enterprise. John Gray had acquired Shell Castle, a warehouse and store on Shell Island near Ocracoke Inlet. The merchandising, lighterage service, and pilotage there offered to ships developed a thriving and absorbing business. Largest new prospect, however, was the agreement of the brothers to send James Mountflorence to France to sell lands. The origin of this idea was a general plan of land sales by the Frenchman, but the Blounts narrowed the operation to the sale of his and their lands only, furnished him with cash, and prepared to send him abroad on their brig *Russell*.[3] Consultations with and advice to this agent occupied considerable time, and it was not until early December that the governor, his wife, their two sons (the governor's daughters were left with their aunt in Carolina), and Willie completed their arduous journey and arrived on the upper Holston. Here, until the new house at Knoxville should be finished, the Blount family made their home with the hospitable Cobbs.

Blount was not long in finding that, despite some

---

[1] Memorandum of November 22, 1791, in Blount Collection, P.C. 898; David Allison to William Blount, October 16, 1791 (copy), in Rodman Papers.

[2] David Allison to William Blount, October 16, 1791 (copy), in Rodman Papers; *Report of the Select Committee,* 16.

[3] William Blount to James C. Mountflorence, November 1, 1791, in Dreer Collection; James C. Mountflorence to William Blount, November 17, 1791, January 22, 1792, in Blount Collection.

successes, affairs were rather worse than on his departure. On the side of accomplishment, acting-governor Smith had again blocked the energetic Cox's further effort, this time from Virginia, to colonize near the Shoals.[4] Support for the territorial administration had appeared with the first edition, on November 5, 1791, of George Roulstone's newspaper, which, though entitled the Knoxville *Gazette,* was presently printed at Rogersville. Prospects were also good for a Federal mail route from Staunton to replace the sadly inadequate person-to-person system hitherto used.[5]

Also, the Holston treaty had been agreed to by the Senate and proclaimed by the President, and the latter had tendered to the proud governor his thanks for Blount's ability and his "zeal . . . uniformly evinced to promote the interests of the United States, in endeavoring to fix a peace on the basis of justice and humanity," to which Knox had added assurances of executive support. On Blount's suggestion that the Holston treaty line should be run as soon as possible, David Campbell, Daniel Smith, and Landon Carter had been named for the task.[6]

On the other hand, the Indian scene had darkened ominously. Robertson had been hopeful of holding Creek friendship, but the crushing defeat of Arthur St. Clair in November, 1791, had plunged the frontier in despair and necessitated an entire reorientation of policy. This second annihilation of their forces in the Northwest reduced the whites' prestige to a low ebb, and all the elements of Indian

[4] Daniel Smith to Thomas Jefferson, October 4, December 9, 1791, in Carter (ed.), *Territorial Papers,* IV, 83–84, 105.

[5] Douglas C. McMurtrie, *Early Printing in Tennessee* (Chicago, 1933), 20; Knoxville *Gazette,* November 5, 1791; Thomas Jefferson to William Blount, December 24, 1791, in Carter (ed.), *Territorial Papers,* IV, 105–106.

[6] Lowrie and Clark (eds.), *State Papers, Indian,* I, 135, 629; Carter (ed.), *Territorial Papers,* IV, 67–68, 103–104; Henry Knox to William Blount, November 19, 1791 (extract), in "Robertson Correspondence," *loc. cit.,* I, 196.

discontent in the South gathered to burst upon the returning governor and his frantic citizens. In the western areas
of the Territory, the friendlily disposed Chickasaw and
Choctaw were becoming increasingly restive under the
continuing white advance; several delegations of them
traveled toward New York, to be turned back by the governor with increasing difficulty. The Cherokee, angry over
their small compensation at the last treaty, had taken advantage of Blount's absence to send a delegation of their
chiefs to the President. The more unsophisticated, younger
members of that tribe, meanwhile, expressed their dissatisfaction in bloody reprisals, protected by the difficulty
in a skirmish of identifying Creek from Cherokee. The
Chickamauga, unbound even by the technicality of treaty
obligation, were especially venomous. Though that nation
finally refused to heed Shawnee envoys who urged a North-
South coalition against the frontiers, still, individual bands
joined Shawnee groups to kill, burn, and steal.[7]

Worst scourge of all were the Creeks. That nation,
riven by the rival leadership of the pro-Spanish McGillivray and the English adventurer William Augustus
Bowles, were quick to note the American defeat in the
Northwest. In addition, Spanish policy, at all times more
influential with the Creeks than with other tribes, now
shifted. On December 30, 1791, Baron Hector Carondelet
replaced Miró as governor and intendant of Louisiana and
West Florida. The new governor brought to his post considerable, if misdirected, energy and a fixed determina-
tion to nullify all the American gains in the treaty of New

[7] William Blount–Henry Knox correspondence, January, March, 1792, in
Carter (ed.), *Territorial Papers,* IV, 115–17, 129–30; Lowrie and Clark
(eds.), *State Papers, Indian,* I, 629; David Craig to William Blount, March
15, 1792, *ibid.,* 264–65; William Blount to Henry Knox, April 22, 1792, in
Palmer and McRae (eds.), *Virginia State Papers,* V, 500–501; Samuel Newell
to Arthur Campbell, February 1, 1792, in Draper Collection, 9DD67.

York by welding the Creeks—and if possible all the Southern tribes—into an offensive-defensive coalition against the Americans.[8]

The results of this concurrency of circumstances were soon evident in the Territory, and during the six months following his return the governor grappled daily with problems of Indian harassment and white retaliation. His first effort was an attempt to hold the bulk of the Cherokee to a state of at least nominal peace, to which end the national Administration co-operated with the governor. The Cherokee deputation to Philadelphia received there a courteous reception. Their annuity was raised to fifteen hundred dollars, supplies were furnished them, and promises made both to combat Cox's Muscle Shoals project and to consider the question of the whites' homes illegally raised across the boundary. James Carey, John Thompson, and George Miller were named, at Cherokee request, as official interpreters, and young Leonard Shaw, a recent Princeton graduate, was sent as a resident agent to the nation. The deputation was loaded with gifts, and other donations were sent to Chickasaw and Choctaw chiefs, with strong arguments in favor of their joining the next American campaign in the Northwest. As a further effort to avoid friction and, if possible, to enlist the aid of the Indians in future Northwestern expeditions, the running of the Holston boundary was deferred.[9] For the Chickasaw and Choctaw, the Administration approved Blount's suggestion of a treaty to be held in June, 1792, at Nashville. In its Creek relations, the United States relied on its agent

[8] Whitaker, *Spanish-American Frontier*, 153–54, 163–66. For Bowles, see also Hamer, "The British in Canada," *loc. cit.*, 107–12.

[9] Lowrie and Clark (eds.), *State Papers, Indian*, I, 629; Henry Knox to Leonard Shaw, February 17, 1792, *ibid.*, 247–48; *id.* to the President, January 17, 1792, in Carter (ed.), *Territorial Papers*, IV, 111–15; *id.* to William Blount, January 31, February 16, 1792, *ibid.*, 115–17, 118–19.

James Seagrove, and supported McGillivray against Bowles.[10]

To implement these policies and to restrain both the white homeseekers and the Indian renegades, a few Federal troops were planned for the Territory in addition to the construction of permanent forts at strategic spots. Also, active service for two companies of militia was authorized at the governor's insistence, and a small quantity of small arms and ammunition and two brass howitzers were sent to beleaguered Mero District. This entire, slowly evolved policy rested on the treaties of Hopewell (with the Chickasaw and Choctaw), of New York (with the Creeks), and of Holston and its amendments (with the Cherokee). Unfortunately, the first of these had been stillborn; the second, through Spanish pressure, was soon to be repudiated by McGillivray himself; and the third, even with its amendments, was incomplete and violently unpopular with large groups of both Indians and whites. In addition, the inability of both white and Indian leaders to restrain their followers, the one from encroachment, the other from the excitement and spoils of marauding expeditions, was a basic weakness. Finally, burdened with the strain of the Northwestern expeditions and faced with the international problems arising from the presence of Spanish and British neighbors, the national government was not in a position to be realistic about, even had it been accurately informed of, actual conditions on the Southwestern frontier.

Nevertheless, the governor, stimulated by the praise of

[10] Henry Knox to William Blount, March 31, 1792, in Carter (ed.), *Territorial Papers*, IV, 131–32; William Blount to Daniel Smith, January 6, 1792, *ibid.*, 111; Henry Knox to James Seagrove, February 20, 1792, in Lowrie and Clark (eds.), *State Papers, Indian,* I, 249–50; *id.* to Alexander McGillivray, February 17, 1792, *ibid.*, 246–47.

his superiors, loyally exerted himself to carry out the difficult and unpopular policies. Attorney general Andrew Jackson of Mero was ordered to make horrendous examples of white violators of the Holston treaty. Robertson was authorized to present vouchers for past and future good-will tokens to visiting chiefs. A detachment of militia was at once ordered to six months duty at the strategic spot where the road to Mero District crossed the Cumberland River. The governor made a special trip for a conference with the influential Cherokee chief John Watts to strive for his co-operation in restraining the marauding Cherokee. The judges (Campbell in particular) by their charges to grand juries, gave zealous support to the governor in his efforts to lead public opinion, and Robertson exerted all his influence in Mero. Blount himself was assiduous in a morale building campaign to assure influential leaders of the progress being made toward peaceful Indian relations and to prove the good will of the Administration toward both the governor and his citizens.[11]

This benevolence, however, was not apparent to the supposed recipients. As depredations and murders reached new peaks, the enraged frontiersmen, especially in exposed Mero, found assurances unconvincing. Those more legalistic turned to further memorials; the more hot-headed or deeply afflicted resorted to volunteer retaliatory campaigns. Even Robertson's firm control of his district slipped, and he suffered unprecedented personal attacks. When the expected Federal troops were diverted to Georgia a council of officers met in Mero and on their own authority determined to dispatch troops to patrol to the southward; where-

[11] William Blount to James Robertson, January 2, 5, April 29, 1792, in Carter (ed.), *Territorial Papers,* IV, 108–110, 145–47; *ibid.,* 122–28; Knoxville *Gazette,* December 31, 1791; William Blount to Governor Shelby, December 31, 1791, February 24, 1792, in Draper Collection, 11DD48, 11DD49; *id.* to John Sevier, December 30, 1791, *ibid.,* 4XX25.

upon the governor was compelled to legitimize the expedition by issuing a militia call.[12]

Few men have been more acutely aware of criticism than was Blount, and few more readily have reciprocated personal ill will or dislike. Nevertheless, under the lengthening lash of public criticism it was necessary to secure all possible political support. John Tipton, perennial foe of Sevier and always a resourceful antagonist, had chosen these months of discontent to strike back at the Blount-Sevier faction in the Washington District. A petition was being drawn up citing grievances against the administration of affairs, and the governor was forced to conciliate the growing opposition. Through Judge Campbell, an associate of Tipton since Franklin, overtures were made to that fiery oppositionist. The negotiations bore fruit and resulted in a "kind" and "satisfactory" interview of "Conciliation and Public Happyness." At the same time, the governor exerted all his famous charm to keep Sevier in harness with his old enemy.[13]

Under pressure of constant if concealed criticism, Blount even considered calling a territorial legislature to silence a demand which had reached the columns of Roulstone's paper. Judge Campbell, however, was opposed to the idea, at least until the public was under better control; also, Benjamin Hawkins in Congress advised against "an expedient so fraught with inconveniences, perhaps dangers," [14] and so the possibility was discarded. Blount's

[12] Tennessee County petition, February 1, 1792, in "Robertson Correspondence," *loc. cit.*, I, 284–85; ? to James Robertson, July 10, 1792, *ibid.*, II, 68–69; William Blount to *id.*, April 1, 1792, *ibid.*, I, 287–91.

[13] Benjamin Hawkins to William Blount, January 31, 1792, in Rodman Papers; William Blount to John Sevier, January 2, March 8, 1792, in Hamer (ed.), "Letters," *loc. cit.*, 126–27; Samuel C. Williams, *Phases of Southwest Territory History* (Johnson City, 1940), 8.

[14] Knoxville *Gazette*, December 17, 1791, March 10, 1792; David Campbell to the President, November 9, 1791, in Carter (ed.), *Territorial Papers*, IV, 101–102; Benjamin Hawkins to William Blount, April 1, 1792, in Rodman Papers.

personal following, meantime, was built up by strategic appointments of friends and the relatives of friends, who were usually already leaders of public opinion.[15] At the same time to distract discontent the governor engaged in well-publicized controversy with Virginia over the boundary and with North Carolina over the continuation of land grants.[16]

March of 1792 also saw Blount's removal to his new capital. A large log house on a knoll by the river was at length ready, and the family left the relative comforts of Cobb's for the new raw settlement on the Holston. Mrs. Blount's apprehensions were allayed by plans for a more luxurious future mansion shortly to be built and by reports of the growth of the new capital to which soon even the *Gazette* would move its presses—and a newspaper to a Blount was a hallmark of civilization. The governor, of course, allowed neither affairs of state nor family to come before personal business activity. His investment in it made possible the enlargement of King's ironworks, an event celebrated for two days with games, races, wrestling, and various feats of strength rewarded by prizes bestowed by the governor himself. As a climax, the new furnace having been charged with charcoal and ore, Mrs. Blount walked to a raised platform, and with a bottle of rum christened the furnace "The Barbara" in honor of the governor's mother.

Other mercantile interests with Allison and certificate speculation required some thought, but land loomed largest

[15] William Blount to John Sevier, January 2, 1792, in Hamer (ed.), "Letters," *loc. cit.,* 126–27; Carter (ed.), *Territorial Papers,* IV, 447.

[16] Blount–Jefferson–Martin correspondence, December, 1791, August, 1792, in Carter (ed.), *Territorial Papers,* IV, 107, 164–66; Knoxville *Gazette,* March 10, 1792; William Blount to Thomas Jefferson, April 23, 1792, in Jefferson Correspondence (photostats in Lawson McGhee Library); Arthur Campbell to William Blount, June (n.d.), 1792, in Draper Collection, 9DD69a; North Carolina *Journal,* November 24, 1792.

The Blount Mansion, Knoxville, Tennessee

in Blount's plans. Despite the publication of Secretary Jefferson's report that little available land remained unclaimed in white territory, the all-absorbing game of speculation was as active as ever, and Blount's advantages over the ordinary speculator were manifold. Robertson was instructed to survey purchases recently made in North Carolina, and patents went regularly to Secretary Smith to be recorded.[17] Both William and Willie Blount were anxious that the surveys be completed before December 22, 1792, the date set by North Carolina for the completion of military grants issued by that state, and with discrimination as to value rather than legality. The same governor who directed the prosecution of violators of the Holston Treaty instructed his surveyors, "Lay as many of the Warrants within the present Indian Bounds as you can, taking Care to avoid disputes in the Titles, but in case you cannot find good land within the Boundary and have got Surveys without the Bounds already made, then let such locations rest as they are." [18]

Scarcely was the family settled in the new capital, however, when increasing Indian warfare necessitated positive action. April proved to be a particularly violent month, filled with murders, ambush, and attacks by both savages and whites. The murders of the prominent settler Harper Ratcliff and his family in the upper Clinch Valley brought to Washington District the anger and fear which in Mero were habitual. The incessant irritant of horse stealing, which Blount termed the "grand source" of hostility in Washington, reached new heights through systematized operations of corrupt traders with the Indians.

[17] William Blount to James Robertson, January 2, 1792, in Carter (ed.), *Territorial Papers*, IV, 108–109; *id.* to Daniel Smith, April 29, 1792, *ibid.*, 147–48.

[18] William Blount to James Robertson, April 29, 1792, in "Robertson Correspondence," *loc. cit.*, I, 392–93.

At the same time, attacks on friendly Indians further aroused the peaceable elements among the Cherokee. From Muscle Shoals and Walnut Hills came deeply alarming reports of a Creek-Chickamauga-Spanish alliance, the first goal of Governor Carondelet. Blount was forced to divert militia raised for Mero to guard the eastern district, and to order another company for the western. Then, impressed by the apparent reasonableness of the half-breed, John Watts, now leading the Chickamauga, he determined to accept an invitation to visit the Indian town of Coyatee for the distribution of the gifts brought by the Cherokee delegation from Philadelphia. At the meeting, Blount hoped to correct for the record the stories the Indians were said to have told in Philadelphia concerning his dishonesty at the Holston treaty and to cement good relations with most of the Cherokee chiefs, since he was convinced, through the inaccurate reports of Indian trader Joseph Sevier, that only the Creeks were responsible.[19]

The governor planned to attend the meeting on its opening and as a gesture of confidence to be accompanied by his wife, but the killing of three whites on the Cumberland Road on May 16 and 17 induced him to postpone his appearance pending a second invitation and then to leave his wife in Knoxville. At length, on May 20, he set off down the Holston River, and after several delays at the Indians' request in order to give them time for a proper reception, arrived at Coyatee at the junction of the Holston and the Little Tennessee to find a large flag pole with the national emblem, a hut built for his reception, and some two thousand Indians firing salutes and showing more "joy" than he had ever seen. That evening and the next day were spent in eating, "seasonable drinking of whis-

---

[19] William Blount to Daniel Smith, April 27–29, 1792, in Draper Collection, 4XX28; Samuel Newell to Arthur Campbell, February 1, 1792, *ibid.*, 9DD67.

key," private conferences, and the Indians' favorite game of ball play, accompanied by the usual heavy betting. On Tuesday the governor prepared for business, but Chief Bloody Fellow, according to Blount's solemn account, "said he had been drinking too much whiskey to be capable of public business; that it was an accident might have happened to any man; that . . . [if the meeting were postponed one day] he would let every body know the fault was his, not mine." [20]

After another day of gambling, eating, and more truly "seasonable" drinking, Blount opened the conference with a carefully written speech. In it, he approved of the decisions at Philadelphia but emphasized his powers of negotiation and the confidence which the President had reposed in him. He then detailed the Indian atrocities which had occurred since Holston and which had cost over fifty white casualties, besides loss of property and prisoners. He did not charge the Cherokee with all of these but insisted that they co-operate in finding and punishing the perpetrators. He explained the defensive function of the militia now on duty and invited close co-operation. On the question of running the Holston treaty boundary, the governor announced that he would send word to the more representative national Cherokee council which was to meet at Estanaula on June 23, and he also postponed the Indian replies until then, fearing, he later said, the effect of Indian confessions of guilt on the frontiersmen present. His hosts promised a reply from the grand council, and even the Chickamauga representatives present assured satisfaction to the whites from that gathering. To conclude the meeting on its happy note, Blount announced that the influential chief Bloody Fellow would henceforth be known by the "more honorable name of General Eska-

[20] Lowrie and Clark (eds.), *State Papers, Indian*, I, 267–68.

qua," and also consented to add to the Philadelphia gifts more presents which he had foresightedly brought. He then left the division of the gifts to the Indians and departed.[21]

This friendly but inconclusive meeting had two important results. The first was an instant and mortal antagonism between Blount and the new Cherokee agent, Leonard Shaw. The second was Blount's mistaken conviction that the Cherokee, including the five Chickamauga towns led by Watts, were now friendly to the United States.[22] This decision was most unfortunate, since Watts immediately after the meeting accepted a Spanish invitation to a conference at Pensacola, during which he became violently pro-Spanish. Furthermore, despite the efforts of the Blount agents present, the proceedings of the Estanaula national council showed conclusively that the chiefs of the nation were exceedingly dissatisfied with the Holston line and white encroachments and were fast losing confidence in negotiation. Not only was Watts absent, but the pro-American new "General Eskaqua" prudently declined to attend, and some of the principal Chickamauga chiefs withdrew.[23]

Indeed, the sharp increase in open attack belied Blount's optimism. On the opening day of the Estanaula council, the most daring and successful attack thus far was carried off against Ziegler's Station, a fort in Mero, during which five whites were killed and twenty-five captured. This attack, followed by others, forced the governor to raise the militia levies to five companies of foot and a

[21] *Ibid.*, 268–69; William Blount to James Robertson, May 20, 1792, in "Robertson Correspondence," *loc. cit.*, II, 61–63.

[22] William Blount to James Robertson, May 26, 1792, in "Robertson Correspondence," *loc. cit.*, II, 63–66; *id.* to Henry Knox, June 2, 1792, in Carter (ed.), *Territorial Papers*, IV, 153–54.

[23] Goodpasture, "Indian Wars," *loc. cit.*, 187–89; Lowrie and Clark (eds.), *State Papers, Indian*, I, 327–29; William Blount to Henry Knox, July 4, 1792, *ibid.*, 270; *ibid.*, 271–73; Carter (ed.), *Territorial Papers*, IV, 175–76.

troop of horse, despite the worried householders' increasing reluctance to answer such calls. The governor also relied for results on the efforts of agent James Seagrove to treat with the Creeks at Rock Landing, Georgia, and on personal appeals to McGillivray.[24]

Meanwhile, at the request of Knox, Andrew Pickens joined Blount on June 10 for the Nashville conference with the Chickasaw and Choctaw. Delay in transporting the goods through the mountains, in addition to a drought which made the Cumberland unfit for transport, caused postponement of the conference until August 7 when an innocuous meeting occurred between the whites, the Chickasaw, and a few Cherokee; the Choctaw, through Spanish pressure, did not attend in large numbers. Knox, still persisting in his hopes for Indian allies for the Northwestern expedition, had instructed Blount to make no claims or statements to offend the savages. The meeting, therefore, although it aroused Spanish fears, concerned itself principally with the distribution of pay and gifts. Finding sentiment opposed to the project, Blount made no public request for aid in the Northwest and was perforce content with a mere explanation of the cause of the war from the United States' point of view. The chiefs even ignored the governor's request that they expel marauding Cherokee from their lands, and their insistence that no trading post be established on Bear Creek as provided at Hopewell was agreed to. In short, the accomplishment of the meeting was merely to hold ground: Chief Piamingo, keen-witted, and always a friend of the whites, was kept attached.

[24] Phelan, *History of Tennessee*, 153; Knoxville *Gazette*, June 2, July 28, 1792; Roosevelt, *Winning of the West*, III, Pt. 1, 272–77; William Blount to Henry Knox, June 2, July 4, 1792, in Carter (ed.), *Territorial Papers*, IV, 153–54, 157–59; Henry Knox to William Blount, April 22, 1792, *ibid.*, 137–42; William Blount to James Robertson, May 26, 1792, in "Robertson Correspondence," *loc. cit.*, II, 63–66; *id.* to Alexander McGillivray, May 17, 1792, in Lowrie and Clark (eds.), *State Papers, Indian*, I, 269–70.

Wolf's Friend, a wealthy Indian who appeared in scarlet and silver lace and seated himself under a crimson umbrella, was enlisted in the American cause, and the Spanish influence in the western end of the Territory was temporarily checked.[25]

Three months of treaty-making had now passed, and the Administration, the frontiersmen, and their governor eagerly scanned the scene for portents of peace. Of such signs there were none. The dreary roll of plunder, fire, and death continued. Even during the conference at Nashville, seventeen horses had been stolen, and this irritant steadily grew to contribute considerably to a major crisis. Meanwhile, the wily John Watts at Pensacola had been deeply impressed by the Spanish war policy of Governor Carondelet and trader William Panton and yet more impressed with the Spanish offers of arms, ammunition, and supplies. At Wills Town, therefore, he easily carried a combination of Chickamauga, Shawnee, and Cherokee in a decision for open war, for which preliminary harassment began in August and September. McGillivray, reduced to subservience by Carondelet's active measures and virtually superseded by the Spanish agent Pedro Olivier, acquiesced in a similar policy, although enough Creeks showed friendship for the United States to mislead Seagrove. Even the Chickasaw accepted the residence among them of a Spanish agent and became less friendly to the Americans.[26] In short, the activities of Carondelet and the

[25] Henry Knox to Andrew Pickens, April 21, 1792, in Lowrie and Clark (eds.), *State Papers, Indian,* I, 251–52; *ibid.,* 284–88; Baron Carondelet to the Marquis de las Casas, October 1, 1792, in Papeles de Cuba; Henry Knox to William Blount, March 31, April 22, 1792, in Carter (ed.), *Territorial Papers,* IV, 131–32, 137–42; George Washington to Henry Knox, August 5, 1792, in Samuel L. Wilson, "Washington's Relations to Tennessee and Kentucky," in East Tennessee Historical Society's *Publications,* V (1933), 18–19; J. W. M. Breazeale, *Life as It Is; or, Matters and Things in General* (Knoxville, 1842), 98–100.

[26] Goodpasture, "Indian Wars," *loc. cit.,* 188–90; Whitaker, *Spanish-*

pro-Spanish–Scottish-Indian trading firm of Panton, Leslie & Company, coupled with the inability or refusal of
the Washington Administration to restrain its land seekers, rendered futile all Blount's diplomacy of the past
summer.

As he observed his citizens guarding each other while
they worked in their fields and as daily reports arrived
of attack and reprisal, the governor gradually abandoned
all hope of peace. His principal objective became that of
holding off open hostilities until the harassed and disor-
ganized frontiersmen could be rallied and his superiors induced to take the inevitable decision for an offensive campaign. Step by step he increased the numbers of active
militia companies and garrisoned more stations. To spy
on Spanish plans, he sent to the Pensacola conference
Father James Alexander Douglas, a Scottish Jesuit, tutor
of Pickens' children, who was familiar with French and
Spanish and the habits of Indians. To acquire support in
Philadelphia, he urged Sevier to go there and forwarded
all the evidence he could secure on Spanish, Creek, and
Chickamauga collusion. On September 26, 1792, he proposed to Secretary Knox to bring in troops from Virginia
and North Carolina for the inevitable war.[27]

In Philadelphia, meanwhile, the Secretary of War
was a harassed man. Involved deeply in preparations for
a third, and, he prayed, finally successful expedition in
the Northwest, he was extremely loath to be convinced that

American Frontier, 167–68; Lowrie and Clark (eds.), *State Papers, Indian,*
I, 288–92.

[27] William Blount to Henry Knox, September 26, 1792, in Lowrie and
Clark (eds.), *State Papers, Indian,* I, 288; Downes, "Indian Affairs," *loc. cit.,*
247–48; William Blount to John Sevier, September 15, 1792, in Conarroe Papers (Pennsylvania Historical Society); *id.* to Henry Knox, July 4, August
31, September 15, 27, 1792, in Carter (ed.), *Territorial Papers,* IV, 157–59,
166, 171–72, 175; Andrew Pickens to William Blount, September 12, 1792, in
Rodman Papers; William Blount to Arthur Campbell, July 1, 1792, in
Palmer and McRae (eds.), *Virginia State Papers,* V, 635–36.

all was not well in the Southwest, whither he had sent considerable money and even more advice. Agent Seagrove from the Creeks reported their peaceful intent, and from Blount himself came assurances of progress or convincing explanations of stalemate. Further, the Secretary himself was troubled with occasional doubts over the correctness of the Holston Indian boundary in the Cumberland area.[28] Most important of all, negotiations with Spain over the Florida boundary and the Mississippi were at an extremely delicate state, and it was essential that no untoward events upset the United States' policy of wait-and-see. Spanish attachés, Jose de Jaudenes and Joseph I. de Viar, might fill the diplomatic air with wild and vapid protest over Blount's gifts of medals to Indian chiefs,[29] but they must not be permitted to have real grounds of complaint lest the United States lose its present initiative in the diplomatic game over the West. Hence the Secretary gave relatively free rein to the governor in matters of detail, requesting only that costs be kept down and a general Indian war, a "very great" and even "insupportable evil," be avoided.

But the decision was not to be made by either governor or Secretary. On September 11, reports from friendly chiefs and from interpreters Carey and Thompson informed Blount of the Wills Town decision of the Chickamauga and the Creeks for war and of their plans to attack with a force of three hundred to five hundred, including about one hundred Creeks. Immediately thereafter the news was confirmed by Joseph Sevier, who had been in the

28 Henry Knox to the President, July 28, 1792, in Carter (ed), *Territorial Papers*, IV, 159–61; *id.* to William Blount, August 15, 1792, *ibid.*, 162–64.

29 Whitaker, *Spanish-American Frontier*, 151–52; Joseph Viar and Jose Jaudenes to Thomas Jefferson, August 10, 1792, in Carter (ed.), *Territorial Papers*, IV, 161–62.

Cherokee country, and by Leonard Shaw from the upper Cherokee towns.[30]

The governor immediately ordered out the militia regiments of Washington and Mero districts and reported the news to Knox, taking care to demonstrate that the proposed attack could not be of a retaliatory nature. Panic prevailed among the whites, the settlers fled their fields to collect in stations or towns, and the militia was raised with difficulty and confusion. Fortunately, the Indians were delayed by the arrival and consumption of some whisky sent earlier from Knoxville and by the delaying strategy of Richard Findleston and Joseph Deroque, friendly traders. The governor utilized the pause by ordering some reinforcements from Washington to Mero, where he expected the blow to fall; but the cunning Watts, too, was capable of strategy. Indian chieftains The Glass and "General Eskaqua," who opposed the war, were induced to write Blount that the whole force was a marauding party caused by a supposed indiscreet threat of Robertson's, and that they, the chiefs, had managed to halt the attackers.[31]

Blount's earlier misjudgment of Watts now led him to fall completely into the trap. On September 14 he disbanded the Knox Regiment and the Mero Brigade, although he added slightly to the militia in service in the western district. Then, four days later, news of a large Indian force crossing the Tennessee induced him, deeply puzzled, to order out seven more militia companies, bringing the total for Washington District to fourteen companies of infantry and a troop of cavalry, the whole commanded

[30] William Blount to Henry Knox, September 11, 1792 (with enclosures), in Lowrie and Clark (eds.), *State Papers, Indian,* I, 276–79.

[31] William Blount to Henry Knox, September 15, 1792 (with enclosures), *ibid.,* 279–82; *id.* to John Sevier, September 15, 1792, in Conarroe Papers; *id.* to James Robertson, September 14, 1792, in "Robertson Correspondence," *loc. cit.,* II, 76–77; Goodpasture, "Indian Wars," *loc. cit.,* 190–91.

by Sevier. Yet the Mero disbanding order remained in force. Robertson, meanwhile, failed to share the governor's faith in Watts, "Eskaqua," or The Glass. Suspicious of the savages and reinforced in his opinions by the reports of Findleston and Deroque, the old general kept his troops alerted and sent out scouts, though the latter were killed by Watts' advancing army.

On the night of September 30, 1792, the blow fell on Buchanan's Station, four miles south of Nashville. Warned by disturbed cattle, the few settlers rushed to the loopholes to battle some two to three hundred frenzied savages. An epic fight resulted, with the whites maintaining amazingly hot and accurate rifle fire, and the Indians shooting both arrows and bullets and hurling burning brands on the little fort. At length, discouraged by the serious wounding of Watts, the Indians drew off, and their force broke up into small harassing bands.[32]

The effect of this attack and victory was immediate and electric. Frontiersmen of both Washington and Mero surged forward at the militia call. All felt the occasion had arisen for the long-awaited offensive campaign which should castigate the savages and secure peace. The governor was chagrined at being duped, but his deep alarm over the threat to Cumberland was transformed by the victory into a "Joy" which "really surpassed that experienced on the surrender of Cornwallis." Through printer Roulstone he glorified the settlers' triumph and, anonymously, of course, rebuked his critics. The mounting expense of the militia found him with "not one dollar public or private," but he personally guaranteed the payment of

[32] Goodpasture, "Indian Wars," *loc. cit.,* 193–95; James Robertson to William Blount, September 26, 1792, in "Robertson Correspondence," *loc. cit.,* II, 77–79; William Blount to Henry Knox, October 10, 1792 (with enclosures), in Lowrie and Clark (eds.), *State Papers, Indian,* I, 294–95; Ramsey, *Annals,* 564–67.

salaries and supplies.[33] He wrote to Governor Martin to secure Carolina's aid in the coming war and pressed Secretary Smith into service to write Jefferson soliciting support for the frontiersmen, while Sevier attempted, though vainly, to convert the Secretary of War to the doctrine of preventive warfare. Robertson, ever baffled by paper work, was carefully instructed in the details of bookkeeping practice in order to forestall criticism from the Administration accountants. Though so ill as to be bedridden, the governor still directed events, while eagerly anticipating authorization and help for a full scale war.[34]

But the elated excitement of the Territory was not matched in Philadelphia. Knox's spirits had oscillated in phase with the optimism of Blount's reports, and when the news of actual war finally came, it brought disappointment, bafflement, and anger to the Secretary. Though he should have been prepared by increasingly grave reports from even the usually optimistic Seagrove, Knox found the Indians' actions and motives "involved in obscurity." His first reply to Blount's reports was therefore chilling. He taxed the governor with being misled by Watts and requested a statement of the actual and alleged causes of the war. These barbs were followed by two unrealistic suggestions: that the upper Creek "banditti" be "restrained" by sending "a faithful and intelligent agent" and that the upper Cherokee be enlisted to "punish" the

[33] William Blount to Henry Knox, October 7, 10, 1792, in Carter (ed.), *Territorial Papers*, IV, 193, 195–97; *id.* to James Robertson, October 17, 1792, in "Robertson Correspondence," *loc. cit.*, II, 80–82; *id.* to Colonel Robert Hays, October 26, 1792, in Andrew Jackson Papers (Division of Manuscripts, Library of Congress); Knoxville *Gazette*, October 6, 20, November 3, 1792.

[34] William Blount to Alexander Martin, October 2, 1792, in Governors' Papers; *id.* to North Carolina frontiersmen, October 2, 1792, *ibid.*; Daniel Smith to Thomas Jefferson, October 27, 1792, in Carter (ed.), *Territorial Papers*, IV, 198–99; Knox–Lear correspondence, November 25, 1792, *ibid.*, 219–20; Henry Knox to William Blount, November 26, 1792, *ibid.*, 220–26; *id.* to James Robertson, October 27, December 11, 1792, in "Robertson Correspondence," *loc. cit.*, II, 82–84, 172–74.

lower towns. Finally, he informed the governor that, since Congress alone could declare war, therefore all military operations must be purely defensive, with no attacks made on Indian towns or in Indian country until March when Congress would meet and might act.[35]

On receiving this unpromising reply in November, 1792, Blount, though still ill, composed a long, careful explanation and argument. The principal alleged cause of the war, he said, was encroachment of the whites on Indian lands, whereas actually the war was the result of machinations of "the Officers administering the Government of Louisiana and their Instrument Mr. Panton." He enclosed a list of persons killed, wounded, or carried into captivity by the Indians since January, 1791, which totaled 119 names, and another list of outrages dated October 3–14. Most of these depredations, he said, were attributable to the Indian law of retaliation, which the savages had distorted by the substitution of white victims in tribal feuds. He devoted considerable time to the crime of horse theft and its bloody results and then presented a long argument denying completely any Creek or Cherokee title to the lands in Cumberland on which they alleged white encroachment. He concluded with a warning of rising anger among his citizens and urged the ease with which an expedition could be raised against the Chickamauga and the Creeks.[36]

In actual fact, Blount was striving earnestly in an impossible situation. Though his analysis of the basic causes of the war was biased in favor of white settlers and further land acquisitions, his views were those of thousands of his fellow citizens, and in statesmanship were far superior to the grasp of the distant and poorly informed

[35] Henry Knox to William Blount, October 9, 1792, in Carter (ed.), *Territorial Papers*, IV, 194–95.

[36] William Blount to Henry Knox, November 8, 1792, *ibid.*, 208–16.

Knox. Moreover, in the face of great popular opposition, he honestly sought to carry out the directions of his superiors while regularizing Indian-white relations. Thus, despite silence from the chiefs he sent commissioners according to his promises to run the Holston treaty line. The commissioners appointed in November, 1791, by President Washington had been Judge David Campbell, Secretary Daniel Smith, and Colonel Landon Carter. However, a series of delays had occurred through American fears of antagonizing the Southern Indians during the Northwestern campaigns and through Indian dissatisfaction with the treaty provisions. In October, 1792, therefore, Blount named Charles McClung and John McKee to serve for Smith and Carter and instructed them in case the Indians failed to appear when expected to run an "experimental line," which was done.[37]

In military affairs, too, he strove to mediate between Administration wishes and popular demand. In spite of the clamor for an offensive campaign, Blount compromised by sending only three militia companies from Washington to Mero, while Sevier, under orders to act defensively only, led others to the mouth of the Clinch River to build a strong post and dispatch scouts. Friendly Indians who came to get promises of protection for their towns were kindly and diplomatically received and sent home guarded against white malcontents. James Carey, the interpreter, was sent to spy on Creek towns.

Blount's obedience to the Administration proved costly to him. The steadily growing opposition to a policy of Indian diplomacy had reached dangerous proportions by September, and when news came of the Chickamauga declaration of war, the chance for capitalization on this

[37] *Ibid.,* 213; *Letter from the Secretary at War Accompanying His Report Relative to the Running of a Line of Experiment. . . .* (Philadelphia [1798]), 6, 11–12.

debacle was too great for Blount enemies. William Cocke, ambitious for an eventual Congressional seat and envious of the Blount-Sevier regime, launched an attack which Roulstone dared not refuse to print:

The war appears inevitable. . . . The idea of forming treaties and purchasing peace of the Cherokee Indians, is as absurd to me as the fabulous story of the goat treating with the wolf, for the security of her kids, and I blush to think that the policy of the Indians has so far exceeded that of the inlightened nation in which we live, but it may be that the great wisdom of our councils have been employed on objects more interesting. . . . Last year John Watts was our beloved confident. We now learn, that he is commander of the army that is marching against us. Will experience never teach men wisdom. . . . I fear that even a discretionary power is not lodged with the first officer of this government, to punish the Indians for the crimes they commit . . . or I am confident he would think the present a proper time to exercise that power.[38]

Blount struck back in the same medium. A letter signed "Hanging Maw" and paid for by a promise of *"two pounds of Beaver Fur"* replied,

they who talk much do not always tell the truth. I suppose you wish it to be thought that you are a man and a warrior. . . . What have you to talk about treaties? you know nothing about them. . . . You say fear is the best and only assurance of the friendship of an *Indian*. This is the language of a bad heart. . . . Our great Father the President did not tell you to speak to us, and he will not hear your talks, nor will I hear them any more. . . .[39]

Another "talk" signed "Red Bird" continued the defense with advice to the man who "talks very strong and runs very fast . . . . make the people believe you are a great man and a warrior; may be their hearts will become soft, and send you to the big council, the place where some of the white pretended warriors want to go." [40]

However, the issue was not always handled verbally.

[38] Knoxville *Gazette*, October 6, 1792. For other attacks, see *ibid.*, July 28, September 24, 1792.

[39] *Ibid.*, October 20, 1792.   [40] *Ibid.*, November 3, 1792.

Following a daring Indian horse theft, fifty-two angry men marched for the destruction of near-by Indian towns and were stopped only by the orders (and persuasion) of Sevier. While thus saved from embarrassment at the cost of personal prestige, Blount was harassed by divisions in his own followers. The Tipton schism broke open afresh, and Colonel James Winchester became miffed at a certain Blount directive. Young protégé McNairy remained loyal, but the governor was forced to rescind his former political approval of Judge Anderson. Campbell's personal timidity, too, excited Blount's scorn, and only that judge's mortal hatred of Cocke kept him politically useful. However, the Blount stalwarts—Sevier, James White, James Robertson, and Daniel Smith, joined now by mustermaster Robert Hays—closed ranks and supported unpopular decisions. The campaign for calling an assembly was met with the threat of the taxes which would inevitably result.[41]

The war between the governor and his political rivals was concurrently carried on outside the Territory. David Allison's dual position as Blount agent and army paymaster was the occasion for widely circulated attacks in Philadelphia. Blount was accused of trafficking in slaves and merchandise with government money and of falsifying accounts. Such charges required the closest attention of Steele and Williamson, his political guardians in Philadelphia, who received in return his advice on political strategy in North Carolina.[42]

[41] William Blount to Henry Knox, November 8, 1792, in Carter (ed.), *Territorial Papers*, IV, 208–16; Knoxville *Gazette*, July 14, November 17, 1792; William Blount to James Robertson, April 29, May 28, September 6, 1792, in "Robertson Correspondence," *loc. cit.*, I, 392–93; II, 66, 88; *id.* to Daniel Smith, April 27–29, July 24, 1792, in Draper Collection, 4XX28, 4XX29; *id.* to John Steele, November 8, 1792, in Wagstaff (ed.), *Papers of John Steele*, I, 84–86.

[42] Hugh Williamson to John Gray Blount, November 25, 1792, in Blount Collection; William Blount to John Steele, November 8, 1792, in Wagstaff (ed.), *Papers of John Steele*, I, 84–86.

Harassed by personal and family illness, the conduct of an Indian war, the discontent of his people, and the disagreement of his superiors, Blount still struggled to carry on the routine administration of office and the demands of private business. In the former category, he continued the endless task of militia and petty civil appointments and laid out new counties (Knox and Jefferson) and a new judicial district (Hamilton). With the judges he enacted law for the collection of taxes by the county courts. Nor was private business neglected. Despite the veiled attacks by his rivals, he continued to deal in certificates. With Allison and Hays he entered both mercantile and land transactions in Philadelphia, whence the paymaster often traveled, and he kept up close connections with influential friends in North Carolina concerning mutual interests.[43]

Private successes, however, were not matched by those in public policy. In November, Knox crushed Blount's laborious explanation of the war with a scathing letter. He repeated that a general war was to be avoided at all costs and that a decision on the question was up to Congress. Admitting the possibility of Spanish activity, he still insisted that the Indians must have some cause for their enmity to the Cumberland settlers, and he demanded that the governor report it. Relying on Seagrove's reports, he informed Blount that the great body of both Creeks and Cherokee were peacefully inclined and that Seagrove would soon remove the Creeks from the war. The Chickamauga should then be bought off. He admitted the number

[43] Carter (ed.), *Territorial Papers,* IV, 218–19, 447–52; Knoxville *Gazette,* March 10, 1792; Hugh Williamson to John Gray Blount, January 26, 1793, in Blount Collection; Benjamin Hawkins to John Gray Blount, January 30, 1793, *ibid.*; William Blount to Colonel Hays, May 28, 1792, in Andrew Jackson Papers; *id.* to James Glasgow, June 6, 1792, in Papers of the Secretary of State (North Carolina State Department of Archives and History).

of militia called out was at present necessary but rebuked the former calls as too large and expensive and even presumed to outline the Territory's exact military needs. Finally, after a long lecture on the necessity for economy, he announced the appointment in Philadelphia of a new quartermaster and paymaster and the impending dispatch of two brass cannon and a company of volunteers from North Carolina.[44]

This blast drew from Blount an even longer reply, denying the Indian claims and justifying his own expenses, and so the fruitless rounds of epistolary controversy continued. In the meantime, however, Blount carried out, in the face of violent opposition, the orders of the Secretary. He dismissed Sevier's whole brigade except for a company of infantry and one troop of cavalry and ordered a similar demobilization in Mero. At the same time, the governor was encouraged by the Indians' return of a captured militia officer to hope for a better state of affairs. He therefore sent letters and an emissary, John McKee, to the wounded Watts, and prospects for peace brightened, at least with the Chickamauga.

Indeed, the month of January, 1793, saw the possibilities of a considerable easing of Indian troubles. True, some responsible chiefs were even then returning from Spanish conferences looking toward a general anti-American confederation, but the increasing ill-feeling between Cherokee and Chickasaw and between Creeks, Choctaw, and Chickasaw, made such a confederation unlikely. Watts, with typical half-breed inconsistency, appeared entirely friendly and unruffled by his late defeat and accepted the governor's invitation for a conference on April 17,

[44] Henry Knox to William Blount, November 26, 1793, in Carter (ed.), *Territorial Papers*, IV, 220–26.

1793. The Chickasaw and Choctaw were reportedly resisting all anti-American blandishments.[45]

On the other hand, elements of the Creeks remained hostile, and their attacks and thefts kept the homesteaders furious and the politicians active. The first five months of 1793, therefore, brought little real calm. Even in Knoxville, which was less exposed to savage incursions, feeling ran high, and upon the murder of one Pate, his neighbors assembled a punitive expedition which the governor by order, proclamation, and entreaty had the greatest difficulty in halting.

In Mero the crash of the settlers' last hopes for an offensive war brought violent reaction, and it required every ounce of Robertson's influence to hold the settlers in check. As the toll of dead, wounded, and captured lengthened, the reputation of the governor fell ever lower. At the same time, he was attacked from a different quarter. Leonard Shaw, the young Cherokee agent, had married an Indian girl, and this attachment coupled with his youth and an addiction to drink made him of questionable value as an official. His enmity towards Blount had not lessened since their meeting at Coyatee, and because of an unfavorable report, possibly by Blount, Knox had authorized the governor to discharge him. Blount had done so, but very tactfully, and Shaw had left for the Cherokee nation, supposedly in a friendly mood, to gather his belongings. Once there, however, he sensed in the Indian unrest a chance to strike back, and when Blount's peace envoy, James Carey, arrived, Shaw denounced the governor, claimed equal authority, and pledged himself to lead the Indians

---

[45] A. P. Whitaker, "Spain and the Cherokee Indians, 1783–1798," in *North Carolina Historical Review*, IV (1927), 257–60; Goodpasture, "Indian Wars," *loc. cit.*, 196, 203–204; William Blount to Henry Knox, January 24, 1793 (with enclosures), February 12, 1793, in Lowrie and Clark (eds.), *State Papers, Indian*, I, 434, 435; *id.* to James Robertson, January 5, 8, 1793, in "Robertson Correspondence," *loc. cit.*, II, 174–75.

to the President and to recover the lands they had lost by treaty or encroachment.[46]

The governor meanwhile was bombarded with various proposals for securing peace. The frontiersmen, without exception, demanded an offensive expedition. A Georgia trader urged an accommodation with George Welbank, the British trader who was keeping alive the old Bowles faction among the Creeks, and Blount's failure to accept this advice cost him heavy attacks later. Knox, on February 8, ordered Blount to accompany Watts and the other Chickamauga and Cherokee chiefs to Philadelphia for a conference with the President.[47]

The worst problem, however, was the utter disorganization of the Indians themselves. The Creeks remained divided by American and Spanish rivalry, some following Seagrove, some pinning their hopes on Carondelet and the coming Indian congress. The nation's leadership was still contested. On McGillivray's death on February 17, 1793, Governor Carondelet and trader Panton continued their influence through agent Pedro Olivier and others, while Welbank sought to create a personal faction to deliver to the highest bidder. Indian traders confused the situation further with advice in favor of Spain or America. Worst of all, the chiefs exercised no real control over the young warriors, whose main interest was war and plunder. The upper Cherokee towns were fairly consistently pro-American under the leadership of Hanging Maw and other friendly chiefs, but the Chickamauga were by no means controlled by Watts, who followed rather than formed opinion. In addition, the younger warriors of the lower towns were powerfully influenced by Creek bellicosity and

[46] Lowrie and Clark (eds.), *State Papers, Indian*, I, 436–37, 440–41.

[47] Jacob Townshend to William Blount, February 15, 1793, *ibid.*, 439–40; Henry Knox to *id.*, February 8, 1793, in Carter (ed.), *Territorial Papers*, IV, 237–38; "General Lincoln's Journal," *loc. cit.*, 171–72.

by the promptings of hostile Shawnees who resided among them.[48]

In these shifting sands, Blount at first made some progress toward his double policy, which was still one of peace while he convinced the Administration of the necessity of offensive war. Robertson's influence was steady and invaluable in Mero. James Winchester was brought over to the waiting policy and was dispatched by the governor to Philadelphia to "complain loudly of everything that deserves to be complained of." Despite Watts' indecision, Creek attacks, and the defection of Shaw, the governor achieved a conference with Cherokee and Chickamauga leaders on April 6, 1793, near Knoxville and there obtained a half-promise from the chiefs to go to Philadelphia. With the Creeks, however, he could make no progress, and parties of this tribe, including the young Cherokee warriors, kept up a steady stream of guerilla assaults on the settlers and their possessions. Furthermore, the constant passage of Creeks through the Cherokee nation to and from these attacks on the Territory, coupled with the outbreak of a Creek-Chickasaw war, caused the Cherokee leaders to hesitate over the Philadelphia visit. Hence, the utmost claim of success for Blount's policy could only be that of holding off warfare with the upper Cherokee and keeping the Chickasaw and Choctaw satisfied, while the Creeks and the Chickamauga struck at will.[49]

Even this modest success was accomplished only with great effort. The marauders spared not Washington, Mero,

[48] A. P. Whitaker, "Alexander McGillivray, 1789–1793," in *North Carolina Historical Review,* V (1928), 303–309; William Blount to Henry Knox, April 9, 1793, in Lowrie and Clark (eds.), *State Papers, Indian,* I, 443–44; miscellaneous correspondence and reports, *ibid.,* 444–51; Haywood, *History of Tennessee,* 373–74.

[49] William Blount to James Robertson, February 13, 1793, in "Robertson Correspondence," *loc. cit.,* II, 278–79; James Winchester to James Robertson, February 2, 1793, *ibid.,* 176; minutes of Henry's Station conference, February [April?] 6, 1793, in Lowrie and Clark (eds.), *State Papers, Indian,* I, 447–48.

nor the new Hamilton District; fire, theft, and murder struck in all parts of the Territory, and the settlers on the extreme frontier were driven to live in miserable crowds within the walls of the various stations.[50] Under this bloody scourge the frontiersmen's rage rose steadily. Pages of the *Gazette* teemed with angry letters. Some suggested local defensive "associations" the better to repel the attacks. Congress was ridiculed and excoriated for sending corn to the distressed parts of the Creek nation, thus "invigorating" the savages for the war. The reports of Seagrove, on the pacific disposition of the Creeks, evoked savage irony. The *Gazette* reminded its readers in each issue that " 'Delenda est Carthago.' The Creek nation must be destroyed." From Mero came the frequent query, "Where will all these mischiefs end? What are the blessings of government to us? Are we to hope for protection? If so, when?" [51] Inevitably, the fury of some took direct form, and several ambushes of friendly Indians occurred. The governor was especially alarmed when, on May 25, three friendly Chickasaw visiting him were fired upon by unknown assailants in Knoxville and one was killed.

Political enemies also made capital of the settlers' discontent. In addition to the perils and discomforts of the Indian harassment, another basis of opposition appeared. Considerable doubt had always existed as to the continuation of North Carolina's fiscal procedures in the Territory. Blount and Judges Campbell and Anderson, therefore, found it necessary to enact various new ordinances on procedure. One of these empowered county courts to lay and collect poll and land taxes to pay the county ex-

[50] Haywood, *History of Tennessee,* 292–99; Catherine Bledsoe to Daniel Smith, April 19, 1793, in Draper Collection, 7ZZ36; E. Douglass to Daniel Smith, April 29, 1793, *ibid.,* 7ZZ37; Knoxville *Gazette,* January 12–June 15, 1793, *passim.*

[51] Knoxville *Gazette,* January 12, April 6, May 18, June 1, 15, 1793.

penses; another, aimed at regularizing financial routine, required that the county clerks and registrars account for and pay their receipts from fees and fines to Secretary Smith. Taxation was anathema to the frontiersmen, especially when the most-desired attribute of government, protection, was not in evidence. Aspiring politicians were, therefore, not slow to point out to an angry people that "these new acts and late instructions to the differant courts appear to be after the cash of the citizens which they have not given their consent to part with, and if I understand the matter, a conduct similar to this was the primary cause of opening the vains of so many brave Americans in the last WAR." [52]

Both oblique and direct arguments in favor of a representative assembly reappeared in the *Gazette*. County courts buzzed with angry clamors of "usurped legislative authority" by the governor and judges. The vote against an assembly in 1791 was explained as the result of a too hasty and unexpected poll. Campbell and Robertson were denounced even in Mero as "the Governor's tools." Blount was referred to as "the head of the Trinity," and his connection with fellow-speculator Allison denounced, since "from him [Blount] or his speculative views as the only source" flowed "all the evasive abuses practiced by Allison as paymaster." The Sumner County grand jury presented the lack of an assembly as an abuse, and such abuses were readily connected with the Indian warfare by Blount's opponents. [53] Cocke, because of illness and his former defeat, was quiescent, but John Tipton now broke into open opposition. In late February and March, he began an agi-

[52] William Blount to Henry Knox, May 24, 1793, in Carter (ed.), *Territorial Papers*, IV, 261–62; *ibid.*, 218–19, 242–43; Henry Bradford to Daniel Smith, May 12, 1793, in Draper Collection, 7ZZ38.

[53] Henry Bradford to Daniel Smith, May 12, 1793, in Draper Collection, 7ZZ38; William Blount to John Sevier, June 2, 1793, *ibid.*, 4XX31.

tation for a punitive expedition to destroy the Indian towns and named March 10 as the date of a rendezvous at his home in Jonesboro. In April, General Logan of Kentucky prepared to march south into the Territory on a similarly bellicose mission.[54]

Blount met these assaults with characteristic vigor. Anonymous assurances and rumors of a general offensive were cautious but constant in the *Gazette,* and letters of encouragement went forth to Mero and Hamilton districts. The suggested defensive "associations" were denounced as unconstitutional. The rage of the settlers was directed at Seagrove's reports, while a stream of official letters to Knox carried detailed lists of the latest atrocities. The arrival of a company of Federal troops under Captain Rickard was heralded by the *Gazette.* In its pages also, letters from "a gentleman to his friend," from "A Citizen," and from "A Fellow Sufferer" expressed concern over the dissension and opposition to the government, especially in "a mobish way," counseled patience, and assured the settlers of the national government's solicitous care. "All our friends over French Broad" were reminded that acts of violence might result in having a "land office opened on an unfavorable footing to their views and interests" (i.e., without pre-emption rights). A letter of Benjamin Franklin's was printed in which he had excoriated the Indian murderers of 1764. When the visiting Chickasaw were fired on in Knoxville, a reward was offered for the assailant, and the murdered Indian was buried with military pomp, the governor being chief mourner.[55] Tipton's reap-

[54] William Blount to Henry Knox, March 20, 1793, in Carter (ed.), *Territorial Papers,* IV, 244–47; *id.* to Governor Shelby, April 12, 1793, in Lowrie and Clark (eds.), *State Papers, Indian,* I, 448–49.

[55] Knoxville *Gazette,* March 9, April 6, 20, June 1, 15, 1793; Lowrie and Clark (eds.), *State Papers, Indian,* I, 436, 440, 443, 448, 453; William Blount to Henry Knox, May 24, 28, 1793, in Carter (ed.), *Territorial Papers,* IV, 261–64.

pearance on the political scene was met by a paragraph of ridicule in the *Gazette* over the small turnout in Jonesboro (although the governor admitted to Knox that if Tipton had come on to Knoxville his following would have considerably increased). Further to discredit this opponent, Blount, through the judges, had a warrant issued against him for breach of the peace and also proceeded on an earlier suit for "trespass on the case" (slander) in the sum of $10,000. To repel General Logan's anti-Indian filibuster from Kentucky, Blount wrote in protest to Governor Shelby of that state, and also, to the intense annoyance of the frontiersmen, ordered Robertson not to permit Logan's passage into Indian territory.[56]

In spite of every effort, however, the governor realized that his position was becoming increasingly untenable. He therefore determined to make a supreme effort to get the Administration to approve a war against the Creeks by availing himself of Knox's order of February 8 to bring the chiefs to Philadelphia in person. Although the Cherokee and Chickamauga chiefs, in the uncertainty of the Creek-American and Creek-Chickasaw wars, could not decide whether to go, the governor resolved to make a swift trip alone. Besides the Indian situation, there were other reasons for such a journey. Blount's commission as governor specified a three-year term, which would technically expire June 8, and he desired to canvass the possibilities of reappointment. His wife, unenchanted with the frontier, and Willie had for some months planned a trip to Carolina, and the governor could now accompany them part of the way. He was also planning even vaster land operations, and conferences with Williamson and other businessmen in

---

[56] Knoxville *Gazette,* March 23, 1793; William Blount to Henry Knox, March 20, 1793, in Carter (ed.), *Territorial Papers,* IV, 244–47; sheriff's writ, March 12, 1793 (Blount Mansion, Knoxville); Y. Ewing to Isaac Shelby, May 11, 1793 (extract), in Draper Collection, 11DD19d.

Philadelphia were in order. Finally, the governor, though he desired peace to be maintained during his absence in order that his Philadelphia negotiations might not be embarrassed, no doubt felt that a strategic absence at this highly explosive period might help save his official reputation.[57]

Before leaving, however, he felt impelled to act on the increasing clamor for a territorial legislature. Therefore, as he had in 1791 in connection with the census, he addressed circular letters to the colonels of the counties, calling for a poll on the question, and determined, despite Sevier's urging (for "Nollachucky Jack" had extensive personal political plans), not to call an assembly unless the poll so advised.[58]

Having distributed the circular, largely as a means of quieting the dissentients, and having advised Knox on affairs to date, the governor at length was ready to depart with his family. The efforts of White and Sevier produced a concourse of citizens on June 7, 1793, to witness the departure and the delivery of the usual formal address, to whom the governor pledged his thanks and undying efforts; afterwards the whip cracked, and the carriage rolled down the dusty street and took the road for the upper valley and Abingdon.

[57] Absolom Tatum to John Gray Blount, September 1, 1792, in Blount Collection; Hugh Williamson to *id.*, January 27, February 16, 1793, *ibid.*; William Blount to *id.*, October 22, 1793, *ibid.*; Carter (ed.), *Territorial Papers,* IV, 24; William Blount to Daniel Smith, June 17, 1793, *ibid.*, 274–75; *id.* to John Sevier, June 2, 16, 1793, in Draper Collection, 4XX31, 4XX32.

[58] William Blount to John Sevier, May 31, June 2, 1793, in Draper Collection, 4XX35, 4XX31; *id.* to Daniel Smith, June 9, 1793, in Carter (ed.), *Territorial Papers,* IV, 270.

CHAPTER IX

REPULSE AND ADVANCE

THE JOURNEY to Philadelphia was not swift. The lumbering coach, the rutted roads, and the care of Mrs. Blount and the children all slowed their progress. Land business and the hospitality of official and personal friends required lengthy stops. Printer Roulstone rode with the governor up to Jonesboro, and Sevier later joined for a ten mile ride and a long, confidential talk. On June 16, still traveling in the Territory, Blount received alarming news which almost induced him to turn back. Captain Hugh Beard and a company of wild militia had, in cold blood, slaughtered the family of Hanging Maw, the most influential pro-American chief among the Cherokee. The possible results of this atrocity were frightening, but as Smith had done all he could to stay the Indians' wrath until the President could act, Blount continued his journey. Planning with Sevier for general white and Indian pacification allowed time for a considerable number of directives to be sent back to Smith, and not until June 19 did the party cross the mountain barrier in Virginia. The next day Blount left his family and turned northeast toward Richmond.[1]

[1] William Blount to Daniel Smith, June 9, 16, 17, 1793, in Carter (ed.), *Territorial Papers*, IV, 270, 272–73, 274–75; *id.* to John Sevier, June 16, 1793, in Draper Collection, 4XX32; Daniel Smith to Henry Knox, June 13, 1793 (with enclosures), in Lowrie and Clark (eds.), *State Papers, Indian*, I, 459.

As he traveled his hopes rose. Allison in Philadelphia wrote that the President was anxious for his arrival and that his advice would probably be followed. This to Blount meant "a vigorous *national* war" that would "bring the Indians to act as they ought." A letter from Knox indicated that the Creek incursions in Georgia had cast doubts on Seagrove's supposed accuracy; and the Secretary even seemed to be swinging to the opinion that, despite the Spanish negotiations, a Creek-American war might have to be undertaken. The governor's spirits improved daily even though at Richmond he was attacked by his old enemies, fever and ague. On the night of July 9, 1793, he rode wearily into the capital to find Allison ill and shops and businesses closed as a yellow fever epidemic swept the city.[2]

Knox, though cordial to the governor, was disappointed over the failure of the expected Indian chiefs to arrive and querulous because of the Beard massacre. Also, the Administration was much concerned with the Anglo-French war and with French Minister Edmond Genêt's imprudent conduct, and so the governor's conferences with the War Secretary were necessarily intermittent. Andrew Pickens, too, had been summoned to confer, and the two Southerners worked hard, and, for once, in unison to bring Knox to their views. By conference and written memoranda they urged a Sevier-led war on the Creeks and gave estimates of forces needed. They also urged that the United States at once establish a military post at Bear Creek, near Muscle Shoals, a post agreed to at the Hopewell treaties but later refused by the Indians. Such an installation, when

[2] William Blount to Daniel Smith, June 17, 1793, in Carter (ed.), *Territorial Papers,* IV, 274–75; Henry Knox to William Blount, June 26, 1793, *ibid.,* 278–79; William Blount to Judges Campbell, McNairy, and Anderson, August 28, 1793, *ibid.,* 301–303; *id.* to John Gray Blount, July 10, 1793, in Blount Collection; John Bach McMaster, *A History of the People of the United States* (New York, 1883–1913), II, 125–31.

supplemented by trading establishments, would divert the Chickasaw trade and resultant political affiliations from Spain to the United States.[3] More immediately, it would prevent hostile alliances between the Northern and Southern tribes, protect Mero, and serve as a means of assisting the Chickasaw in their current hostilities against the Creeks. This last assistance had long been strenuously urged, first by Robertson on Blount, then by the latter on the Administration. The Cabinet had debated urging the Choctaw to join the Chickasaw and then supporting both secretly but had split on the question. Blount and Pickens, now regarding a Creek-American war as inevitable, strongly urged some such American intervention.[4]

As the days of conference passed, Blount found that Washington was inclined towards his arguments for "chastising" the Creeks, but that the possible international concomitants of such an action combined with the recent breakdown of Indian negotiations at Detroit and the reluctance of Congress to undertake such a war were too strong for his arguments.[5] The Beard massacre also turned official sentiment against a white offensive. The Secretary of War, at least in regard to the Southwestern Indians in 1793, showed no sign of a desire to exercise his military powers. On August 5, he asked for suggestions as to the best means to "postpone a Creek war." The frontier leaders replied wearily that sending someone disguised as a trader to distribute occasional presents would probably "induce the Creeks to commit fewer Murders and Rob-

[3] Carter (ed.), *Territorial Papers*, IV, 283–89; William Blount to Judges Campbell, McNairy, and Anderson, August 28, 1793, *ibid.*, 301–303; Blount Memorandum, July 31, 1793, in George Washington Papers; Andrew Pickens and William Blount to Henry Knox, August 1, 1793, *ibid.*

[4] Andrew Pickens and William Blount to Henry Knox, August 1, 1793, in George Washington Papers; Cabinet minutes, June 1, 1793, in Carter (ed.), *Territorial Papers*, IV, 266–67.

[5] William Blount to Judges Campbell, McNairy, and Anderson, August 28, 1793, in Carter (ed.), *Territorial Papers*, IV, 301–303.

beries than they otherwise would," and, they added hopefully, might "collect much Information that would be
useful in the War with that Nation." [6] For the pacification
of Cherokee anger over the Beard murders, the Westerners
recommended gifts and a conference. As the meetings
ended in late August, Blount gradually realized that the
only possibility for an offensive war lay in a change of
sentiment in Congress, and he pinned his hopes on Wayne's
success in the Northwest and a subsequent diversion of
troops to the Southwest.

But if official business went badly for the governor,
private operations beckoned appealingly for the speculator.
The alarms and excursions of the past year had in no wise
diminished his interest in or pursuit of land. Acting with
the greatest secrecy, using dozens of aliases, numerous
surveyors, and various partners, he built up an imperial
domain in land claims. At the same time, the firm of John
Gray & Thomas Blount was acquiring enormous tracts of
several hundred thousand acres on the Mississippi, and
John Gray Blount himself was plunging in Carolina and
Georgia lands. [7]

The business schemes of the capital always fascinated
Blount, and the private conferences and dinner table con-
versations of this visit convinced him of the wisdom of a
change of technique in land operations. Although, as a
Blount he never disdained small purchases or sales, he
now began to specialize in transactions involving the sale

[6] Henry Knox to William Blount and Andrew Pickens, August 5, 1793,
ibid., 295; William Blount and Andrew Pickens to Henry Knox, August 6,
1793, *ibid.*

[7] William Polk to John Gray Blount, January 18, 1794, in Blount Col-
lection; John Hall to *id.*, April 8, 1791, *ibid.*; Daniel Smith to Francis Walker,
June 6, July 13, 1793, in William C. Rives Collection, Papers of Thomas
Walker (Division of Manuscripts, Library of Congress); Knox County Deeds,
Book A-1, 254, 258; Book B-2 (I), 121; Book C-1, 106; John Preston
Arthur, *Western North Carolina* (Raleigh, 1914), 135–36; Keith, "Three
North Carolina Blount Brothers," 276–78.

of enormous tracts, this change paralleling one in family methods in Carolina and Georgia, where whole counties were now insufficient to meet the unending stream of their land warrants. Captivated by accounts of Robert Morris' gigantic sales to Dutch investors, the Blounts began to acquire claims to fantastic amounts of acreage for the purpose of disposal overseas.[8] Mountflorence's sales trip to France had been blighted by the flames of the French Revolution, but the speculating brothers were convinced of the existence of a European market, and a beginning was now being planned in England and Holland. To reach this market as well as Eastern seaboard speculators, Hugh Williamson for months past had combined attendance in Congress with extensive preparations of a detailed map of the Territory and a prospectus of Western land which he planned to sell to speculators and possible investors. Blount, unsure of his friend's success, had already in the Territory assisted William Tatham in the preparation of a similar map, and he now gave information and assistance to Williamson, whose prospectus was to be included in Matthew Carey's geography.[9]

Of vastly greater portent to himself, Blount took up with old friend Nicholas Romayne a project they had discussed earlier—namely an association to sell in England the huge tracts which Blount was now acquiring. Romayne had sent his family on to London, whence he planned to follow soon for permanent residence. His connections with

[8] William Blount to James Robertson, December 7, 1793, January 19, 1794, in "Robertson Correspondence," *loc. cit.*, III, 269–70, 282–83; Peter Mallett to John Gray Blount, June 13, July 13, 1791, in Blount Collection; Benjamin Smith to *id.*, September 24, 1793, *ibid.*; Hugh Williamson to *id.*, February 16, 1792, January 10, 1793, *ibid.*; Thomas Blount to *id.*, February 18, 1794, *ibid.*; correspondence of James C. Mountflorence, 1792–93, *ibid.*; John Gray Blount to John Strother (n.d.), *ibid.*, P.C. 905.

[9] Hugh Williamson to John Gray Blount, August 20, 1793, in Blount Collection; William Blount to John Gray Blount, September 18, 1793, *ibid.*; Knoxville *Gazette*, March 23, 1793.

wealthy Englishmen were good, and he and Blount drew up formal articles of association in the enterprise.[10]

Several other affairs engaged the governor. He arranged for a meeting of those landholders whose grants had been placed in Indian territory by the Treaty of Holston, in order to urge on the December North Carolina assembly the passage of compensatory legislation and a petition to Congress. Then too, agent Mountflorence was in prison on the charge of a lady for breach of promise, as well as on the less romantic charge of debt, and hence needed the assistance of his patron. The latter was involved also in negotiations to sell his shares of the old Bend Company to Joseph Martin, who, with other Virginians, was planning to resume the Tennessee Yazoo Company's attempts at a Muscle Shoals settlement.[11]

Since the Administration proved adamant against a Creek war, these land and other matters of personal interest would have led the governor to visit his brother John Gray in Carolina, but the blackening news of Indian troubles persuaded him to go at once to the Territory. The summer had been full of sickness in Carolina, though, and his wife was needed there by the family. Relieved to have her far from "the *Jacobin* Part of the Cherokee and Creek Nation," Blount decided that she should stay in Carolina for the winter while he joined the ailing Allison and Joseph Sevier in a carriage for the long trip to the Territory. At Abingdon, Virginia, they encountered John McKee, a Blount lieutenant, with Piomingo and other

[10] *The Debates and Proceedings in the Congress of the United States* (Washington, 1851), 5 Cong., II, 2357 (hereinafter referred to as *Annals of Congress*); Hugh Williamson to John Gray Blount, August 20, 1793, in Blount Collection.

[11] William Blount to John Gray Blount, July 10, August 14, 1793, in Blount Collection; Hugh Williamson to *id.*, November 10, 1793, *ibid.*; William Blount to Joseph Martin (and John Gray Blount), September 18–19, 1793, *ibid.*; petition of land proprietors, December 26, 1793, in Carter (ed.), *Territorial Papers*, IV, 314–15; Haywood, *History of Tennessee*, 417–18.

Chickasaw on the way to see the President, but by means of accounts of the yellow fever epidemic the Indians were persuaded to turn back, as Blount explained to Knox, to save expense.[12]

As the governor approached his Territory, he was conscious of the failure of his mission. Though he felt the next Congress should "be gullatined" if they failed to declare and execute a punitive war on the Creeks, yet he well knew the strong Eastern opposition to such a war. As for the Administration, the President was impotent, if not secretly unwilling, Knox was indecisive, and Hamilton opposed. The exigencies of the Northwestern campaign, and especially of Spanish-American relations, clearly came first in the minds of President and Cabinet. Blount therefore became obsessed with the conviction that Spain was in several respects the primary enemy of the West—a conviction of eventful consequences.[13]

In early October, 1793, the Territory to which the governor returned was still in considerable turmoil. The rising swell of anger which had so disturbed him before his departure had broken in a wave on the less influential Smith who presided in the governor's absence. The usual Indian depredations were answered by volunteer punitive expeditions which Smith was powerless to halt, and which even included officers of the government. Though Beard's massacre of friendly Cherokee had signaled the opening of special violence, he was acquitted of a murder charge by a partisan jury. Others led expeditions at will into Indian territory and killed Indians usually innocent of the

[12] Thomas Blount to John Gray Blount, September 22, 1793, in Blount Collection; William Blount to *id.*, September 19, 1793, *ibid.*; *id.* to Henry Knox, October 5, 1793, in Carter (ed.), *Territorial Papers*, IV, 307; *id.* to John Sevier, August 28, 1793, *ibid.*, 303–304; *id.* to James Robertson, October 11, 1793, in "Robertson Correspondence," *loc. cit.*, II, 373.

[13] William Blount to John Gray Blount, September 19, 1793, in Blount Collection.

immediate outrage which provoked the attack, but harassment was continual from the Creeks, the Chickamauga, and small Cherokee bands.[14] On September 24, the climax had come. An Indian "army" of six or seven hundred Creeks, Chickamauga, and Cherokee under John Watts moved across the Tennessee River and toward Knoxville. That settlement had been spared only by Indian indecision and the sacrifice of the family of Alexander Cavet, whose small station eight miles from Knoxville was destroyed; and on September 30 Smith had dispatched General John Sevier with several hundred men to pursue the Indians into their own territory. The governor's arrival found this expedition still absent, but it returned on October 25 with accounts of success in several skirmishes and the destruction of a considerable quantity of Indian provisions.[15]

The consequences of this, the last of Sevier's Indian campaigns, were almost immediately felt in the Territory; for, while Indian attacks continued, their number and ferocity temporarily declined. Blount was therefore able to heed Knox's orders to reduce the militia somewhat, though the settlers individually or through grand juries complained bitterly of the lack of protection.[16] From the Creek nation, Seagrove wrote of the strong sentiment for peace, and Blount in reply assured the agent the sentiment was

[14] Daniel Smith to Henry Knox, June 13, 22, July 19, 27, August 31, 1793, in Carter (ed.), *Territorial Papers,* IV, 271–72, 276–78, 280–83, 290, 304–305; Knoxville *Gazette,* July 13, 27, August 13, September 14, 1793; Haywood, *History of Tennessee,* 300–306.

[15] Ramsey, *Annals,* 580–88; Goodpasture, "Indian Wars," *loc. cit.,* 208–210; John McDonald to Governor White, September 12, 1793, in Papeles de Cuba; Daniel Smith to Henry Knox, September 27, 1793, in Carter (ed.), *Territorial Papers,* IV, 305–307; William Blount to *id.,* October 12, 18, 28, 1793, *ibid.,* 307–308, 310.

[16] William Blount to John Sevier, October 28, 1793, in Draper Collection, 4XX34, 4XX36; General Orders, November 8, 1793, in "Robertson Correspondence," *loc. cit.,* III, 80–81; William Blount to James Robertson, November 28, 29, 1793, January 18, 1794, *ibid.,* 81–83, 278–81; *id.* to Daniel Kennedy, November 8, 1793 (Blount Mansion, Knoxville).

mutual but recounted at length the nation's crimes against the territorials and warned that his aroused citizens could no longer be held in check if the attacks continued.

In this relative lull in Indian hostilities, the governor was able to devote closer attention to private business. He saw to it that the speculators' meeting for an assault on Congress was well advertised. He bought and sold land and rented on shares, although he thoroughly disliked the latter system. Titus Ogden, his general agent for mercantile transactions, died, and the governor made haste to claim his estate. Through another agent, Robertson, he continued to seek out vendors of large tracts in order to purchase for European clients, and George Farragut was kept busy bearing communications between the Territory and Carolina. With his old friend Thomas Hart, Blount began a correspondence concerning speculation and land sales in Kentucky, which was "more full of Money arising from . . . the army North of Ohio than any other Part of America." Blount was particularly concerned that the Transylvania Company's members obtain legal titles to their tract in the Territory, as both he and his brother John Gray had purchased from the company and were trustees for others. Still other involved financial transactions occurred between the governor and Robertson through the former's secret financial agent, Sheriff Sampson Williams.[17]

With all the distractions of public and private business, Blount was lonely. The absence of his wife and

[17] Knoxville *Gazette*, October 12, 1793; William Blount to John Gray Blount, October 22, 1793, January 21, 1794, in Blount Collection; *id.* to James Robertson, December 7, 1793, January 19, March 7, 1794, in "Robertson Correspondence," *loc. cit.*, III, 269–70, 282–83, 286–87; Thomas Hart to William Blount, December 23, 1793, in Roosevelt, *Winning of the West*, III, Pt. 1, 251–52; William Blount to Thomas Hart, October 25, 1793, February 9, 1794, in Thomas J. Clay Papers (Division of Manuscripts, Library of Congress).

children made a void in his daily existence. In earlier days
in the exposed cabin, Mrs. Blount had lived in terror of
the murder or kidnapping of her children by the savages.
Lately, the greater security of Knoxville's growth had led
her to make the governor's home a place of family warmth
and gaiety, and no absorption in affairs of state or business
dimmed Blount's delight in his young ones, for whose
future prominence and wealth he unceasingly planned.
Now, with his wife, his half brother Willie, and all his
children in Carolina, the governor felt keenly the emptiness
and silence of the house.

Loneliness was accentuated by a sense of growing popular disfavor. Upon his arrival from Philadelphia he had
felt the trip and the return well-timed. Radical popular
feeling had been eased by Sevier's campaign, while conservative settlers, alarmed by Smith's helplessness, showed
such pleasure at the governor's return that he was convinced his popularity was then "as high as ever it was."
But the continued Indian attacks coupled with the growing realization of the failure of his Philadelphia mission
brought a further reaction against him. Cocke, desperately
ill, had concluded a truce with Sevier, but Tiptonians were
vociferous critics. In December, 1793, some Mero citizens
sought to join the Genêt-Clark expedition against West
Florida. When the governor denounced "these Schemes
[which] must proceed from the Machenations . . . of
that jacobin Incendiary Genet," and issued stern orders
to repress the expedition, he incurred further resentment.
David Henley, the newly appointed paymaster-agent of
the War Department, viewed with critical eye Blount's
personal business relations with Robertson and other officers, and made no secret of his disapproval. The fiscal
enactments of the governor and judges were in some places

flatly denied obedience. Robertson yet held his district in surface loyalty, but even that sorely tried lieutenant was weary and talked of resignation.[18]

Such an admission of defeat was, however, not in Blount's mind; he had other plans than retreat. Between the increasing clamor on one hand, and the firm antiwar policy of the Administration on the other, he decided on a neat finesse by a call of the long-demanded legislature. Through an entente between William Cocke and the supporters of Robertson and Sevier he might control the legislators while the public discontent was silenced, and at the same time the Administration in Philadelphia might hear other and perhaps more convincing arguments for war than his own had been. Statehood would then follow, with a senatorship as a prize for his labors. On October 17, the grand jury of Hamilton District presented a strong complaint of Indian marauders, coupled with a reminder, amid polite compliments, of their right to an assembly. The governor returned equally polished thanks for their congratulations on his return and for other felicitations but pointedly said nothing about a legislature. Two days later, however, he called for an election in late December and according to the Ordinance of 1787 assigned the methods of voting, the number of representatives (13), and the terms (two years).[19]

Elections took place accordingly, to the great interest

[18] William Blount to John Gray Blount, October 22, 1793, in Blount Collection; William Cocke to John Sevier, August 15, 1793, in Draper Collection, 11DD103; William Blount to Thomas Hart, October 25, 1793, in Thomas J. Clay Collection; id. to Daniel Smith, November 29, 1793, in "Papers of Daniel Smith," loc. cit., 226; David Milsom to id., July 23, 1793, ibid., 225–26; William Blount to James Robertson, November 29, 1793, January 18, 1794, in "Robertson Correspondence," loc. cit., III, 82–83, 278–81; David Henley to Gabriel Duval, March 3, 1808, in David Henley Papers (Duke Archives, Duke University).

[19] Knoxville Gazette, November 23, 1793; Carter (ed.), Territorial Papers, IV, 309–10.

of both the people and their governor. The former expressed their views in elections riots amid charges of bribery and illegal voting worthy of a far more politically sophisticated electorate; the governor expressed his in careful understanding with his followers as to candidates. Opposition or loyalty to him and his administration was, in fact, a principal issue of all the various campaigns.[20] On January 1, 1794, he called for the successful candidates to assemble in Knoxville in late February to nominate ten councilors from whom the President would name five. The early date was selected in order that Congress might still be in session when the record of the meeting of the representatives reached Philadelphia, for the governor was sure such a record would include a demand for punishment of the Creeks.[21]

In this belief he was not disappointed. When the delegates gathered in Knoxville on February 24, the matter of Indian defense was uppermost in all minds. The governor's message cited the Ordinance of 1787 as their constitution and remarked facetiously that the work of the session was limited to the nomination of councilors. But after marching with Blount to hear the Reverend Samuel Carrick's prayers and sermon on Paul's Epistle to Titus, the representatives on reconvening showed no disposition to limit their activities. Cocke introduced and Tipton seconded a motion for an address to Congress, and a committee was named to write it. The house then nominated ten councilors, after which it adopted the report of the Congressional address committee. This report strongly requested a Creek war and reminded Congress that they

[20] Knoxville *Gazette,* December 7, 1793, January 16, March 13, 1794; William Blount to James Robertson, January 19, 1794, in "Robertson Correspondence," *loc. cit.,* III, 282–83; *id.* to John Gray Blount, October 26, 1794, in Blount Collection.

[21] Carter (ed.), *Territorial Papers,* IV, 319.; William Blount to Daniel Smith, January 19, 1794, in Miscellaneous Manuscripts.

who had borne a part in the Revolution had suffered two hundred murders and a loss of $100,000 in property since 1791. They warned that "self preservation" might induce the frontiersmen to act "unauthorized by your declaration," for the consequences of which they were not responsible, and they closed with an ironic congratulation on the measures adopted against the Algerines and a reminder that poor frontiersmen should claim equal protection with those who "roll in luxury, ease, and affluence" in Eastern cities.[22]

The governor too received the delegates' attention. They again complained sharply of too little protection and besought him to extend his authority to encompass the erection of a chain of forts at places named. They also recommended that militia tours be reduced to two months and requested a guard for the returning Mero members.

On being informed that the business of the session was completed, the governor prorogued the representatives until the fourth Monday in August. He was not dissatisfied with the work of the delegates, for the pain of their censure was allayed by the satisfaction of a fairly friendly set of nominees and a strong remonstrance to Congress. The nominee list was dispatched by express to Congress, and Dr. James White followed with the address.

In the months which followed, Blount was primarily absorbed by the two major concerns of his entire administration—the Indian problem and his private land transactions. Four days after the representatives were prorogued, a letter from Robertson, stained with the blood of the wounded courier, announced larger scale Indian depredations in Mero, and Blount was forced to revoke his late orders and enlarge the militia bands. As the fierceness and

---

[22] Knoxville *Gazette,* March 13, 27, 1794; Ramsey, *Annals,* 621–22. For the nominees, see Carter (ed.), *Territorial Papers,* IV, 328, 329.

frequency of murders, assaults, and thefts increased, the frontiersmen's rage soared against both Indians and Spanish. The replacement of Genêt removed the governor's worries over expeditions against Florida; but the Indians' brutal slaughter of William Casteel and his entire family roused the French Broad settlers to plan another incursion into Indian territory, which was stopped with difficulty by the persuasions of Blount supporters under Knoxville's General James White. In the face of rising anger, the governor could do little save urge patience in awaiting the outcome of Dr. White's mission to Congress and to preach the "Republican Virtue" of economy in calling out militia. He encouraged Robertson by pointing out the prospects of a Chickasaw-Chickamauga war. He also sent John McKee and Joseph Sevier to the lower Cherokee to urge a peace conference and mingled appeals with orders to his militia officers to protect the conference.[23]

However, even these frail reeds of hope withered in the winter of Administration disapproval. Despite the most urgent pleas of Doctor White, Knox, faced with the approaching climax of Anthony Wayne's campaign, could not bring himself to advocate the dispatch of regular troops to the Southwest nor to authorize offensive operations by the militia. In response to the pleas of the territorial representative, a bill was introduced in the House for more effectual defense, and passed on May 29, but heavy amendments by the Senate were rejected by the House, and no further action was taken. The best that White's representations could obtain, therefore, was a post at the Cumberland crossing, an increase of standing militia, and six

[23] William Blount to Daniel Smith, April 3, 1794, in Miscellaneous Manuscripts; Ramsey, *Annals,* 592–94; William Blount to John Gray Blount, May 26, 1794, in Blount Collection; *id.* to James Robertson, April 3, 15, 1794, in Carter (ed.), *Territorial Papers,* IV, 334, 340–41; *id.* to Captain Campbell, May 23, 1794, in David Campbell Papers (Duke Archives, Duke University).

howitzers with ammunition to be sent from Philadelphia
to Nashville. With such meager results the governor was
deeply disappointed, but he gave orders to Robertson accordingly and awaited the assembling of the legislature.

Meanwhile, the spring and summer months had wit-
nessed an accelerating tempo in Blount's land operations.
The great land boom of 1795 was building up in the East,
while in the Territory farsighted speculators such as the
governor, foreseeing statehood and the possible loss of vast
tracts of public domain, hastened to buy on every occasion.
Armed with Tatham's and Williamson's maps, borrowing
more and more heavily from every source, even diverting
public funds for his private uses,[24] Blount plunged again
and again into huge transactions. His association with
Paymaster Allison, formerly largely mercantile, now became a partnership in land speculation, with Blount buying in the territory and Allison selling on his trips to the
capital. Allison had invested in lead mines in the territory
and in 1794 was buying land wildly with both William
and John Gray Blount in order to fill an eastern contract
for three million acres. In this same year the firm of John
Gray & Thomas Blount loaned him $150,000, and in
1795, $82,340.[25] Robertson, too, was pressed to divide
with the governor the lands they formerly held in common,
to secure yet more purchasers, and to manipulate funds for
the governor's benefit.[26]

While using fictitious names or those of agents (except
when he wished to frighten off rival bidders) Blount also

[24] William Blount to John Pitchlynn, October 14, 1793, in "Robertson
Correspondence," *loc. cit.*, II, 374; affidavit of John Pitchlynn, September
4, 1795, in David Henley Papers; John Overton to David Henley, December
10, 1795, *ibid.*; Hugh Williamson to John Gray Blount, February 9, 1793,
in Blount Collection.

[25] Correspondence of David Allison, 1794–95, in Blount Collection, P.C.
852, 853, 854; memorandum of Allison notes in Rodman Papers.

[26] William Blount to James Robertson, January 19, March 7, 1794, in
"Robertson Correspondence," *loc. cit.*, III, 282–83, 286–87.

continued to do much of his business through the firm of John Gray & Thomas Blount, Merchants. Nevertheless, operations of such magnitude inevitably came into public view. One grand jury in North Carolina indicted the Blount firm for fraudulently obtaining 105,000 acres of Western lands. Another presented as a "public grievance" and "insufferable monopoly" the engrossment of land by "land jobbers," among whom it named John Gray Blount and a number of his associates. Meanwhile in the territory, Paymaster David Henley sent to Secretary Knox evidence of malfeasance in office and attempted to rally sentiment against the governor.[27]

These attacks annoyed but did not in the least deter either brother. John Gray Blount entered a partnership with one John Hall, a representative of Eastern speculators, and began the task of securing four million acres in North Carolina, of which the Blounts were to keep five hundred thousand in addition to their fees for the rest. Allison, plunging deeply, counted on another one to two million acres from his Carolina partner.[28] William Blount was deeply involved through the firm in his brother's commitments and on May 1 journeyed to the "Moravian Town" (Salem, North Carolina) for the double purpose of meeting his own returning family and making land plans with John Gray. Moreover, schemes of his brother and of Allison were by no means the entire scope of the governor's large scale activities, for his project with Romayne also required vast acquisitions. Through Stockley Donelson, his principal surveyor, he had maps made of

<hr>

[27] Copies of presentments of grand juries, 1794, in Blount Collection, P.C. 881, 884; John Overton to David Henley, December 10, 1795, in David Henley Papers; David Henley to Gabriel Duval, March 3, 1808, *ibid.*

[28] Land plats and warrants in Blount Collection, P.C. 884; Thomas Blount to John Gray Blount, January 11, March 27, December 4, 11, 26, 1794, in Blount Collection; Blackledge correspondence, 1794, *ibid.*, P.C. 852, 853; Sumner County Deeds, Book A, 209.

various holdings and sent James Grant, his agent, to sell them in Philadelphia, planning to realize $100,000 on one tract alone. In July, another survey of 95,370 Hawkins County acres followed. For the Fall, he planned with Donelson to make a "sweeping Survey between the Clinch & Holston" rivers to include about 150,000 acres more, and other projects were initiated to buy out all the Transylvania Company partners or subpurchasers resident in the Territory. Further sales to Allison totaled 164,000 acres, while smaller tracts of 3,000 acres each were also vended to Eastern purchasers directed to him by Allison. John Chisholm, the governor's personal Indian agent and general handyman, was sent to Thomas Hart in Kentucky to confer on sales.[29] Thus, by town lots and by parcels from a few acres to many thousands, the governor's holdings grew steadily into a colossal total acreage. On occasions he sold tracts of various sizes, but the overwhelming trend was accretion in the Eastern area, in Mero, and even on the Mississippi.

These pleasant excursions into futures were complicated in August, 1794, by the gathering of the first territorial assembly. Prodded and advised by Dr. James White, the Administration had named as legislative councilors Griffith Rutherford, John Sevier, James Winchester, Stockley Donelson, and Parmenas Taylor, all of whom were Blount's friends, and whose selection, in every case but Taylor's, was preordained. With immense self-

[29] William Blount to John Gray Blount, March 27, May 26, July 2, 18, 29, October 26, 1794, in Blount Collection; Knox County Deeds, Book A-1, 202–203, 213, 254, 258, 260; Book B-2, I, 124, 126, 127–28, 131, 212; Book C-1, 1, 107, 139, 140; Book N-1, 375; Sumner County Deeds, Book A, 209; Davidson County Deeds, Book C, 342; William Blount to James Robertson, September 9, 1794, in "Robertson Correspondence," *loc. cit.*, III, 358; *id.* to Thomas Hart, November 18, 1794, in Thomas J. Clay Collection; Keith, "Three North Carolina Blount Brothers," 278–89, 291–95, 296–99.

conscious satisfaction the Knoxville citizens on August 25, 1794, watched the assembling of these five councilors and the eleven, later thirteen, representatives.[30] Nearly two hundred travelers arrived along with the representatives from Mero, and this invasion coupled with that of the interested and the curious of the eastern area put some strain on the hospitality of Knoxville's forty dwellings; but Chisholm's, Stone's, and Carmichael's taverns took nightly care of some distinguished guests. The governor's mansion, too, although once again crowded with family, was always open to the legislators, most of whom stayed, however, in the homes of friends outside of but near the settlement.

After preliminaries on August 25, including a "suitable and well adapted prayer by the Rev. Mr. Carrick," the two houses on Tuesday settled to their work. The council met in the fort's barracks; the representatives met in Carmichael's tavern or another room of the barracks. Conferences and occasional meetings were scheduled in the courthouse, for which General James White, the city founder, was paid five dollars. Roulstone, through Blount and Sevier influence, secured both the council clerkship and the public printing. Griffith Rutherford, for his parliamentary experience in Carolina, was chosen president of the council, and David Wilson speaker of the house. Carolina precedent was closely followed in procedure and rules. The steering committees included William Cocke,

---

[30] James White to Edmund Randolph, April 16, 1794, in Carter (ed.), *Territorial Papers*, IV, 342; William Blount to Edmund Randolph, July 28, 1794, *ibid.*, 350–51; Knoxville *Gazette*, August 25, 1794; *Journal of the Proceedings of the Legislative Council of the Territory . . . Begun and Held at Knoxville, the 25th Day of August, 1794* (Knoxville, 1794; Nashville, 1852), 3 (hereinafter referred to as *Council Journal*); *Journal of the Proceedings of the House of Representatives of the Territory . . . Begun and Held at Knoxville, the 25th Day of August, 1794* (Knoxville, 1794; Nashville, 1852), 3, 5 (hereinafter referred to as *House Journal*).

Joseph Hardin, James White, John Sevier, and James Winchester. John Tipton, though late in arrival, was very active.[31]

The governor had anticipated the session with considerable misgivings, but events proved that in most cases he had no cause for anxiety. Through Sevier and, for a while, Winchester, he controlled the action in the council with fair success. The careful bestowal of offices and favors in the past now produced results in Blount supporters such as Dr. James White and Joseph Hardin. The representatives defeated Sevier's attempt to have bills referred to the governor before final passage, but despite the presence of Tipton, the lower body was not openly hostile, due in part to the able work of young Hugh Lawson White, the governor's secretary and son of Knoxville's founder, General James White.

The passage of legislation, therefore, was swift and generally unopposed. Cocke secured for Knoxville a college (named for the governor), and another, Greeneville College, was set up under Reverend Hezikiah Balch in Greene County. The judicial code was reworked by Sevier with the assistance of Blount's half brother, Willie, and the acts of the governor and judges were accepted, although their tax enactments were repealed and replaced by those of the legislature.[32] Mero's wishes were heeded in a provision for a lottery in order to build county buildings in Nashville. The French Broad people received considerable attention in that the old Franklin division of Sevier County was re-established (though that of Blount was not), and a memorial of citizens from the French Broad requesting pre-emption rights and the validation of their land purchases from Carolina was forwarded to Con-

[31] Ramsey, *Annals*, 630; *Council Journal*, 3, 4, 8–9; *House Journal*, 4–5, 43.
[32] *House Journal*, 8, 16, 36–37; *Council Journal*, 12, 30, 34.

gress. With it went another petition for measures to "punish those two faithless and bloodthirsty nations, the Creeks and Cherokees," along with a painstaking account showing that from February to September, 67 persons had been killed, 10 wounded, 25 captured, and 374 horses stolen. The memorial denounced the policy of official gifts to Indians, and assured the Administration that "fear, not love, is the only means by which Indians can be governed." [33]

Only occasionally did the houses clash, reflecting the divergent economic and social status of their respective constituents. The representatives refused to allow the "artists" employed in iron works and bloomeries to be exempt from militia duty, while the councilors killed a rate of fees for attorneys. The principal fight, however, came over taxation, as had similar struggles in North Carolina. The upper house refused a tax on stud horses, while emphasizing a poll tax on free males and a tax of twelve and one-half cents per hundred acres on land. The representatives, willing to compromise on other provisions, steadfastly insisted on a twenty-five cents per hundred acres tax. As days passed in disagreement, the council sought to compromise on eighteen cents, but finally was compelled to capitulate. This action marked defeat for the governor, one of whose reasons for accepting his office had been to secure a favorable land tax policy.[34] But his forces still showed the strength to control when, on September 3, Dr. James White was elected territorial delegate to Congress over William Cocke, by eleven votes to seven.[35] A victory of value to the governor, this placed a friend in an influential position in the coming campaign for statehood.

[33] *Council Journal,* 21, 25; *House Journal,* 8, 23–24, 28–30.

[34] *House Journal,* 40; *Council Journal,* 29, 30–33; Williams, "Admission of Tennessee," *loc. cit.,* 294.

[35] *Council Journal,* 11; Knoxville *Gazette,* September 9, 1794.

A considerable impetus for this campaign was Blount's growing absorption with huge land tracts, for extraterritorial speculation inevitably drew his interests more and more continually to Philadelphia. At the same time, the refusal of the Administration to permit a Southwestern Indian war on the one hand, and the mounting demand for legislative participation in the Territorial government on the other indicated clearly that the days of his political domination were numbered. This conclusion was reemphasized also by Sevier's growing restiveness. "Nollachucky Jack's" popularity, being based on Indian chastisement, never dropped as did the governor's; in fact, the repressive role forced on Blount pointed up all the more the well-known impetuosity of his general. The latter knew this and felt he had paid the penalty for Franklin by his secondary role in the Territory, while he increasingly savored the sweets of power which could be his under statehood. Blount's course was therefore clear: statehood as quickly as possible and the national Senate, leaving to Sevier the coveted governorship. Well before the legislature met, the governor had begun his campaign. Through the press, private conferences, and correspondence, he urged the change. Talk of Federal taxes now gave way to arguments that only by statehood could the Territory achieve protection from the Indian attacks. With his blessing if not through his authorship the legislature adopted a resolution for a new census and coupled with it the explicit requirements for a poll on statehood.[36]

At length on September 30, the houses concluded their work. Blount was, with the exception of the tax law, very pleased with the legislature's labors and with its cordiality, as well as with his reviving popularity. Thanks and congratulations were exchanged and the governor upon re-

---

[36] Knoxville *Gazette*, August 28, 1794; *House Journal*, 17, 40.

quest furnished a guard for the Mero members and a prorogation until the first Monday in October in Knox-ville,[37] whereupon, after a farewell round of calls and entertainment, the legislators departed for their respective homes.

The intricacies of guiding a legislature were only a part, however, of the governor's Fall diplomacy. Even while the legislature sat, he was absorbed in the results of a calculated risk in Indian relations. During the summer months the usual pattern of half-peace, half-war had con-tinued. The Administration in pursuance of its appease-ment principle brought delegations of both Cherokee and Chickasaw to Philadelphia. The former had the Holston Treaty further financially revised in their favor, and the latter were loaded with gifts and assurances of good will (though not actual assistance) in their hostilities with the Creeks. The Creeks, however, with the assistance of some Chickamauga, maintained the sporadic but continual harassment under which the restless tempers of the settlers rose steadily. In May, General Robertson visited the gov-ernor and broached his favorite scheme of an expedition against the Chickamauga towns. He received cautious sympathy and unofficial approval and quietly proceeded. During the summer, scouts, by Robertson's orders, dis-covered a more direct route to the towns, and Blount re-newed his pressure on Knox to secure authorization for an attack. In August, however, an order of the Secretary's flatly refused this,[38] whereupon, with public sentiment rising over this rebuff, the governor and his general pro-

---

[37] *House Journal*, 36, 37, 40, 41; William Blount and Willie Blount to John Gray Blount, October 25, 1794, in Blount Collection; William Blount to *id.*, October 26, 1794, *ibid.*; *id.* to James Robertson, October 1, 1794, in Carter (ed.), *Territorial Papers*, IV, 356–57.

[38] William Blount to Henry Knox, September 21, 1794, in Carter (ed.), *Territorial Papers*, IV, 354–55; Ramsey, *Annals*, 606–609; Putnam, *History of Middle Tennessee*, 436, 471–72.

ceeded to devise their strategy. A company of sixty-nine men under Major James Ore of Hamilton District was sent to Mero for a scouting expedition under Robertson's orders. Sampson Williams was dispatched to Kentucky with secret suggestions to the ever ready and aggressive Colonel William Whiteley who at once agreed to raise forces and join Ore.[39]

It was clearly understood between Blount and Robertson that the former would give no official sanction, and the latter, long seeking to escape further official duties, would assume full responsibility and tender his resignation to appease official wrath. The resignation was, in fact, written out by the governor, and Robertson's successor was agreed upon by the conspirators. The good news of the expedition was, however, impossible to keep, and in his enthusiasm Robertson authorized the raising of further troops in the neighborhood, as well as those he himself raised in Nashville.[40] On August 6, 1794, taking advantage of one of the more or less frequent reports of an impending Creek invasion, he ordered the troops to destroy the lower Cherokee towns and on the seventh, the frontiersmen left. Six days later, they fell upon the surprised Chickamauga Muscle Shoals towns of Nickajack and Running Water, dealing out complete destruction.[41]

Blount, meanwhile, carefully covered himself from official blame by both private and official letters, and when publicly informed of the expedition, went through every motion of official displeasure. Robertson's resignation was duly tendered and accepted, although no action on it was

[39] Reverend John Kidwell account, in Draper Collection, 32S257; Ramsey, *Annals*, 609–10; Putnam, *History of Middle Tennessee*, 476–77.

[40] James Robertson to William Blount, October 23, 1794, in "Robertson Correspondence," *loc. cit.*, III, 363; Ramsey, *Annals*, 609–10; Thomas E. Matthews, *General James Robertson* (Nashville, 1934), 399–401, 406–10.

[41] Ramsey, *Annals*, 610–16.

taken in Philadelphia.[42] The general meanwhile, though assuming responsibility, calmly defended himself and followed up with threats to John Watts of further action if peace were not secured.[43] These threats, coupled with the Nickajack campaign and Wayne's victory at Fallen Timbers, were in the case of the Cherokee and Chickamauga strikingly effective; and, although occasional bloody incursions continued from the Creeks, the backbone of the Chickamauga offensive was broken. As the winter began, the victorious frontiersmen were further reassured by the Federal troops stationed at South West Point, Fort Grainger, and Tellico Block House. Public confidence so rose, in fact, that in November, Blount had considerable difficulty in restraining another white incursion under Whiteley.[44] In November and December, Watts and other Cherokee and Chickamauga chieftains met the governor at Tellico Block House for the exchange of prisoners and for assurances of future peaceful intent.

Thus, as the attacks of the Creeks continued, the Westerners' interest shifted during the closing months of 1794 and early 1795 from antagonism toward the now broken Chickamauga to intensified sympathy for the Chickasaw in their deepening hostilities with the Creeks. The same period found the governor in optimistic mood.

[42] *Ibid.*, 617–18; William Blount to James Robertson, September 9, October 1, 1794, in "Robertson Correspondence," *loc. cit.*, III, 357, 360; *id.* to Henry Knox, September 22, 1794, in Carter (ed.), *Territorial Papers*, IV, 356; Abishai Thomas to John Gray Blount, October 20, 1794, in Blount Collection; Matthews, *General James Robertson*, 406–408, 410, 412, 413.

[43] James Robertson to William Blount, October 8, 1794, in Lowrie and Clark (eds.), *State Papers, Indian*, I, 529–30; *id.* to John Watts, September 20, 1794, *ibid.*, 531.

[44] Downes, "Indian Affairs," *loc. cit.*, 261–62; William Blount to Colonel Whiteley, November 1, 1794, in "Robertson Correspondence," *loc. cit.*, III, 365; *id.* to General Logan, November 1, 1794, *ibid.*, 366–67; *id.* to James Robertson, November 1, 1794, *ibid.*, 366; *id.* to Henry Knox, November 3, 1794, in Carter (ed.), *Territorial Papers*, IV, 361–64.

The belligerent Carondelet's proposed anti-American confederation of 1793 had been watered down by the more realistic Governor Gayoso to a mere protective treaty of little practical effect. Further efforts by the bellicose Spaniard to bring on an American-Indian war had been overruled by the Spanish court, which felt the need of American friendship in its unsure European position. Meanwhile, Wayne's victory and the suppression of the Whisky Rebellion convinced Blount that the long expected offensive against the Creeks would soon be sanctioned, and probably aided by Federal troops.[45] Therefore, while awaiting the glad tidings, and encouraged by Cherokee and Chickamauga passivity, he expanded Robertson's proposal for aid to the embattled Chickasaw into an ambitious plan for a general Indian confederacy against the Creeks. He was careful to deliver the Administration's presents to the Chickasaw and allowed Robertson to give that tribe strong hints of American aid, while he was punctilious in keeping the Choctaw satisfied. At Tellico in December, 1794, and January, 1795, he pressed the Cherokee to keep the Creeks back from the white settlements and to join the Chickasaw. To Robertson, he approved of all possible secret measures to support the Creek enemies. To Knox, he constantly urged the inevitability of a Creek war and the practicality of supporting Creek foes: "If the Citizens of the United States, do not destroy the Creeks, the Creeks will kill the Citizens of the United States, the alternative is to kill or be killed." [46]

[45] Whitaker, "Spain and the Cherokee Indians," *loc. cit.*, 260–62; William Blount to James Robertson, December 4, 1794, in "Robertson Correspondence," *loc. cit.*, III, 375–76.

[46] William Blount to James Robertson, October 8, 1794, January 6, 1794 [1795], February 2, 1795, in "Robertson Correspondence," *loc. cit.*, III, 272–73, 362, and IV, 171–72; Little Turkey and others to James Robertson, April 10, 1795, *ibid.*, IV, 191–92; Ecooe to John McKee, February 1, 1795, *ibid.*, 169–71; James Robertson to William Blount, January 13, 1795, *ibid.*,

For a time the governor's plans seemed to flower. The President requested information concerning logistics and manpower for a Creek war, and even Knox wavered in his pacifism. But on December 31, the bumbling if well-intentioned Secretary left office, and on January 2, 1795, his place was taken by one who was to play a large and fatal role in Blount's career. Much like the governor in several respects, Timothy Pickering was in others his exact antithesis. Both were strong haters, both were land speculators, both were snobs. Both, curiously enough, admired England, feared France, and despised Spain. Both grew to loathe John Adams. But the New Englander's thin frugality, his icy venom, his Puritan self-righteousness were alien to Blount's sense of fitness, even of decency. Blount's faults were chiefly those of character, Pickering's those of personality. The former are perhaps more serious, but the latter more often antagonizing. Conceivably they might have understood one another better in Blount's early years, but his Western career had produced changes in outlook which opened chasms between the frontier governor and the New England ultra-Federalist.

By the time the new Secretary came into office, he had formed a distinct and highly unfavorable opinion of Blount. He had read the accounts of the partisan George Welbank concerning the governor's activities, especially at the Treaty of Holston, and he was, or soon became, the recipient of Paymaster Henley's accusations. The latter charged Blount with duplicity toward the Indians, with using his office for private gain through illegal contracts

---

163–65; Willie Blount to Daniel Smith, December 13, 1794, in Draper Collection, 4XX41; agreement of David Moore and William Blount, October 12, 1794, in Blount Manuscripts (Tennessee State Archives); William Blount to John Pitchlynn, November 3, 1794, in Emmett Collection; *id.* to the Secretary of War, November 10, 16, 28, 1794, January 9, 10, 20, 1795, in Carter (ed.), *Territorial Papers,* IV, 364–70, 373, 380–81.

for supplies, and with disregard of United States policy in the interest of his private land speculations.[47] From his first days in office, therefore, the Secretary was convinced that Blount was a self-seeking swindler, and he refused to consider rationally any Blount suggestion, whatever its merits. On January 20, he opened with a complaint that six Chickasaw and Choctaw had "strolled to Philadelphia without an interpreter or Guide," and no one knew the object of the stroll except "that they might expect to be clothed and to receive presents." The Secretary wrote that he was "desirous of discouraging such irregular visits," and "must request you as far as lays in your power to prevent them." [48]

A further indication of the direction of the wind came from territorial delegate White on March 19. He informed Blount that Sevier's troops ordered out by Smith in 1793 would not be paid because the expedition was deemed not defensive, but offensive, and that Congress refused to "act with spirit" against the Creeks, despite the representations of the governor. In fact, of these representations he reported that "your candid & generous Statement of the necessity of Congress resenting the outrages committed against your Government by the Creeks, occasioned a Person high in office to observe that the ardor you Showed for that object indicated a disposition interested for that Purpose: which mistaken idea I had the mortification to hear uttered in my own presence." [49]

The real blast, however, came on March 23, 1795, when the Secretary devastatingly reviewed Blount's whole

[47] David Henley to Gabriel Duval, March 3, 1808, in Henley Papers.

[48] Timothy Pickering to William Blount, January 20, 1795 (copy), in "Robertson Correspondence," *loc. cit.*, IV, 275.

[49] James White to William Blount, March 19, 1795, in Carter (ed.), *Territorial Papers*, IV, 385–86.

policy. He informed the governor that Congress had refused to declare war against the Creeks, and "all ideas of offensive operations are therefore to be laid aside and all possible harmony cultivated with the Indian Tribes." The "small parties of plundering Creeks" would be restrained by "some pointed declarations to the Creeks" by Seagrove, from whom had been received reports indicating the probability of entire peace. Flatly the Secretary told Blount that the United States would not support the Cherokee nor the Chickasaw against the Creeks and ordered that the first two of these nations should so be informed. The Cherokee were not to be encouraged to attempt to stop Creek attacks on the whites, and the governor was censured for his Tellico implications of approval of such attempts. The Secretary could see no inevitable general Chickasaw-Creek war unless the governor continued to incite one; this he ordered the latter to cease doing, both in the case of Chickasaw and Cherokee. "Upon the whole, Sir," the acid pen went on, "I cannot refrain from saying that the complexion of some of the Transactions in the South western territory appears unfavorable to the public interests." The posts at Fort Grainger and at Tellico Block House were ordered removed if they continued to displease the Indians. Even South West Point was to be reduced unless it was guaranteed in writing to the Indians not to involve further land cession. Settlers on the Indian lands, "an unlooked for ground of complaint," were to be at once removed, if necessary by the Federal troops. The frontiersmen's complaint of horse stealing, the Secretary said, was nullified by such encroachment and by the purchase of the stolen animals by other whites. Furthermore, he strongly implied that recent murders of whites had been due to illegal hunting on the Indian lands where the game was to the Indians "as essential to their comfortable living as the Horses of the White men to their convenience and Support." [50]

This letter cut Blount the more for the elements of truth it contained. Not hampered, as Knox had been, by the exigencies of the Northwestern campaigns, Pickering was able to give closer scrutiny to Southwestern events and to pick upon undesirable conditions which there occurred with or without Blount's connivance. On the other hand, the Secretary, a rigid bureaucrat ensconced in Philadelphia, failed, perhaps through his hatred of Blount, to assess the actual temper of the West and the conditions surrounding a civil officer on a frontier. His logical legality missed the point, though to his cast of mind legality outweighed reality.

In any event, the importance of the letter on Blount's career was enormous. His immediate reaction was typical —a mobilization of counter sentiment. He sent copies to his lieutenants for popular information and excitation. He promised that, while the Secretary's letter was not "a very acceptable one to me, perhaps my answer to it may not be more pleasing to him." He also arranged with his Mero lieutenants to have drawn up grand jury grievances, complaining of the Federal policies laid down by Pickering and executed by Henley, which were identical with those he personally engineered in Knoxville. At the same time he suggested that Robertson send, but not appear to direct, some Chickasaw chiefs to accompany a Choctaw party on a trip to the President.[51]

Most important, however, was the long range effect of

[50] Timothy Pickering to William Blount, March 23, 1795, *ibid.*, 386–93.

[51] William Blount to James Robertson, April 26, 1795, in "Robertson Correspondence," *loc. cit.*, IV, 249–50; Putnam, *History of Middle Tennessee,* 506; grand jury protest, April, 1795, in *American Historical Magazine,* II (1897), 336–37; Haywood, *History of Tennessee,* 476.

Pickering's rebuke on Blount's attitude. The long exerted pressure of Western dissent from national policies had worn thin the governor's allegiance to the Eastern Administration. Intensely sensitive both to praise and blame, he had suffered much in popularity and, worse, prestige, to carry out the program of the Federalists. This letter from an ultra-Federalist snapped the frayed link of loyalty. At the same time, Blount's land involvement in the West had become economically vital to him. Regardless of his personal opinions, the prosperity and peopling of the West were from a purely economic standpoint his paramount concern. Thus his interests had become completely identified with those of his citizens, and in a clash of policy between them and the Administration, there could now be no question of his first loyalty.

Fortunately for both Blount and Pickering, the Indian situation was clearing during 1795. Carondelet had been working hard to heal the Chickasaw-Creek breach and to keep the Cherokee neutral, for an intertribal war meant the end of his pet theme of an anti-American confederacy. At the same time, his revival of the Kentucky intrigue took precedence in his efforts over his battered Indian policy. Furthermore, the Spanish government itself, anxious to incur no further foes on the eve of and after its desertion of England for a peace with France, desired that Creek attacks on the frontiersmen should not, at any rate, be abetted. The collapse of Chickamauga belligerency further tended to discourage Creek marauders and give more weight to the pacific advice of Seagrove. Also, the refusal of the Cherokee to join the Chickasaw in war and the Choctaw messages to the Creeks advising peace tended to close the Creek-Chickasaw hostilities.[52]

[52] Baron Carondelet to Mad Dog, March 25, 1795, in "Robertson Correspondence," *loc. cit.*, IV, 186–87; Whitaker, *Spanish-American Frontier*, 205, 208, 209–13.

Events of the Spring proved that Creek peace would come with the whites before the end of intertribal troubles. In March, raiding parties continued, but on April 3 the chiefs promised to return their captured property and prisoners and to "bury the Hatchet, guns and all other sharp weapons. . . ." With hard-won skepticism, the governor attributed the change to the Creek-Chickasaw war and awaited concrete results. May saw the Creeks asking the Chickamauga for an alliance against the Chickasaw and Cumberland settlements, but before the middle of June, a defeat inflicted by the Chickasaw induced a peace conference with Seagrove and a formal renunciation of further anti-American warfare. After a few more Creek waverings, on October 10, 1795, Blount met a full delegation of Creek and Cherokee chieftains at Tellico Block House at which peace and an exchange of prisoners were agreed on, and the last of April, 1796, was set as the time for running the long delayed Holston boundaries.[53]

For the relative calm which gradually settled upon the Territory both Blount and Pickering adduced explanations. To Pickering it was the result of his policies, his control of Blount, and the work of Creek agent Seagrove. To Blount it was the Nickajack expedition, the Chickasaw war, and the labors of his emissaries among the Indians, especially John McKee, John Chisholm, and Silas Dinsmoor. Time sharpened rather than allayed the virulent mutual antagonism of the two men. Blount, for the most part, confined his aspersions to the spoken word among his cronies, but Pickering felt no hesitancy in discharging his

[53] Choctaw Chiefs to the Creeks, June 10, 1795, in "Robertson Correspondence," *loc. cit.*, IV, 269–70; Creek chiefs to Governor Blount (n.d.), 1795, *ibid.*, 190–91; Mad Dog and others to James Seagrove, April 22, 1795, *ibid.*, 253–54; John McKee to William Blount, June 9, 1795 (extract), *ibid.*, 269; conference minutes, June 15, 1795, *ibid.*, 272–74; Tim Barnard to William Blount, September 16, 1795, *ibid.*, 69–70; Haywood, *History of Tennessee*, 479–83.

barbs openly.[54] He continued to lecture the governor and at one time had almost persuaded Washington to supersede Blount with Seagrove for the important Indian negotiation at Tellico in October.[55]

Throughout 1795, however, while he yet struggled under the lash of Pickering to secure peace in his Territory, the governor was primarily engaged in private campaigns, the chief of which was the acquisition of still more colossal land holdings. The plan for partnership with Romayne and English investors took more definite form. In October, 1794, Romayne sent a series of searching questions on prospects, to which Blount in February, 1795, made equally acute, if optimistic, replies. The governor, after a shrewd analysis of territorial lands, suggested the military reserve lands south of the Cumberland as the best field for the company efforts. He explained that the holders of these lands were chiefly nonresident veterans or their heirs and estimated that an agent could buy $100,-000 worth at 33 ⅓ cents per acre, including traveling costs. Blount proposed that he direct the agent and receive a one-tenth share and that he be loaned his capital investment at interest for three years. He estimated a sales profit of 6 per cent to the company even without a rise in land values. John Chisholm, the innkeeper-storekeeper-speculator whom Blount used as an Indian agent and personal messenger, bore the governor's letter to Romayne and was recommended by Blount as purchasing agent. This plan was not accepted, but a new one was devised before Romayne sailed for England in July. The new plan had even more grandiose features including a scheme to lay out Palmyra,

[54] William Blount to James Robertson, April 24, 1795 in "Robertson Correspondence," *loc. cit.,* IV, 256–58; Timothy Pickering to Bartholomew Dandridge, June 27, 1795, in Carter (ed.), *Territorial Papers,* IV, 395.

[55] George Washington to Timothy Pickering, September 18, 1795, in Carter (ed.), *Territorial Papers,* IV, 401–402.

a city two miles square next to Knoxville, in order to realize an $80,000 profit.[56]

In addition to Romayne's project, Blount continued to correspond with his agent James Mountflorence, who had transferred his operations to England. But overseas operations were only a fraction of the Blount program. Correspondence was maintained with Thomas Hart in Kentucky with a view to mutually advantageous trades and Transylvania company lands. In a constant stream of private letters to Robertson, the governor bought land for one or another project, ordered surveys, and gave advice. From the general he bought tens of thousands of acres in Cumberland and in east Tennessee surveys lying in yet Indian-owned lands.[57]

With his brother John Gray, of course, the closest cooperation continued. To assist his brother to fulfill his enormous commitments to speculators John Hall and David Allison, Blount devoted time, advice, and even some of his scarce and precious cash, and Blount acreage on occasion reached a total of over 1,000,000 acres in a single North Carolina county.[58] Together they planned numerous projects. In one of them the brothers would sell to William Cocke, now purchasing agent for an Eastern speculator, 200,000 acres in Mero; in another Blount urged priority for a requisition of Stockley Donelson's for "*as much* Western Lands as I can procure to the Bank's

[56] William Blount to Nicholas Romayne, February 5, 1795, in Blount Collection; id. to John Gray Blount, April 20, 1795, *ibid.*

[57] James Mountflorence to William Blount, November 24, 1795, in Keith (ed.), "Letters of James Cole Mountflorence," *loc. cit.*, 283–86; John Gray Blount to Thomas Hart, January 6, 1795, in Thomas J. Clay Collection; Thomas Hart to William Blount, February 15, 1795 (extract), in Roosevelt, *Winning of the West*, III, Pt. 1, 253; William Blount to John Gray Blount, March 28, September 22, 1795, in Blount Collection; id. to James Robertson, February 26, March 30, October 3, 1795, in "Robertson Correspondence," *loc. cit.*, IV, 74–75, 174–75, 188–89.

[58] George Ragsdale to William Blount, February 26, 1795, in Blount Collection; William Blount to John Gray Blount, March 28, 1795, *ibid.*

of the Mississippi" in order to sell it to an agent of Robert Morris of Philadelphia.[59] Still another transaction aimed at the double profit so beloved of Blounts. John Sommerville, merchant of Knoxville, was secretly set up in a branch store in Raleigh with capital which Blount and Stockley Donelson raised by the sale of Indian lands on the Mississippi. The store was supplied by John Gray Blount's warehouses and sold the goods in return for military land warrants which were cheaper in Raleigh than in the Territory, to which they were then forwarded.

Thus, to meet the needs of these associations with Allison, Romayne, and Donelson, and the requirements of his brother's various partnerships, as well as to exploit every rising opportunity, Blount plunged deeper and deeper into land speculation, straining every financial resource and utilizing every possible claim. In addition, he worked hard for his partners and absentee friends and investors. He successfully urged Secretary Daniel Smith to produce a new and better map of the Territory; he pressed Robertson on the need to cut the best road possible from Mero to Knoxville; he used all his address and influence with Territorial officials to prevent the seizure of absentee-owned lands for taxes; and through the correspondence both of himself and of Willie Blount he "planted" in Carolina newspapers highly colored propaganda on the peace, salubriousness, and fertility of the Territory.[60]

[59] William Blount to John Gray Blount, March 28, April 20, 24, 1795, in Blount Collection.

[60] William Blount to John Gray Blount, April 24, September 16, 22, 1795, *ibid.*; Willie Blount to *id.*, September 22, 1795, *ibid.*; William Blount to Elisha Rice, September 18, 1795, in Thomas Ruffin Papers (University of North Carolina); Knox County Deeds, Book B-2, I, 213, 214, 216–17, 219; Sumner County Deeds, Book A, 213; William Blount to Daniel Smith, April 27, 1795, in "Papers of Gen. Daniel Smith," *loc. cit.*, 229; *id.* to James Robertson, May 30, 1795, in "Robertson Correspondence," *loc. cit.*, IV, 267; *id.* to Reverend Joseph Dorris, October 11, 1795, *ibid.*, III, 363–64; *id.* to Andrew Jackson and others, September 2, 1795, in Andrew Jackson Papers; North

Meanwhile the new Yazoo grants of January, 1795, marked the revival of Cox's old enterprise, and this time Blount, his Bend scheme dead and his resentment roused against the Federal government, planned to join Sevier as an adventurer in a project he had once strongly opposed.[61]

One of the most daring of Blount's projects, in the face of Pickering's animosity, was a letter to Delegate James White in which the governor, with the aid of his brother Thomas, now a member of Congress, sought to circumvent the Secretary of War and persuade the President to acquire more land from the Indians. Blount urged that White seize upon a precedent set by Washington in naming a commission, at the request of two members of Congress, to purchase Cherokee lands. White was asked to act likewise and secure the purchase of two hundred thousand acres north of the Tennessee between the Clinch River and Chilhowie Mountain. Securing this tract, Blount urged, would provide a natural defensible boundary where especially needed; would save several military posts which under Pickering's orders would otherwise have to be given up; would overawe the Chickamauga towns; and would secure the only land at present purchasable from the Cherokee. Following his invariable premise that men act primarily from self interest, the governor pointed out to White that such a purchase would afford peace, whereas the Delegate's district of Mero suffered first and worst in war. The archenemy of Pickering disingenuously explained that while his own application to the War Department for the purchase "would have been officious rather than official," yet for the sake of patriotism he would have done so "had I

Carolina *Journal,* December 21, 1795; *id.* to Judge Campbell, October 15, 1795, in Knoxville *Gazette,* October 23, 1795.

[61] Whitaker, *Spanish-American Frontier,* 144–45; Haskins, "Yazoo Land Companies," *loc. cit.,* 83; Lowrie (ed.), *American State Papers, Public Lands,* I, 225. The date in the latter work is an obvious misprint.

not feared that it would have been supposed as I am known to be a large Landowner that it was some Interest of my own which prompted me and now to avoid that Imputation I declare to you that I am by no means personally interested upon the Event of the Purchase. . . ." [62] Despite these tender sensibilities, however, White was too aware of the governor's growing unpopularity in official quarters, and the matter was never pushed.

Yet while land remained the foremost, it was by no means the only economic interest of the businessman-governor. He urged his brother John Gray to join him in a nail factory in Tennessee. With Colonel King, a partner, territorial official, and land agent, he established another bloomery near his namesake village of Blountville and planned a slitting mill. He bought and sold slaves. He advised his brother on warehousing and shipping investments in North Carolina. Despite the dazzle of ambitious land schemes, his eye for detail remained keen. Thus he sought to prevent his friend and agent Robertson from becoming a competitor in the iron business by emphasizing the necessary capital outlay and by announcing his intention to extend his own works into Mero District. Likewise, in directing his brother to advise Joseph Martin on land purchases in the Territory (to which Martin planned to immigrate) he cautioned John Gray Blount to act secretly since "the Report of Men of his Rank going may raise the Price." [63]

In 1795, also, Blount's social life was busy and happy. The governor's new mansion was imposing. Two stories

[62] William Blount to James White, December 14, 1795, in Carter (ed.), *Territorial Papers*, IV, 411–14.

[63] William Blount to John Gray Blount, March 23, April 20, 1795, in Blount Collection; *id.* to Daniel Smith, May 13, 1795, in "Papers of Gen. Daniel Smith," *loc. cit.*, 229–30; *id.* to James Robertson, October 3, 1795, in "Robertson Correspondence," *loc. cit.*, IV, 74–75; *id.* to John Gray Blount, October 12, 1795, in Draper Collection, 2XX48.

of straight, planed lumber, gleaming transoms and win-
dow panes, long porch, shingled roof, and commodious
chimneys were the admiration of the passers-by. In the
rear, Mrs. Blount's flowers and carefully planted shrubs
filled the air with fragrance, and behind these an orchard
and a tilled field sloped downward toward the river. The
favored citizens whom the governor entertained gazed with
admiration at the hand-carved mantels and broad paneled
floors, the Windsor chairs, and the elaborate sideboard.
The ballroom, reached by a separate entrance, was the
scene of formal levees, gay balls, and elaborate weddings.
Dinners—if small, in the dining room; if large, in the
ballroom—were graced by monogrammed crystal, fragile
china, and gleaming flat silver. Bustle mingled with formality. Visits from the Carolina family and friends
brought excursions to nearby points of interest. Local magnates—Sevier, Robertson, Jackson, Archibald Roane, or
W. C. C. Claiborne—were familiar guests. Into the governor's little office behind the home streamed the generality
of men to petition the governor or to scheme with the
speculator. Their very existence was to be forgotten, but
the glitter and charm of the big house was to remain for
many generations.[64]

Through it all, through Indian conference, legislative
session, business scheme, or social activity, Blount's mind
never left his new objectives: statehood for the Territory,
the Senate for himself. To his brother he confided that
"we expect at least 10,000 People to settle by the 10th
October which I hope will complete our Number 60,000 &
make us a State of Rights and If I did not sincerely indulge
in this Hope I would resign my Appointment the first Hour
I had Leisure to write it. I am disgusted of the rascally

[64] Blount Mansion, Knoxville, Tennessee; William Blount bill of sale,
June 9, 1797, Knox County Record Book, Book E, I, p. 99; Blount Collection, *passim*.

Neglect of Congress and weary of the Duties of Office. However this is my Country under all Circumstances, a great Field is yet to open." [65]

The "great Field," like all fields, needed cultivation to produce fruits, and this the governor furnished politically as well as economically. From the end of the first territorial legislature he worked tirelessly for statehood. By personal letters to his political lieutenants Robertson, Sevier, and John Gray Blount, and by public letters in the press he urged on all occasions the advantages of statehood status. Unwilling to wait for the assigned date in October for the next legislative session, he called upon the delegates to be in Knoxville on June 29 and strongly pressed his followers to be present when the session should begin. [66]

The exact legal procedure for acquiring statehood was not well understood either in Congress or the Territory, since the only precedent was the irregular Kentucky one. Blount had urged Delegate White to introduce a bill authorizing statehood after a favorable referendum in the Territory, but White informed the governor in March, 1795, that Congress would not act. He reported that opinion in Philadelphia seemed to favor a referendum in the Territory to be followed by the governor's call for a constitutional convention whose work would take effect after Congress admitted the state. [67] When the legislature met

[65] William Blount to John Gray Blount, March 28, 1795, in Blount Collection.

[66] William Blount to James Robertson and Captain Gordon, November 22, 1794, in "Robertson Correspondence," *loc. cit.*, III, 374–75; William Blount to James Robertson, February 2, 26, May 4, 30, June 9, 15, 1795, *ibid.*, IV, 171–72, 174–75, 258–59, 267, 268–69, 271; S. Mitchell to Isaac Shelby, May 8, 1795, in Draper Collection, 16DD34; William Blount to John Sevier, March 20, 1795, *ibid.*, 4XX40; *id.* to John Gray Blount, April 24, 1795, in Blount Collection; Willie Blount to *id.*, September 22, 1795, *ibid.*; Philadelphia *Aurora and General Advertiser*, September 7, 1795; North Carolina *Journal*, November 30, 1795.

[67] William Blount to John Sevier, December 4, 1794 (extract), in Ramsey, *Annals*, 639; *id.* to James Robertson, February 2, 26, 1795, in

on June 29, therefore, Blount announced that its principal business was to be that of providing for a referendum and measures for statehood (as well as repealing the obnoxious absentee-landowner tax so injurious to the plans of the governor-speculator).[68] Opposition to the measures for statehood immediately arose from the Middle Tennessee area, whose spokesman, Thomas Hardeman of Davidson County, argued that statehood meant taxation without equivalent advantages, and that the census, for which the people had not asked, would be unfairly taken by counting travelers. However, Blount's control of this assembly was firm, and the delegates, who were assembled but eleven days, responded with assurances that statehood was the will of the majority and enacted that a census be taken by the sheriffs commencing September 15.[69]

Some complaint resulted from the census-taking, anti-state frontiersmen objecting to its rapid and irregular methods, and antistate Easterners declaring that the time for the enumeration was purposely set so that a large number of Fall travelers, who were mere transients, were included as inhabitants. The governor and his friends were well satisfied, however, for the final count showed 77,262 inhabitants and a vote of 6,504 to 2,562 in favor of statehood. Blount, therefore, on November 28, called for an election of delegates to a constitutional convention to be held at Knoxville on January 11, 1796.[70]

"Robertson Correspondence," *loc. cit.,* IV, 171–72, 174–75; James White to William Blount, March 19, 1795, in Carter (ed.), *Territorial Papers,* IV, 385–86; Knoxville *Gazette,* December 18, 1795, February 17, 1796.

[68] *Journal of the Proceedings of the Legislative Council of the Territory . . . Begun and Held at Knoxville the 29th Day of June, 1795* (Knoxville, 1795; Nashville, 1852), 3, 4.

[69] *Ibid.,* 9. Through error, final action by the council is not recorded. *Ibid.,* 12. *Journal of the Proceedings of the House of Representatives of the Territory . . . Begun and Held at Knoxville the 29th Day of June, 1795* (Knoxville, 1795; Nashville, 1852), 16, 17.

[70] Sampson Williams to David Henley, November 17, 1795, in David Henley Papers; Rufus King report, May 5, 1796, in Walter Lowrie and Walter S

In the interim, the governor divided his time between preserving the public calm, advertising the advantages of the Territory's lands and climate, and exerting strong pressure for a favorable membership in the convention.[71] He had become acutely conscious of his Territorial "enemies," including the apostatized Sampson Williams, Judge Anderson, the Cocke-Tipton alliance, now reviving, and above all, David Henley. With the latter, Blount of necessity had considerable dealings, and official relations were studiously polite; but the governor had learned of the agent's reports to Pickering and of his position as a focus of discontent. He therefore warned Robertson, "Don't let that man deceive you, he is a spy & will seize any occasion to report everything he can against the country and with a few Exceptions against every Individual in it . . . . you *must be* a member of the Convention. Take care of your popularity as it will be necessary to punish your & my Enemies upon the change of Things." [72]

At the same time the governor strengthened his coalition for the shock of battle in the convention and in the elections to follow. With confidence that "my popularity here is at the greatest Perfection & I believe will hold," he prepared to guard his economic interests in the new frame of government, and to take a new role, this time on the national political scene.[73]

Franklin (eds.), *American State Papers, Class X, Miscellaneous* (Washington, 1834), I, 150; Carter (ed.), *Territorial Papers*, IV, 404–405, 406–408.

[71] William Blount to Samuel Wear, December 27, 1795, in Philadelphia *Aurora and General Advertiser,* February 18, 1796; William Blount to Alexander Kelley and Littlepage Sims, December 1, 1795, in Carter (ed.), *Territorial Papers*, IV, 408–10; *State Gazette of North Carolina,* December 24, 1795.

[72] William Blount to James Robertson, October 3, 1795, in "Robertson Correspondence," *loc. cit.*, IV, 74–75; Henley correspondence, *passim* (typed copies, Lawson McGhee Library); Rickard–Henley correspondence, October, 1795, in David Henley Papers.

[73] William Blount to James Robertson, October 3, October 25, November 5, 1795, in "Robertson Correspondence," *loc. cit.*, IV, 74–75, 77–78.

CHAPTER X

"VAULTING AMBITION WHICH O'ERLEAPS ITSELF"

The year 1796 found a different scene in many respects from that which had met William Blount's eyes when he arrived in east Tennessee in 1790 to begin his governorship. As the territorial period moved toward its close, the social transformations of the last five and a half years were everywhere evident. On expanding shelves and in growing wardrobes, silks and brocades joined calicoes and muslins, broadcloth appeared with homespun and buckskin. In numerous towns—Greeneville, Jonesboro, and Rogersville, as well as Knoxville and Nashville—frame houses and shingle roofs were rising to rebuke the formerly admired log cabins. Porches, flower gardens, and stone walks invited leisure moments. Dancing masters, fencing masters, dressmakers, the shops of artisan specialists encouraged rivalry in elegance in a rising generation. Like the Reverends Balch and Doak in Greeneville and Washington colleges, the Reverend Carrick in Knoxville strove to implant a smattering of classicism in the sons and daughters of Indian-fighters. Parties were becoming receptions, dances were now balls. At the governor's levee the flattered guest might meet a traveling scientist, a writer, or a foreign politician. While the older towns grew, new rivals thrust outward from the forest clearings—Clarksville, Maryville, Sevierville. Still narrow and rutted were the roads, but they lengthened and branched; flats and ferries crossed former fords. The wagon and the riding horse still ruled, but the carriage and the chair were soon to come. Civilization was in full progress—the frontier was moving on.

It was a reflection and a phase of this development which, on January 11, 1796, brought a notable gathering to Knoxville. The great and the near great of the Territory were among the fifty-five delegates who scraped the winter mud from their boots as they entered David Henley's office, rented for the use of the convention. The Knox County delegation was headed by the governor and included James White, Knoxville's founder, and Charles McClung, Blount's business and political follower. From Washington County came, with others, John Tipton; Landon Carter, former speaker in the Franklin legislature; Leroy Taylor; and Samuel Handly, all leaders of their localities. Sullivan's delegation included John Rhea, later Congressman for eighteen years, and the future Mississippi territorial governor W. C. C. Claiborne. Hawkins County sent ambitious William Cocke along with Joseph McMinn, later to be speaker of the senate and governor. Mero District's representatives were led by James Robertson, Judges McNairy and Anderson, Attorney General Jackson, and Secretary Daniel Smith. Even the new counties of Tennessee, Sevier, Jefferson, and Blount sent able leaders, including the Franklin chieftain Alexander Outlaw, the future Governor Archibald Roane, James Houston, father of Sam Houston, and Thomas Johnson, later a brigadier general under Andrew Jackson. Of the Territorial leaders, only Delegates Dr. James White and John Sevier were absent, the latter being represented by his namesake son. The state chiefly represented was Virginia, birthplace of sixteen delegates; eight had been Pennsylvanians and seven North Carolinians. Eight delegates had served in the Territorial legislatures, and a number of others were or had been local officers.[1] It was a group experienced in leadership, and a fair cross section of frontier society from the aristocratic element of Blount through the professional classes of Jackson, McNairy, and Anderson to such extreme frontiersmen as Samuel Wear and Thomas Hardeman.

The delegates chose Blount as president, with other officers, and adopted the usual rules of procedure. On Carter's motion a special rule allowed the president of the convention (with the house's permission) to speak on any subject before the body, provided he did not speak last and thus carry undue influence. A grand committee composed of two members from each county was appointed to prepare a draft of the constitution and a bill of rights. On January 15, the committee reported out the latter draft and on the same day the convention in committee of the whole house under Robertson began a consideration of it; three days later the convention debated it.[2]

As discussion began, it became apparent that the membership was fluid in a political sense. Though loose groupings formed, there was much shifting about on specific measures. The governor's forces numbered almost half of the convention members, and in more or less continuous opposition to his group were perhaps one half to three fourths as many, led by Outlaw, Judge Anderson, and

[1] John D. Barnhart, "The Tennessee Constitution; A Product of the Old West," *loc. cit.*, 539–40.

[2] *Journal of the Proceedings of a Convention Began and Held at Knoxville, January 11, 1796* (Knoxville, 1796; Nashville, 1852), 3, 4–6, 7, 8 (hereinafter referred to as *Convention Journal*).

Thomas Hardeman. The remainder shifted, and both of
the more coherent groups were constrained to compromise
in order to attract the votes of this "center" as well as to
hold intact their own membership.[3] In addition, Blount,
Cocke, and other aspirants to office were aware of the wisdom of conciliation in view of the coming Federal elections. The result was a confused political scene.

On a number of issues, however, the clash of interests
was direct and bitter. The minority made a strong and
nearly successful fight for a unicameral legislature. It took
all the governor's influence to defeat this during two re-
considerations and then to preserve the powers of the
senate.[4] On procedural matters, too, the Blount group
held firm and defeated an effort to bestow the franchise
on all those subject to militia duty, just as they also beat
down an attempt to establish viva-voce voting.[5] Frontier
democracy asserted itself, however, in providing for male
suffrage limited only by age and residence requirements
(or property ownership in a county).

As usual, a battle developed over taxation, and the
cohesion of the groups' votes broke rather badly since the
blocs were not formed on purely economic lines. The main
objective of the Blount group, however, was accomplished,
namely the protection of their property by the constitutional mandate that all lands were to be taxed equally
regardless of location. Town lots, for which taxation rate,
like that for slaves, was guaranteed not to exceed 200
country acres, were excepted. To the larger speculators
such as Blount this was a real victory, for their town property was proportionately not so extensive as their rich
country tracts or strategic holdings next to the towns. They

[3] Barnhart, "Tennessee Constitution," *loc. cit.,* 543.
[4] *Convention Journal,* 6, 8, 9, 10, 25–26.
[5] *Ibid.,* 21–22.

were therefore willing to concede a similar maximum (the equivalent of 100 acres) to the poll tax.[6]

The businessmen were also careful to secure inclusion of a prohibition of taxes (except inspection fees) on domestic industry. Blount himself, increasingly concerned over Western land prices, wrote and secured the inclusion of the resounding alliterative declaration, "That an equal participation of the free navigation of the Mississippi, is one of the inherent rights of the citizens of this State; it cannot, therefore, be conceded to any prince, potentate, power, person or persons whatever." [7] In accordance with invariable practice, however, he took no open part in the convention sessions, and his name appears nowhere in the proceedings save in the roll calls.

The convention, like its famous predecessor in Philadelphia, spent considerable time on matters of detail, and on these there was no consistency of voting. Jackson, in the interest of Mero, shortened the period of Knoxville's position as the capital to an earlier date than first contemplated. The Outlaw group made determined efforts, for which there was strong public sentiment, to keep official salaries low. Outlaw also reverted to his old Franklin crusade with a motion that if Congress refused to confer membership in the Union, then "we should continue to exist as an independent state." Considerable interest centered around the dates for the first elections and the inauguration of state administration. Similar agitation occurred over a religious qualification for office and over barring ministers from public office, these latter questions being eventually settled by requiring a belief in the existence of God and of a

    [6] *Ibid.*, 27, 29.
    [7] *Ibid.*, 18; Ramsey, *Annals*, 654; Miscellaneous Manuscripts, R37R (Tennessee State Archives); Wallace McClure, "The Development of the Tennessee Constitution," in *Tennessee Historical Magazine*, I (1915), 300; Knoxville *Gazette*, February 17, 1796.

future state of rewards and punishments, and by barring ministers from the general assembly only instead of from all civil office.[8]

The final draft of the constitution, which showed a moderate but definite movement toward democracy, was the product of Pennsylvania and North Carolina backgrounds. In the legislative and executive provisions, and in the bill of rights especially, the weight of Pennsylvania precedent was noticeable, through the influence of Judge Anderson, a native of that state. North Carolina, of course, was also influential, though notable departures were made especially in a stronger executive department.[9] The constitution was never referred to a popular vote, for a copy was sent by express to the Secretary of State, and the governor was directed to issue writs of election bearing the date of the convention's final session, which he did.

This rapidity of action, entirely in accord with Blount's wishes, was due to the convention's desire to bring the question of admission before the present session of Congress, which had been sitting since December. But it did not fail to rouse opposition from rival interests, including Arthur Campbell who, in a letter to President Washington, cast doubts on the census and the convention and suggested that, while it would "disappoint a few aspiring Spirits," a two-year wait before admission would be beneficial to the majority of territorials.[10]

Protest was vain, however, for the propaganda campaign for statehood had been effective, and with Blount and Sevier leading it the movement was irresistible. At the same time, in maintaining their initiative by the early

[8] *Convention Journal,* 20–21, 23–24, 26–28; Valentine Sevier to John Sevier, December 31, 1795, in Draper Collection, 11DD122.

[9] Barnhart, "Tennessee Constitution," *loc. cit.,* 546–48.

[10] Arthur Campbell to George Washington, February 18, 1796, in Carter (ed.), *Territorial Papers,* IV, 420; Knoxville *Gazette,* October 23, 1795.

February election call, the Blount-Sevier group prevented the formation of effective opposition in the first election. For the governorship, Sevier's popularity in the eastern districts was so great as to defy the best efforts of the Tiptonians. In Mero District there was a campaign for Judge Anderson, led by Thomas Hardeman and Colonels Robert Hays and James Winchester; however, the Robertsons, the Lewises, and McNairy, with William Maclin from Knox County, led the Sevier forces strenuously and successfully.[11] Blount himself, despite the undesirable popularity and ambition of Sevier, greatly preferred his election to that of the officious Anderson. His relations with Sevier, especially now that he was about to leave the Tennessee stage to the latter, were entirely harmonious even though he was also close personally and politically to the rising Andrew Jackson; for the Jackson-Sevier breach was not yet a wide one, and Blount was able to hold these two fiery personalities in reasonable harmony.[12]

Upon the convening of the legislature on March 28, 1796, Blount's territorial administration came to an end. Two days later the nominations for the office of United States Senator took place, the house naming Blount, Cocke, and Anderson, and the senate adding Dr. James White, erstwhile territorial delegate. The election of the former governor was assured from the first, especially after the withdrawal of Anderson on the morning of the election; but that of Cocke was in doubt until Tipton in the senate secured Dr. White's withdrawal a few moments later. Before information of this could reach the house, the two

---

[11] Valentine Sevier to John Sevier, March 18, 1796, in Draper Collection, 11DD123.

[12] See Abernethy, *Frontier to Plantation*, 164–65, and A. V. Goodpasture, "Genesis of the Jackson–Sevier Feud," in *American Historical Magazine*, V (1900), 115–23.

bodies met in the representatives' room to ballot, and Cocke's son, John, a representative from Hawkins County, unaware that his father's election was already certain, brought over George Rutledge from the opposition by a bill to name the Grainger county seat in that gentleman's honor. The election, therefore, was swift, and the Senators were quickly named, along with Sevier's lieutenant, William Maclin, as secretary of state. Congratulatory addresses framed by White were sent to both Senators, with Blount's excelling considerably in fervor, and were entered in the Journal.[13]

Blount had, meanwhile, regarded his gubernatorial administration at an end and devoted his attention to Indian arrangements, such as sending John Chisholm to quiet the Creeks, arranging another visit of Creeks and Cherokee chiefs to the President, and combating the effects on the Indians of the new Spanish Fort Fernando on the Mississippi. Robertson had finally resigned his generalcy but continued as Chickasaw agent, and to him Blount relayed messages from the new Secretary of War, James McHenry, to whom he took care to discredit Agent Henley whenever possible. He engaged in some correspondence with John Haywood on seeking office in the new state, and with André Michaux, the traveling French botanist, on the presence of wood dyes in the Territory, but was much more interested in private plans, which included moving the household to Philadelphia and bolstering up his financial resources, now cracking badly under a slipping land market. He bought and sold lands and slaves,

[13] *Journal of the Senate of the State of Tennessee* (Knoxville, 1796; Nashville, 1852), 7, 9, 10, 13, 20; Valentine Sevier to John Sevier, December 31, 1795, in Draper Collection, 11DD122; William S. Spears, *Sketches of Prominent Tennesseans,* 265, cited in Williams, "Admission of Tennessee," *loc. cit.,* 301.

and watched closely the activities of Cox's new Yazoo Company, in which he was now considerably interested.[14]

At length in mid-April, the ex-governor left for Philadelphia to take part in a developing battle for the admission of the new state. President Washington had, on April 8, referred the Tennessee convention's proceedings to Congress without advisory comment. Of this Congress the House of Representatives was dominated by an anti-Administration majority and the Senate by a Federalist one. By April, 1796, members of both houses realized clearly the Antifederalist proclivities of the Westerners, and the probable vote of any Western state in the coming Presidential election. The reception accorded the Tennessee request for admission therefore differed widely. The House immediately referred the matter to a committee, but the Senate delayed and finally referred it to one made up entirely of stout Federalists.[15] From this point, the dictates of political strategy dominated the question. In the House the committee reported on April 12 in favor of statehood, but consideration of the report was delayed by a debate on the Jay Treaty until May 5, by which time the House Federalists had received an arsenal of oral weapons from anti-Blount forces in Tennessee. They therefore argued that prior action by Congress was necessary before the state could be formed; that the census was improperly taken and illegal; and that the Tennessee con-

---

[14] William Blount to James Robertson, April 6, 11, 1796, in "Robertson Correspondence," *loc. cit.,* IV, 279–80; James McHenry to William Blount, February 27, 1796, *ibid.,* 275–76; William Blount to David Henley, January 5, March 25, April 10, 1796, in "Correspondence of William Blount," 83, 90–91, 93–94; *id.* to Timothy Pickering, March 29, 1796, in Carter (ed.), *Territorial Papers,* IV, 422–23; John Haywood to William Blount, March 11, 1796 (copy) in Rodman Papers; Andrew Jackson to *id.,* February 29, 1796 (copy) *ibid.;* André Michaux to William Blount, March 2, 1796, in *North Carolina Minerva and Fayetteville Advertiser,* May 12, 1796; William Blount to André Michaux, March 8, 1796, *ibid.;* Knox County Deeds, Book B-1, 85.

[15] *Annals of Congress,* 4 Cong., 68, 72, 892.

stitution was imperfect and in conflict with the Federal Constitution. In the two-day debate which followed, the defense of the new state was carried on by Jeffersonian stalwarts, including James Madison and Blount's newly elected brother, Thomas. On May 6 the rambling debate closed, and the committee's original report was first accepted by the Committee of the Whole House and then approved by a very sectional 43 to 30 vote in the House.[16]

In the Federalist Senate, the new state's cause suffered far more. The committee waited a month to report and then used every argument of the House Federalists in recommending that statehood be denied, while a sop was tossed in the report permitting admission after a Congressionally supervised census.[17]

At this juncture Blount arrived from Tennessee to join Cocke. On May 9 they presented their credentials, but the Senate postponed consideration of them, and the debate on King's unfavorable report went languidly on. On May 13 a new five-day debate opened, and unsuccessful efforts were made by Antifederalists to expunge the entire report, but upon these attempts being defeated 14 to 9, the report was adopted 14 to 11, and a bill introduced for a Congressional census in the Territory. On May 23, the Senators-elect addressed a letter to the obdurate house offering to prove their constituents' rights to immediate statehood and demanding to be seated; but the Senate by a 12 to 11 vote merely provided chairs for their accommodation as spectators. The Southerners desperately offered a concession (that the state's quota be reduced to

[16] *Ibid.*, 916, 1300–12, 1313–29; Charlotte Williams, "Congressional Action on the Admission of Tennessee into the Union," in *Tennessee Historical Quarterly*, II (1943), 307; Williams, "Admission of Tennessee," *loc. cit.*, 304–309.

[17] *Annals of Congress*, 4 Cong., 81; Lowrie and Franklin (eds.), *American State Papers, Miscellaneous*, I, 150; Williams, "Congressional Action," *loc. cit.*, 308.

one Representative) to no avail. On May 26, King's bill passed its third reading. At this crisis, however, King, a Federalist stalwart, enraged his fellows by resigning to become ambassador to England, and to the ensuing conference committee with the House, the Senate named Caleb Strong and Aaron Burr. To the latter Blount devoted all his charm and persuasion in pointing out the dangers of a rejection of the state: the possible separation, the Spanish allurements, and the complication of the Creek-Georgia problem. The Antifederalist nominee for Vice President also heard a detailed description of the political sentiments of Tennesseans. A closely kindred soul to the ex-governor, he was persuaded without too much difficulty, and he and the Representatives overbore Strong. The Senate thereupon capitulated on May 31, 1796, but in the last vote of the session Blount and Cocke by an 11 to 10 vote were refused their seats.[18]

The political significance of this contest was by no means lost on the baffled Senators-elect, who faithfully reported to Tennesseans both the activity on the floor of Congress and the cloakroom politics of the issue.[19] Since a reduction to one Representative and their own re-election was the price of admission, new elections were necessary in the state, and Cocke returned to Tennessee for the formality of the second election of himself and Blount to the Senate and of Andrew Jackson to the House of Representatives.

For Blount himself, the effect of these weeks of wrangling was of immense importance. While the majority of Tennesseans raged at the Senate's refusal to accept their

[18] *Annals of Congress,* 4 Cong., 83, 85, 87–94 *passim,* 97, 103–104, 106–107, 108–109, 116, 117, 120–21; Williams, "Admission of Tennessee," *loc. cit.,* 311–12.

[19] William Blount and William Cocke to John Sevier, June 2, 1796, in Blount Manuscripts (Lawson McGhee Library).

wishes, he underwent the added humiliation of hearing himself, his administration, and his methods roughly handled and openly sneered at by the Federalists. In addition, he found the tone of the Administration decidedly unfriendly. Pickering, now Secretary of State, and well-briefed by Agent Henley and Collector Overton, was ever more icy, and of McHenry Blount wrote to Sevier, "You can't conceive what a puppy of a Secretary of War we have. He was by the author of the Creation intended for a diminutive Taylor." [20] Even Washington, tired and disillusioned, regarded his old appointee coolly. In a dozen minor ways, Administration disapproval of Blount himself was manifest. Occasionally, as in the appointment of the Indian-minded Benjamin Hawkins to be Blount's successor as Indian superintendent, rejection of the ex-governor's policies was also clear. Nowhere save in the anti-Administration circles, which he increasingly frequented, did he find the appreciation he felt was deserved for those six years of exhaustive services in representing law, order, policy, and patriotism to the frontiersmen who regarded all these principles as of highly doubtful value.

Thus, searing personal and public humiliations doused the last embers of Federalist loyalty in the ex-governor. The Administration—its agents and its policies, foreign and domestic—became anathema to him. At last he was completely at one with the great majority of his fellow-Tennesseans. He therefore plunged immediately into the work of defeating the Federalists, and his motives and activity are revealed in a private letter to Sevier:

Permit me to say that it will be the true interest of Tennessee in particular and the Union in general to promote the interest of Jefferson-Burr for President and Vice-President at the ensuing election. . . .

[20] William Blount to John Sevier, September 26, 1796, in Miscellaneous Letters (New York Public Library).

That Jefferson is a friend of our country I suppose no body in Tennessee doubts and I pronounce positively that Mr. Burr from a combination of circumstances may be ranked among its very warmest friends. None of the Southern States except South Carolina will vote for Mr. Pinckney for Vice-President, but generally for Burr and it is generally believed that such of the Northern states as talk of Mr. Pinckney mean only thereby to prevent Mr. Adams' election and in the end not vote Mr. Pinckney—perhaps this business had not best be spoke of aloud at least I would not like to have it understood that there was any premeditated Plan in the Business. . . . Truth is that I have taken a great agency in this election and have been induced so to do by the part the adverse party took against the admission of the State of Tennessee.[21]

While the last six months of 1796 thus saw the final phases of Blount's political metamorphosis and while he immersed himself in political strategy, he was at the same time faced with far graver personal problems. This same crucial year of 1796 found him at the apogee of his land proprietorship. Carried away by the raging mania of speculation that was sweeping the country in the middle 1790's, the Blount brothers had reached dizzying heights of landownership. Through the incessant calls of partner Allison, the schemes of Romayne, the commitments of his brother John Gray, and the vast plans of Stockley Donelson, as well as his innumerable personal schemes, the Senator-elect had bought or committed himself personally to buy at least 1,000,000 acres of land. John Gray Blount, besides even more enormous commitments, had *secured* at least another 1,660,355 acres in which operations William Blount was more or less involved.[22] To obtain this colossal acreage, Blount had strained every personal resource, including his credit, to its utmost limit and had drawn upon those of his friends and even upon public funds. He was

[21] *Ibid.*; William Blount to John Sevier, September 27, 1796, in Emmett Collection.

[22] Blount Collection, P.C. 854–859, *passim*; Keith, "Three North Carolina Blount Brothers," 287.

utterly and irretrievably committed to a realization on his land interests with no alternative save absolute ruin.

But as the summer months waned into Fall, the prospects for such realization grew steadily darker. Allison, in January of 1795, had engaged to sell to the speculating Judge James Wilson of Pennsylvania 2,500,000 acres for twenty-five cents per acre, and in June of the same year 2,000,000 more. But the lands thus "sold," while actually surveyed and entered in the name of John Gray or William Blount, or of Allison himself, were in most cases not in the "owner's" possession, since the cash required for their final purchase and completion of title was to come from their sale by Allison, and the Philadelphia purchasers would not advance the cash without the title. In the meantime, taxes fell due; countersuits were filed; local antagonisms prevented the completion of titles; banks refused to accept further notes from any of the partners; and, although Allison employed four brokers to sell his promissory notes to private buyers, they did so if at all only at enormous discounts. From the treasurer of North Carolina, Allison borrowed $30,000 on the credit of John Gray & Thomas Blount, Merchants. He also took bonds from both Wilson and Robert Morris, although he could raise but little cash on either.[23] Ill, harassed, and defeated, this indomitable and incurable speculator had struggled on through 1795, and while all personal credit was lost, he still managed by some sales to keep a small flow of cash or notes to his partners for further purchases. But by the fall of 1796, he was very near the brink. He still sold lands to Robert Morris, but his own notes were now completely worthless, and those of Morris were rapidly becoming so. Other Blount associates, too, were suffering from Allison's

[23] Correspondence of David Allison, John Gray Blount, and Thomas Blount, 1795, in Blount Collection, P.C. 855, 856; Keith, "Three North Carolina Blount Brothers," 289–98, *passim.*

shaky position; Andrew Jackson through him had also become liable for large sums and was considerably in need of Blount's assistance.[24]

Yet his failing partner was only one, if the largest, of Blount's land troubles. In October, Dr. Nicholas Romayne, newly arrived in New York from England, wrote that he had accomplished nothing in their plan to sell Western lands to wealthy Englishmen. Stockley Donelson failed in his last plan to sell the Blount claims to lands in the Bend. From North Carolina came the wails of his thoroughly frightened brother John Gray, who this time realized later than the usually less acute Thomas that partner Allison was slipping into the ruin that had already engulfed another partner, John Hall. Furthermore, the appointment of Benjamin Hawkins to be Southern Indian superintendent inevitably meant a sympathetic approach to the Indians' land claims, and the unfinished boundary of the Treaty of Holston would now without doubt be run so as to cause Western speculators and homesteaders to lose valuable land to the Indians.

Blount met these blows with characteristic vigor. He contracted with a Philadelphia company's westward-bound agent to sell 90,000 acres (although one half of these were not yet even surveyed), and sent instructions to satellite Charles McClung and to brother Willie Blount to delay the sale but not lose the buyer until the survey and title were complete. Realizing Allison's fatal position, he became yet more cautious in committing more land to that unfortunate gambler, but with Jackson his financial relations continued to be close. Then, on October 21, 1796, he went to Carolina to confer with John Gray,

[24] John Spencer Bassett (ed.), *Correspondence of Andrew Jackson* (Washington, 1926), I, 16, 21–22.

to attend his brother Thomas' wedding at Halifax, and to meet his wife in Raleigh.[25]

However, affairs worsened with the winter months as the inexorable penalty of over-speculation fell on the business world. Money vanished; Western land prices dropped to ten cents an acre; the mercantile communities, already harassed by war, became semiparalytic; credit collapsed; old and respectable firms were shaken or struck down; and the myriad marginal speculators were swept away in disgrace, bankruptcy, and prison. Allison was saved temporarily only by the very complexity of his transactions, coupled with a few fortunate sales; but the failures of Wilson and of Morris sealed his doom. Jackson was plunged yet deeper into debt. All this to Blount meant a variety of dangers. He himself was by Allison's collapse thrown into virtual bankruptcy, and creditors hounded him in Raleigh; but the greatest ultimate danger lay in the collapse of land values in the West, where lay his hundreds of thousands of acres. A large portion of these holdings awaited final action and fees to become legally his, and worse still, any creditors from whom he had borrowed in order to pre-empt the land were now increasingly importunate for immediate payment. Other partners than Allison were also in dire straits, and their impending fall meant his own. Above all, even those lands to which he personally held complete title now appeared unsalable in the panic market.

For this crisis in values more than the financial crash was responsible. In October, 1796, war broke out between

[25] William Blount to Willie Blount and Charles McClung, September 27, 1796, in "Correspondence of William Blount," 95–96; note of William Blount, June 11, 1796, in Papers of Andrew Jackson, II, 204 (Division of Manuscripts, Library of Congress); Allison correspondence, 1795–96, in Blount Collection, P.C. 856–59; David Allison to John Gray Blount, October 21, 1796, *ibid.,* P.C. 859.

Britain and her former ally Spain, and all America believed that the astonishingly vigorous and successful French Republic would now demand Louisiana and the Floridas from Spain as the price of alliance. Such a transfer would mean the end of all those dreams, which had so often filled Western minds, of seizing those lands from the feeble Spanish monarchy. The Mississippi and its vital traffic would then be forever at the mercy of foreign whim and yet secure from seizure.[26] Western slaveholders, too, as neighbors of the egalitarian and emancipating Revolutionists, could never be sure of the possession of their property or of its value. In this crisis of so many hopes, statesmen might eventually plan to "marry ourselves to the British fleet," but marginal speculators and soldiers of fortune thought of more violent and lucrative employment.

An outstanding example of the latter category of individuals arrived in Philadelphia during Blount's absence in Carolina. This was the Blount henchman, lusty and irrepressible John Chisholm, who in November, 1796, accompanied some twenty-odd Creek chiefs on a visit to the President. Much brooding, considerable drinking, more talk, and a sense of grievance and of possible gain had all produced in this Spanish-hating Englishman the outlines of a plan of deep consequences. Though a sometime innkeeper and merchant, the British ex-soldier's principal means of livelihood, or at least his principal interest, lay in Indian relations as a trader or general emissary of the whites, and in the latter capacity he had been of considerable use to Blount. With Congress now devoting increasing attention to the regulation of the Indian trade and relations in general, it became important to this free lance

[26] Knoxville *Gazette and Weekly Advertiser,* December 19, 1796; William Cocke to George Roulstone, January 2, 1797, *ibid.,* February 6, 1797; Whitaker, *Mississippi Question,* 107, 110.

to regularize his position and enhance his prospects by American citizenship. This move would also improve chances for compensation for his services to the former governor, a reward the latter had often promised him. Therefore, on this trip to the capital, Chisholm brought with him a petition for citizenship on behalf of himself and about twenty other such British adventurers in the Southwest, which petition he presented to Secretary Mc-Henry.

In the event of failure, however, or perhaps in addition to his citizenship plans, Chisholm was prepared for more drastic action. As a veteran of Spanish imprisonment at Pensacola he had developed, along with his violent hatred of that nation, a firm confidence in his own influence over the Indians; hence, with other similarly placed Loyalists of the border region, he had often planned a coup against the Spaniards in the Floridas. From Bowles and possibly Welbank the plan had received support, though their meager resources could not make headway against the influence of McGillivray and of Panton & Leslie's supplies. But the outbreak of Anglo-Spanish hostilities in 1796 raised the ex-Loyalists' hopes, and Chisholm, nothing if not bold, was prepared as their spokesman to offer the British government their services in an attack against Spanish possessions in return for British supplies, naval assistance, and any necessary complement of men.[27] Meanwhile, Secretary McHenry, well-convinced by Pickering that no good thing could come out of Nazareth, treated Chisholm's citizenship petition with great "coolness" and thus furnished any needed incentive to boldness. Thus by late November, 1796, Chisholm was

[27] *Annals of Congress*, 5 Cong., 2366; F. J. Turner (ed.), "Documents on the Blount Conspiracy, 1795–1797," in *American Historical Review*, X (1905), 595–96; Whitaker, *Mississippi Question*, 107–108; John McDonald to Governor White, December 31, 1795, in Papeles de Cuba.

quite prepared to proceed with his filibuster plans. Accordingly, he presented himself to the British minister in Philadelphia, Robert Liston, and explained his project of a joint British and Indian assault on East Florida, the British to furnish a privateer and stores, and Chisholm and his associates to induce the Indians to join under their leadership.[28]

Minister Liston was both intrigued and uncertain. He was probably aware (despite subsequent denials) that his government had, since October, 1795, been considering the possibilities of an attack on the Spanish possessions should it become necessary, and Chisholm was a convincing intriguer. On the other hand, the minister hardly dared assume responsibility for furthering such an enterprise from a neutral country. Hence he temporized, announcing disapproval but continuing to have meetings with Chisholm.[29]

Blount, therefore, returned from Carolina in early December, 1796, to find his former agent full of enthusiastic plans.[30] The Senator listened closely while his active mind considered possibilities with the agility and suppleness developed in a lifetime of scheming. The plan had great merit from his point of view, for to save the Floridas and Louisiana from the French would afford tremendous support to the sagging land values of the West and open vast possibilities for the development of his Yazoo interests and others yet more ambitious. Great prizes undoubtedly

[28] *Annals of Congress,* 5 Cong., 2389; Turner (ed.), "Documents," *loc. cit.,* 600–601.

[29] Turner (ed.), "Documents," *loc. cit.,* 575–76, 596. For Liston's role, see Posey, "William Blount: the Land Speculator," 108–109, and W. B. Posey, "The Blount Conspiracy," in *Birmingham-Southern Bulletin,* XXI (1928), No. 6, p. 15.

[30] *Annals of Congress,* 4 Cong., 1517; *ibid.,* 5 Cong., 2378, 2390; Turner (ed.), "Documents," *loc. cit.,* 596, 601; Joseph Martin to John Gray Blount, November 26, 1796, in Blount Collection. See also Whitaker, *Mississippi Question,* 108.

awaited the leaders of the enterprise, and if Chisholm could go thus far, Blount interests could go much further. The vision gained splendor since the ex-governor's Carolina visit had been made unpleasant by two attempted arrests for Allison's debts—attempts which were thwarted only by his Senatorial immunity. To Chisholm, therefore, the bankrupt statesman gave indications, if not of commitments, assuredly of close support. It was apparent to Blount, however, that much more was at stake than the rewards of what he termed Chisholm's "petty enterprise," and since the stakes were higher, the resources and planning needed likewise to be greater.

Meanwhile, the December session of Congress proving dull, the Senator devoted most of his official time to a bill to replace territorial officers with permanent ones and to efforts to secure payment of the unofficial military expeditions of 1793 and 1794. He and Cocke reported regularly to Sevier and agreed on recommendations of some Tennesseans for appointments and opposition to others, notably that of David Campbell. Blount especially, but unavailingly, attempted to influence the selection of more favorable commissioners to replace his 1792 "experimental line" with the final definitive Holston treaty boundary line.[31] In his private affairs the Senator gave his attention to raising money to meet his ever more pressing creditors and to adopting and perfecting Chisholm's scheme. Dr. James White, both a political crony and a Yazoo associate, was sent to Natchez in the guise of peddler in order to contact British sentiment there and sound out Western senti-

[31] Knoxville *Gazette and Weekly Advertiser,* January 2, 1797; *Annals of Congress,* 4 Cong., 1526, 1530, 1531; William Blount to James McHenry, December 23, 1796, in Myers Collection (New York Public Library); *id.* to John Sevier, January 3, 1797, in Simon Gratz Collection; *id.* to *id.,* January 4, 1797, in Miscellaneous Letters (New York Public Library); *id.* and William Cocke to the President, January 17, 1797 (with enclosures), (Tennessee State Archives).

ment, now antagonized by disappointed hopes from the Pinckney Treaty.[32]

In late January, 1797, Blount went to New York for the double purpose of salvaging a protested note which he had endorsed and of seeing Romayne. He was as deeply depressed as only such intense natures can be. His credit was steadily slipping and his future prospects ever gloomier. The war between France and Britain continued fiercely, and any day might see the announcement of the transfer of Louisiana to France. Also, the defeat of Jefferson now appeared increasingly probable, and hence the continuation of an anti-Western Administration.

Romayne's views were yet more depressing. He refused to press the land sales in England because of the unsettled state of international affairs; he further confirmed Blount's fears of the transfer of Louisiana to France, whose great power, he felt, would enable her to seize the whole of Canada and the Mississippi valley; and he expressed the opinion that Western land was worthless. Such views from so well-qualified a judge moved the Senator deeply. He in turn discussed his continuous care of the Tennessee West, his private and public concern for that area, and his shameful treatment by the Administration, a recital which reduced him to rare tears. From this point, in the course of several visits, the conversation of the gloomy speculators turned on the desirability of English rather than French neighbors in the West, and Blount unfolded to his old friend the nature of Chisholm's plan (without at first naming the author) in which the doctor became highly interested. But, while he agreed readily with Blount that a trip by the latter to England might be helpful, on hearing of Chisholm's activities he expressed strong dissatisfaction with them as "coming from a person of

[32] Whitaker, *Mississippi Question,* 109; Papeles de Cuba, 1500, No. 60.

that description"; and he urged Blount to prevent further activity by the soldier of fortune. Realizing that Romayne regarded intrigue as a proper sphere for gentlemen only, Blount disclaimed connection with Chisholm, whom the Senator confessed "he could command . . . when near but could not answer or control . . . at a distance." However, Blount kept in mind both plans: the Chisholm project, which at first, at least, was directed primarily at East Florida; and the Blount-Romayne discussions in which by implication both Louisiana and the Floridas would be attacked, with the former being retained by England and the latter going to the United States as a price for acquiescence.[33]

In actual fact, the details of the proposed enterprise were never worked out and probably varied in the later Chisholm and Romayne versions, but in general the project involved a three-fold attack. The first, on New Madrid and the Red River silver mines of Spain, would be made by Northwestern volunteers with British aid from Canada. The second, under Blount, would be carried out by Southwesterners and Indian allies against New Orleans. The third attack, on Pensacola, would be by whites and Indians under Chisholm. A British fleet would assist at New Orleans and Pensacola, and Britain would secure either Louisiana or the Floridas or both, with New Orleans becoming a free port and free Mississippi navigation being guaranteed to British and Americans.[34] Blount and Romayne agreed that the doctor would write letters introducing Blount to influential Englishmen, and meanwhile the Senator would sound out "persons of importance in Philadelphia, both in the Government and out . . . certain persons in Virginia, the frontiers of North Carolina, the State

---

[33] *Annals of Congress,* 5 Cong., 2357–60.
[34] Turner (ed.), "Documents," *loc. cit.,* 600–601.

of Tennessee, and generally throughout the Southern States." Particular attention was to be given to those formerly engaged in Genêt's project and to the Indians.[35]

Full of his new project, the Senator returned to Philadelphia and plunged at once into his assigned activities. Well-known speculators and adventurers began to be uncommonly active. The controversial figure of George Matthews appeared on the frontier on a mysterious errand. His arrival and that of certain other taciturn figures aroused the consternation of United States agent Andrew Ellicott and Spanish governor Gayoso, then engaged in a controversy over the Natchez posts. Both immediately became highly suspicious of practically everyone not their avowed adherent, and Ellicott in particular began to sniff treason in every breeze. Lachlan McIntosh, another Yazoo associate of Blount's, was busy in the East. Blount himself questioned Oliver Pollock, George Turner, and other Western travelers or residents who were possessed of information on Spanish forts and troop disposition in the Mississippi Valley. His house on Chestnut Street became a center of frequent and mysterious visits.[36]

Chisholm, still waiting for Liston's decision, was as active as he was garrulous. He interested frontier agents such as Indian interpreter James Carey, Loyalist John Rogers, and surveyor John Mitchell, as well as substantial citizen James Ore, along with a Knoxville merchant, and Chisholm's Loyalist frontier friends. In fact, the talkative intriguer seemed unable to converse long with anyone without unfolding his scheme, and the number of those informed of it grew to include almost casual acquaintances

[35] *Annals of Congress,* 5 Cong., 2359–60. For Romayne as a British agent, see Posey, "Blount Conspiracy," *loc. cit.,* 16; Turner (ed.), "Documents," *loc. cit.,* 599.

[36] Whitaker, *Mississippi Question,* 109–10; *Annals of Congress,* 5 Cong., 2355–56, 2376–77.

in all walks of life. Either by personal emissary or circular letter, he approached Indian chiefs both of the upper and lower Mississippi Valley, including the famous Joseph Brandt and James Colbert, and, to his own belief at least, he enlisted the efforts of Canadians, including a member of the Canadian assembly. With a certain native shrewdness, Chisholm came to understand that Blount's and Romayne's decision "to carry on the plan on a much larger scale" might well mean his own dismissal; hence he became more reticent with his former patron and proceeded, to Blount's alarm, without the Senator's knowledge or direction.[37] At length in March Chisholm determined to go to England to consult British officials on the plan. Liston gave him letters of introduction to the British foreign secretary, Lord Grenville, to George Hammond, late minister to the United States, and others, and, after some rather *opera bouffe* incidents connected with getting aboard the ship, the adventurer left, his expenses paid by the Minister.[38]

Meanwhile, through the months of February and March, 1797, Blount continued to try to keep both Chisholm's and Romayne's plans in harness. Chisholm's departure was not at his instigation, and Romayne was so alarmed at the minister's dalliance with the soldier of fortune that he even wrote Liston seeking to prevent any further connivance between the two. Toward his own project with Blount, however, the doctor continued to be highly enthusiastic. He advised Blount closely on current European developments and shrewdly on arguments to gain Western converts; and he himself made careful soundings of the politicians in his wide acquaintanceship, including, he told Blount, "your friend Mr. Burr." The

[37] Turner (ed.), "Documents," *loc. cit.*, 596–600, 603; *Annals of Congress, 5 Cong.*, 2387.
[38] *Ibid.*, 2365–69; Turner (ed.), "Documents," *loc. cit.*, 596.

appearance in the Blount project of this conspirator of the future was to rouse the interest of both contemporaries and later historians, but the connection of the two conspiracies remains undefined.[39]

It was at first planned that Blount should go to England in May, but since he hoped to go to Carolina and to Knoxville on both personal and conspiratorial business, Romayne agreed to go abroad in his stead. The Senator, therefore, continued to observe his confederate's advice "to appear a pure, dignified political character." He quietly gathered his resources to hold off his creditors, meanwhile conferring with Cocke and the President on appointments and other official matters. The strong efforts of the Tennessee delegation, especially Jackson, at length obtained authorization for the payment of Sevier's troops in the 1793 campaign; but all efforts to secure land titles for the squatters south of the French Broad River were unavailing, as were efforts to call upon the President to secure a new land cession from the Indians. Blount was careful to have printed in Tennessee his efforts in behalf of his constituents since the great conspiracy was to him merely a business matter, and in no way affected his plans for re-election to the Senate in 1799.[40]

At the same time, the Blount flair for society and the polished world was not neglected. His wife and some of his family had joined him in Philadelphia, and the Blounts were an attractive couple who moved with grace and

[39] *Annals of Congress,* 5 Cong., 2340–45, 2346, 2347–49, 2351–55, 2373–75; Whitaker, *Mississippi Question,* 110; William Tatham to Thomas Jefferson, April 12, 1807, in *William and Mary Quarterly,* 2d ser., XVI (1936), 362–63.

[40] William Blount to Charles Simms, February 24, 1797, in Papers of Charles Simms (Division of Manuscripts, Library of Congress); *id.* to *id.,* March 4, 1797, in Manuscript Collection (Pennsylvania Historical Society); *id.* to the President, February 9, 1797, in State Department Miscellaneous Letters (National Archives); *id.* and William Cocke to the President, February 13, 1797, *ibid.*; Knoxville *Gazette and Weekly Advertiser,* April 10, May 1, 1797; Ramsey, *Annals,* 676–77, 684–85.

pleasure in the round of plays, balls, dinners, and receptions that engaged the amusement-loving capital even amid
financial panic and political acerbities. Despite the trag-
edy and danger of a miscarriage Mrs. Blount entered into
all possible social life of the capital, where her graces
drew grudging admiration even from stanch Federalist
Justice Iredell. The Senator was honored with a membership in the Massachusetts Historical Society and exchanged information with geographer Jedediah Morse.[41]
On March 4, 1797, while his wife watched from the gal-
lery, he gathered with his fellow Senators to witness with
little joy the inauguration of Adams and Jefferson. Then,
although the Senate was adjourned, he lingered in Philadelphia, laboriously gathering money for a lengthy trip
south. Mrs. Blount, who at last thought of Tennessee as
home, insisted on going to Knoxville, and he himself had
much to do in both Carolina and Tennessee.

At length in mid-March the couple left the capital for
Carolina from whence, after a brief stay, he rode west
in April toward Tennessee. But at the ironworks which
he and King owned just south of the Virginia line, he received word of Adams' message of March 25, calling Congress in session on May 15. This bespoke foreign news,
and the Senator gave up his Tennessee visit. However, a
thorough drenching on his journey from Carolina brought
crippling rheumatic pains, and in an enforced stay at
the works he wrote letters to serve in lieu of his visit to his
state. To Sevier he urged an interim appointment to replace Cocke, who had drawn a short term, giving lip
service to his colleague's services but a strong (though
unsuccessful) hint for Jackson. To Jackson, Winchester,

[41] James Iredell to Samuel Tredwell, March 10, 1797, in McRee, *Life of
Iredell*, II, 495–96; Massachusetts Historical Society *Collections*, 3d ser.,
I (1825), 290; William Blount to Jedediah Morse, June 20, 1797, in Blount
Manuscripts.

and Robertson, he counseled attention to the coming Tennessee elections with a view to his own re-election, recommended Jackson for the United States Senate, Claiborne for the House of Representatives, and Sevier for re-election as governor. Despite his embarrassed financial position resulting from Allison's collapse, he also wrote on land acquisition to Hart, on ironworks to Robertson, and to others to disburse and to collect money.[42]

A major incentive for the Western trip, however, had been to forward the conspiracy, and for this purpose he wrote several letters to Colonel John McClellan at Knoxville, to Major James Grant, John Rogers, and to James Carey. To the latter he was especially explicit, advising the interpreter that, while it was not entirely certain that the plan would be attempted, if Romayne's mission to England were successful, he, Blount, would "have a hand in the business, and probably shall be at the head of the business on the part of the British." Carey was especially warned against interpreter Dinsmoor, storekeeper Byers, Indian superintendent Hawkins, or any other pro-Federalist official and was advised to be extremely discreet. The characteristic letter continued:

Among things that you may safely do, will be to keep up my consequence with Watts and the Creeks and Cherokees generally; and you must, by no means, say anything in favor of Hawkins, but, as often as you can with safety to yourself, you may teach the Creeks to believe he is no better than he should be. Any power or consequence he gets will be against our plan. Perhaps Rogers, who has no office to lose, is the best man to give out talks against Hawkins. . . .

I have advised you, in whatever you do, to take care of yourself. I have now to tell you to take care of me too, for a discovery of the plan would prevent the success, and much injure all parties concerned. It may be that the Commissioners may not run the line as

[42] William Blount to John Sevier, March [April] 17, 1797, in Etting Papers (Division of Manuscripts, Library of Congress); *id.* to James Robertson, April 24, 1797, in "Robertson Correspondence," *loc. cit.*, IV, 342–43; *id.* to Thomas Hart, April 24, 1797, in Thomas J. Clay Papers.

the Indians expect or wish, and in that case, it is probable the Indians may be taught to blame me for making the Treaty.

To such complaints against me, if such there are, it may be said
by my friends, at proper times and places, . . . that, though I made
the treaty, that I made it by the instructions of the President, and,
in fact, it may with truth be said, that I was by the President instructed to purchase much more land than the Indians would agree
to sell. This sort of talk will be throwing all the blame off me upon
the late President, and as he is now out of office, it will be of no consequence how much the Indians blame him. And, among other
things, that may be said for me is, that I was not at the running of
the line, and that if I had been, it would have been more to their
satisfaction. In short, you understand the subject, and must take care
to give out the proper talks to keep up my consequence with the
Creeks and Cherokees. Can't Rogers contrive to get the Creeks to
desire the President to take Hawkins out of the nation? for, if he
stays in the Creek nation, and gets the good will of the nation, he
can and will do great injury to our plan.

When you have read this letter over three times, then burn it.
I shall be at Knoxville in July or August. . . .[43]

This incriminating missive needed a safe messenger,
and the Senator left for Philadelphia before finding such,
but in Washington, Virginia, he met James Grant and sent
it south by him.

When Blount reached the capital he found Cocke re-
elected and the political scene, from his anti-Administration view, dark and depressing. On May 16, Adams' message reviewed the rejection of Pinckney by the French
government and urged attention to military and naval
preparations. The Senator found the message "high tempered" and lamented the Federalist gains in the House,
where the clerk was displaced "not because he is not a
good clerk for I believe he is the best upon earth but
avowedly because his politics is not as theirs is—a rascally
procedure." [44]

[43] William Blount to James Carey, April 21, 1797, in *Annals of Congress,*
5 Cong., 2349–50.

[44] William Blount to ?, May 16, 1797, in Miscellaneous Manuscripts
(Tennessee State Archives).

Foreseeing a long and bitter session, he settled down with brother Thomas in a rooming house at 68 North Eighth Street. His personal convenience was becoming increasingly disturbed by angry creditors. However, he forestalled many of them by a nominal deed to Willie of much of his land, all of his 26 slaves, household belongings, and his farm stock and equipment.[45] Unimpressed by creditors' anger, he watched closely the unfolding political strife and faithfully performed the routine of his office. He informed Governor Sevier minutely on the official reports reaching Congress from Benjamin Hawkins and his fellow commissioners, who were striving to run the final Holston treaty line, to which effort thus conducted Blount was unalterably opposed. He sent legal publications to Tennessee; he pressed for militia payments; and he carefully reported to the governor on international developments. As these grew steadily more menacing, the now thorough Antifederalist observed with alarm the rising military sentiment in Philadelphia, fearing a majority were becoming "desirous to embrace the present alarm of war to rivet upon the U.S. the expense of a standing army and an expensive and useless Navy." In his attitude toward foreign relations, Blount revealed one of his most characteristic traits; namely, his clear distinction, when necessary, between political tenet and private advantage. Thus, on the one hand, his conspiracy was directed against Spain and France, and it depended on British co-operation; also, since 1793 he had loathed "Jacobins" and their leveling doctrines. Yet, after his break with the Federalists in 1796, he never flinched from admiration of France and disparagement of Britain in their Napoleonic struggles. He followed the Antifederal party line faithfully, kept informed

[45] Knox County Deeds, Book E (I), 61, 87, 90, 92, 96, 99.

on the current status of all military bills, and sent long letters on these to Sevier for publication.[46]

Throughout May, while Senator Blount thus performed his political duties, conspirator Blount pursued his secret machinations. He kept in touch with accomplice James Grant on the frontier, from whom he received encouraging reports of white and Indian unrest. Confederate Lachlan McIntosh arrived in the city seeking to extricate Zachariah Cox from the bankruptcy which had befallen Morris and Nicholson, and on departing he carried orders from the Senator to the Western conspirators.[47] In New York, however, Romayne, alarmed at the appearance of France's success and England's financial burdens, appeared to be cooling toward the project; he and Blount were unable to arrange a meeting, and the doctor began a letter to Blount renouncing the whole plan.[48]

Then, on July 3, while the Senate debated consular salaries and taxes on parchment, Senator Blount, bored with the proceedings, strolled from the chamber, to meet on the steps Fate in the humble form of Samuel B. Malcom, the President's secretary. Recognizing the bearer of a Presidential message, Blount stopped the secretary and asked the nature of the message, to which Mr. Malcom confusedly replied that it was confidential and secret and pushed on into the chamber, while the Senator continued on his walk.

A short time later he returned to find the Senate in an

[46] William Blount to Alexander J. Dallas, May 18, 1797, in Simon Gratz Collection; *id.* to John Sevier, May 27, 1797, in North Carolina Manuscripts; *id.* to *id.*, June 19, 1797, in Personal Miscellany (Division of Manuscripts, Library of Congress); *id.* to *id.*, June 23, 1797, in Miscellaneous Papers (North Carolina State Department of Archives and History).

[47] James Grant to William Blount, May 8, 1797 (extract) in *Annals of Congress,* 5 Cong., 2352; William Blount to James Grant, May 27, 1797, in Miscellaneous Manuscripts (Tennessee State Archives).

[48] *Annals of Congress,* 5 Cong., 2352–55.

uproar. Every head turned at his entrance. Cocke wore a satisfied but frightened look. A quick motion to re-read something followed, and the horrified Senator heard an excited clerk read out his damning letter of April 21 to James Carey. The Vice-President then inquired whether it was the Senator's letter. Pale and shaken, Blount replied that he had written a letter to Carey, but could not identify this letter without reference to his papers, for which purpose he requested a delay in his answer until the next day. This was granted, and the Senate reluctantly turned to a debate on liquor taxes, while Blount summoned all his power of will to walk calmly from the chamber.[49]

In the nightmare events that followed he learned the method of his undoing. Carey, influenced perhaps by his recent oath of allegiance to the government but more by the loosening effect of his beloved alcohol, had after some delay shown the letter to James Byers, the government factor at Tellico. Byers secured the letter and took it to Blount's mortal enemy, agent David Henley, who at once forwarded it express to Philadelphia and the eager hands of McHenry and Pickering.[50] The former, who had with Henley despaired of bringing down their adversary, was now delighted; but the more astute Pickering perceived at once that this bouquet of delight contained thorns. The British were strongly implicated, and, though Blount was known to be an Antifederalist, the coupling of the British minister with such a prospect would discredit both the pro-British Administration and the "good understanding"

[49] *Ibid.,* 33–34; Abigail Adams to Mary Cranch, July 6, 1797, in Stewart Mitchell (ed.), *New Letters of Abigail Adams, 1788–1801* (Boston, 1947), 100–102.

[50] *Annals of Congress,* 5 Cong., 2390–91; Benjamin Hawkins to David Henley, June 4, 1797, in David Henley Papers; Turner (ed.), "Documents," *loc. cit.,* 590; James McHenry to David Henley, June 21, 1797 (excerpt), in Catalogue of Bernet Galleries, Miscellaneous Papers (New York Public Library).

which the Secretary enjoyed with Liston. The latter, informed at once by his baffled friend, reinforced these arguments and persuaded both Pickering and McHenry not to make public the disclosure.[51] President Adams, however, had other views. Both to strike a blow at his enemies and to keep his administration clear of later recrimination, he first secured the opinion of the Attorney General that Blount's actions constituted a crime subject to impeachment and then directed that the papers be marked confidential and laid before Congress.[52]

The explosions which followed were thunderous if not illuminating. Amid wild flying rumors Pickering constituted himself a "committee of safety" for the dual purpose of getting Blount indefinitely imprisoned and of demonstrating to the world the purity and innocence of the British government and especially of Minister Liston. As a concomitant he undertook the imposing task of proving the whole matter to be a French or Spanish plot in which Jefferson had a major share. Oliver Wolcott, William Bingham, and other Federalists took up the Secretary's theme with variations, such as an explanation that it was merely a shallow attempt to blackmail Spain or the Administration.[53] Washington's rage boiled, and he expressed hope for thorough punishment. The party presses battled with venomous delight, and anonymous corre-

[51] James McHenry to David Henley, April 20, 1797 (excerpt) in Catalogue of Bernet Galleries, Miscellaneous Papers; Robert Liston to Lord Grenville, June 24, 1797, in Turner (ed.), "Documents," *loc. cit.,* 589–90.

[52] Robert Liston to Lord Grenville, July 8, 1797, in Turner (ed.), "Documents," *loc. cit.,* 593–94; opinion of Charles Lee and others, June 22, 1797, in Pickering Papers.

[53] Timothy Pickering to J. J. U. Rivardi, July 7, 1797, in Pickering Papers; Pickering correspondence, July–August, 1797, *ibid.*; Oliver Wolcott to Oliver Wolcott, Senior, July 4, 1797, in George Gibbs (ed.), *Memoirs of the Administrations of Washington and John Adams* (New York, 1846), I, 548; William Bingham to Rufus King, July 10, 1797, in C. R. King (ed.), *Life and Correspondence of Rufus King* (New York, 1895), II, 199–200; Timothy Pickering to Rufus King, August 5, 1797, *ibid.*, 209–10.

spondents in their pages contributed new hints and clues for the indefatigable Pickering. The President's lady joined the pro-Federalist writer "Porcupine" in lamenting the absence of a guillotine in Philadelphia.[54] In London, Ambassador Rufus King, laboring under several delusions (including that of the identity of Blount), directed efforts to create an elaborate conspiracy and to browbeat Chisholm into a pro-Spanish position, mildly remonstrating the while to Lord William Grenville over the activities of Liston. King was spurred on by William Tatham, who, as early as 1794 or 1795 in Knoxville, had detected some plot (probably the germ of Chisholm's plan) and had gone to Britain and Spain to disclose it. The whole affair convinced Spain's minister Godoy of the necessity of a rapid compliance with the 1795 Pinckney Treaty, but it also gave renewed arguments to the reluctant Spanish agents in the United States for the continued retention of the Mississippi posts.[55]

On the frontier, repercussions had begun before the Senate explosion. As soon as he received the Carey letter, Henley made sure, through correspondence with Washington, that the latter knew the agent's part in saving the Union and preserving the ex-President's reputation. He

[54] George Washington to David Henley, July 3, 1797 (excerpt), in Catalogue of Bernet Galleries, Miscellaneous Papers; George Washington to James McHenry, August 14, 1797, in George Washington Papers (New York Public Library); *Virginia Gazette and Petersburg Intelligencer*, July 10, 14, 18, 1797; North Carolina *Journal*, July 17, 24, 31, August 7, 14, 1797; *State Gazette of North Carolina*, August 10, 1797; *Annals of Congress*, 5 Cong., 2406–13; Abigail Adams to Mary Cranch, July 6, 1797, in Mitchell (ed.), *New Letters*, 100–102; William Cobbett, *Porcupine's Works* (London, 1801), IX, 135–80 *passim*.

[55] Turner (ed.), "Documents," *loc. cit.*, 595–605; Rufus King correspondence, August–November, 1797, in King (ed.), *Rufus King*, II, 216, 218, 236–37, 253–58; Tatham–King correspondence, January–August, 1797, in State Department Miscellaneous Letters (National Archives); Samuel C. Williams, "William Tatham, Wataugan," in *Tennessee Historical Magazine*, VII (1924), 166–67; Whitaker, *Spanish-American Frontier*, 215–16, 220–21; *id., Mississippi Question*, 66, 115.

then informed influential friends of Blount's villainy, joined Hawkins for an examination of Carey, and sent that interpreter first to Judge McNairy for another inquisition and then, with Rogers and Grant, to Philadelphia for still more interrogation. Other frontier politicians, notably Arthur Campbell, also saw a chance to discredit the ruling clique and opened correspondence with Pickering to denounce Sevier and other opponents and to impress the Secretary with their own capable availability. Ellicott mixed gratification over his perspicacity with further accusations. The trapped speculator's friends, according to their degree of complicity in the affair, either dived for cover, or, like Sevier, displayed a monumental calm over Blount's "very imprudent conduct." [56]

Meanwhile, the author of this wide commotion vacillated between flight and defiance. His first decision was a letter to the Senate asking for further time to prepare his defense, and this Cocke read to the Senators the next day, July 4. But the legislators responded by naming a committee headed by James Ross and empowered to send for persons and records and report on proper procedure to be followed. The following day, July 5, panic seized the Senator. To the committee's request for attendance at nine o'clock to make explanations, he wrote to Ross that he did "not recollect" having written Carey since his own relinquishment of the Indian department but that no letter he ever wrote was intended "to injure the United States or either of them," and that he could, if given time, justify

[56] David Henley to George Washington, June 11, 1797, in George Washington Papers; John Wade to David Henley, June 11, 1797, in Secretary of War, Official Correspondence (National Archives); *Annals of Congress*, 5 Cong., 2381–88, 2393–98; Arthur Campbell to Timothy Pickering, July 29, August 8, October 7, 1797, in Pickering Papers; Andrew Ellicott to Timothy Pickering, September 12, 1797, in Ellicott Papers (Division of Manuscripts, Library of Congress); John Sevier to James Robertson, July 15, 1797, in "Robertson Correspondence," *loc. cit.*, IV, 343–44; Thomas Dillon to John Sevier, July 20, 1797, in Draper Collection, 11DD126.

or refute "whatever may be deemed offensive" by testimony. Dispatching this highly equivocal missive, the Senator fled to the wharves, chartered a boat for a voyage to Carolina, and brought his belongings aboard. Meanwhile, however, the Senate had commanded his appearance, and upon the doorkeeper not being able to find him, peace officers dispatched by Ross's committee descended on the wharves and seized the ship. Since they had no knowledge of their quarry's personal appearance, however, they permitted the ship's quietly dressed passenger to go ashore, and the fugitive escaped his pursuers.[57]

After these dramatics, Blount surveyed the situation. The House of Representatives had appointed a committee under Samuel Sitgreaves, whose labors, it was clear, would result in an attempt at impeachment. On the other hand, Congress was to rise on July 10, and a delaying action might well be successful. The Senator, therefore, prepared for a legal fight and marshaled his reserves. He had the Carey letter printed with an accompanying circular in which, while not admitting his authorship of the letter, he asked the citizens to disregard the clamor and to judge for themselves "if the contemplated plan, let whoever may be the author, had gone into effect—what would have been the result to the citizens of Tennessee, whose good it ever has been, and will be, my happiness and duty to promote. . . ." To his friends in Tennessee, he also wrote an admission of his authorship of the Carey letter: "In a few days you will see published, by order of Congress a letter said to have been written by me to James Carey. It makes a damnable fuss here. I hope, however, the people upon the Western Waters will see nothing but good in it,

[57] *Annals of Congress*, 5 Cong., 34, 35–36; William Blount to James Ross, July 5, 1797, in Records of the Senate, 5 Cong. (National Archives); *id.* to William Cocke, July 6 [4?], 1797, in North Carolina *Journal*, July 17, 1797; McMaster, *History*, II, 342.

for so I intended it—especially for Tennessee. . . ." [58]
He engaged as attorneys Alexander J. Dallas and Jared
Ingersoll, themselves speculators. He informed the president of the Senate that he would appear to answer that
body's summons, and asked Secretary of the Senate Otis
for transcripts of all journal entries regarding himself.
From his place in the Senate he read a carefully written
declaration that he would henceforth be present to answer
charges and hoped for a full investigation. The Senate
thereupon voted to hear him by counsel the next day. [59]

That day, July 7, 1797, saw excitement at a high pitch
both in and out of Congress. The houses were packed. A
motion to allow printers to be present and take notes was
defeated. Blount arrived, with his counsel, in a white rage.
The Senatorial committee had seized his clothes, trunks,
and papers, and his application to Secretary of the Treasury Oliver Wolcott, whom he thought had them, received
a rude refusal even to answer the Senator's "insolent letters." Ross, to whom he had next applied, [60] countered with
a resolution, which the Senate passed, specifically authorizing the committee to seize Blount's letters.

The president pro tempore then flatly requested Blount
to confirm or deny his authorship of the Carey letter, and
the Senator declined to answer. His counsel asked a three-
day postponement to prepare his case, and while debate
raged about this request, Sitgreaves entered with the impeachment charge of the House of Representatives (passed
there by a vote of 41 to 30) and its promise to prove the

[58] *Annals of Congress*, 5 Cong., 2356; *State Gazette of North Carolina*,
August 10, 1797; Philip M. Hamer, *Tennessee, A History, 1673-1932* (New
York, 1933), I, 198.

[59] William Blount to the Vice President, July 6, 1797, in Records of the
Senate, 5 Cong.; *id.* to Samuel Otis, July 6, 1797, *ibid.*; Blount statement, July
6, 1797, *ibid.*; *Annals of Congress*, 5 Cong., 37–38.

[60] William Blount to James Ross, July 7, 1797, in Records of the Senate,
5 Cong.

charge at a future date. The message also requested that the Senator's seat be "sequestered" and that he be held on bonds of himself and sureties. An anti-Administration motion to postpone consideration of the message was defeated, but the Senate having set Blount's bond at $20,000 and those of his sureties at $15,000 each, did postpone action on expulsion until the morrow.[61] At that time, after testimony of Martin and Cocke on the identity of Blount's handwriting to that of the fatal letter, debate raged over the question of adopting Senator Ross's committee report. This report admitted that the matter was not fully sifted; but on the evidence of the letter to Carey, which it maintained was certainly Blount's, it pronounced him guilty of several abuses of public trust and guilty of a high misdemeanor, and it announced his expulsion from the Senate.[62]

At length, an effort to postpone consideration of the report was beaten down 19 to 7, and the question of expulsion taken. Stony-faced, Blount heard the roll call as voice after voice condemned him. Even colleague Cocke and North Carolina friends Bloodworth and Martin joined the denouncement. The final vote stood 25 to 1 with only Henry Tazewell of Virginia supporting the expelled legislator on a technicality of procedure. The expulsion and Blount's appearance cleared the air of some suspense, for Thomas Blount and Pierce Butler then surrendered Blount to the Senate and were released as sureties, while Blount himself was delivered to the Senate messenger until he should enter a bond of merely $100 for himself and secure his sureties for only $500 each to appear for the impeachment trial.[63]

On Monday, the day of adjournment, the messenger reported Blount had filed his bond and had been released,

[61] *Annals of Congress,* 5 Cong., 38–40.
[62] *Ibid.,* 41–44.
[63] *Ibid.,* 41, 44; North Carolina *Journal,* February 5, 1798.

but the Senate saw him not. While the legislators angrily ordered the recording of his nonappearance and sent transcripts of their proceedings to the Tennessee governor, the fallen statesman was pushing his horse down the Valley road to safety.

CHAPTER XI

THE OPPOSITIONIST

THE HURRYING FUGITIVE chose back roads, avoiding towns to stop at smaller hamlets. Flight, not from Pickering and Sitgreaves alone, but also from creditors—the holders of his myriad notes and promises—kept him from the accustomed hospitable halts and cheering visits. By-passing Staunton, he nevertheless met an acquaintance whose later mention of the encounter sent a citizens' troop of horse pursuing the fallen speculator to catch up with him near Lexington. The zealous posse forced him to return to Staunton, but the timely arrival from Richmond of news that he had been released on bail led to his discharge, to the disgust of Pickering, who was hastening legal matter and instructions for arrest and return to Philadelphia.[1]

At Abingdon the fugitive turned his course to the Carolina road, for his wife was in Raleigh, her arm badly shattered by a fall from her carriage. Through the hot months of August and September, 1797, he stayed with her at Colonel Ben Williams' or quietly visited his brother John Gray, meanwhile spreading conflicting rumors of his future plans, analyzing public opinion, and corresponding with McClung, Robertson, and other lieutenants in Knox-

---

[1] *State Gazette of North Carolina*, August 10, 1797; Timothy Pickering to Archibald Stewart, July 28, 1797, in Pickering Papers.

ville.[2] These stalwarts worked steadily for the rehabilitation of their chief, aided by the prejudices of party politics
and the Antifederalism of the West. Gradually results became apparent. Friendly items appeared in newspapers;
criticism of the Senate increased; a loyal nucleus of Blount
followers was joined by old friends who had fled the storm
and by new adherents actuated by anger or by disappointment with their rulers. Sevier and Robertson were, in
public at least, carefully noncommittal; Robertson, in fact,
appeared to turn to Cocke, but Jackson remained fiercely
loyal and was now joined by Blount's old antagonist,
Judge Anderson, more Antifederalist than anti-Blount.[3]
Willie Blount, now a prominent lawyer-landowner, gave
cautious but valuable support to his half brother.

Against these adherents and the ex-Senator's rising
popularity Agent Henley, John Wade, commander at
South West Point, and Superintendent Benjamin Hawkins
strove mightily, while from Virginia Arthur Campbell
continued to console the furious Pickering. But such
Blount friends as McClung, James Ore, Claiborne, and
James White were shrewd and powerful.[4] They and their
chief decided that the best gauge of strength would be to
boom the fallen Senator for re-election to the Senate which
had so ignominiously expelled him, and feelers were ac-

[2] Governor Ashe to General Robert Smith, August 18, 1797, in Council
Journal, 1795–1855 (North Carolina State Department of Archives and History).

[3] John Sevier to David Henley, August 16, 1797, in Samuel C. Williams
(ed.), "The Executive Journal of Governor John Sevier," in East Tennessee
Historical Society's *Publications,* II (1930), 142; circular of August 17, 1797,
ibid., 142–43; James Robertson to William Cocke, August 1, 1797, in "Robertson Correspondence," *loc. cit.,* IV, 344–45; William Blount to John Gray
Blount, November 7, 1797, in Blount Collection.

[4] William Blount to John Gray Blount, November 7, 1797, in Blount Collection; Benjamin Hawkins to David Henley, August 28, 1797, in David
Henley Papers; John Wade to *id.,* September 22, 1797, in Papers of the Secretary of War (National Archives); Arthur Campbell to Timothy Pickering,
October 7, 1797, in Pickering Papers.

cordingly put out. The result was surprisingly favorable, showing that the Antifederalist Tennesseans were no whit intimidated or converted by the supposed misdemeanors of their representative. Adams, with his unpopular Western policies and without the personal prestige of the first President, was scarcely a frontier favorite. His officers of the stamp of Pickering and McHenry were anathemas. The recent Indian negotiations of Hawkins and his fellow Federal agents over the Holston line threatened to lay the holdings of some hundreds of settlers in the Indian country, and everyone so displaced was a potential follower of Blount.

As these encouraging developments were relayed eastward across the mountains, Blount, though ailing from fever and ague, determined to return to Knoxville. Since his wife was still unable to travel, he went alone. On September 16, he approached the Tennessee capital to be met, possibly through prearrangement, by an honorary escort of volunteer cavalry and a "large concourse of citizens," headed by General White, the city's founder, and James Stuart, speaker of the state house of representatives. After the usual amenities and refreshments, he was conducted in state to his mansion.[5] These volunteer horsemen and the welcoming "citizens in files," however contrived, nonetheless represented a sentiment whose reality even Blount enemies were forced to admit.[6] The fallen politician himself was deeply moved. But it was not his plan actually to run for the national Senate, though urged to do so and convinced that he had "nearly a Majority" of "very warm Friends" in the legislature. He therefore declined to run,

[5] North Carolina *Journal,* October 16, 1797.

[6] John Wade to David Henley, September 19, 1797, in Papers of the Secretary of War; Oliver Wolcott to James McHenry, September 15, 1797, in Gibbs (ed.), *Memoirs of the Administrations of Washington and John Adams,* I, 562; James McHenry to Oliver Wolcott, September 22, 1797, *ibid.,* 563.

and this was widely advertised by his enemies as a sign of his political demise. The Tennessee legislature, then in session, elected Blount's friends Jackson and Anderson to fill his and Cocke's terms.[7]

The ex-Senator himself now entered upon an existence as impressive in style and nearly as influential in public affairs as that of his governorship had ever been. Despite Eastern disgrace and financial ruin, his manner of living was as elaborate as ever and far outshone that of Governor Sevier's modest ménage. His health was bad, for, while he loyally insisted on the superiority of the Tennessee climate, he was shaken by chills and fever. He lost some thirty pounds, and failing sight now compelled him to wear spectacles. His friend, Dr. Fournier, lived at the mansion to minister to the ailing politician. Nevertheless, despite illness and longing for his invalid and absent wife, he entered his son Billy in Mr. Carrick's school and took up an active program of social life.

At the same time, despite his weak financial position, Blount pursued the acquisition of land with unabated ardor. He believed that in the Mero District Hawkins and the Holston line commissioners had unintentionally erred in the white's favor. Encouraged by this and by the swelling westward migration, he plunged into plans to realize profits on his Transylvania lands and to acquire yet more middle Tennessee lands before the rise in value that he was convinced was coming. Finding prices in Tennessee too high for his slim resources, he and his associates by agents and letters filled the Carolina press with a flood of falsehoods depicting threatened Indian hostilities, bad titles, and lack of water in Cumberland areas. Sole pur-

[7] William Blount to John Gray Blount, November 7, 28, 1797, in Blount Collection; Arthur Campbell to Timothy Pickering, October 1, 1797, in Pickering Papers; *North Carolina Minerva and Fayetteville Advertiser*, November 4, 1797; North Carolina *Journal*, November 6, 1797.

pose of these stories was to "raise the *Horrors* with timid land Holders" in North Carolina and thus depress prices for the Blount agents, since the unregenerate speculator assured his brother John Gray that Cumberland lands were the best investment in America. Completely convinced of their great appreciation in three to seven years, and despite tremendous losses through delinquent tax sales on his former possessions, he further burdened an almost nonexistent credit with ever more land purchases and schemes.[8]

With this economic program he allied an intense political activity. More bitter and vindictive, even more devious and secretive than before his fall, the ex-Senator found himself at home among a restless people, and he made himself a focus and a leader of opposition to the policies, members, and agents of the national administration, on whom his comments were open and scathing. Opportunity for such opposition was at hand. In accordance with War Department orders of February, 1797, to run the long-delayed Holston Treaty boundary, Benjamin Hawkins and Andrew Pickens had in March proceeded to Tellico, there to encounter the determined opposition of the local citizenry, the procrastination of their fellow commissioner, James Winchester, and the official obstruction of Governor Sevier.[9] All concerned fully understood that if the line were properly run some two or three hundred families would inevitably be found to have settled in Indian terri-

---

[8] William Blount to John Gray Blount, November 7, 28, 1797, in Blount Collection; Knox County Court Minutes, I, 316 (Knoxville, Tennessee); William Blount to Thomas Hart, May 18, 23, 30, 1798, in Thomas J. Clay Papers.

[9] Pound, *Benjamin Hawkins*, 119–21; Royce, "Cherokee Nation," *loc. cit.*, 165–69; John Sevier to the Tennessee Senators, June 6, 1797, in Williams (ed.), "Executive Journal," *loc. cit.*, II, 136; *id.* to William Cocke, July 6, 1797, *ibid.*, 139–40; Benjamin Hawkins and Andrew Pickens to John Sevier, April 16, 1797, in Emmett Collection; Silas Dinsmoor to James McHenry, June 4, 1797, in Steiner, *James McHenry*, 261–62.

tory. Moreover, reassured by the "favorable" running of Blount's "experimental line" of 1792, these squatters had made considerable improvements in the way of orchards, barns, and the like and were determined to prevent the present line-running, or at least to have it also run "favorably." Hawkins and Pickens—the first rigorously correct, the latter anti-Blount, and both considerably irked by Sevier's opposition—had proceeded inflexibly in the face of open and implied popular threats, and, after considerable delay, the actual surveying took place in August, 1797. Moreover, with unheard-of firmness, the Administration had ordered two companies of Federal troops under Captains Richard Sparks and John Wade to remove by force if necessary those settlers found to be in Indian territory. This removal was carried out in the Fall of 1797, and though no open clashes occurred, popular anger was extremely high.[10]

Blount did not overlook the opportunity thus presented. Immediately after his arrival he conferred with Sevier on obstructionist measures; he ordered tenants on his own lands in the disputed area not to move off until dispossessed by the army; and he tirelessly attacked the *"Military Gentry"* and warned the citizens to defend their "civil liberties." [11] Through typical Blount strategy the Tennessee legislature was induced on October 5 to name three commissioners to trace the boundary as designated by the Federal commissioners, determine the number of families

[10] Royce, "Cherokee Nation," *loc. cit.*, 168; Pound, *Benjamin Hawkins,* 123–25; Report of commissioners, July 24, 1797, in David Henley Papers; Williams (ed.), *Early Travels,* 428–30; correspondence and journal, April, 1797, in "Letters of Benjamin Hawkins," *loc. cit.*, 122–25, 129–30, 145, 148, 152–53, 154; *Virginia Gazette and Petersburg Intelligencer,* July 4, 1797; Wilmington [North Carolina] *Gazette,* September 7, 1797.

[11] Charles Wright to David Henley, October 7, 1797, in Papers of the Secretary of War; William Blount to John Gray Blount, November 7, 1797, in Blount Collection; *id.* to James Robertson, January 2, March 12, 1798, in "Robertson Correspondence," *loc. cit.*, IV, 346–48, 351–53.

displaced, and decide whether the Federal commissioners' line "as marked, be run agreeably to the Treaty of Holston, and if not for what reason—and how far it is above where the true line ought to cross the Holston [Tennessee] river. . . ." [12] These commissioners, simple frontiersmen, reported in language strangely polished that the Federal commissioners' line was not run according to the treaty and that if it had been it would have saved many of the settlers who were soon "by the extension of an erroneous line to be turned out of house and home by military force. . . ." The state commissioners also felt it necessary to refer to an official report of Hawkins claiming the concurrence of many citizens in the justice of the line. To this the Tennessee commissioners replied that "no citizen whatever unconnected with office 'does concur in the justice of their decision.' In other words Mr. Hawkins has given the Secretary of War official information which is not true." [13]

The Tennessee legislature, on receiving this report on October 18, passed resolutions also written by Blount declaring the Hawkins line to be erroneous and denouncing any attempt of the troops to remove settlers as "an act of violent oppression, and an undue exercise of the military over the civil authority." These resolutions formed part of a general memorial and remonstrance to the President, which complained of treaty regulations which deprived the settlers of lands legally bought from Carolina's land office and prayed for legal arrangements to be made to extinguish the Indian claim.[14]

The mixture of personal revenge and politics which

[12] *House Journal of the Second General Assembly of the State of Tennessee* (Kingsport, 1933), 174.

[13] *Ibid.*, 200–201.

[14] *Ibid.*, 201–202; William Blount to John Gray Blount (n.d., probably 1797), in Blount Collection, P.C. 860.

actuated the ex-governor are evident in letters to his brother:

Mr. Hawkins has been very conspicuous in this State for his Egotism, his Vanity his self Importance, his official Consequence & his Want of Veracity. . . . It is certain that Mr. Hawkins and his Disciple Pickins took several indirect Means to injure the writer in the estimation of his Frontier Neighbors such as insinuating in very plain Terms that it was his Fault or they might have been included in the Treaty of Holston. . . . Never was man more exercrated in any Country than Hawkins in this and as to Pickens he has no character but that of his being his humble Follower. It is to be observed this conduct of H & Pickins towards the writer was at their first arrival in this State & before the letter to Carey appeared.[15]

If the national Administration's agents were thus attacked, that Administration itself was excoriated. Blount rejoiced at the establishment of a newspaper in Nashville under an editor who was "not a Ministerial Printer"; and he himself never wearied of assaults on Adams' military, naval, and foreign policies, which he, like his fellow Antifederalists in Congress, constantly reiterated would inevitably bring a costly and useless French war.[16] Through friends at the capital he was kept informed on affairs in the Congressional session which lasted from November, 1797, into July, 1798. This session, despite the urging of Blount's old enemy, Joseph McDowell, now a North Carolina Representative, made but little progress in the impeachment procedure. Sitgreaves' committee continued to gather evidence, drew up formal charges, and dispatched a summons to Blount; but the Senate defeated any effort to start proceedings before the next session, while Antifederalists under Jefferson began to plan the ex-Senator's defense.[17]

[15] William Blount to John Gray Blount (n.d., probably 1797), in Blount Collection, P.C. 860.

[16] William Blount to James Robertson, January 2, 1798, in "Robertson Correspondence," loc. cit., IV, 346–48.

[17] Annals of Congress, 5 Cong., 672–79, 809–970 passim, 1143–45, 1376–77,

Meanwhile the object of this strategy was involving himself in another illegal scheme of desperation. Blount, always a dangerous opponent, was now, through threat of financial ruin and loss of prestige, especially ruthless. In 1796, Representative Andrew Jackson, on the way to Congress, had by chance discovered something more of the wholesale frauds in the land office transactions of North Carolina's Secretary of State James Glasgow, a Blount friend but long an object of suspicion in that state. Jackson informed Governor Ashe, and the latter requested Governor Sevier to forward the records of Martin Armstrong of Nashville, an official of the old military reserve. Sevier, deeply implicated, did his best to hamper the investigation by a refusal to send the papers, but copies were made and an investigation began in Carolina.[18] The legislature's committee of inquiry sat at Raleigh, and by its orders the books and papers of Glasgow were stored in the comptroller's office for their use. Blount, Sevier, Stockley Donelson, and other speculators were badly frightened. Consequently, the comptroller's office was broken into and a large chest and trunk were stolen; but the robbery was interrupted and most of the papers recovered, although all the thieves escaped except an uncommunicative slave. Then, on the night of February 11, a meeting was held in Blount's home and the prospects reviewed. A public exposure of the crimes of Glasgow, a land partner of Donel-

---

1412–13, 1426, 1559; John Dawson to James Madison, December 10, 1797, in Madison Papers; Thomas Jefferson to Edmund Pendleton, January 14, 1798, in *Jefferson Papers,* Massachusetts Historical Society *Collections,* 7th ser., I (1900), 59–60; *id.* to James Madison, February 8, 1798, in Madison Papers; Andrew Jackson to Willie Blount, February 21, 1798 (copy), in Rodman Papers.

[18] Legislative Papers, 1797, *passim* (North Carolina State Department of Archives and History); Governors' Papers, XXI, *passim;* Abernethy, *Frontier to Plantation,* 171–72; Williams (ed.), "Executive Journal," *loc. cit.,* III, IV, V, *passim.*

son and often an associate of Blount's, was unthinkable, involving as it would all the speculators. The meeting, therefore, designated William Tyrrell, a Donelson accomplice in various land frauds, to go to Carolina and destroy the papers by another attempt at theft or, if that again failed, by burning the building which housed the comptroller's office.[19]

But the author of the Carey letter was an unfortunate plotter. This time one of the lesser conspirators, frightened by his associates' ruthlessness, betrayed the plot to Tennessee judges John McNairy and Howell Tatum, who, by express rider, informed Governor Ashe. The latter doubled guards in the comptroller's office, thus foiling the plot, while the investigating committee completed its work and reported one of the most comprehensive records of fraud and land thievery in the history of public lands.[20] Though Blount was implicated, the chief malefactors were Stockley Donelson, William Tyrrell, Glasgow, and, to a less extent, the firm of John Gray & Thomas Blount, and John Sevier.[21] While the Blount-Sevier influence could not save Glasgow or Donelson from prison in Carolina, it could in Tennessee protect fugitive Tyrrell, who was valuable to the Blounts "for he is loudly our Friend, he travels much & has several active young men under his Command besides he is a sensible designing Man of Boldness and Enterprise." [22] This same influence which saved

[19] State Gazette of North Carolina, February 1, 1798; Howell Tatum to Governor Ashe, February 13, 1798, in Governors' Papers; John McNairy to Governor Ashe, February 13, 1798, ibid.

[20] John McNairy to Governor Ashe, February 13, 1798, in Governors' Papers; Journal of the Council of State, April 11, 1798, in Governors' Office Papers, 122; Abernethy, Frontier to Plantation, 172–73.

[21] For the report of the commissioners, see Glasgow Land Frauds, 1798–1800, IV (North Carolina State Department of Archives and History). North Carolina Minerva and Fayetteville Gazette, December 15, 1798; North Carolina Journal, December 24, 1798; Abernethy, Frontier to Plantation, 173–76.

[22] William Blount to John Gray Blount, November 17, 1797, in Blount Collection.

Tyrrell also protected Blount's and Sevier's reputations by the suppression of the committee's report.

The exposure of some of his illegalities, however, did not in the least dampen Blount's ardor for more land, his pride, or his optimism. To his brother John Gray, despondent over reverses, he wrote a series of enticing letters to come and settle in Tennessee for reasons which lay deep in Blount's character. His complete conversion to Western interests and his pride and faith in family are alike reflected in these pages:

It is certain that every man who arrives here and determines to become a Citizen appears to feel and I believe does in reality feel an Independence and Consequence to which he was a Strainger in the Atlantic States—This must be owing to some Cause, which can be no other than that the Richness of the Soil and the Healthfulness of the Climate will afford him a certain Prospect to Plenty & Health if not to greater Riches. . . .

. . . .

meet your difficulties with Firmness be them of what Description they may and since Credit is fallen and cannot be recovered with any advantage don't make Sacrifices to pay debts for paying as soon as you can or at the Extremity of the law will be the same thing to your Credit . . . but yet I advise sell your House in Washington & every Thing in No Car⁰ but your Negroes in preference of Cumberland lands. . . . It's a Country affording Health & Plenty and such Luxuries as we have been accustomed to can be had if care is taken at a moderate Price. . . .

. . . .

If Nothing else is left but our Wives and our Children I consider them of inestimable Value and after so bold an Essay I have become if posible more anxious that our Sons should be well educated to the end that they may have it in their Power to become distinguished Characters and keep up the Family and Name . . . and it appears to me that these Objects could be the better secured and our Happiness promoted if you and I were settled near each other. . . .[23]

It was these deep motives of prestige, wealth, and family, which, despite public exposures, personal ill

[23] William Blount to John Gray Blount, November 7, 17, 28, 1797, *ibid.*

health, and near-bankruptcy drove Blount on. He entertained Moses Fisk, who was on a Western trip as agent for
a land syndicate, and interested him in a forty thousand
acre purchase. He planned extensive tenancy and stock
raising schemes in middle Tennessee. His involvement in
Zachariah Cox's Yazoo enterprises continued, for Major
Lachlan McIntosh, the company's attorney, had been involved with Blount in the Romayne-Chisholm debacle,
had fled Philadelphia with him, and was a three-months
visitor in his Knoxville home. In March, 1798, Blount
sent this confidential friend to Mero District with warmest
recommendations to Robertson to obtain an attorney's
license and to ingratiate himself with the Mero citizens.[24]

It was primarily this interest in the Yazoo enterprise
which aroused Blount's and Sevier's enthusiasm for a new
Indian treaty. Under pressure from the national government, Sevier, closely advised by Blount, was making unconvincing motions to thwart the progress of the indefatigable Cox, but the involvement of both Sevier and Blount
in the speculation insured that nothing drastic would be
done to stop him.[25] Meanwhile, national events afforded
a chance to further Cox's aims legally. The legislature's
memorial of 1797 concerning the Holston line, of which
Blount's resolutions had formed a part, had been pressed
in Philadelphia by the state's Congressional delegation.

[24] William Blount to John Gray Blount, November 7, 1797, *ibid.*; *id.* to
James Robertson, March 12, 1798, in "Robertson Correspondence," *loc. cit.*,
IV, 351–53; Lowrie (ed.), *American State Papers, Public Lands,* I, 225, 226.
[25] Williams (ed.), "Executive Journal," *loc. cit.*, II, 144, 148, III, 159–61,
166–67, IV, 151–52; Isaac J. Cox (ed.), "Documents Relating to Zachariah
Cox," in Historical and Philosophical Society of Ohio *Quarterly Publications,*
VIII (1912–14), 34–35, 97–103; Manuel Gayoso de Lemos to the Count of
Santa Clara, November 30, 1797, in Papeles de Cuba; William Blount to
James Robertson, March 12, 1798, in "Robertson Correspondence," *loc. cit.*,
IV, 351–53; Lowrie (ed.), *American State Papers, Public Lands,* I, 225;
George Elholm to John Sevier, January 28, 1798, in Draper Collection,
11DD130; William Polk to William R. Davie, August 9, 1797, in Steiner,
James McHenry, 266–67.

Adams referred the matter to Congress; Pinckney's House committee reported favorably; and, after some disagreement on personnel, three commissioners were named to negotiate a new treaty for the purpose of buying the lands in question. When Fisher Ames and Bushrod Washington declined to serve, George Walton and John Steele were substituted and, with Alfred Moore, were provided with elaborate instructions.[26] But here lay the elements of future discord. The instructions aimed primarily at the acquisition of the area south of the French Broad; Jackson and the other Congressmen looked further, to the Bend of the Tennessee River; Blount and Sevier wanted all of southern Tennessee in order to open the way to the Yazoo company's vast purchase.[27]

However, before these divergencies were known, Blount and Sevier worked eagerly for the success of the treaty. Together they chose Robertson, James Stuart, and Yazoo associate Lachlan McIntosh to be present as Tennessee agents and to push for wider acquisitions. They sent speculator-settler James Ore to the Cherokee chiefs to prepare their minds for a land cession proposal.[28]

In July, 1798, the Federal and state commissioners met the Indians at Tellico Block House. The native chiefs, threatened by their warriors, were unwilling to cede land and were further confused by the two sets of commissioners and frightened by the presence of McIntosh and other

[26] Royce, "Cherokee Nation," *loc. cit.,* 175–79; Lowrie and Clark (eds.), *State Papers, Indian,* I, 638–41; miscellaneous correspondence in Papers of the Secretary of State, Box 1 (Tennessee State Archives).

[27] Andrew Jackson to James Robertson, January 11, 1798, in "Robertson Correspondence," *loc. cit.,* IV, 348–49; *ibid.,* IV, 357–64, *passim*; Willie Blount to John Gray Blount, February 6, 1798, in Blount Collection.

[28] William Blount to John Sevier, February 18, 1798, in Miscellaneous Manuscripts (Tennessee State Archives); John Sevier to James Robertson, May 13, 1798, in "Robertson Correspondence," *loc. cit.,* IV, 354; William Blount to *id.,* May 14, 1798, *ibid.,* 353; Royce, "Cherokee Nation," *loc. cit.,* 179–80.

well-known land robbers. They therefore shrewdly took advantage of the open dissension between the two white delegations and despite every inducement refused to sell any land, whereupon the conference was adjourned until September.[29] Recriminations at once broke out between the settlers and the Federal commissioners. The latter were convinced that the homesteaders and their leaders had sought to prevent a treaty and bring on a war to obtain lands. The secretary to the Federal commissioners, Elisha Hall, was particularly convinced and published a conversation with Robertson in which the latter had allegedly admitted the desire of the frontier leaders for the treaty meeting to fail. Judge Campbell, too, indulged his unquenchable officiousness in an anonymous letter in Roulstone's paper denouncing the supposed obstructionism of Sevier and McIntosh. The leaders, thus assailed, replied with spirit. McIntosh replied vigorously to Hall's publication. Blount brought suit for slander and needled Robertson into a public letter denying the alleged statements. Sevier likewise sued Campbell for defamation. Thus, in the early Fall of 1798, the political scene livened noticeably.[30]

This field was, in fact, exerting all its old attraction for the ex-Senator, who, never blind to the advantages of office, by mid-1798 was again feeling the urge for official power. The suit against Hall for slander was a part of this program, designed to prove to the skeptical that Blount wished an Indian treaty, as in fact he did. Then in com-

[29] E. Harris to John Gray Blount, July 16, 1798, in Blount Collection; James Robertson, James Stuart, and Lachlan McIntosh to the United States Commissioners, July 19, 1798, in "Robertson Correspondence," *loc. cit.,* IV, 357–64.

[30] Putnam, *History of Middle Tennessee,* 546–50, 560; William Blount to James Robertson, August 5, 1798, in "Robertson Correspondence," *loc. cit.,* IV, 355–57; *ibid.,* 365–68; Alfred Moore to James McHenry, June 30, 1799, in Steiner, *James McHenry,* 445–50.

missioning officers for the new provisional army in July, 1798, Adams, to Washington's intense disgust, named Sevier a brigadier general, and the governor planned to accept. When this was followed in September by Speaker James White's resignation in order to accept a Federal office, Blount immediately announced his availability for White's seat in the senate for Knox County. If successful in the election, he could hope, upon the convocation of the assembly in December, 1798, to be named speaker. Then with Sevier's expected resignation following the rise of the assembly, the way to the governorship would be open.[31]

Meantime, when the treaty negotiations commenced on September 20, Steele and Moore had been replaced in the Federal commission by George Walton and Lieutenant Colonel Thomas Butler. In the Tennessee delegation Robertson failed to appear, White replaced Stuart, and Sevier himself followed Blount's earlier suggestion to attend in person. The achievements of these second negotiations were more successful, partly because the Indians, in the presence of "Nollachucky Jack," read the possible results of further refusals.[32] The cession of lands obtained was due in Blount's view to the "good sense of the Indians" rather than "the good conduct of the commissioners," of whom Walton was "certainly the most crafty blockhead that has ever filled so important a Commission";[33] but

[31] Steiner, *James McHenry,* 313–14; George Washington to James McHenry, July 22, September 9, 1798, in John C. Fitzpatrick (ed.), *The Writings of George Washington* (Washington, 1941), XXXVI, 356–60, 430–34; James White to John Sevier, September 6, 1798, in Sevier Papers (Tennessee State Archives); Robert Love to John Gray Blount, November 2, 1798, in Blount Collection; William Blount to James Robertson, August 5, October 1, November 11, 1798, in "Robertson Correspondence," *loc. cit.,* IV, 355–57, 370–71.

[32] Royce, "Cherokee Nation," *loc. cit.,* 174–75, 180–83; Lowrie and Clark (eds.), *State Papers, Indian,* I, 640.

[33] William Blount to James Robertson, October 1, 1798, in "Robertson Correspondence," *loc. cit.,* IV, 370.

whatever the cause of the cession, it was a valuable asset to the ex-Senator's political plans.

Another element in these arose in the unpredictable Judge Campbell, who, in November, quashed Blount's slander suit against Hall without even hearing it. To crush the ambitious judge, "the most meddling blockhead that ever crept into such high office in any Country," Blount took up the weapon of his Philadelphia enemies and with Sevier's aid prepared impeachment charges.[34]

A third potential issue in Blount's campaign was the arrival of the Sergeant at Arms of the United States Senate to take the ex-Senator to Philadelphia for his own impeachment proceedings. Such an arrival might well have spelled doom to another political aspirant, but the Blount-Sevier control was too strong in Tennessee for any embarrassment. The Senatorial officer was handsomely entertained as Blount's house guest; however, he was informed that his host could not conveniently accompany him to Philadelphia, and in the face of this all the influence of Henley, Cocke, Hawkins, and Tipton proved insufficient to raise a posse for a forcible removal.[35]

Thus, in his political resurgence, Blount overrode or turned to advantage the events of the Fall, and his reward came with election in October to White's seat. On December 3, 1798, he met with Robertson and his other fellow senators, and the second portion of his plans succeeded upon his elevation to the speakership over Edward Douglass, a Campbell adherent.[36]

With so much accomplished, Blount now primarily had to consolidate his position and wait for Sevier's ex-

[34] William Blount to James Robertson, August 5, 1798, *ibid.*, 355–57; Knox County Court Minutes, I, 406.

[35] Ramsey, *Annals,* 699–700; James Ramsey to Governor Porter, February 14, 1876, in Miscellaneous Manuscripts (Tennessee State Archives).

[36] *Senate Journal of the Second General Assembly of the State of Tennessee* (Kingsport, 1933), 269–70.

pected resignation. Part of this consolidation was the punishment of Judge Campbell. Accordingly, on December 5, Sevier laid before the representatives a letter from Blount complaining of Campbell's denial of justice by the illegal quashing of the suit against Hall. The governor added to this the charges of the judge's failure to hold the designated Spring session of court in Mero and of inciting, by a charge to the Grand Jury of Hamilton, armed resistance to the general government. The house of representatives appointed a committee which took testimony and reported in favor of impeachment on the grounds of illegality in the Blount slander action and of failure to attend the Mero court, but not to incitement of rebellion. To this report the house agreed, and on December 17 the charges were presented to the senate.[37]

The eleven senators were somewhat at a loss on the formalities of an impeachment trial but received expert advice from the speaker. They summoned Campbell to answer the charges, subpoenaed witnesses, and set December 24 for the trial date. The house managers, too, were busy collecting witnesses, Blount among them; and Campbell himself selected witnesses and lawyers and acted vigorously in preparing his defense. From the beginning affairs did not go well for the prosecution. Campbell had a host of witnesses, including even Blount adherents, and when his objection to Blount's participation as prosecutor, witness, and judge was overruled by the senate, there were ominous dissents from the Greene and Sullivan County senators. Since the votes of two thirds of the eleven senators were necessary for impeachment, it was clear that the vote would be close, and when Alexander Kelly of Blount County absented himself on December 23, Blount sent the

[37] *House Journal of the Second General Assembly*, 391–96, 399, 400, 407–18, 422–24.

sergeant at arms with a demand for attendance at the trial. But Kelly, like the speaker in a similar situation, could not be found.

On December 24 the ten remaining senators took the trial oath and arguments were heard on that day and the next, by which time it was clear that the judge's case had several friends. On December 26, the vote was taken and found to be 6 to 4 for impeachment. Thus, the absence of Kelly was decisive, and the speaker had the mortification of pronouncing his enemy not guilty.[38]

Meanwhile, as Blount judged, he was the object of judgment. On December 6, 1798, in Philadelphia, the Sergeant at Arms returned his unexecuted writ of summons to the Senate, and Ingersoll and Dallas reported to that body that they were ready to defend the ex-Senator. On the seventeenth, rules of procedure were adopted and the first national impeachment trial in the nation's history began before an audience that included justices of the Supreme Court, judges of the District of Columbia, "Officers of the late revolutionary Army and such Gentlemen as may be introduced by Members of either house," "Ladies of Members of Congress," foreign ministers, and other notables.[39] Counsel for Blount argued that the Senate lacked jurisdiction since 1) Blount was no longer a Senator; 2) when a Senator he was not a civil officer within the meaning of the impeachment clause of the Constitution; 3) the impeachment articles did not charge any crime, malconduct, or abuse of trust while in such civil office; 4) if any criminal act was committed, the remedy lay in the courts of local jurisdiction. After a brief delay at the managers' request, the formal answers and rejoinders were

[38] *Senate Journal of the Second General Assembly,* 305–10, 311–12, 319, 321, 327, 328–30.

[39] *Annals of Congress,* 5 Cong., 2190, 2196, 2197, 2245; seating chart, Records of the Senate, 5 Cong.

heard, from which the trial proceeded to lengthy argument by counsel and managers.[40] At length, on January 7, 1799, a motion to overrule Blount's plea was offered, debated for three days, and on January 10, the motion lost, 14 to 11.[41] The following day, by an exactly reverse vote, the Senate upheld the ex-Senator's plea and ruled that Senators are not impeachable civil officers by dismissing the impeachment for want of jurisdiction; on January 14, this decision was communicated to counsel and the court adjourned.[42]

This victory, however welcome to the Tennessee speaker, was nullified by fatal political blows at home. His failure to impeach Campbell showed serious political weakness, but far more fatal was Sevier's refusal to fulfill his expected role by resigning. "Nollachucky Jack" had been impressed by the Campbell fiasco and had observed the lagging prospects of martial glory through a war with France. Perhaps, too, Blount's advocacy of the rising Jackson disturbed him, though he followed Blount's recommendation in appointing the young politician to the bench upon his resignation from Congress. Hence, with an eye to re-election or at least continued control of the state, Sevier determined to fill out his present term. This decision, preceded by the election of Cocke to the national Senate to replace Jackson, was fatal to Blount's political plans. His protégés and friends were well placed, Jackson on the bench,[43] and Claiborne and Anderson in Congress; but the old political master himself was for once at

---

[40] For the proceedings, see *Annals of Congress,* 5 Cong., 2245–2319. For evidence gathered by Sitgreaves' committee, see *ibid.,* 2319–2416.

[41] *Ibid.,* 2318; Thomas Blount to John Gray Blount, February 1, 1798, in Blount Collection.

[42] *Annals of Congress,* 5 Cong., 2319; Homer Carey Hockett, *The Constitutional History of the United States* (New York, 1939), I, 311.

[43] William Blount to John Sevier, July 6, 1798, in Miscellaneous Manuscripts (Tennessee State Archives); Willie Blount to John Sevier, August 12, 1798, *ibid.*

loose ends. His real desire was the governorship, but he could not at this late date hope to challenge Sevier's popularity.

The year of 1799 was therefore marked by political doldrums for Blount personally, although it saw rising factionalism in the state, centering around Adams and Jeffersonian policies on the one hand, and on the other the ambitions of Jackson and Roane against Sevier.[44] Hence, plagued by ill health, he devoted his interests primarily to family and business.

His wife, accompanied by her mother, had at last been able to join her husband, and the activity of seven children filled the house. The two older daughters, Ann and Mary Louisa, now claimed the admiration of Henry Toole, Pleasant Miller, and the other young men of the town. Billy Grainger Blount, the eldest son, was studying under the Reverend Mr. Carrick, and Richard was soon to follow. The varied activities of these four and the care of the three smallest babes kept Mrs. Blount fully occupied.

The ex-governor was the object of attention at all civic and social functions. His thorough knowledge of Indian affairs brought him into correspondence with President John Wheelock of Dartmouth on the establishment of Cherokee mission schools, and he was the host of Moravian missionaries on the same subject.[45] With his wife he attended balls and banquets, and his charm and address were as admired in the social world as his influence was courted in the political.

But public and private life were alike circumscribed by financial weakness. The collapse of partner Allison had immediately brought up for settlement obligations to

[44] Putnam, *History of Middle Tennessee,* 562; Thomas Johnson to Willie Blount, June 16, 1799 (copy), in Rodman Papers.

[45] Moses Fisk to President Wheelock, September 25, 1799, in Dartmouth College Archives; Williams (ed.), *Early Travels,* 458–59.

the amount of hundreds of thousands of dollars. In addition, as further commitments fell due, new judgments for more thousands were awarded other creditors. His prospects for help remained dark; John Gray Blount and the firm were also close to the financial brink, and in addition, this brother was indicted to stand trial for "high crimes" as a result of the Glasgow exposures. These same exposures had depressed Western land prices, despite the 1798 treaty, and since war continued to be a strong possibility, prices were further depressed. Cox's Yazoo plans were temporarily if not permanently ruined by his arrest in Natchez and subsequent flight.[46]

Blount as usual struggled steadily against his adversities. He worked hard and took a leading part in the division of the Transylvania lands in which he was interested as an attorney and executor for subpurchasers. He kept close watch on land values as reported by friends, for the use of agents was less feasible than before.[47] Allison, in prison since 1797, finally closed his stormy life and to Blount fell the duty of executor of the speculator's tangled estate—a post involving yet more difficulties. To pay off a part of his own obligations, he endeavored to sell some remaining North Carolina lands,[48] and, according to the

[46] Willie Blount to John Gray Blount, April 23, 1800, in Blount Collection; John Gray Blount to Willie Blount, May 11, 1800, *ibid.*; Benjamin Orr to John Gray Blount, April 18, 1800, *ibid.*; Knox County Court Minutes, II, 36; William B. Grove to James Hogg, January 18, 1798, in H. M. Wagstaff (ed.), "Letters of William Barry Grove," in *The James Sprunt Historical Publications,* IX (1910), No. 2, pp. 67–69; John Steele to David Campbell, October 14, 1798, in Draper Collection, 9DD66; Thomas Butler to John Sevier, March 11, 1799, in Sevier Papers.

[47] William Blount to Thomas Hart, March 13, June 1, 1799, in Thomas J. Clay Papers; Articles of Agreement, December 3–4, 1799, in Draper Collection, 1CC222–225; Sampson Williams to William Blount, December 4, 1799 (copy) in Rodman Papers; John Strother to *id.,* October 7, 1799 (copy), *ibid.*; Edward Jones to John Gray Blount, May 6, 1799, in Blount Collection.

[48] Knox County Wills, Book O, 14 (Knoxville); Knox County Court Minutes, II, 106; Knox County Estate Book, I, 69; Benjamin Orr to William Blount, April 2, 1800, in Blount Collection.

Spanish at least, the ex-Senator never lost sight of the aim of his old conspiracy; it is certain that he kept closely in touch with his old agents.[49]

But his progress from this financial swamp was slow if perceptible and was made with terrific cost to his health. When the Fall elections for the legislature occurred he felt unequal to the political pressure and declined to run, though he kept in touch with events and as a Knox County Justice faithfully attended the county court. The first months of the new year brought some improvement both in his finances and his health. On February 22, 1800, he took part in the somewhat grim celebration of Washington's birth—a funeral procession, complete with casket and funeral oration [50]—at the same time anticipating with great interest the coming national election, with the hope of seeing the first President's successor turned out of office.

Public functions became fewer during the winter months of 1799–1800, as Knoxville suffered a series of various epidemics. In March, disaster struck Blount's family. Mrs. Grainger, Blount's mother-in-law, who had been living with the Blounts, first fell ill of a malarial disease, and during her illness Mrs. Blount and two children were also bedridden by similar attacks. The old lady was unable to meet the assault and died; on March 11, the day after her funeral, Billy, Blount's eldest son, was very severely stricken.

As the ill boy labored through the nights, his father was constantly up and moving through the chilled house and as a result caught a severe cold. On March 15 he felt

---

[49] Martinez de Yrujo to the Marquis of Someruelos, March 6, 1800, in Papeles de Cuba; Marquis of Someruelos to Martinez Yrujo, April 23, 1800, *ibid.*

[50] "The Diary of John Sevier," in Samuel G. Heiskell (ed.), *Andrew Jackson and Early Tennessee History* (Nashville, 1920), II, 576.

better and took his customary evening coffee on the porch, absorbed in the newspaper until dark. A half-hour later a violent chill struck, followed by a fever and a day and night of delirium. Dr. Fournier and friends were faithful and devoted, and when the delirium passed, the sick man felt so much better after two days that he insisted that the night vigil at his bed be stopped. During that night he caught more cold. Further tortures of blistering and purging were applied; for two days his condition seemed static until a relapse on Friday morning, March 21. The strong vitality of the ill man fought this until late evening when, after a sudden paroxysm, he lost the power of speech. Two large tears coursed down the stricken face, and he turned his face to the wall and died.[51]

The unexpectedness of the attack and his unrealized danger made Blount's death a complete surprise to all. With Willie in Nashville, and Mrs. Blount and Billy prostrate in illness and shock, the funeral in the First Presbyterian churchyard was attended only by his children, Sevier, and other friends. Willie, who hastened back, took over the education of the children and sought, with John Gray Blount's help, to salvage what little was possible from the ruined estate. The children were made the legal charges of Willie and that other successful lawyer-protégé, Hugh Lawson White, son of Blount's associate, James White. Mrs. Blount lingered two years more, until jaundice relieved her too from what John Gray called "the School of adversity" and its lessons of "that cunning now so necessary."[52]

Blount's passing evoked varied reactions. Enemies

[51] J. Sommerville to Thomas Blount, March 27, 1800, in Blount Collection; *id.* to John Gray Blount, March 27, 1800, *ibid.*; Willie Blount to Jacob Blount, Jr., May 25, 1800, *ibid.*

[52] John Gray Blount to Willie Blount, May 11, 1800, *ibid.*; Knox County Wills, Book O, 25, 28, 29, 34; "Diary of John Sevier," *loc. cit.,* 577.

were strangely silent, absorbed, perhaps, in preparing for
the coming political battle of 1800. Obituaries in the press
recorded his services in the usual glowing terms,[53] and
news of his death was widely printed. "Many will de-
plore . . . his death," wrote Moses Fisk. "He had a winning address and had been very humane to many of the
first settlers in this country, and seemed to take peculiar
pleasure in bringing forward to business and consequence
young men of narrow circumstances and good genius." [54]

The era of Blount was over with his death, for the
triumph of Western interests after 1800 and the color of
the Sevier-Jackson feud in Tennessee politics removed
the issues and shifted the personalities of his day in the
public mind. It was left to those less astute—such as
Sevier—or more fortunate—such as Jackson—to reap
greater rewards from contemporaries and greater praise
from posterity. His own relatives saw little chance for his
fame. "As that is a new country the face of which will
be in a few years totally changed I hope you will procure
to be engraved on some lasting stone his name, age etc
which will for a time point out the place of his inter-
ment," [55] wrote his brother John Gray to his executor,
Willie Blount.

Yet his work was of importance, and his influence
was vital alike in the history of his state and in the lives
of three governors and a President—three of them his
"young men of narrow circumstances and good genius."

[53] Tennessee *Gazette,* April 16, 1800; Virginia *Argus,* April 18, 1800.

[54] Moses Fisk to John Wheelock, April 17, 1800, in Dartmouth College
Archives.

[55] John Gray Blount to Willie Blount, May 11, 1800, in Blount Collection.

EPILOGUE

A MAN AND A LIFE

Certain figures of history appear destined to be written down as either heroes or villains. Such a man was William Blount. Of his contemporaries, those within reach of his influence were usually cautious in criticism, but those at greater distance, such as Pickering, Henley, Ellicott, or Arthur Campbell, were vitriolic. Campbell, indeed, mixed animosity with shrewd appraisal when he wrote to Pickering that Blount "possesses considerable abilities, a restless ambition, griping avarice, much vanity and pride; and as he seemed to have a prospect to gratify his favorite pursuits he was a republican or an admirer of royalty." [1]

This characterization is closer to the truth than that of some historians who have lost the man in the figure, and, encouraged by the secrecy of Blount's operations, have laid an overcharge of villainy at his door. On the other hand, for many historians of his area, the clouds of patriotic incense have never risen to reveal the truly significant features of the territorial governor. With a few exceptions, these writers have substituted for fact the flowery rhetoric of Ramsey and Haywood. [2]

[1] Arthur Campbell to Timothy Pickering, October 7, 1797, in Pickering Papers.
[2] For example, see Marcus J. Wright, *Some Account of the Life and Services of William Blount* (Washington, 1884).

William Blount was neither god nor devil; he was a Federalist thwarted by Fate. His tastes were those of his upper-class landowner-merchant father. He thus loved authority, order, and all the properties of his eighteenth-century social world. At the same time, while neither Jacob Blount nor his son was born at the very top of the economic or social order, in eighteenth-century America, and especially in the yet unformed society of North Carolina, to rise to the top was always possible, given energy, ingenuity, and ambition. These qualities, which to others were "concern with twopenny matters" and "restless ambition and grasping avarice," Jacob and his sons possessed to a superlative degree.

In the social convulsion which attended the Revolution, William Blount, through his inborn and acquired knowledge of economics, rose into a new class, that of the leaders of his state. He thereupon placed himself in the halls of government—partly because that was the place of a gentleman, but primarily because he, like Hamilton, realized the nexus of governmental and economic power, and he aimed at both. But the social philosophy of Hamilton was not the primary concern of Blount. The latter's interest was not principally in the stability of society but in his own advance in society; in short, he was a businessman in politics for business. When his observing eye saw that the ultra-Whigs would control the assembly and the state, he wasted no time in the impotent rage of a Hooper or Maclaine but rather used the ultra-Whig tenets, paper money and anti-Loyalism, to advance his business interests and, incidentally, his political power.

Thus, from his first army office, political place and power were to Blount the handmaidens of business profit. He loved authority for its concomitant dignities and deference, but he cherished it more highly for the economic opportunities it presented. In an age when the public and private purse of rulers was but by few persons differentiated, when official salaries were small and official and private duties were of equal weight to nearly all officeholders, in such an age the climbing businessman naturally and easily combined office and enterprise. Business was the prime motive of his service in the Continental Congress, business was the rationale of his uncomfortable and unprofitable wilderness sojourn at Hopewell. As a businessman he realized the values even to a speculator of a more perfect union; therefore, as a businessman he cautiously supported the Constitution before a hostile constituency.

As a businessman, too, he was caught up in the overwhelming business project of his age—land speculation. A climber who had come far, he was dazzled by the prospect of a continent for sale, and he gambled with the daring engendered by hundreds of profitable speculations in his past. To this supreme project he naturally brought every resource, including politics, and he secured the Western governorship.

Yet to Blount, while business was, in this instance as always, first, yet position and prestige were, as always, present. He envisioned a Western empire of incalculable profit to its leaders, rulers who were to bring the dignified orderliness and social system of the East across the mountains. Upon closer contact, he found the average Westerner unenchanted with such a vision, and so modified his own views somewhat; but he skillfully chose his agents and pursued his course even while he lost his cherished deference and popularity. Still, something happened in Blount, the man. Beyond the speculator's optimism, beyond the official's role, he grew to love the Western country. His labor as governor was for gain and for self, but it was also for the Territory whose trials had been his trials, whose victories his victories, and whose viewpoint now became his own. He remained primarily a businessman, but he became a Westerner.

Then came the realization that the Federalism of the East, of which he had dreamed to be the evangelist, rejected the West—its people, its economic and social order, and its aspirations. A titanic clash occurred in Blount loyalties—and the West won.

At this critical juncture in his career, Blount once again demonstrated the unity of his business and political systems. His greatest gamble, the conspiracy, was in essence purely a business speculation, the greatest of many hundred such. It failed, the Eastern world castigated him, and he fled to the people he knew would understand and applaud. But his other speculative failures struck simultaneously, and it was their loss, specifically the Allison failure, that brought Blount low, not the conspiracy, which destroyed him only in the East. Then, at the same time that his business edifice crashed, his political scaffolding also fell, for the less complicated and more truly popular Sevier had come at last into his own and had no thought of again yielding primacy to his old mentor and chief.

Thus, Blount the businessman in politics, at fifty years of age failed in both. The question of ultimate rehabilitation was cut short by death.

Yet his personal failure should not obscure his role in his section's history. He was no national figure; his activities were often in that sphere, but seldom his influence. Still, he moved with certainty and effect in Carolina and Tennessee, where he and his family and his kind often played decisive parts in determining the states' histories. In particular he was a bulwark of early nationalism in an Antifederal society in both states. In Carolina, besides his dominant role in internal policy-making, his influence and that of his associates was of tremendous, probably decisive, significance in securing that state's adherence to the Union. On the Tennessee frontier his activities, personal and official, molded the history of the 1790's and caused repercussions in the foreign policies of nations. In Tennessee, too, he performed his greatest personal contribution to the nation by his territorial administration during a most delicate and difficult period. It is the irony of his life that this really valuable labor resulted only in his disaffection and ultimate disgrace.

As a man, Blount was not heroic but intensely human. His faults are clear: pride and a certain snobbishness, intense acquisitiveness, a marked capacity for personal enmity, and a willingness to act dangerously close to and even into illegality for economic gain or social prestige. His virtues, including intelligence and a sense of civic responsibility, are equally evident in his record. But William Blount's greatest significance lies not in his personal stature but in his role as the archetype of thousands of his countrymen. His influence was greater than many others', but his aspirations were theirs and his methods were often the same. His activities, therefore, like others of his kind, must be more thoroughly studied for a true picture of the American past.

CRITICAL ESSAY ON AUTHORITIES

Manuscripts

From the wide range of his private interests and public life, one might expect a considerable amount of manuscript material on Blount's activities, but such is not the case. Although his correspondence was extensive, his ultimate disgrace and the confusion of his personal affairs following his sudden death resulted in the destruction or loss of the great majority of his personal papers, of which there remains only one collection of any size. Likewise, his practice of self-effacement in public and his preference for devious methods of operation combined to remove him from the written notice of others. Consequently, the story of his personal life must largely be pieced together from occasional and widely scattered letters of himself and others in various collections.

The one large and indispensable collection of Blount manuscripts is in the John Gray Blount Collection of approximately 10,000 items in the North Carolina State Department of Archives and History in Raleigh. This collection comprises the business letters and papers of John Gray Blount and of the firm of John Gray & Thomas Blount, and it contains the most valuable of William Blount's extant letters, although it lacks purely personal ones. The collection is now in the process of publication by the State Department of Archives and History, and the first volume has been published as Alice Barnwell Keith (ed.), *The John Gray Blount Papers* (Raleigh, 1952). Letters used in the present work which are found in Miss Keith's book are so cited unless a difference of rendition makes reference to the collection advisable. Letters and papers which are not dated or are not in chronological order in the collection are cited in the present work by their drawer or (P.C.) number.

Smaller though very important collections of Blount's letters are in the Blount Manuscripts of the Lawson McGhee Library, Knoxville, where there are also typed copies of Blount letters from various repositories (not named), in "Correspondence of William

Blount, 1771–1797." The Tennessee State Archives, Nashville, has valuable Blount letters in the Blount Manuscripts and in the Sevier Papers. The Draper Collection (Wisconsin Historical Society, Madison) has a very considerable number of extremely valuable letters of Blount and of Sevier, Robertson, and other contemporaries concerning Blount and his activities. The Rodman family of Washington, North Carolina, owns a number of papers concerning the Blounts as well as copies of letters to William and to John Gray Blount of which the originals are no longer available. Some of these are being given to the North Carolina State Department of Archives and History.

One or two of the very rare Blount letters on North Carolina Revolutionary events are in the Thomas Jefferson Papers (Division of Manuscripts, Library of Congress), and important letters of others in this period are in the Richard Caswell Papers (North Carolina State Department of Archives and History), in the letters of Hardy Murfree in the Emmett Collection (New York Public Library), and of Benjamin Hawkins in the Madison Papers (Division of Manuscripts, Library of Congress). Material on Blount's service in the Continental Congress is in the Papers of the Continental Congress (Division of Manuscripts, Library of Congress), the Purviance-Courtenay Papers (Duke University Archives), and the Charles McClung Papers (Lawson McGhee Library).

More manuscript material exists on Blount's later career in Tennessee. Most of his known letters of that period have been published, but there are in the Library of Congress Blount letters in the Andrew Jackson Papers, the Harry Innes Papers, and the George Washington Papers, besides some in the already-mentioned Thomas Jefferson Papers. Other Blount letters are in the Conarroe Papers (Pennsylvania Historical Society, Philadelphia), the Charles E. Johnson Collection (North Carolina State Department of Archives and History), the David Campbell Papers (Duke University Archives), and the Miscellaneous Manuscripts (Tennessee State Archives). The Emmett Collection also contains several letters of this period. The letters of David Henley and others concerning Blount in the David Henley Papers (Duke University Archives) are of great importance, since they contain some of the rare open attacks on the territorial governor and his administration. Typed copies of some Henley Papers are also in the Lawson McGhee Library.

William Blount's short Senatorial career is relatively well represented in surviving letters. In the New York Public Library there is material in the Emmett Collection, the Myers Collection, and Miscellaneous Letters. In the Pennsylvania Historical Society, there are

Blount letters in the North Carolina Manuscripts, the Simon Gratz Collection, and the Manuscript Collection. The Division of Manuscripts of the Library of Congress has Blount letters in the Papers of Charles Simms, the Blount Collection, and the Etting Papers. A few important Blount letters are also in Miscellaneous Manuscripts (Tennessee State Archives) and Miscellaneous Papers (North Carolina State Department of Archives and History).

In the matter of the Blount conspiracy, manuscript letters of Blount himself are lacking; however, there are letters on the events of the conspiracy in the Timothy Pickering Papers (Massachusetts Historical Society, Cambridge), the Miscellaneous Letters and the Washington Papers (New York Public Library), and the Ellicott Papers (Division of Manuscripts, Library of Congress). The National Archives also have material on this subject in Miscellaneous Letters, State Department, and in Official Correspondence, Secretary of War. The evolution of the Democratic-Republican defense of Blount is illustrated in letters in the Madison Papers (Division of Manuscripts, Library of Congress).

A very large proportion of William Blount's correspondence concerns land matters. Besides collections already mentioned, there are Blount letters on this subject in the Thomas Ruffin Papers (University of North Carolina), the Dreer Collection (Pennsylvania Historical Society), and the Papers of Thomas Walker (William C. Rives Collection) and the Thomas J. Clay Papers (Division of Manuscripts, Library of Congress). The last-named collection's letters are especially valuable for the Blounts' connections with Thomas Hart, Richard Henderson, and the Transylvania project. There are also a number of interesting manuscripts on the subject of land in the Tennessee State Archives, including the field notes of James Robertson and other land papers.

Three small groups of Blount manuscripts deserve final mention. The Blount Mansion in Knoxville has Blount letters of the territorial period formerly in the possession of Mrs. Edith LaRue of Greeneville, Tennessee, and also a legal writ involving Blount and John Tipton which is of value in the political story of the Southwest Territory. The Johnston Collection (Hayes Library, Edenton) has several noteworthy items on the politics of North Carolina and the Territory, and the Dartmouth College Archives has an interesting commentary on Blount by Moses Fisk.

Published Correspondence

The lack of many large collections of manuscripts by Blount or directly concerning him is alleviated by a considerable body of published correspondence. Among this correspondence is the volume of letters from the John Gray Blount collection already mentioned, Alice Barnwell Keith (ed.), *The John Gray Blount Papers* (Raleigh, 1952). Other essential material is in Walter Clark (ed.), *The State Records of North Carolina,* 16 vols. (Raleigh, 1896–1907). In addition to Blount's own letters, other letters of private individuals and government officials concerning Blount or matters in which he was involved are extremely valuable. W. L. Saunders (ed.), *The Colonial Records of North Carolina,* 14 vols. (Raleigh, 1886–90), contains similar though earlier material. For Blount's Tennessee career, the most important published correspondence is that in Clarence E. Carter (ed. and comp.), *The Territorial Papers of the United States,* 17 vols. (Washington, 1934–50), of which Volume IV deals with the Southwest Territory. This work contains much of the available official correspondence from the archives of the State and War Departments, records of the Senate, some manuscripts from the Library of Congress, and certain other papers. It is well edited by a scholarly historian. Another highly important printed collection of official Blount correspondence is in Walter Lowrie and M. S. C. Clark (eds.), *American State Papers, Class II, Indian Affairs,* 2 vols. (Washington, 1832–34). This collection contains highly important letters and their enclosures written by Blount as governor and Indian superintendent, and subsequent loss of the manuscripts has made the papers especially important.

A very valuable corollary to the above official papers is the collection, partly official and partly private, printed in "Correspondence of General James Robertson," in *The American Historical Magazine and Tennessee Historical Society Quarterly,* I (1895), 72–91, 189–95, 280–91, 390–96, II (1896), 59–86, 172–77, 278–79, 355–75, III (1897), 74–83, 267–98, 348–94, IV (1898), 66–96, 163–92, 247–86, 336–81, V (1899), 67–96, 162–90, 252–86. Philip M. Hamer (ed.), "Letters of Governor William Blount," in East Tennessee Historical Society's *Publications,* IV (1932), 122–37, has some valuable Blount letters, and there are a few others in Theodore Roosevelt, *The Winning of the West,* 3 vols. (New York, 1889–94).

A phase of Blount's earlier career is represented by his and others' correspondence in Edmund Cody Burnett (ed.), *Letters of Members of the Continental Congress,* 8 vols. (Washington, 1921–

36). Griffith J. McRee, *Life and Correspondence of James Iredell*, 2 vols. (New York, 1847–57), has an indispensable collection of letters of North Carolinians and others on the political and social life of that state. H. M. Wagstaff (ed.), *The Papers of John Steele*, 2 vols. (Raleigh, 1924), contains two very important Blount letters and significant letters of others. William Wirt Henry, *Patrick Henry: Life, Correspondence, and Speeches*, 3 vols. (New York, 1891), has a number of informative letters on Southwestern affairs. Other important figures in Blount's career have letters in "Letters of Benjamin Hawkins, 1796–1806," in Georgia Historical Society *Collections*, IX (1916), and in "Papers of Gen. Daniel Smith," in *American Historical Magazine*, VI (1901), 213–35.

Material on events and personalities in Blount's later career is found in several other printed collections: Isaac J. Cox (ed.), "Documents Relating to Zachariah Cox," in Historical and Philosophical Society of Ohio *Quarterly Publication*, VIII (1912–14), 31–114; Alice B. Keith (ed.), "Letters from James Cole Mountflorence to Members of the Blount Family," in *North Carolina Historical Review*, XIV (1937), 251–88; Bernard C. Steiner, *The Life and Correspondence of James McHenry* (Cleveland, 1907); and Henry M. Wagstaff (ed.), "The Letters of William Barry Grove," in *James Sprunt Historical Publications*, IX (1910), No. 2. Elizabeth G. McPherson has published two interesting groups of correspondence in "Unpublished Letters of North Carolinians to Washington," in *North Carolina Historical Review*, XII (1935), 149–72, and "Unpublished Letters of North Carolinians to James Madison and James Monroe," *ibid.*, XIV (1937), 156–87. Other correspondence concerning Blount and his affairs is in such standard works as John Spencer Bassett (ed.), *Correspondence of Andrew Jackson*, 6 vols. (Washington, 1926–33), and John C. Fitzpatrick (ed.), *The Writings of George Washington*, 39 vols. (Washington, 1931–44).

The best single source on the Blount conspiracy remains the evidence uncovered by the impeachment committee, which is printed in *The Debates and Proceedings of the Congress of the United States . . .* , 42 vols. (Washington, 1834–56). The evidence, consisting largely of correspondence and affidavits, is in the record of the Fifth Congress, pp. 2319–2416, and although it was later republished separately with the addition of at least one additional pamphlet, the fundamental material is in the original printing. Supplementary to this are two publications by F. J. Turner. The first is his edited "Documents on the Blount Conspiracy, 1795–1797," in *American Historical Review*, X (1905), 574–606, which gives valuable European perspective, and the second, "The Policy of

France toward the Mississippi Valley in the Period of Washington and Adams," *ibid.*, 249–79. For the impact of the conspiracy in Philadelphia and abroad, there is correspondence in George Gibbs (ed.), *Memoirs of the Administrations of Washington and John Adams,* 2 vols. (New York, 1846); Charles R. King (ed.), *The Life and Correspondence of Rufus King,* 6 vols. (New York, 1894–1900); and Stewart Mitchell (ed.), *New Letters of Abigail Adams, 1788–1801* (Boston, 1947). The Democratic-Republican defense of Blount is illustrated in the *Jefferson Papers,* Massachusetts Historical Society *Collections,* 7th Series, 10 vols. (Boston, 1900–15), I.

Diaries and Travel Accounts

Works of this category have not been extensively used in this study; two, however, contain valuable though brief criticisms of Blount. Such contemporary criticism, though often hinted at, is very rarely found in explicit form. This valuable material is in "Diary of Jacob Lindley," in *Michigan Pioneer and Historical Collections,* XVII (1890), 536–632, and "General Lincoln's Journal," in Massachusetts Historical Society *Collections,* 3rd Series, 10 vols. (Boston, 1825–49), V, 109–76. The "Diary of John Sevier," in Samuel G. Heiskell, *Andrew Jackson and Early Tennessee History,* 2 vols. (Nashville, 1920), II, 503–614 provides disappointingly little significant information but does indicate something of Sevier's cordial relationship with Blount. Lida T. Rodman (ed.), "Journal of a Tour to North Carolina in 1787 by William Attmore," in *James Sprunt Historical Publications,* XVII (1922), 5–46, provides a good contemporary view of North Carolina in the late eighteenth century and gives a glimpse of the Blount family. Samuel C. Williams (ed.), *Early Travels in the Tennessee Country* (Johnson City, 1928), is an excellent compilation of travel accounts extremely well edited.

Biographies

Few biographies furnished information. Carl S. Driver, *John Sevier: Pioneer of the Old Southwest* (Chapel Hill, 1932), though on a most important subject, is too biased in Sevier's favor to be as useful as it could be. Thomas E. Matthews, *General James Robertson* (Nashville, 1934) suffers more acutely from the same weakness. Merritt B. Pound, *Benjamin Hawkins—Indian Agent* (Athens, 1951) is a useful study in a too little known area of Southwestern history.

Histories and Monographs

Blount's participation in so many of the events of his day, even though this participation was unobtrusive, has made useful a number of studies of this type. The works listed here have in some cases very little or no direct information on Blount himself, but they have all been found of value and some are indispensable for reconstructing the events of his life.

Because of its attention to social history and its use of newspaper sources, John Bach McMaster, *A History of the People of the United States,* 8 vols. (New York, 1900–14), is informative on conditions in Philadelphia in the 1790's, and especially the atmosphere during the Blount impeachment. The most useful general histories of North Carolina and Tennessee were: Samuel A. Ashe, *History of North Carolina,* 2 vols. (Greensboro, 1908; Raleigh, 1925); R. D. W. Connor, *Colonial and Revolutionary Periods* (New York, 1919), Volume I of *History of North Carolina;* and William K. Boyd, *Federal Period* (New York, 1919), Volume II of the same work; John Haywood, *The Civil and Political History of Tennessee* (Nashville, 1891); James Phelan, *History of Tennessee* (Boston, 1888); A. W. Putnam, *History of Middle Tennessee* (Nashville, 1859); Philip Hamer, *Tennessee—A History, 1673–1932,* 4 vols. (New York, 1933); and J. G. M. Ramsey, *The Annals of Tennessee to the End of the Eighteenth Century* (Charleston, 1853; Chattanooga, 1926). The last-mentioned book, despite findings of modern scholars, is still the best single volume source of information on the Tennessee of that period.

Of regional studies, Thomas P. Abernethy, *From Frontier to Plantation in Tennessee* (Chapel Hill, 1932), is by far the most penetrating work on North Carolina and Tennessee politics and speculation. The author overemphasizes the power of the large speculators and lays perhaps too heavy a charge against Blount personally; but his book is a clear-sighted analysis of the North Carolina and Tennessee of the late eighteenth and early nineteenth centuries. Two other excellent regional studies are Arthur P. Whitaker, *The Mississippi Question, 1795–1803* (New York, 1934), and *The Spanish-American Frontier, 1783–1795* (Boston, 1927). These two books not only approach Southwestern history from the extremely important point of view of Spain, but they also give valuable accounts of influential if shadowy figures in Indian and frontier affairs. Comparable studies dealing with British, French and Spanish relations with the Indians are F. J. Turner, "The Policy of France toward the Mississippi Valley in the Period of Washington and

Adams," in *American Historical Review,* X (1905), 249–79; Archibald Henderson, "The Spanish Conspiracy in Tennessee," in *Tennessee Historical Magazine,* III (1920), 229–43; and Philip M. Hamer, "The British in Canada and the Southern Indians, 1790–1794," in East Tennessee Historical Society's *Publications,* II (1930), 107–34.

Of works dealing with the Southwestern Indians, Merritt Pound's biography of Benjamin Hawkins, already mentioned, deals largely with the Creeks. For the Cherokee, an excellent and comprehensive work is Charles C. Royce, "The Cherokee Nation of Indians," in Bureau of Ethnology *Fifth Annual Report,* 1883–84 (Washington, 1887), 129–378. Two other good articles are by Randolph C. Downes, "Cherokee-American Relations in the Upper Tennessee Valley, 1776–1791," in East Tennessee Historical Society's *Publications,* VIII (1936), 35–53, and "Indian Affairs in the Southwest Territory, 1790–1796," in *Tennessee Historical Magazine,* Third Series, II (1937), 135–50. A more extensive and detailed treatment is A. V. Goodpasture, "Indian Wars and Warriors of the Old Southwest, 1730–1807," in *Tennessee Historical Magazine,* IV (1918), 3–49, 106–45, 161–210, 252–89. Other useful articles on the Indians are: Arthur P. Whitaker, "Spain and the Cherokee Indians, 1783–1798," in *North Carolina Historical Review,* IV (1927), 252–69, and "Alexander McGillivray, 1789–1793," *ibid.,* V (1928), 289–309; Samuel Watson, "William Augustus Bowles," in *American Historical Magazine,* V (1900), 195–99; and Stephen B. Weeks, "General Joseph Martin and the War of the Revolution in the West," in American Historical Association *Annual Report,* 1893 (Washington, 1894), 403–77.

Of the large number of local histories, only a few were of use in this study, and only one dealt directly with Blount. For the scenes in which he moved the following were useful: John H. Wheeler, *Historical Sketches of North Carolina,* 2 vols. (Philadelphia, 1851); John Preston Arthur, *Western North Carolina* (Raleigh, 1914); Francis Nash, "History of Orange County," in *North Carolina Booklet,* X (1910), 55–113; Oliver Taylor, *Historic Sullivan* (Bristol, 1909); John Allison, "The Mero District," in *American Historical Magazine,* I (1896), 115–27. A. V. Goodpasture, "William Blount and the Old Southwest Territory," *ibid.,* VIII (1903), 1–13, is a pioneer article on the subject which misinterprets the complex figure of Blount as territorial governor. The State of Franklin is the subject of an excellent book, Samuel C. Williams, *History of the Lost State of Franklin* (Johnson City, 1924), which also contains a number of very useful short sketches of western leaders.

The "lost State" is also dealt with in F. J. Turner, "Western State-Making in the Revolutionary Era," in *American Historical Review*, I (1895–96), 70–87, 251–69, and a later study is W. F. Cannon, "Four Interpretations of the History of the State of Franklin," in East Tennessee Historical Society's *Publications*, XXII (1950), 3–18.

The important subjects of land ownership and speculation and the parts they played in early Tennessee history have not yet received the attention they deserve. Abernethy's work already mentioned is the best study at present. Aaron Morton Sakolski, *The Great American Land Bubble* (New York, 1932) is a popularly written and generalized treatment of the subject throughout the United States. Payson Jackson Treat, *The National Land System, 1785–1820* (New York, 1910) is useful. Albert L. Bramlett, "North Carolina's Western Lands" (Ph.D. dissertation, University of North Carolina, 1928) provides information on the Tennessee situation. P. T. Glass, "Sketch of Henry Rutherford," in *American Historical Magazine*, V (1900), 225–29, throws some light on land practices of that day, as does James McCallum, "Brief Sketch of the Settlement and Early History of Giles County," *ibid.*, II (1897), 303–24, and A. V. Goodpasture, "Education and the Public Lands in Tennessee," *ibid.*, IV (1899), 210–28, traces the legislation concerning Tennessee lands.

Two excellent studies deal with land companies in which Blount was interested. Arthur P. Whitaker, "The Muscle Shoals Speculation, 1783–1789," in *Mississippi Valley Historical Review*, XIII (1926), 365–86 is the best work on the Bend of the Tennessee company, and Charles H. Haskins, "The Yazoo Land Companies," in American Historical Association *Papers*, V, Part 4 (1891), 61–103 remains authoritative despite new evidence since its publication. Archibald Henderson, "The Transylvania Company; A Study in Personnel," in *Filson Club History Quarterly*, XXI (1947), 229–42, and Rev. John D. Shane (ed.), "The Henderson Company Ledger," *ibid.*, 22–48 are informative on Henderson's company and its operation. James Clarence Posey, "William Blount, the Land Speculator" (M.A. thesis, Vanderbilt University, 1929) deals specifically though not intensively with Blount's land operations, and Alice B. Keith, "Three North Carolina Blount Brothers in Business and Politics" (Ph.D. dissertation, University of North Carolina, 1940) devotes considerable space to a deeper study of the Blounts' land business.

William Blount was deeply engaged in political activity all his mature life, and he played influential and decisive roles; yet, as in other spheres, his activity was as quiet and unobtrusive as he could make it, and most political studies of the period do not mention his name. The works listed here, therefore, were chiefly useful in making clear the scenes, issues, and problems in which he worked.

For the colonial and Revolutionary periods, a number of special works were helpful in economic matters. Christopher C. Crittenden, *The Commerce of North Carolina* (New Haven, 1936) is a scholarly study, and Arthur M. Schlesinger, *The Colonial Merchants and the American Revolution, 1763–1776* (New York, 1918) contains North Carolina material. Adelaide L. Fries, "North Carolina Certificates of the Revolutionary Period," in *North Carolina Historical Review,* IX (1932), 229–42, helps unravel the intricacies of the disordered finances, while R. L. Hilldrup, "The Salt Supply of North Carolina During the American Revolution," *ibid.,* XXII (1945), 393–417, presents other economic problems.

For the social history of Blount's early neighborhood, Francis H. Cooper, "Some Colonial History of Craven County," in *The James Sprunt Historical Publications,* XVII (1922), 29–74, is good, and Alonzo Thomas Dill, Jr., "Eighteenth Century New Bern: A History of the Town and Craven County, 1700–1800," in *North Carolina Historical Review,* XXII (1945), 1–21, 152–75, 293–319, 460–89, XXIII (1946), 47–78, 142–71, 325–59, 495–535, is a detailed study of Blount's county. The crisis of the Revolution in North Carolina is the subject of David Schenck, *North Carolina, 1780–1781* (Raleigh, 1889). Published correspondence already mentioned, especially in the *Colonial Records* and the *State Records,* was especially valuable.

For the political story of Revolutionary North Carolina, a number of works deserve mention. Allan Nevins, *The American States During and After the Revolution* (New York, 1924) has good if somewhat biased sketches of political leaders and issues. Edmund Cody Burnett, *The Continental Congress* (New York, 1941) has numerous references to the activities of the state's delegates. John S. Bassett, "The Regulators of North Carolina," in American Historical Association *Annual Report,* 1894 (Washington, 1895), 141–212, has excellent political material of the late colonial period. Three works on Loyalists were also useful: Isaac S. Harrell, "The North Carolina Loyalists," in *North Carolina Historical Review,* III (1926), 575–90; Bessie M. Steinle, "The Confiscation of Loyalist Property During and After the Revolution in North Carolina" (M.A. thesis, University of Texas, 1935); and Robert O. DeMond, *The Loyalists of North Carolina During the Revolution* (Durham, 1940).

The story of late eighteenth- and early nineteenth-century North Carolina politics, unlike that of Tennessee, has been well told by a number of authors. Among the best are: Delbert H. Gilpatrick, *Jeffersonian Democracy in North Carolina, 1789–1816* (New York, 1931); Fletcher M. Green, *Constitutional Development in the South Atlantic States, 1776–1860* (Chapel Hill, 1930); Louise Irby Trenholme, *The Ratification of the Federal Constitution in North Carolina* (New York, 1932); Julian P. Boyd, "The Sheriff in Colonial North Carolina," in *North Carolina Historical Review*, V (1928), 151–81; A. R. Newsome, "North Carolina's Ratification of the Federal Constitution," *ibid.*, XVII (1940), 287–301; Thomas M. Pittman, "The Revolutionary Congresses of North Carolina," in *North Carolina Booklet*, II (1902), No. 6; William C. Pool, "An Economic Interpretation of the Ratification of the Federal Constitution in North Carolina," in *North Carolina Historical Review*, XXVII (1950), 119–41, 289–313, 437–61; Enoch W. Sikes, *The Transition of North Carolina from Colony to Commonwealth*, in Johns Hopkins University *Studies in History and Political Science*, XVI (1898), Nos. 10–11; St. George L. Sioussat, "The North Carolina Cession of 1784 in Its Federal Aspects," in Mississippi Valley Historical Association *Proceedings*, II (1908), 35–62; Henry M. Wagstaff, "Federalism in North Carolina," in *The James Sprunt Historical Publications*, IX (1910), No. 2, and *States Rights and Political Parties in North Carolina, 1776–1861*, in Johns Hopkins University *Studies in History and Political Science*, XXIV (1906), Nos. 7–8.

Constitutional problems and events in North Carolina and Tennessee are also dealt with in most of the works mentioned above and also in others. Max Farrand, *The Framing of the Constitution of the United States* (New Haven, 1936), and Max Farrand (ed.), *The Records of the Federal Convention*, 3 vols. (New Haven, 1911), contain a number of references to North Carolina, although Blount appears but rarely. For the North Carolina constitution itself, Earle H. Ketcham, "The Sources of the North Carolina Constitution of 1776," in *North Carolina Historical Review*, VI (1929), 215–38, is helpful. Several works deal with Tennessee constitutional developments. Joshua W. Caldwell, *Studies in the Constitutional History of Tennessee* (Cincinnati, 1907) is fairly thorough, but legalistic. John D. Barnhart, "The Tennessee Constitution: A Product of the Old West," in *Journal of Southern History*, X (1943), 532–48, is perhaps the best discussion of the subject; Wallace McClure, "The Development of the Tennessee Constitution," in *Tennessee Historical Magazine*, I (1915), 293–314, is also excellent. Edward

S. Sanford, "The Constitutional Convention of Tennessee of 1796," in Tennessee Bar Association *Proceedings,* 1896, is a printed address containing some unique information. Two good articles relate to the constitutional and political problems arising from Tennessee's request for admission to the Union: Charlotte Williams, "Congressional Action on the Admission of Tennessee into the Union," in *Tennessee Historical Quarterly,* II (1943), 291–315, and Samuel C. Williams, "The Admission of Tennessee into the Union," *ibid.,* IV (1945), 291–320.

Since the publication of Walter B. Posey, "The Blount Conspiracy," in Birmingham-Southern *Bulletin,* XXI (1928), No. 6, pp. 11–21, there have been several articles on the conspiracy. One of the best discussions of it is in A. P. Whitaker's *The Mississippi Question,* already mentioned elsewhere. A less satisfactory treatment is Isabel Thompson, "The Blount Conspiracy," in East Tennessee Historical Society's *Publications,* II (1930), 3–21, and the beginning of a completely unconvincing defense is in Marcus J. Wright, *Some Account of the Life and Services of William Blount* (Washington, 1884), which has little else.

Besides the book-length biographies mentioned elsewhere, a number of shorter biographical sketches furnished information on Blount's contemporaries and indirectly on himself. The influential figure of Richard Caswell has received some attention in three articles by C. B. Alexander, "The Training of Richard Caswell," in *North Carolina Historical Review,* XXIII (1946), 13–31; "Richard Caswell, Versatile Leader of the Revolution," *ibid.,* 119–41; and "Richard Caswell's Military and Later Public Services," *ibid.,* 287–312. An anonymous article, "An Outline of the Life of Governor Caswell, with a Selection of His Letters" in *University of North Carolina Magazine,* March, 1855, pp. 68–85, furnishes interesting letters. Kemp D. P. Battle, "Life and Services of Brigadier General Jethro Sumner," in *North Carolina Booklet,* VIII (1908), 111–40, has brief but significant politico-military information. Blackwell P. Robinson, "Willie Jones of Halifax," in *North Carolina Historical Review,* XVIII (1941), 1–26, 133–70, is an all too brief sketch of this potent political leader, as is also Stephen B. Weeks, "Thomas Person," in *North Carolina Booklet,* IX (1909), 16–35. Samuel C. Williams, "George Farragut," in East Tennessee Historical Society's *Publications,* I (1929), 77–94, has brief mention of Farragut's early Tennessee career with Blount. Other useful brief sketches of this type are Rev. P. L. Cobb, "William Cobb—Host of Governor Blount," in *Tennessee Historical Magazine,* IX (1926), 241–64; A. V. Goodpasture, "Genesis of the Jackson-Sevier Feud," in *Amer-*

ican Historical Magazine, V (1900), 115–23; and Samuel C. Williams, "William Tatham, Wataugan," in *Tennessee Historical Magazine,* VII (1924), 154–79.

Some helpful genealogical information on Blount and related families was found in Stuart Hill, "The Hill Family," a large and careful manuscript study in the North Carolina State Library, and in Helen M. Blount Prescott, *Genealogical Memoir of the Roulhac Family in America* (Atlanta, 1894). More concise but even more useful was Worth S. Ray (ed.), *Index and Digest to Hathaway's Historical and Genealogical Register* (Austin, 1945), and Edythe R. Whitley (ed.), *Tennessee Genealogical Records,* 5 vols. (Nashville, 1932–36).

Finally, three publications deserve mention as of use in a study of Blount: W. R. Garrett, "Northern Boundary of Tennessee," in *American Historical Magazine,* VI (1901), 18–40; George F. Bentley, "Printers and Printing in the Territory of the United States South of the River Ohio, 1790–1796," in *Tennessee Historical Quarterly,* VIII (1949), 332–44; and Douglas McMurtrie, *Early Printing in Tennessee* (Chicago, 1933).

Contemporary Newspapers and Pamphlets

By far the most valuable newspaper in Blount's career was the Knoxville *Gazette,* later the Knoxville *Gazette and Weekly Register.* A few items of interest at the end of his life are in the Tennessee *Gazette.* In North Carolina, since both the Blounts and their enemies used newspapers for propaganda, several newspapers are of interest: the North Carolina *Journal, State Gazette of North Carolina, North Carolina Minerva and Fayetteville Advertiser,* and, to a less extent, the North Carolina *Gazette.* Because of the close political connection between North Carolina and Virginia, as well as the Blount interest in both states, two Virginia newspapers are useful, the Virginia *Argus,* and the *Virginia Gazette and Petersburg Intelligencer,* the latter, at least, read by William Blount. These newspapers also carried considerable news of the conspiracy exposé.

For the same reasons, four Northern newspapers are important in a study of Blount: the Pennsylvania *Packet and General Advertiser,* the Philadelphia *Aurora and General Advertiser,* the New York *Daily Advertiser,* and the New York *Journal and Weekly Register.*

From the period of high controversy in which Blount lived there naturally arose a vast array of pamphlet literature. However, apart from its background value, this contains little of value for the student of Blount, for his hand, though possibly employed in it, was too skillfully hidden to be glimpsed, and he was not often a target of public attack or defense. The best collection of pamphlet literature used in this work was William K. Boyd (ed.), "News, Letters, and Documents Concerning North Carolina and the Federal Constitution," in *Trinity College Historical Papers*, XIV (1922), 75–95. Editorial comment on the Blount conspiracy is in William Cobbett, *Porcupine's Works*, 12 vols. (London, 1801), and a good sampling in John B. McMaster's *History* already mentioned.

National, State, and Local Government Documents

Because of the gaps in the personal correspondence of William Blount and his reticence in public, a great deal of the story of his life must be gleaned piece by piece from government documents, both in manuscript and printed form. No single type of material except the John Gray Blount Collection furnishes so large a part of the story of his activities.

For his service in the Continental Congress, there is manuscript material in the Papers of the Continental Congress (Division of Manuscripts, Library of Congress). Gaillard Hunt *et al.* (eds.), *Journals of the Continental Congress, 1774–1789*, 34 vols. (Washington, 1904–37), contains the journals during his attendance and the record of his committee work. For Blount's Senate career, *The Debates and Proceedings in the Congress of the United States*, already mentioned, contains his brief record, as well as the impeachment evidence and proceedings and the story of the fight over the admission of Tennessee. The National Archives contain Blount material on territorial events in the Papers of the Secretary of War, and a small amount on his Revolutionary War service in the Records of the Office of the Adjutant General. The Records of the Senate there also contain interesting correspondence and papers on the impeachment trial.

On North Carolina affairs, Walter Clark (ed.), *The State Records of North Carolina*, already cited, is the indispensable source, containing the legislative journals, the text of the enacted legislation, and the official correspondence of the entire period of Blount's activity there. That state is also fortunate in the preservation in the North Carolina State Department of Archives and History (Raleigh) of a large number of official manuscript collections to supplement the *State Records*. The material on Blount in each of these is small but invaluable in conjunction with his correspondence and includes the Council Journal; the Governors' Letter Books; Land

Fraud Commission Report; North Carolina Legislative Papers, 1789; North Carolina Revolutionary Army Accounts; Papers of the Commissioners of Confiscated Property; Papers of the Convention of 1789; Papers of the House of Commons (for the years of Blount's service); and Papers of the Secretary of State. Extremely valuable is the collection of Governors' Papers.

For Blount land records in North Carolina, there is scattered material in the Returns of Taxes and Fees and the vouchers in the Comptroller's Office, the Glasgow Land Fraud Papers, and the Governors' Warrants. The actual grants, often accompanied by survey plats, are filed by counties in the State Land Office in Raleigh. There are also land records in the Pitt County Papers in the State Department of Archives and History. In addition, the ultimate details of Blount's activity in the land market are spread over the deed books, entry books, and records of wills of Beaufort, Craven, Pitt, and other counties, although the full story of this activity can never be traced because of poor administrative methods as well as Blount's use of fictitious names and third parties.

Blount's political and economic story in Tennessee is also widely scattered. The political material available is principally in printed form. For the territorial period, the *Journal of the Proceedings of the House of Representatives of the Territory of the United States South of the River Ohio . . . at Knoxville the 25th Day of August, 1794* (Knoxville, 1794; Nashville, 1852) is paralleled by the similarly titled journal of the 1795 session, also reprinted in 1852. Likewise, the *Journal of the Legislative Council of the Territory . . . Knoxville . . . 1794* (Knoxville, 1794; Nashville, 1852) and the 1795 journal of that body are extant. The constitutional convention journal of 1796 is also useful but only in a limited degree because of the time spent by that body in committee of the whole house. For Blount material in the period of early statehood, there is the *Journal of the Senate of the State of Tennessee* (Knoxville, 1796; Nashville, 1852), and the *House Journal of the Second General Assembly of the State of Tennessee* (Kingsport, 1933), bound with the corresponding senate journal. The legislation of the territorial and early state periods is in George Roulstone, *Laws of the State of Tennessee* (Knoxville, 1803). In print also is Samuel C. Williams (ed.), "The Executive Journal of Governor John Sevier," in East Tennessee Historical Society's *Publications*, I (1929), 95–153; II (1930), 135–49; III (1931), 154–82; IV (1932), 138–67; V (1933), 155–77; VI (1934), 104–28; VII (1935), 128–64.

A very few accessible manuscripts supplement this political material, principally in Papers of the Secretary of State (Tennessee

State Archives). Spanish reaction to events in the Tennessee country is found in the Papeles de Cuba (typed translated copies, Lawson McGhee Library, Knoxville).

The Blount land record in Tennessee, like that in North Carolina, is widely scattered. For Davidson County, the Deed Book (County Court House, Nashville) and the copies of deeds in the State Library should both be used. Other land material is in the court minutes, deed books, estate books, and will books of Knox County, and the Deed Book of Sumner County (Gallatin). A large amount of Tennessee land business is in the files of the North Carolina State Land Office, Raleigh.

A very helpful document in tracing the story of the running of the Holston Treaty line is the *Letter from the Secretary at War Accompanying His Report Relative to the Running of a Line of Experiment* . . . (Philadelphia, 1798?), printed by Joseph Gales in response to a House resolution.

Two government documents throw some light on two private land operations dear to Blount. For tracing the tortuous career of his Bend of the Tennessee company, information is found in *The Report of the Select Committee to Whom was Referred the Petition of Andrew Jackson* . . . . , House Document No. 31, 15th Congress, 2nd Session, Vol. II. A little light is thrown on Blount's participation in Zachariah Cox's second Yazoo enterprise in Walter Lowrie *et al.* (eds.), *American State Papers, Class VIII, Public Lands,* 8 vols. (Washington, 1834–61), I, 238, 243, 244.

The printed state records of two other states were found useful in the study of Blount. Allen D. Candler (ed.), *The Revolutionary Records of the State of Georgia,* 3 vols. (Atlanta, 1908), furnishes further information on Blount's Bend company, and there is correspondence on North Carolina's Revolutionary War and Indian affairs and on some territorial matters in W. P. Palmer *et al.* (eds.), *Calendar of Virginia State Papers,* 11 vols. (Richmond, 1875–85).

INDEX

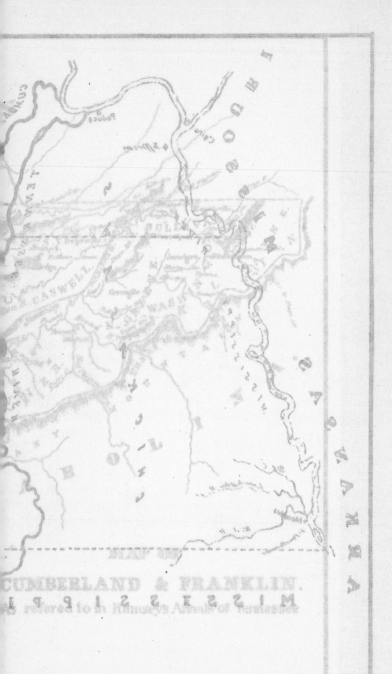

MAP OF
CUMBERLAND & FRANKLIN.

as refered to in Ramsey's Annals of Tennessee